G. W. Mudge
3080 Telegraph Rd.
Mill Bay. B.C.

FOR
SERVICES
RENDERED

Also by John Sawatsky:
Men in the Shadows

FOR SERVICES RENDERED

Leslie James Bennett and the RCMP Security Service

John Sawatsky

1982
Doubleday Canada Limited, Toronto, Canada
Doubleday & Company, Inc., Garden City, New York

Library of Congress Catalog Card Number: 82-45272

Copyright © 1982 by John Sawatsky
All rights reserved
FIRST EDITION

Design by Irene Carefoot
Typeset by ART-U Graphics Ltd.
Printed and bound in Canada by T.H. Best Printing Company Ltd.
Jacket design by David Wyman

Canadian Cataloguing in Publication Data

Sawatsky, John, 1948-
 For services rendered

Includes index.
ISBN 0-385-17660-0

1. Bennett, Leslie James.   2. Royal Canadian Mounted
Police. Security Service — Biography.   3. Intelligence
officers — Canada — Biography.   4. Spies — Canada —
Biography.   I. Title.

HV8157.S38   363.2'092'4   C82-094927-2

To Allan Fotheringham,
who taught me that journalism is more than a job.

Acknowledgements

WRITING THIS BOOK was a lonely exercise, but not a solitary one. I received contributions from many people, including research and other help from Janet Inksetter and Sally Bennett (no relation). Erik Spicer personally opened to me the full facilities of the Library of Parliament. People across Canada provided shelter so that I could stretch a lot of research out of a limited budget. They are Jay and Marta Armin, Doug Riley and Adele Armin-Riley, Lee Carter, Jan O'Brien, Geoff Meggs, Neil and Herta Neumann, Edward and Ingrid Suderman, John McHugh, Sandy McCormick and my parents.

Irene Carefoot of Doubleday Canada's publicity department conceived a most fitting title when I and others could not. My editor, Janet Turnbull, contributed in many ways, particularly with her editing, which did much to improve the manuscript without tampering with its character.

A special thanks is owed to Mark Budgen, who volunteered time and effort at his own expense, for doing field research I could not do. The Ottawa *Citizen* and the City of Ottawa Archives deserve a special thanks for going out of their way to provide photographs.

My biggest thank you must go to the many people whose interviews provided the substance for this book. Unfortunately I cannot name them but without their help this book would have been impossible.

Parliamentary Press Gallery
Ottawa, Canada
July 1982

Contents

FOR
SERVICES
RENDERED

1

Leaving Canada

"JIM'S OUT," REPORTED one breathless officer in the RCMP Security Service.

"What happened?"

"They think he's working for the KGB."

The speculation could not be stopped. Veteran Mounties who normally lived by the rules of secrecy and the "need to know" principle could not restrain themselves. A few months earlier, Leslie James Bennett, without notice or explanation, had suddenly stopped appearing for work at headquarters in Ottawa. Jim Bennett knew more secrets than almost anybody. He had spent sixteen of his eighteen years with the RCMP in the Counterespionage Branch and for most of that time ran the Russian Desk. The frantic rumours now accused him of having sold out to the KGB since joining the Force in 1954. Each piece of speculation spawned further rumour until the normally secretive Security Service Mounties seemed no different than any other group of gossipers.

How circumstances had changed. One day Bennett held the highest level of security clearance the Canadian government provided—higher than Top Secret—and ran the branch with the largest staff and biggest budget. The next day he could not walk through the main door of RCMP headquarters, not even to clean out his desk. Bennett, because of his knowledge, experience, authority and intellect, had been one of the most sought-after officers in the Force. People, whether high or

1

low, needing a solution usually came to him. His door always stood open. Despite the mountains of paper on his desk and the self-imposed schedule that made him the first to work in the morning and the last to leave at night (with work taken home and trips to the office in the evenings and on weekends), he found time to talk to colleagues whenever they needed him. Even if he did not exactly know the answer he gave the impression he did and that was good enough for most people. If Bennett did not know, then nobody else knew anyway.

Nobody came to see him now. Nobody wanted to be seen with Bennett. The guru of counterespionage had become a loser and, possibly worse, a traitor. There were no phone calls following his week-long interrogation in March, 1972 and his wife chose that time to take their two daughters and leave. So suddenly, he was totally alone.

"It's a very human thing," says one of Bennett's former colleagues. "If there's any suspicion it's difficult to find someone who will come out and defend your position because if you're proven wrong, then the question was why was the person defending a KGB spy? Why? Is he one of the co-opted workers? Or was it just incompetence? If it is just incompetence, what is your career potential after that? So everybody just lies low. But when the dogs really start to bite, then everybody runs with the pack. I know the syndrome, I've seen it and experienced it. This goes back many years. I was going to be kicked out of the Force for being AWOL a couple of days and then turning around and telling the sergeant-major to commit an impossible sexual act upon himself. I was just a constable at the time. You just don't do that. Bets were on that I was out of the Force. I was saved somewhere along the line, I don't know by whom. But the fellows were reluctant to be seen talking to you during the day. That would be lending moral support. So everybody backs off. Once I was reinstated, fine. All the old friends come back."

In late 1947, when Bennett still worked for the U.K. government, he went to Istanbul while Kim Philby, later exposed as a Soviet agent, worked there in another arm of the British intelligence community. The two met. When Philby defected to Moscow sixteen years later this connection returned to haunt Bennett, and he spent years down-playing and even hiding this connection. Now his colleagues in the RCMP ran from him the way he had run from Philby.

The Soviet Union disposes of leaders the same way. The removal comes quickly—no warning, no commotion and, once done, no announcement. People learn only when the victim stops appearing and becomes a non-person. Now, Bennett no longer existed. The RCMP *Quarterly*, which dutifully records retirements, ran a picture of Miss Nora Mary Attree and a notice saying she was retiring as RCMP dietician in Toronto, while Bennett, the master of counterespionage, the fount of all knowledge, got no special mention. He appeared only as another name in a long list of retirees—Reg. No: C/40; Rank: C/M; Name: L. J. Bennett; Div.: HQ; Retirement Date: July 28. That brief entry closed out the career of the most influential officer in the history of the Security Service.

There was one concession, probably the consequence of the new awareness of workers' rights inside the Force, and the fact that Bennett still had a few loyal supporters. His staff in E Branch took a collection and bought him a farewell gift, a crafted piece of mahogany mounted with three weather instruments, a thermometer, a barometer and a hygrometer. Since Bennett was physically barred from headquarters, he couldn't come into the office for a ceremony. Two Mounties drove out to his home in East End Ottawa and privately made the presentation there.

His hair had been dark when he entered the security and intelligence business thirty-two years earlier, but now it was grey and turning white. The years taught him, if anything, to understand the consequences of his predicament. It didn't require much understanding since his career was smashed at fifty-two. As victimized as he felt about everything that had happened, he knew that he could not vent his anger with colleagues, even in a restrained way. Secrecy was the trademark of his professional upbringing and he was not planning to take on the system. Still, he felt a few of his close friends deserved to know what had happened just as a matter of human decency. After a couple of months he began to call some of them and propose little get-togethers.

Among his intimate colleagues was Dick Rowan, an assistant in E Branch. Bennett phoned and proposed lunch at the Chez Pierre, a fancy French restaurant strategically located halfway between headquarters and his home. Rowan was naturally curious about what had happened. He had worked well with Bennett until one day he came in to work and was told to report to Superintendent Al Nowlan. No more

Bennett. Rowan knew Bennett was suspected of being a Soviet agent who had penetrated the Security Service; he knew Bennett had been the object of an intensive internal RCMP investigation lasting nearly two years; he knew before the "retirement" that Bennett had been cut off from vital secrets; and he knew furthermore that he had been formally interrogated. Rowan knew all this because during the internal investigation he had been instructed to keep back certain information from Bennett, which was unusual because Bennett, after all, was his superior in the chain of command. The internal investigation team had interviewed Rowan in the search for little telltale clues that might betray Bennett's alleged secret life as a Russian mole. Later Rowan learned from a source that Bennett had been interrogated but didn't know the result. Had he broken down and confessed? If so, why wasn't he behind bars? Had he been exonerated? Then why wasn't he back at work? Rowan was curious and to satisfy his curiosity he accepted the luncheon invitation. But he was also cautious. Before going he made a few checks with superiors to see if it was all right. It was okay, he was advised, not necessarily politic, but okay. This pleased Rowan because in addition to getting the lowdown he wanted to go because he considered Bennett a pretty decent guy.

It was impossible for Rowan to cleanse himself of Bennett because they had worked together so closely. If Bennett had been passing information to the KGB, Rowan would have been among the foremost to have been manipulated. He wanted to find out what happened to Bennett so he could get a feel for what was likely to happen to him—he had little doubt E Branch would be purged and he would be among the first victims. Would he be transferred to some remote post, the RCMP's equivalent of exile in Siberia, or stay in Ottawa and merely be moved into different and less sensitive work? Rowan was waiting for notice to arrive and was surprised only because it hadn't yet come.

Bennett, punctual as usual, arrived at the Chez Pierre slightly before the 11:45 A.M. luncheon appointment. The tightness of his face revealed the strain of the last few months and he was thinner, but seemed generally healthy. In fact he seemed healthier than the last time Rowan had seen him, which was in winter when the Ottawa cold would swell up his sinuses and block his breathing. Even a block-long walk outside in the cold rendered him semi-helpless as he wheezed and gasped for breath. Now it was June, a good time of year, that restful interlude between the winter cold and the summer pollens that triggered his chronic allergies.

Bennett kept up a good face. He joked about the diet his new doctor put him on, saying his triglyceride level was a little high, forcing him to cut back on fat and sugar. Fortunately, he said, the diet didn't restrict his alcohol intake unduly and he ordered a rusty nail. When the discussion turned serious, Bennett, knowing that Rowan knew, said he was sorry and hurt about the recent developments and assured Rowan the allegations were untrue and without foundation. He advised Rowan to quit the RCMP and find work elsewhere because now that they had gone after him they were sure to extend the purge to his associates, although the brass had assured Bennett this wouldn't happen. "You can't trust those sons of bitches," he counselled. Besides, a house cleaning had taken place in Britain after Philby. Bennett provided names of several people in the government who might give Rowan a job. Rowan agreed his standing with the Force was precarious but said no more.

Bennett revealed that Shev, his wife of twenty years, had left, saying his circumstances with the Force brought his marital situation to a head but hadn't caused the separation. The house had already been sold and Shev was returning to her native Australia with both girls. It was clear the break-up of the marriage hurt him, particularly losing his two daughters. At the moment he had no definite plans for himself other than to fly to Florida and see his aunt, then leave Canada for Britain where he would visit his father and relatives in Wales. After that everything was a blank. He was in the process of arranging a medical pension but that wouldn't sustain him and his children, so he was looking for work almost anywhere in the world except in Canada and had only a few possibilities so far.

Tables in the Chez Pierre were emptying as the luncheon crowd drifted back to work. Bennett hadn't told very much and Rowan's appetite for information was not satisfied, so when Bennett invited him to his home, he accepted. If Bennett was a good teacher, Rowan was one of his star pupils. The civilian Bennett often privately complained that some of the flat-footed Mounties he had to work with were useless, or worse, for counterespionage work. Rowan, a Mountie, did not fall into this category since he was bright and quick and made the switch from policeman to security officer with ease. Bennett relied on him.

At Bennett's split-level home, already half empty, Rowan started pressing for details on what had happened. Something must have gone on, otherwise Bennett wouldn't be leaving his career and the country at age fifty-two. Bennett insisted the rumours were untrue and unfounded and that he had never been a Russian agent and had never been in any way disloyal to Canada.

"They must have something on you or else they wouldn't have interrogated you," insisted Rowan.

Bennett maintained his claim of innocence and argued that the charges against him were groundless, yet he seemed reluctant to delve into the matter. The two left the living room and moved out to the back of the house where there was a small screened-off nook tucked beside the garage, underneath the overhang of the upstairs bedrooms. Here, removed from the listening range of any bugs, Bennett felt free to talk.

Now Bennett was getting more adamant about his innocence and the weakness of the RCMP's case. If the Force decided a mole had infested the ranks, it needed to find somebody and picked him because he was not a Mountie and one of the few civilians in a senior position. Also, he had come from the tainted British service and was involved in the running of virtually every Russian Desk case between 1954 and 1970.

"The organization needs a scapegoat and I am it," he said.

Rowan needed no lesson on the inequalities of treatment given Mounties such as himself and civilians such as Bennett. He realized civilian members had to be twice as good to get half as far and he knew that the Force when looking for a mole would look at the civilians first because the RCMP believed its own myth that Mounties were superior individuals. But Rowan didn't believe the Force would expel somebody, even a civilian, without reasonable evidence.

"They must have had something stronger than that on you, Jim," responded Rowan. "You must have been caught in a meet with the Russians."

"No, Dick," answered Bennett. "I'll go upstairs and get my rebuttal and you can read it for yourself."

Bennett returned a minute later with a sheaf of typed sheets answering each of the RCMP allegations against him. It was his rebuttal, which, after receiving legal counsel, he filed with the RCMP so that the record would show his response. Rowan flipped through the documents. The first was an affidavit from Bennett swearing he had never been an open or secret member of the Communist party or any front group and that he was completely innocent of any charge of having been disloyal to Canada. The second was an affidavit sworn by Shev saying she agreed he was innocent and stating that their decision to separate was brought on by the interrogation but not caused by it. The third document, marked TOP SECRET—PERSONAL, constituted a point-by-point rebuttal of each point the RCMP pressed at the week-long interrogation just three months earlier. On one page of this document Bennett was replying to the allegation that he was an ideological recruit to communism while on another page he answered the contradictory charge that he had infiltrated the Canadian services on behalf of British intelligence. Nevertheless, the thrust of the RCMP case was clear: Bennett had deliberately caused the RCMP's counter-espionage cases to fail in the service of the KGB.

There were more documents written by Bennett setting out his family background, describing his achievements in thirty-two years of anti-communist service with the Canadian and British governments, but Rowan did not read this far. His faith in Bennett was restored and he couldn't understand how the Force could have interrogated him based on so little information. He shook his head and muttered that it was unbelievable.

Conversation then turned to cases. Bennett had been the guiding light behind scores of cases against both the KGB and its military cousin the GRU and some of his decisions had been wrong. Rowan asked about some of these. "Damn it," replied Bennett, "when you sit in the driver's seat and make decisions every day on the spur of the moment you have to live with them. Then somebody pops up six weeks later and says, 'You did it wrong. If you had done it this way, things would have developed differently.' Well you never know. It's easy to say that in retrospect. Hindsight is great."

Bennett said it was unfair to make comparisons. The Soviets put more resources into espionage than Canada did into counterespionage, thus weighing the odds in their favour. The Russians saved some of their brightest university graduates for the KGB while Canada picked policemen and then gave them virtually no training. Besides, he said, in an open society like Canada's, conducting espionage is much easier than stopping it.

It was like a high school reunion as they reminisced about specific cases, old and not so old operations from their mutual past. The afternoon shadows lengthened into evening and Rowan, already having missed dinner, had to get home because he had invited some friends over for a game of bridge.

Bennett drove Rowan the short distance home and the guests, a Mountie and his wife, were already waiting inside. They saw the car pull up and park in front of the house. Rowan and Bennett had been talking for eight hours and by now the discussion was freewheeling and, for Rowan at least, fascinating. Bennett was providing a complete defence of his actions and, in a way he had never done openly with the Force, a thorough and unabashed critique of the weaknesses of the RCMP as a counterespionage unit. In Bennett's opinion, under existing circumstances, it would always remain weak. By now Bennett was talking cases and describing details Rowan had not known before. Rowan couldn't pull himself out of Bennett's Rambler as there always seemed to be another point and another case to prolong discussion a few more minutes. Another two hours passed before he finally left Bennett and joined his waiting guests.

One night several days later, Bennett went to the home of his close friend Ken Green, a fellow civilian with whom he had fought a lot of wars for the improved status of civilian members. Green knew that Bennett had been interrogated and dismissed, but Bennett thought he should know more. They went to the basement to be alone and Green listened to his story with interest but was not overly sympathetic. Sensing that Green did not necessarily believe his claim of loyalty, Bennett only mentioned evidence about left-wing connections in his family background and said this shouldn't be a reflection on his status. The meeting didn't last long and Bennett left without further discussion.

Time was now running into July and the day of Bennett's departure from Canada was approaching. Four months had passed since the interrogation but time did nothing to ease Bennett's anxiety. In fact the fourth month was worse than the third and as the burden grew it began to wear away the veneer of good spirit that had protected him during chance encounters with friends on the street. He still recited the cover story arranged with the Force: his health forced early retirement and he was leaving Canada to escape the debilitating cold. His medical pension was genuine in that he was about to receive a disability pension, but maintaining the cover was becoming more difficult. Nobody would challenge his cover story but after eighteen years in Canada and adopting Canadian citizenship, strong emotions sometimes betrayed this professional soldier.

During their marathon discussion a few weeks earlier Rowan had promised to invite Bennett for dinner before he was to leave the country; when Bennett arrived his usual spirit was subdued. Soon he would be gone and he still had nowhere to settle. The sixty letters he had sent applying for work around the world had produced nothing solid. It was beginning to appear he would have no job to go to upon leaving Canada.

After dinner the Rowan children went to bed and Bennett's mood and the drinks put him into an expressive disposition. He talked about his two daughters, Vivienne, fifteen, and Hilary, eleven, and as he did tears dropped from his eyes. It was the first time anybody had seen him cry. He knew the Security Service had a long and insidious arm which could quietly plague his daughters wherever in the world they chose to work. They might fail the physical or the eyesight test or just lose to a superior candidate when in fact nobody wants to employ the daughter of a suspected traitor.

As the night wore on he talked about the interrogation and Rowan used this opportunity to ask him about the carrier pigeons he was suspected of using to send messages to the Soviets. A source of Rowan's told him the Watcher Service spent hours charting one of Bennett's suspicious activities while at home. Bennett was repeatedly seen putting a cage into his car trunk and driving to the spacious grounds of the National Research Council to make a release. Fearing the worst, the watchers theorized he was releasing carrier pigeons and that the National Research Council was chosen as the launch site because it was on high ground. It was an age-old system of communications for agents. This story produced a sarcastic chuckle from Bennett followed by the retort that the entire investigation had been incompetent. The cage, he explained, contained not pigeons but squirrels who were threatening the birds in his yard. He decided they had to be moved, trapped them in a cage with a trip wire, and one by one drove them to their new home in the vicinity of the National Research Council. Black squirrels populate the city of Ottawa from the outlying suburbs to the inner core and about twenty trips were needed to clear the squirrels out. Evidently, Bennett theorized, the RCMP's observation post on his home gave the watchers an obstructed view of his wooded lot that allowed them mere glimpses of what was going on, thus precluding them from seeing what was in the cage. The view at the National Research Council must not have been much better since trees there also blocked the view and the watchers would have had to stay well back to avoid detection, thus not seeing what kind of animal was being released. The watchers at some point must have discovered what was happening because the subject of releasing carrier pigeons was never raised at the interrogation. Upon learning of these shenanigans, Bennett snorted derisively.

Talk continued into the night and until the hours were no longer small. Bennett became repeatedly exasperated, exclaiming that he couldn't understand how anybody could believe he was a traitor. The more he dwelled on the thought the more disconsolate he became and tears again rolled from his eyes. He had dedicated his life to security work against communism and he loved Canada and did so much in bolstering the RCMP's fight against the espionage threat. These scenes solidified Rowan's faith in Bennett and made him think that if Bennett was acting he deserved an Academy Award. Rowan believed Bennett was incapable of feigning such grief; besides, there was no need to impress him especially now, since he carried no weight with the brass at the top.

Bennett had never before revealed passion over nationality or political ideology. He was a tough operator who happened to be stationed on the anti-communist side of the secret war. In his youth he was sympathetic to socialist views but in later life he never talked about it. In fact, until the interrogation, nobody knew, at least not definitely. During the interrogation he confirmed that in his youth he had strongly supported the British Labour party and still believed that Britain acted correctly in nationalizing the coal mines in South Wales. But he had become disenchanted with the Labour party in the early 1950s and had voted Liberal ever since coming to Canada in 1954, although he was tempted once or twice to vote NDP. Many colleagues routinely assumed he was a socialist although they couldn't say why they felt this way and nobody had any misconceptions about him being a bleeding heart. He was a centralist who believed in the state as a good and efficient administrator. The fact was that this technocrat was now in tears.

"I can't go back," cried Bennett. "How could I face my colleagues now?"

A touch of the old Bennett remained, for even now he tried to maintain his dignity and leave the impression that he had been cleared and could stay with the Force when in fact he had been sacked and could never return to the RCMP. If Bennett thought the interrogation was incompetent, the RCMP brass felt Bennett had defended himself badly and without enthusiasm.

Bennett felt he owed an explanation and a good-bye to one more former colleague, Janette Keir who, like Bennett, joined the Force as a civilian from Britain in the 1950s. Keir, a Scot, had served in Poland for MI6 after World War Two and possessed excellent counterespionage instincts. Short, plumpish, quiet and self-effacing, she looked out of place at RCMP headquarters, particularly on the highly secret fourth floor. One thought she should be tending her knitting at home. But her keen mind and sound judgement tended to restrain Bennett's enthusiasm for pushing operations too hard and too fast. "I think Jim takes too many risks," she once told a colleague. "Some day it will get him into trouble." So when Bennett showed up for dinner on one of his last nights in Canada she was more disturbed at his plight than surprised.

Keir grieved for Bennett because she was a good friend and colleague. She grieved also because he had worked so hard to build up the counterespionage branch. She knew all about his legendary capacity for work, how he often returned to the office evenings and took work home on weekends. Others in the Security Service may have been equally dedicated, but nobody backed up the dedication with so much work.

Keir also grieved a little for herself because she suspected they had nothing on him that they couldn't accuse her of as well. Their backgrounds were similar and she had been with the Force almost as long as he, witnessing the same case failures. Surely the RCMP investigators would be knocking on her door next. Like a condemned mafia leader, she waited in silence. She received no solace that night when Bennett described what had happened to him.

As Bennett and Keir talked, Robbie Robertson, a tall and lean former Mountie, left a private party in Ottawa and drove to Bennett's home, arriving near midnight to find nobody there. He sat in his car and waited for a rain storm to pass and for Bennett to return. Robertson had headed the Watcher Service but retired a decade earlier to establish a private security company in Toronto. His company was successful and became one of the most respected in Canada but he remained close to the Force and heard quickly enough about Bennett's departure and the surrounding circumstances. He had once worked with Bennett and wanted to satisfy himself that he had not wasted years of effort. He also had a special message to pass on. So he waited.

It was three A.M. before Bennett returned from Keir's place. Bennett was sober but clearly in a shattered emotional state, now little more than twenty-four hours before his departure from Canada. The house was barren except for a camp cot and a case of beer. Robertson asked what he had been doing in the ten years since they last worked together and, more importantly, what had happened to the Force in those years. Bennett figured Robertson had been sent by the Force and offered his cover story about retiring for medical reasons. When Robertson demonstrated that he knew the truth, Bennett yielded as little ground as possible and acknowledged that there had also been an investigation. Robertson persisted, wanting to know the whole story and whether or not he had been a Soviet agent.

As the storm passed and dawn arrived the two moved outdoors where Bennett began opening up. He said the Force had put clandestine closed circuit television surveillance on both his home and office and boasted that he had become aware of it from the first day because the Force had been sloppy and never bothered to clean up the mess on the floor. Robertson figured Bennett was merely guessing. He also had the impression that Bennett, although shaken, was more upset at the break-up of his marriage than the other events. Robertson was reassured by Bennett's claims of innocence but gave him a calculated warning: if he was ever shown to have been a foreign agent a special squad would take care of him. A few individuals, concerned at the damage that he would have inflicted as a Soviet agent, would see to it that justice would prevail.

"Well," Bennett replied, "They'll never prove anything."

By nine A.M. the two departed still friends.

Bennett was well out of the country when John Starnes, the head of the Security Service, was giving a talk to Mounties and staff at an

RCMP instructional course at headquarters. The gathering was routine although usually the Director-General wasn't the speaker. A junior Mountie got up and asked a question about Bennett's departure. Starnes, who made the decision to have Bennett interrogated and then to fire him, turned white and said, "Look, this matter is closed. I do not want questions concerning it."

But questions continued, at formal courses, on the job, and in the mess. The RCMP discovered that cleansing itself of Bennett was easier than clearing out the speculation about Bennett, or, for that matter, ensuring the mole was gone, if there had been a mole. The questions, coming mainly from younger, more inquisitive Mounties, were always hushed up. The Force, in spite of its adherence to discipline, couldn't stop the spread of rumours and questions within the ranks. The affair was too juicy and Bennett was too big and too well known and the alleged crime was too serious for people not to gossip.

Some felt that Bennett actually was a KGB agent and that headquarters was coddling a spy, who knows for what reason—perhaps to play him back to the KGB as a triple agent. Others felt he was innocent and a victim of the RCMP nineteenth century system of discipline and personnel management. Still others felt he was loyal but incompetent and that after years of exaggerating his expertise the many case failures finally exposed his true experience. One Mountie quipped that his feelings depended on which side of the bed he had gotten out of that morning.

"I've talked with a number of people and the thing is I still don't know," says a retired colleague of Bennett's. "If Jim walked into this room and said, 'Yes, I was,' it wouldn't surprise me. I'd say, 'Okay, fine. Now I know.' On the other hand, if he could prove conclusively that he was not, that wouldn't surprise me either. It's a terrible situation to be in. Either he's tremendously lucky or the victim of a tremendous injustice."

2

Joining
the Secret War

THE CYNON RIVER in South Wales meanders gently through the Aberdare Valley. It is so narrow that even small children can throw rocks across its industrially polluted contents with room to spare. The valley floor itself usually spans a mere 100 yards from side to side. At the turn of the century, a continuous ribbon of collieries monopolized the flat land of the valley from Aberdare to Abercynon. Farms and slag heaps, most abandoned and overgrown with grass and spindly trees, dominated the eastern slope at least 100 yards deep, linking village after village for as long as the mines stretched. The only break in this contiguous scarp of houses came from cross streets, occasional semi-detached clusters, and the odd house with a large yard for the local doctor or colliery manager. Each house, built by the collieries, was packed as closely as possible to the mine sites.

Penrhiwceiber (pronounced pen-rue-khyber) sits in the middle of this valley where the floor widens to nearly half a mile and the strip of housing climbs farther up the slope. The best steam coal in the world once came from this valley and the villagers, for decades before World War One, had thrived on the success of the industry. But their strength was their weakness for they had little alternative commerce and when coal suffered bad times the town had no secondary means of economic support. After the War the industry crashed and remained depressed for nearly two decades, teetering much of that time on the brink of total collapse.

The world peace of 1918 provoked this crisis superficially because less coal was needed after the war ended. Later it became apparent that the underlying problem was actually Britain's antiquated coal industry, which had stopped expanding while efficient new foreign mines undercut South Wales and stole her markets. British mines could not fight back without modernization, something the owners could not afford. In 1926 they cut wages to maintain profitability, although miners' incomes for years had lagged behind the cost of living.

Organized labour called a nation-wide general strike in 1926 but, with Prime Minister Stanley Baldwin opposed, the national stoppage lasted only nine days. The miners themselves stayed out six months before capitulating to reduced wages and lengthened hours. Thereafter, as the depression worsened, the miners had their number of work days reduced or were laid off outright. Families fought for survival. Entire communities rebelled against society. "Little Moscows," which elected communist representatives and subscribed to Russia's still untainted vision of utopia, sprang up throughout South Wales and elsewhere in Britain. Penrhiwceiber stayed relatively moderate and continued to support the Labour party. Only about twenty percent of its residents took up communism unlike neighbouring Aberaman, about three miles away, where about ninety-five percent supported communism.

Ted Bennett was born in 1896 of working class parents in the heart of this South Wales mining district. A fun loving, adventurous and inquiring lad, he might have escaped work in the mines except that he lacked formal education. But when he reached the age of eighteen and World War One erupted, he left the mines to join the Welsh Regiment where he served for four years. It was during a stay in hospital to recuperate from shrapnel wounds in the leg that he was attended by nurse Rose Long, who he married before the war ended. A merry yet practical woman from a neighbouring village, Rose produced two sons in quick succession: Telford in 1919, and Leslie James in 1920.

The house where Ted and Rose lived after the war was situated in a Penrhiwceiber World War One housing development that overlooked a quarry with 100-foot walls and a railtrack leading to the mine at the bottom of the valley. During the 1926 general strike eight years after their marrige, Ted Bennett, an entrenched Labour party supporter with an undogmatic social conscience, volunteered in the soup kitchens and fixed shoes for children and adults. At night he would sneak over to the colliery grounds and load up coal so he and his neighbours would have fuel. The police knew what was happening and would make the occasional raid, but they always provided plenty of warning. Bennett also helped found the Penrhiwceiber Branch of the British Legion and devoted much leisure time to it, particularly to the Legion's Benevolent Fund where he constantly struggled to coax a meager budget into relieving as much hardship as possible.

While the entire Bennett clan supported the Labour party, Rose's father was staunchly Conservative and her mother a Liberal. Rose a fan of Prime Minister David George, voted Liberal, and when no Liberal ran in the area, would switch to the Conservatives. Only in later years under the influence of the Bennett family and after the Liberals had deteriorated into a permanent splinter party did she passively support the Labour party, and even then a family connection with Lord Hall, the local Labour member of Parliament, smoothed the transition. She loved entertaining and had a knack for playing whist. She combined the two at least once a week, often managing to secure sound financial returns on modest investments.

In January of 1930, Telford, the oldest son of Ted and Rose Bennett, died suddenly at age eleven. He had been the pride of his parents and the idol of his younger brother, and the family went into mourning, never to emerge the same. Mrs. Bennett suffered a nervous breakdown and recovered, but the tragedy always hung over the home. There were no more children. From this point on Leslie James, not quite ten, lived in the shadow of his dead brother. "After this," recalls Gordon Bennett, his cousin, "Jim became somewhat more restrained and quiet, and perhaps later on, something of a 'loner.'"

At fourteen young Bennett was confirmed in St. Winifred's Parish Church in Penrhiwceiber, and under the firm hand of Rose Bennett attended church twice on Sundays, often three times, and kept busy with the church brigade during the week. The church did not command a great deal of authority during the social unrest of the 1920s and 1930s, but it did continue to be popular as there seemed little else to lend hope and optimism. The Bennett family had started out devoutly Baptist, but when the local minister's dalliances with young ladies became known, Rose took her family to the Church of England. Even Ted attended church regularly, although shift work and Legion activity caused him to miss occasionally.

There was never any doubt about the political sympathies of young Leslie James Bennett. From his first moment of awareness his sympathies were planted deeply in the Labour party. One could not remain aloof during those poverty years in South Wales. Circumstances impelled him to take a stand. Even at age six he would stand look-out while his father loaded coal clandestinely during the 1926 general strike. Later young Les—the army would christen him "Jim"—would accompany his father on his rounds to war veterans to determine who most needed support from the Legion's Benevolent Fund. These experiences shocked and depressed him for he witnessed psychological and financial bankruptcy and near starvation festering everywhere. He felt the futility lying ahead for the children whose only course was to enter the mines. These experiences stirred his social conscience and he came to believe that nationalizing the collieries was the only solution for the miners. He went with his father to Labour party rallies and saw the imposing figure of George Hall and other party leaders advocating a more equitable society.

The Bennett family weathered the long lean years better than most. Father had more consistent work than the majority of miners and received a small stipend from the British Legion, and houseproud Mother scrimped to ensure her surviving son ate well and dressed adequately. Young Bennett appreciated his relatively fortunate circumstances. While politically conscious, he was a typical boy who sought fun and spent a good part of his early teens swimming and playing soccer and cricket. Cycling provided some of his most pleasant moments. He would mount his trusty Raleigh three-speed and cycle through the hilly vale of Glamorgan and when he felt like a challenge he would turn north to tackle the mountainous Brecon Beacons. He spurned an approach to try out for professional soccer on his father's advice. Playing for a regional team would inevitably lead to the dirt and grime of the local mines.

Bennett quit school at sixteen and went to work. He wanted to stay in school for the final two years and attain university entrance standing but felt this required too many sacrifices by his parents. In 1936, fortunes were improving in South Wales and he took a job as counter clerk with the Penrhiwceiber Post Ofice, managed by a friend of his father's, where he answered the telephone, sold stamps, dispensed registered letters and took money orders. He enjoyed meeting the public but the work was humdrum and held no future, so he viewed it as temporary employment until something better came along. Less than a year later he won a competition for the position of clerk to the Clerk of the Mountain Ash Urban District Council office a few miles away and became responsible for registering deaths and burials in the district.

At the district council his talent was spotted by Arthur Williams, the district's Engineer and Surveyor, and he was given a clerical-engineering position which could turn an ambitious youngster into a professional engineer. Impressed by the quality and humanitarianism of the district's engineers and their desire to improve local facilities, and lured by the career potential of this work, Bennett soon set civil engineering as his professional goal, and as his ambition took form he aspired to join the colonial service and travel to Africa to build water and sanitation systems. He first, however, had to become an engineer and acquire experience in Britain.

Twice weekly after work he gulped down dinner and boarded a bus for an hour's ride to the Cardiff Technical School for night classes and returned home by eleven P.M., leaving the home-study portion of his class to the other free evenings. His diligence was rewarded at the end of the year with a first-class certificate and a Sandwich Scholarship worth twenty pounds toward the second academic term. He looked forward to returning in September, 1939 but on the eve of the new semester World War Two erupted and civil defence work at the urban district hall consumed his evenings and wiped out his academic plans for the year. The school promised to defer the scholarship until after the war. He wanted to volunteer for the Royal Corps of Engineers and acquire some quick professional experience but his supervisor at work talked him out of it, saying the war effort needed him in his present job and that he could volunteer for the second company of engineers forming later. The second company never formed. Twice he visited the local army recruiting office hoping his initiative would land him an engineering spot in the forces and both times he was told to wait to be called up.

Shortly after his twentieth birthday Bennett was conscripted and assigned to the Royal Corps of Signals. This turn of events devastated him. Signals was a war of its own in which both sides monitored the other's communications for evidence of troop movements and battle intentions. It was the most secret part of World War Two but that meant nothing to him then and he appealed, but Britain was mobilizing furiously and did not hear his complaint. In any case, the army desperately needed signalmen in the Middle East and war requirements took precedence over the career ambitions of a single draftee. So on May 30, 1940, Bennett reported for training to the Royal Corps of Signals Special Battalion at Trowbridge, Wiltshire where they taught him how to be a soldier and a signalman. The hard physical work caught him and the other recruits by surprise. When he was not digging trenches under the hot sun, running cross-country or marching full pack drills, he was learning how to receive and send Morse code for the purpose of intercepting enemy radio communications. He was given sixteen weeks to reach twenty-five words a minute, met this goal in eleven weeks, and joined the first draft sent overseas to Malta.

The troopship *Duchess of Bedford* left Liverpool in August 1940 and headed north to Scotland and into the Atlantic to rendezvous with a convoy of protection ships crawling south at fourteen knots. It by-passed direct entry into the Mediterranean at Gibraltar and sailed around South Africa's Cape of Good Hope and up through the Suez Canal where Bennett climbed aboard a cruiser for Malta. Here he and fellow recruits were thrown directly into top secret work without signing any special indoctrination forms. A simple oath of allegiance ushered these recruits into the heart of the secret war.

The war was cruel to Malta. Only sixty miles from Sicily, this tiny island served as the Allied staging point for bombing raids on Italian ports and Rommel's supply lines in North Africa. Axis planes retaliated by dumping more bombs here than on all England. After being stationed at Id Duera, overlooking the ancient city of Moina, the signals unit split up to achieve protection through dispersal and Bennett spent six months in Valletta until a Luftwaffe raid destroyed the offices and nearly wiped out the unit. After that he moved to Salina Bay. It seemed these evasive measures were merely delaying the inevitable capitulation since everybody believed Malta was doomed. The soldiers knew their fate. With plans complete, the Axis High Command was set to destroy Malta and remove this vexatious sore but Rommel's success in North Africa postponed the need and by the time Rommel was pushed back, Malta was sufficiently reinforced to defend itself.

Through these siege conditions everybody on Malta ate subsistence rations, being allotted each day a slice and a half of bread, a strip of bacon, a few army biscuits mashed with corned beef and maybe a sardine. At tea time, one got a half slice of bread and a cup of tea. Bennett had eaten better than this during the worst days in South Wales. Mail arrived approximately twice a year depending on the carrier's ability to avoid German U-boats. Bennett's twenty-first birthday cake from his mother, sent three months in advance, arrived nicely in time for his twenty-second birthday.

The signals unit, aside from intercepting Axis communications, was charged with responsibility for breaking the low-level codes used on the field and deciphering the traffic for the purpose of analysing strengths and weaknesses as well as predicting intentions. Any significant troop movement, whether an attack, retreat or strategic shift, could be spotted in advance through communications intercepts by a crack signals unit. Communications intelligence was crucial in daily war strategy and had to be fed to army command before time aged the information. With the quick death of British intelligence's entire network of agents on the continent, signals became the Allies' intelligence lifeline all through the war. Without it, the British would not have broken the code of the German High Command and the war would have ended differently.

Starting as a signalman third grade, the lowest rank, Bennett shifted from the intercept side to the intelligence side of operations and became involved in directing which signals should be monitored and ensuring that the hot information was passed on quickly. This work was so secret that still today it remains a forbidden subject except for a few disclosures such as Ultra, the breaking of the German code.

Two years of Malta was taxing for any soldier and Bennett was happy to learn of an impending transfer to Heliopolis, Egypt, outside Cairo. But before he left, hepatitis, which plagued the ranks, struck. Bennett wanted nothing to jeopardize his transfer and promotion and two days before he was scheduled to leave he swallowed gallons of water in the hope of flushing out the infection. The hepatitis largely disappeared but the flow of water stretched his liver toward his rib cage and for the rest of his life he suffered sharp pains from bending in certain ways.

Heliopolis formally transferred Bennett out of the Signals Corps and into the Intelligence Corps. The building which housed the intelligence offices stood isolated on the outskirts of town—the nearest building was the signals encampment half a mile away—and it was called the Intelligence School for cover. From here he journeyed into the desert to places such as Derna and Bengazi where he helped establish intercept posts and stayed on for months to help run them. The desert was the only place Bennett carried a gun during the war. Heliopolis, with weekend passes to Cairo and trips to Palestine, was a haven compared to Malta. In March, 1944 Bennett was sent back to the front lines, this time to Italy to help provide intelligence support for the Eighth Army's onslaught. Italy was Bennett's most professionally rewarding posting and the one in which his aptitude for intelligence grew increasingly apparent. When he was sent back to Britain after four and a half years abroad, the Allied victory was certain and VE Day only months away.

Bennett had tried resuming his engineering studies at Malta briefly but siege conditions defeated him. Now during the leisurely post-war months in army camps in England he tried again and signed up for correspondence courses in engineering and mathematics from the army's educational branch. He gave up after six months. Five years and history's greatest military carnage had changed him and his interests. Engineering held high prospects for a kid growing up in Penrhiwceiber, but now, having seen a piece of the world and experienced the suffering of war, he viewed his future from a different vantage point and engineering no longer had the same glitter. His escape from Penrhiwceiber was already made good and war had given him a new profession, whetting his appetite for spicier experiences. Now the prospect of stealing enemy secrets during the coming peace seemed more invigorating than designing a storm sewer.

The post-war prospect for Intelligence promised to be stimulating. While the public looked forward to peace, the entire intelligence community was re-tooling for the oncoming battle with a more entrenched and ideologically more resistant enemy, communism. Post-war Britain found itself scrambling against the Soviet Union almost the way it had done against Germany six years earlier. New intercept stations were springing up and the entire thrust was changing and Bennett wanted to be part of the action. Excitement and challenge aside, he concluded the work was as important as engineering and in some ways more fundamental.

With the transition to peace the communications intelligence bureaucracy was brought together under a single new civilian roof called Government Communications Headquarters, GCHQ for short. One of Bennett's last duties in the army was to help convert the Radio Security Service, a military unit whose task was to pinpoint enemy agents through their transmitters, into a civilian outfit under the new GCHQ. Bennett was promised an excellent career with the new peacetime organization and in July, 1946, after six years of army life, shed his uniform to start as a probationary executive officer. While that step advanced his career considerably, Bennett had another reason for hiring on. His girlfriend, Pauline Jowett, a civilian in the Intelligence Corps, was also transferring to GCHQ and they planned to marry later in the year. The marriage never took place mainly because her parents wanted a ranking officer and Bennett left the army as a Warrant Officer Second Class, which was two promotions away from commissioned officer status.

If Pauline's family did not appreciate Bennett's qualities, evidently the army did because a couple of decades later it issued Army Form B 108A (Revised) describing Bennett's military conduct as exemplary. "A man of outstanding intelligence, ability and initiative who possesses good powers of organization and determination to get things done. Absolutely trustworthy." (Army's emphasis.)

3

The Philby
Connection

THE VIEW ATOP the hills of Istanbul in 1947 told the story of this historic city's importance in the intelligence world of post-war Europe. Immediately to the east, across the Bosporous and easily visible to the naked eye, Asia opened its doors. Toward the south the Dardanelles offered a route to the Mediterranean and the host of interests there. To the north the Black Sea fended off the behemoth, the USSR. Old Constantinople, the world's only city to bridge two continents, also divided the world's two ideological spheres in a country where the western alliance confronted Russia face to face. The city had lost its official status as capital of Turkey a few decades earlier but carried on as an international metropolis and, among other things, remained the crossroads for the intelligence community. While the British embassy had moved to the new capital Ankara nearly a quarter of a century before, the MI6 station stayed behind and British intelligence continued using Istanbul as a major base for espionage against the Soviet Union and its satellites in the Balkans and central Europe.

Possessing only a small intercept station inherited from the army, GCHQ wanted to send civilians to expand facilities in Istanbul. Bennett, after finishing the conversion of an army unit in Austria, drew this duty and travelled to Turkey in October, 1947 with cover as a foreign service officer in the Consulate-General. Most of his day was cannibalized by paperwork prying loose his small staff one by one from the military and turning them into civilians for integration into the

23

GCHQ structure. When his administration work ended for the day he would pick up the incoming reports and sift through the data to determine which Soviet targets needed chasing. Nobody knew how much non-military intelligence would flow from this corner of the world or what form it might take, so he devoted his time to establishing surveillance priorities for the unit.

As the ranking GCHQ man in the British mission, Bennett, as instructed by headquarters, quickly sought to introduce himself to the MI6 station chief but found he was out of town for several weeks. This station chief had arrived six months earlier and was a young hotshot named Kim Philby whose secret work as a Soviet mole inside British intelligence was completely unsuspected at that time. Philby, then thirty-five, was already being tagged by MI6 insiders as a future head of the organization. Bennett, working in a different organization and not privy to MI6 rumours, had no knowledge of Philby's star quality except to wonder how such a young man acquired such a major posting so quickly in such an established bureaucracy as MI6. Consumed by his responsibilities, he had not sought a meeting out of personal curiosity. His briefings in headquarters had urged him to cultivate MI6 because GCHQ in Istanbul was small and it might from time to time need help.

Considering that both individuals would later become suspects as KGB agents, their meeting several weeks later held portentious promise, a kind of spy-world solar eclipse in which two separate and independent KGB suspects crossed paths on British business. But as it turned out, Philby was remote, limp and uninterested. Bennett, eight years younger and much junior, acted very correctly but, being busy, was pressed for time and made no move to prolong the encounter. The meeting never lived up to its potential and resulted only in two men indifferently acknowledging one another in the pursuit of separate objectives. Even their spheres of intelligence work were different. Philby enlisted human agents with access to secrets. Bennett functioned by listening to radio traffic—ship to shore, air to ground and ground to ground—and distilling it into hard information. Philby's father was an English knight and Bennett's a Welsh coal miner. After some small talk, Bennett secured his sought-after commitment of assistance and Philby, with his stutter, wished Bennett good luck. The meeting lasted only a few minutes. The two occasionally bumped into one another on the cocktail circuit and exchanged greetings, but they never discussed business.

Seven months later, Bennett's unit was established and operating smoothly. His objectives were accomplished, so he handed over control to his assistant and, with Philby still in Istanbul, returned to Britain. He never did need Philby's help and, once gone, never saw him again. As far as Bennett was concerned his stopover was successful and uneventful. He never suspected that this simultaneous posting with Philby would, nearly a quarter century later, return to haunt him.

Bennett took on a new job as Section Head in the old Radio Security Service he had previously helped convert into a civilian unit. He worked on the attack against all forms of Russian communications including transmissions between Moscow and its agents, and his duties made him secretary of the interdepartmental Counter Clandestine Committee consisting of GCHQ, MI6 and MI5 (The British Security Service), drawing him into central planning for the secret war. Here the British security and intelligence community unfolded under full view. His vantage point gave him a privileged glimpse at the three main organizations and taught him things about his own organization few of his colleagues knew, such as how the organizations interacted, fitting and sometimes not fitting together. It was the best instruction available and broadened his professional experience beyond communications intelligence, opening the world of human espionage and counterespionage work. The position was good and the work satisfied his thirst for knowledge. But it still left him hungry for field experience.

When a post in Australia became available in early 1950 he jumped and went to Melbourne as GCHQ's Traffic Liaison Officer to Australia's Defence Signals Division (later called the Defence Signals Bureau). Only three months passed before more pressing work pulled him to Hong Kong to target China after the revolution. His brief stay in Melbourne introduced him to a young Australian telegraphist named Heather (Shev) Quinn and they married in a Catholic church in Hong Kong during the next assignment.

Hong Kong was a gruelling post. Mao's takeover of China jolted western intelligence. China had suddenly defected leaving the West with a major new intelligence target and few existing assets to exploit. Returning missionaries and travellers produced the bulk of the legitimate intelligence and even this was unreliable and thin. The British suddenly needed intercept stations in Hong Kong to monitor developments and this objective became Bennett's major mandate. As a colony, Hong Kong did not require liaison with a foreign agency as was the case in Melbourne. Bennett liaised with other British personnel in the army, navy, air force, MI5, MI6 and the Governor's office, all of whom taxed both his time and humour. Then the tropical disease sprue, a nutritional deficiency with symptoms somewhat similar to dysentery, flattened him in a hospital bed for weeks and forced him onto a non-wheat and non-fat diet.

The Hong Kong tramway connection flourished in the hectic months after the revolution. The "tramway," a collection of defeated Chinese military types and assorted others, sold "intelligence" about events inside China to western agencies. The goods were exaggerated and concocted but fetched millions of dollars. The scam was exposed in time and Bennett, whose ear on the mainland helped expose the phony intelligence, played a role of which he was proud.

The diplomatic circuit absorbed much of his time and made him entertain socially, often at some financial expense. The frugal GCHQ in those days did not reimburse these out-of-pocket expenses, which in the two years in Hong Kong totalled about $1,000. He resented GCHQ's stinginess and really never forgave the organization.

Bennett returned to Britain in 1952 to become Section Head responsible for the Middle East. But as marriage to Shev had coincided with the fervour of establishing the Hong Kong office, the trip back was planned as their real honeymoon. Together they disembarked at Genoa and made their way to Paris, living on fresh air, sunshine and love, arriving finally in England without a penny in their pockets.

Bennett had been abroad most of the six years the Labour government of Prime Minister Clement Attlee held power and his return from Hong Kong followed the defeat of the Labour party and the comeback of Winston Churchill and the Conservatives. The mess under the Labour government disappointed him and he concluded the programs of nationalization were simply not working, except for the 1947 takeover of the coal mines, which he thought saved the industry. He felt that the Labour party did not deserve backing yet he could not bring himself to support the Conservatives. His social conscience would not permit that leap, so from that point on he favoured the remnants of the Liberal party.

Bennett soon moved to General Search Section where as head he supervised the analysis of intercepted clandestine short wave transmitter signals between Moscow and its agents around the world. General Search tried to establish how many separate agent-oriented broadcasts originated from the Soviet Union so the West could estimate the number of Soviet agents being served by radio. It also tried to pinpoint the location and identity of responding agents through tracking illegal transmitters. While in General Search, Bennett and colleague John Rickwood, who would also emigrate to Canada and join the RCMP Security Service as a civilian employee, suspected that secrets were leaking to the Soviet Union. As soon as GCHQ would break a low-grade Russian cipher, the Soviets would switch to a new system. It happened often enough to make them suspect a Russian pipeline into the organization. Where it originated, they did not know because several British organizations received the information from the broken ciphers. Bennett and Rickwood passed on their doubts and were told by superiors to drop the matter. Their superiors left the impression that all was under control. Like good servants they complied and never did learn what was happening. At GCHQ one was not nosy.

Bennett had risen swiftly in Government Communications but had reached the stage where further promotion would be difficult. By the mid-1950s GCHQ had matured and lost much of its old excitement. It was not Bennett but the organization which was becoming mundane. The British intelligence community had completed the massive switch from surveillance of fascist forces to communist, and GCHQ was coasting on comfortable bureaucratic normality. He was told the prospects of going abroad again in the next five years were slight, and his superiors thought he had spent enough time overseas, especially after his serious bout of sprue. GCHQ's new home at Cheltenham in the west country of England brought him about fifty miles from Penrhiwceiber which was convenient, and the Bennetts spent many weekends visiting the folk, but in a way it was too close. Wanderlust remained and intensified so close to home. The prospect of being stuck in Britain held no appeal. General Search was demanding, particularly at this time when Soviet agents started using high-speed transmitters, increasing the challenge of tracking them. But he was tied to a desk in headquarters when the field ignited his enthusiasm.

Shev had come to Britain filled with anticipation and romance, particularly at the prospect of exploring historic sites previously experienced only through school books. But the excitement soon faded, disappointment followed, and finally unhappiness, so much so that she wanted out of Britain. She found British society less rugged and less open than Australia's and the people snobbish. She had been spankingly healthy in Melbourne but the British dampness—especially in Cheltenham, which lay in a valley—and a seemingly endless string of colds, influenza and pleurisy drained away her vitality. Several miscarriages robbed her of motherhood. Her doctor warned that becoming acclimatized to English weather might take five years.

Bennett at this time had become friendly with Joe Gibson who worked for Canada's GCHQ, called CBNRC because it was the Communications Branch under the cover of the National Research Council. Gibson in the early 1950s was CBNRC's liaison officer to Britain and through this connection Bennett inquired about life in Canada and work prospects at CBNRC. Gibson promised to put in a word for him in Ottawa and check out the prospects. So far it sounded good, but when Bennett stopped by the Canadian immigration office in Cheltenham he received a gloomy forecast. The immigration officer there warned him that he would find it tough and that getting established in Canada could take five years or more. But the word back from CBNRC through Gibson held hope. The organization did not promise anything but was interested in meeting him once he arrived in Ottawa. The Bennetts debated their future and, realizing no job may be waiting, decided to take a flyer and emigrate to Canada. Bennett left GCHQ carrying a letter of reference from Robert Amys, the deputy personnel officer.

> I have pleasure in confirming that you have been employed by this headquarters as an established civil servant from the 15th July, 1946, until the 13th March, 1954. During that time your health, conduct and performance of duty have all been very satisfactory. We are extremely sorry that personal reasons have made you decide to emigrate, and will be pleased to recommend you with the greatest confidence, to any prospective employer as a thoroughly capable and reliable person.

The passenger liner *Beaver Burn* from Liverpool docked at Saint John, New Brunswick, on March 28, 1954, and the following day the train carrying the Bennetts rolled into Ottawa's Union Station a few hundred yards from Parliament Hill. Bitter cold and high snowbanks greeted their arrival. Roy Batchelor, alerted by Joe Gibson, was waiting at the station and his greeting overcame, somewhat, the shock of the cold. Batchelor was an old army and GCHQ friend of Bennett's who came to Canada five years earlier, caught on with CBNRC and was now comfortably established. As he took them home for lunch, Batchelor told him that a job interview at CBNRC was arranged for two P.M.

When Bennett met Rod MacAskill, Co-ordinator of Administration at CBNRC, he found him friendly but quick to come to the point. Bennett was not a Canadian and CBNRC's policy was to hire Canadians first. He explained that hiring him required a special reason and, unfortunately, his case did not meet the requirements for an exemption. The session with MacAskill was not an interview but a statement of policy which not only closed the door but locked it.

The rejection, especially its swiftness and finality, stunned Bennett. No job was ever promised but he thought CBNRC would at least interview him, think it over and get back. His only job prospect in Canada had evaporated within hours of his arrival and he had no inkling that nationalism was growing in CBNRC offices as a result of a series of senior hirings from the U.K. So many Britishers were coming to the organization that miffed natives were saying CBNRC stood for Communications Branch—No Room for Canadians. Director Ed Drake, a Canadian from Saskatchewan, decreed he wanted no more British accents in his organization.

Batchelor too was taken aback as was Mary Oliver, the personnel officer. She had wanted to hire Bennett and she was the CBNRC officer in Ottawa who had originally given encouragement to Joe Gibson who in turn encouraged Bennett. In the meantime, MacAskill had moved into a position above her and assumed authority over the matter. She felt personally responsible for Bennett's predicament and, as Bennett left the building, told him she was disappointed and sorry.

More setbacks followed. Shev suffered another miscarriage and, lacking hospital insurance, this jeopardized his temporary financial independence. Currency exchange controls had restricted his withdrawal of money from Britain to $800 and now he was beginning to run short. He began looking for work and applied with the Civil Service but was rejected on residential qualifications. He turned to another old GCHQ friend, Donald Camfield, working at the Joint Intelligence Bureau in the Department of National Defence and got the same forthright refusal that CBNRC gave. Camfield advised him to concentrate on engineering and Bennett applied without success to Alcan Canada for its massive construction project in Kitimat, B.C. He tried the Employment Exchange on Queen Street saying he was prepared to accept anything and was rewarded with a three-week secretarial-clerk job at Canadian Pacific Express. He could type and manage rusty shorthand, so for fifty-eight dollars a week he took dictation, typed letters and checked waybills at the last loading platform in Union Station while the regular employee was on holiday.

Mary Oliver had not forgotten Bennett's plight and invited him to a party at her home where he was introduced to two civilian members of the RCMP, Mark McClung and his assistant, Don Wall. McClung, a Rhodes scholar, was head of the RCMP's research unit and had vacancies on his staff. Through Mary Oliver, McClung and Wall already knew about Bennett's CBNRC experience and brought to the party an employment application form. They arranged an interview for the following week.

Beer flowed freely in the Naval Officers' mess, the HMCS Bytown during the interview. The session with McClung and Wall started over lunch as all three, with trays in hand, picked up their roast beef and moved to the Crow's Nest on the top floor where they could be alone. The atmosphere was warm and proceedings meandered informally for three hours. Bennett got the impression they were testing his ability to hold drink and maintain discretion. McClung and Wall laughed as he described the various systems he had devised for breaking the tedium of those damn waybills at the Canadian Pacific Express platform. The interview went well and McClung and Wall were impressed. They warned him that as a civilian in the RCMP he would be deprived opportunities since civilians were considered support staff to RCMP members who had endured boot camp in Regina and graduated as Mounties to become policemen. The inequities caused some RCMP civilians to quit, but the warning did not deter Bennett. He came from class conscious Britain and, besides, could not be choosy. As the interview ended McClung told him he was best suited for a vacant slot in B Branch under Terry Guernsey and promised to talk to Guernsey who would probably get in touch for an interview.

B Branch excited Bennett because it was the counterespionage section and it ran agents and double agents and did everything else involved in counterintelligence operations. This prospect stimulated him more than writing research reports under McClung. Also, B Branch was an infant only starting to grow, which would allow Bennett the opportunity to get onto the ground floor and rise with the branch.

Then, weeks passed with no word from Guernsey or anybody else at the RCMP. The temporary job ended and Mary Oliver and Rod MacAskill helped him find a summer job at $250 a month as research clerk for a government survey of scientific and engineering salaries across North America. Finally, Guernsey called and arranged an interview. He seemed intrigued by Bennett's engineering background and experience processing intelligence.

Guernsey, the only Mountie with formal counterespionage training, wore an RCMP uniform but did not think with a paramilitary mind. Once a regular policeman, he attended MI6 intelligence school in Britain and returned convinced that a police organization like the RCMP could never be an effective counterespionage force. He also came to believe the RCMP should be split into two organizations—a police force to uphold the law, and an independent civilian security service to safeguard the national interest—since policing and security work were not only different but inherently conflicting duties. At work he continually proposed new techniques, but superiors who failed to perceive this fundamental difference overruled him.

One interview with Bennett convinced Guernsey that he too possessed an innovative, non-police mind and was the type of help needed. On July 2, 1954, Bennett reported to RCMP headquarters as a Research Analyst III earning $4320 a year, and was given an office in headquarters which had once been a Catholic seminary. The only available room had a big horse trough at one end where nuns used to wash their clothes.

Six months earlier, while Bennett was working as head of General Search and preparing for his move to Canada, he had been called into the office of his superior and handed a sensitive assignment. Since everything at GCHQ had been top secret, all assignment work was sensitive. But his boss had emphasized that the secrecy of this matter was to be guarded with special care since it came from the RCMP in Canada and concerned a top-flight counterespionage case against the KGB. Only one of his men could be brought into it.

The case involved a Soviet agent in Montreal under a false identity who had secretly defected to the Canadian authorities and was now being doubled back. The defection represented the western world's first exposure of a Russian "illegal" agent since World War Two. An illegal agent is an alien who enters the country under a false identity and citizenship as opposed to known or suspected agents who enter as diplomats. Moscow had been sending coded instructions over short wave radio while the illegal copied them in the back of his photo studio. Now all this information had fallen into RCMP hands, including broadcast times, frequencies, call signs, code books and the messages themselves. The RCMP wanted to be sure the defector was a genuine spy and not an impostor and therefore needed confirmation that these claimed transmissions from Moscow had actually occurred.

As head of General Search at GCHQ at the time, Bennett had been responsible for Soviet communications to its illegals around the world. He had read the detailed brief and one day summoned his staff expert and, without divulging the case, instructed him to check the logs and verify or refute the transmission schedule. After lunch the next day the staff member had returned with his assessment. The transmissions were real.

Now, six months later, Bennett began work at RCMP headquarters on the same case, this time from the Canadian side with Guernsey. And, although he started at the bottom as a junior functionary, he suddenly found himself in a supporting capacity on one of the most monumental double agent cases the West had going.

4

Operation Keystone

THE SHIP LANDED in Halifax Harbour in the fall of 1952 and the disembarking passengers lined up for the mandatory inspection at the immigration shed. Separating the old-world immigrants searching for a new life in Canada from established Canadians returning from European visits was easy, for their clothes, appearance and manners were different. Almost everybody seemed to fit into either of these categories. A young, short, blond man in his late twenties, waiting alone, defied either category. His prominent cheekbones and deep set eyes tagged him as a European. His face wore the tenseness of an immigrant settling into a foreign land with dreams for a new life. Yet his native tongue was English, spoken with a decided North American accent carrying a slight twang from the Bronx.

He showed all the signs of travel fatigue after a week-long ocean voyage but his faculties were at peak alertness. His instructors at The Centre in Moscow had warned him he was now walking into his most dangerous moment; the customs and immigration check represented one of the riskiest points in his entire mission. He had also been given assurance that there was no reason for anything to go wrong. His identification papers had been assiduously prepared and checked and the authorities had no reason to suspect them. When his turn arrived he produced his American passport calmly and was whisked through in half a minute. What a relief. His heart pounded. He picked up his single suitcase and strolled outside, following the road as it wrapped about to the front of the Hotel Nova Scotian, all the while dreading that he might be called back before he could disappear around the corner, not daring to expose his fear by looking over his shoulder. His inner terror eased as he cleared the corner and subsided with each step until he reached the front of the railway station and felt confident enough to congratulate himself for successfully passing this crucial phase.

Moscow's instructions—drilled into his memory over many months—kept ringing through his mind: "Buy a train ticket to Montreal and board the next departure. Befriend nobody on the journey. Talk to nobody until you become legalized." More instructions rolled out of his memory the next day when the train pulled into Montreal: "Go straight to the washroom in the station." He had no trouble finding the facility and inside a three-inch diagonal chalk mark on the door registered the cubicle he was to use. Inside he found taped underneath the lid of the toilet tank a birth certificate and other papers giving him a new identity as a native Canadian citizen. He ripped up his forged American passport and driver's licence and dropped the bits into the toilet. Two weeks ago in Moscow he was the son of a ranking Soviet trade official. He had learned English as a boy while his father was stationed in New York with the Russian trade company Amtorg. This was his true identity. The KGB made him temporarily the travelling son of a phony American industrialist so he could get into Canada without being traced as either the person he had been in the Soviet Union or as the person he was about to become in Canada. Now that he was safely on Canadian soil his temporary documentation had served its purpose and was flushed into the Montreal sewer system. He was now David Soboloff, the native Canadian son of Russian immigrants and no documentary evidence survived to suggest the man posing as Soboloff had ever been outside Canada. With his previous passport destroyed, no evidence linked David Soboloff to the lone "American" who disembarked the previous day in Halifax and took the train to Montreal. Even if his new identity fell under suspicion, the authorities would be hard pressed to prove he slipped into the country illegally. The Soboloff family had at one time existed and lived in Canada and did have a son named David, but the parents emigrated back to Russia and took young David with them, leaving no official record of having gone. Had the son remained in Canada he would now—1952—resemble in age and appearance the new David Soboloff whose task over the next year would be to acquire a legitimate driver's licence in the Soboloff name and build up a documented identity in Canada for the long range purpose of legitimately emigrating to the United States to help a KGB illegal who was already in place.

Gideon, as he would eventually be called in RCMP reports, got his first shock that evening. Following The Centre's instructions, he had no trouble finding a cheap boarding house but ordering a meal in a restaurant was something Moscow had overlooked and he bolted out the doors on his first attempt. As good as his training had been, it had failed to cover everything. Restaurants, with their booths and complex menus, frightened him. He figured the people in them were doing more than just dining. Hungry, Gideon stood on the street and watched street vendors selling fast food from pushcarts and wondering why people were so eager to eat dog meat. Then he figured out what a hot dog was, and for the next seven days ate nothing but hot dogs and french fries from these vendors.

The public transport system also scared him. Montreal had different kinds of streetcars: trollies operated by one man with passengers entering from the front and exiting at the rear; and trolleys operated by a driver and a ticket taker with passengers entering from the back but exiting at the back on some and at the side on others. Gideon did not know which doors to use and worried about becoming a white crow— the KGB term for somebody who sticks out—so avoided all public transit. He expected at any minute a stranger to stop him on the street and challenge his identity as one might do in Moscow. His trainers at The Centre emphasized above everything else to "maintain your legend; it is the key to survival." Montreal was to become home and shelter his secret life but on this occasion he was staying only a few weeks—just long enough to get a feel for the city. First he had to build cover elsewhere in Canada and learn the country and its customs and this required travelling—first to Toronto.

According to his prepared "legend," David Soboloff had once lived in Toronto so Gideon also had to put in sufficient time there to know the city well enough to answer questions about his past. He toured the area where he claimed to have lived, visited the apartment, inspected his "old" work premises, and learned the bus routes he would have taken. Three weeks later he boarded the train for Vancouver, stopping along the way in Winnipeg and Edmonton where he lived in cheap rooming houses.

Gideon already knew almost as much about Vancouver as a class-room could teach. He had scored well in the KGB's oral tests about the west coast city and even withstood a gentle mock interrogation. Where was the main public library? What street divided Burnaby from Vancouver? Where was Chinatown? KGB efficiency made him learn the names of all Vancouver aldermen, population figures, shipping tonnages and other statistics even most Vancouverites would not know.

The real Soboloffs abandoned Russia in the 1920s as the shocks of collectivization tore up the old society and before the Bolshevists locked the doors of emigration. Canada was booming but the Soboloffs had trouble adjusting to the language and customs of a foreign country and were not sharing in the boom. When the depression hit in the 1930s they felt no better off and concluded that if they were destined to scratch out a living they might as well struggle in the more familiar surroundings of their homeland. So they returned to the Soviet Union via Finland taking young David with them. Whatever became of them back in the old country only the KGB knows.

The Canadian government never knew they had left Canada which made the Soboloffs an excellent identity for a legend. An imposter merely had to apply for birth certificates and passports in the Soboloff name to receive genuine and nearly unchallengeable documentation. Unfortunately, the father had stopped filing income tax returns after leaving Canada and since this would arouse suspicion he was precluded from being used, but David was an excellent cover. The legend had the elder Soboloff die in Canada during the 1930s—hence no income tax returns—and Mrs. Soboloff die a decade later as David supposedly entered adulthood. This way Gideon playing the role of David could roam the country as a native Canadian without worrying about bump-ing into family or relatives.

Gideon regularly reported his progress to Moscow through "dead letter boxes." He would drop his message into a pre-arranged public hiding place such as a hole in a wall, underneath a stairway or in a hole in a tree in a park and an hour later somebody would pick it up. The system was safe because it required no physical contact between the sender and the receiver. Even if the receiver was watched clearing the box the authorities had no clue who had originally filled it. So Gideon could communicate safely with the Soviet embassy in Ottawa no matter how intensively they were being followed. The only weakness was that the communication through this system usually moved one way. While Gideon could send messages to The Centre it would normally not return communications.

Vancouver relaxed Gideon and boosted his confidence. His rugged boyish face, grinning smile, quick wit and blond hair attracted admirers in spite of his shortness. Women savoured him as a cute workingman type. Even his bottled up nervousness broke out into unique and likeable mannerisms. Back in Moscow he was happily married but his devotion to his wife did not stop him from enjoying female attention. He felt his wife would understand that the stress of a dangerous assignment on behalf of the state required him to relax. If his wife did not understand, The Centre did and merely required him to report every affair, which he did except for one.

From Vancouver he returned east, destined eventually for Montreal but stopping off first for a prolonged visit in Kingston. Here he fell in love so passionately he lost his enthusiasm for other women; even his wife in Moscow no longer mattered. His lover made him forget about spying and his duty to the advancement of socialism. She, more than anything else, helped him adapt to Canada, reduce his tensions and make life more comfortable. For the first time he was beginning to enjoy Canadian life.

It seemed no time had passed before his stay in Kingston ran out and The Centre's instructions required him to move to Montreal and open a one-man watch repair shop to provide cover for the spying he was about to begin; Gideon had been taught watch repairing as part of his espionage training. But he did not want to leave his lover so proposed they marry and live together in Montreal without thinking of the consequences. In fact, he would be committing a fundamental error as an illegal. A secret marriage would force him to lead yet another double life. He was already fooling the Canadian government and now proposed to deceive the KGB as well. Eventually The Centre would discover his secret marriage and recall him to Moscow and interrogate him as a traitor. His own marriage aside, Gideon was also conveniently overlooking the fact his lover was married to a corporal in the Canadian military. It was one thing for her to carry on an illicit affair and another to leave her husband for a drifter. Fortunately for Gideon's own security, she told him that although she loved him she could not leave her husband to live with him.

Gideon arrived in Montreal despondent, alone and late. Being behind schedule did not matter much. He was becoming almost casual in attitude and The Centre would never know since the lines of communication were long and slow. Looking for an excuse not to settle in Montreal, Gideon dropped a note in a dead letter box advising The Centre that watch repair competition in Montreal was too heavy for him to build a viable cover. Somehow he believed The Centre would abandon Montreal and let him return to Kingston. The message would at least buy him a few months of time while The Centre decided how to respond and Gideon could use this reprieve to visit Kingston.

The message caught Moscow in an awkward position. Gideon had not quite reached the stage where The Centre could easily send him instructions. Once he set up shop in Montreal he was supposed to buy a short wave radio and listen for weekly encoded instructions through Morse signals directly from The Centre. With Gideon receiving through short wave and sending through dead letter boxes secure communications would flow in both directions and finally make Gideon a serviceable agent. But this was still in the future. First The Centre had to figure out how to handle the case of an illegal agent wanting to alter his legend. The Centre did not want to encourage such independence but neither did it want to ignore the agent in the field.

The Centre responded by signalling Gideon to attend an emergency meeting in Ottawa where he met Leonid Abramov, a KGB resident working under cover as second secretary in the Soviet embassy. Moscow disliked holding meets between a legal officer like Abramov and an illegal like Gideon. Illegal agents were to remain independent of the embassy for security reasons. In case war or a break in diplomatic relations closed the Ottawa embassy and shut down both the KGB and GRU legal residencies, Moscow would rely on self-contained agents such as Gideon to keep on spying in Canada. While The Centre tried to keep these two intelligence efforts separate and independent, sometimes the illegals needed temporary support from the embassy.

Abramov shook hands warmly and congratulated Gideon for having persevered for nearly a year under trying conditions in a foreign country. Gideon enjoyed being made to feel like an accomplished warrior, yet the meet revived the hard realities he had been ignoring. He realized wishing the KGB would disappear did not resolve his problem or bring him back to Kingston. Abramov told him Kingston was too small an espionage target and that a big city offered him better cover protection. Gideon could not at this point confess to falling in love or express misgivings about being a spy or even acknowledge a serious interest in Kingston without arousing the KGB's curiosity. He told Abramov that his reservations about Montreal rested solely on the fact the city already had so many watch repair shops. His outlet would not generate sufficient revenue to protect his cover. Besides, he said, most one-man shops were run by a middle-aged or older immigrant with a European accent and as a young, native Canadian he violated the stereotype.

Abramov listened carefully and asked what cover he wanted. His bluff being called, Gideon had to produce an alternative and came up with photography. A one-man photo studio had all the advantages of a small watch repair shop. He would be independent and could close shop and leave Montreal for intelligence missions. In fact his flexibility would be greater since his absences could be explained as photographic expeditions. Abramov lacked authority to approve the suggestion. Such basic changes needed the blessing of The Centre and Abramov promised to get word back to him. Weeks later word arrived to start setting up shop as a photographer.

Gideon settled on a small shop on Bannantyne Avenue two blocks from the St. Lawrence River in Verdun, a suburb near downtown Montreal. The store had previously been a one-woman beauty salon that succumbed to competition from two other beauty shops within a block. Low-income homes, some with illegal basement suites, mixed with the smattering of mom-and-pop outlets such as the Joe and Alec Restaurant across the street dotted the neighbourhood. Portraits by Soboloff blended in well with this quiet block. Before he had finished purchasing photographic equipment he went out and bought a short wave radio and propped it up in his living quarters.

Now that he accomplished the first goal of settling in as a business-man, The Centre brought on phase two by instructing him to inquire about emigrating to the United States. The move would not happen immediately but re-locating south of the border always had been the long range objective. The Centre figured settlement in the United

States was easier if Gideon was Canadianized first. Entering North America was always easier through Canada because phony documentation was more likely to fool Canadian authorities than their American counterparts and when Gideon was ready to move south he would have real credentials to present. Besides, the Americans would have more difficulty checking his legend if most of it was rooted north of the border. The United States had a consulate in Montreal and its embassy in Ottawa was two hours away by bus, but Gideon travelled to the border city of Windsor to see what must be done to enter the United States.

When Gideon read the U.S. immigration forms the self confidence growing within him over the last year vanished. For the first time since arriving in Canada his legend would be tested and the prospect brought back the old fears. Halifax a year ago had not questioned his background because he was posing as an American visitor and at the time he did not apply for immigrant status as he would be doing now. His closest scrutiny came in Vancouver when he applied for a driver's licence which he got by producing his birth certificate. Gideon had been growing accustomed to the ready acceptance of David Soboloff. He had fooled the Canadian port authorities but U.S. immigration forms convinced him his legend would not withstand American examination. One question nagged him particularly; where was his last income tax return filed? The real David Soboloff never filed a Canadian income tax return because he left Canada as a youngster. In reality the question posed little danger because U.S. Immigration would never know Soboloff had not filed a return for the first ten years of his adult life and even if it did know it could be covered with any number of convincing excuses. But Gideon did not understand this. He wondered what would happen if he was discovered and sent to prison or worse. Spying in the Soviet Union provoked long terms in labour camps and death sentences. He decided the risk was not worth it. Moving to the United States was out.

Gideon had another reason for backing off. Life in the United States would make him a radio operator whose role was to send and receive short wave messages under the watch of the KGB illegal resident. Working under somebody's thumb would subject him to KGB discipline and effectively deny him the North American society he had come to enjoy and put his lover in Kingston beyond reach.

He would lose his freedom for travel. He would be lectured about his duties to the Soviet state and observe but not sample the life of New York City. No, he decided, he would not be moving south and the exacting American immigration forms would give him his out.

Returning to Montreal he stopped off in Kingston and urged his lover to abandon her husband. Now that he was staying in Canada he felt she should be with him, again forgetting about his bondage to the KGB and the security requirements his profession imposed on him to remain low key and keep away from trouble. An undercover Soviet agent in Canada illegally could not afford to lure a Canadian woman from her husband, or become involved with any woman, for that matter. How much would he tell her? How could she avoid noticing his two A.M. monitoring of the short wave radio and his one-time cipher pads? Where did his loyalty lie—with the woman or with mother Russia? A married woman could attract an irate husband and maybe the police which would be the worst authority to have poking around. Worse than no agent was an exposed agent. He could be arrested and tried and the publicity would remind the world again about KGB espionage, ruffle diplomatic relations with Canada and cause the Politburo to demand why the KGB allowed something so stupid to happen.

Gideon's lover again refused to follow him to Montreal. Gideon had not confided his secret life to her. He often hinted about some important clandestine activity and sometimes openly bragged he was a secret agent but she laughed it off as another of his implausible claims. He pleaded with her to join him and she wanted to, but was not prepared to leave her husband. He returned to Montreal without his lover and resigned to maintain his covert life for a while, at least.

Oddly, the KGB readily accepted his claim that entry to the United States was too risky. It seemed unusual that after giving Gideon two years of training and creating a legend and plotting his itinerary with military precision that The Centre would casually accept such a major change. Maybe Moscow decided that Gideon could not be trusted sufficiently to be put into contact with a functioning illegal. KGB surveillance may have uncovered his love affair or The Centre, through studying his messages, deduced a certain weakness in him. He had already failed to establish the watch repair business and now wanted to change plans again. How reliable was he? If the KGB doubted Gideon he would be diverted away from his original assignment to minimize the potential damage as much as possible.

On the other hand the KGB may have agreed that entry to the United States posed some risk and wanted him to stay put while it overcame any hazard. McCarthyism was in full flight and, in the process of ruining a lot of innocent people, was scoring on some Soviet agents as well. The devastation wreaked on the American communist community intimidated Soviet intelligence, which momentarily froze and withdrew some of its espionage activity. The KGB had a big investment in Gideon and would not want to risk wasting him. Successful espionage organizations do not take many chances.

Whatever the motive, the KGB kept him in Canada. In fact The Centre notified him he was being promoted to the status of illegal resident and would thus control intelligence-producing agents. He would work under nobody's thumb. Short wave broadcasts from Moscow would give him his assignments and he would respond by supplying his material through dead letter boxes. Once or twice a year he would meet an officer from the embassy. The new role excited Gideon because it would give him standing with The Centre, allow him to remain independent and, most of all, keep him in Canada.

The latest turn of events seemed almost too good to be true, and it was. Gideon soon discovered he did not like his life as an illegal resident. Illegal residents do not spy—it is too risky and, besides, they do not have the necessary access. Their job is to run agents who have access. But Gideon had not yet acquired any agents so The Centre gave him assignments gathering overt information, presumably to keep him occupied. In doing so, The Centre overloaded him with work and as the deadlines approached the pressure mounted. Almost every broadcast gave him a list of companies to check out, even entire industries, with the expectation that the information would be ready the following week. It was not exciting, just dull. A free spirit like himself did not enjoy the responsibility and liked, still less, the work. Even so, The Centre demanded too much and he could not possibly fulfill his assignments. Living his cover as the proprietor of a hole-in-the-wall photo studio was a full-time job by itself and yet almost every assignment pulled him out of Montreal. It would challenge a seasoned operator. Gideon was a rookie radio operator hastily converted into an agent running officer. The Centre's messages carried the impression that he must execute orders flawlessly. The KGB, as a policy, over-loaded its agents and many of the most conscientious complained about unreasonable demands, but Gideon did not know this. The burden made him privately curse The Centre, the Soviet Union and communism. He hated his predicament and wanted out.

The coup de grace for Gideon arrived at his next meet with his contact from the embassy. Appearing in place of the understanding Abramov was Vladimir Bourdine who was young, handsome, cosmo-politan, openly ambitious and tough. He explained that Abramov had returned to Moscow and from now on he would be the contact. Missing was Abramov's warmth and friendliness. Bourdine quickly wanted to know why he was missing his assignments. Gideon explained and Bourdine did not challenge him but everything from his admon-ishing manner to the ominous tone in his voice frightened Gideon. Any thought of ignoring assignments and coasting vanished with Bourdine as the liaison.

Fear of Bourdine and The Centre spurred him on for a while but he inevitably fell behind his work even at his efficient best and seemed always to be fighting one deadline crisis after another. He had already resolved not to carry on this way but remained uncertain what to do. Since childhood he had been indoctrinated about the evils of western society and was now confronting evidence that his enemy was not the west but Bourdine and The Centre and the somber system behind them. In any case, his official enemy seemed friendlier and more humane than his own organization. He also was not so sure any more that capitalism exploited the poor while communism protected them. Businessmen were not such big ogres. He was one now and compared notes with other small businessmen in his area and nobody was exploiting anybody or getting rich.

He had to break from the KGB but how? Defecting had never crossed his mind. Defecting was treason and he did not consider himself a traitor. He still loved Russia and rather than selling out, wanted to remove the KGB yoke, better his personal circumstances and be with the woman he loved. After pondering it, he boarded the train for Kingston for a frank talk with his only true friend.

At first she laughed at his story because he had always told tall tales. Once he laid it out piece by piece and explained how he had grown up mainly in Moscow she started believing he could be a Russian spy. The pieces fell into place. He had been surprisingly ignorant of things everybody took for granted. At times his ignorance of past events and customs made it seem he had dropped in from Mars. She noticed it at the time but attributed it to Soboloff's ghettoized upbringing in a poor immigrant family and the lack of access to mainstream society, although she wondered how he could be sophisticated in other areas. An aura of mystery had always surrounded him and she had never fully believed his drifter story, thinking he drifted to escape a skeleton in his background, and his compulsion for moving to Montreal did not fit. She urged him to break free and together they started exploring how.

They made an unusual pair; a hopeless romantic and a woman so innocent she had never heard of the KGB, conspired together against the might of Soviet intelligence. They discussed running away and living quietly in western Canada but he feared the sinister arm of the KGB and she the wrath of her army husband. She advised him to call the police but he wanted to avoid the police who in Russia were society's enemy and the instrument of repression. He had been engaging in espionage and the last institution he wanted was the police who would send him to prison or worse. The RCMP, she told him, was different—the Force would listen to his story and do the right thing. She pleaded with him to go directly to RCMP headquarters in Ottawa where they had the smartest and most powerful Mounties. Gideon figured the RCMP could be no worse than the KGB and had no palatable options so en route back to Montreal detoured through Ottawa, slipped into a telephone booth, and called the famous RCMP.

Having dialed the RCMP number in the Ottawa phone book, Gideon assumed he was contacting headquarters. Instead he reached A Division, which was the RCMP's operating division in charge of the Ottawa region. Like any other division in the country, A Division reported to a separate bureaucracy at headquarters, only in this case it stood less than a mile away across the Rideau River. For Gideon's purposes, headquarters might as well have been a thousand miles away, for A Division preoccupied itself with the decaying Communist Party of Canada and had never handled a true counterespionage case.

The corporal on the phone promised to send somebody to see him but his voice revealed little excitement. A stodgy Mountie dropped by and interviewed Gideon who immediately sensed he knew little about the spy business. The Mountie believed Gideon's story but said he would have to check first with the office and get back. He talked about setting up Gideon as a double agent which failed to inspire the Russian because it would drag him further into a world he was trying to escape by defection. What worried Gideon most was the Mountie's desire to chauffeur Gideon in a black car to a dead letter box beneath a rock in an open field in the Hog's Back area of Ottawa. The KGB might have the spot under surveillance. Besides, sloppy tradecraft like driving a double agent through the streets of Ottawa, especially in a police car, could expose him.

In November 1953, the B Branch head, Terry Guernsey, lay in the Veteran's ward of the Ottawa Civic Hospital recovering from a gall bladder operation when the report of the defector came to his attention. Realizing A Division was not equipped to run a double agent, and unable to check out of the hospital, Guernsey brought staff into his room and plotted strategy from his bed. Guernsey wanted to run the Russian as a double agent to give the RCMP a window on KGB tradecraft for running an illegal and offer leads on Soviet techniques which, if followed up, might uncover other illegal agents in place, as well as disclose the KGB's intelligence priorities for Canada. A blanket policy of running double agents in Canada led the KGB to suspect all its agents and forced security precautions that slowed down all the operations there. The fledgling Security Service needed experience running counterespionage cases and would not get it accepting Gideon as a straight defector. Guernsey code-named the case Operation Keystone because it represented not only the Security Service's biggest case against the Russians but the only one.

Guernsey quickly cut out A Division and brought the case entirely under headquarters control. His next move brought in Charles Sweeny who seemed an unlikely Mountie. Short and slight in physique, Sweeny was blessed with the gift for persuasion and practiced the art on his Mountie colleagues who hulked over him, squeezing the advantage with his quick mind, deep voice, modulated speech and relaxed confidence to whittle their arguments until his victim was wondering what happened. Sweeny knew about defectors. When Czechoslovakia went communist in 1948 half the diplomatic staff in the Ottawa embassy secretly defected but stayed in place until recalled home when, one by one, they would officially seek political asylum. As a constable, he ran these agents. Now a corporal, he had been plucked by

Guernsey from the Satellite Desk because he was easily the best available Mountie to run Gideon.

Sweeny ripped a one-dollar bill into two and gave half to Mitch Hanna, the non-commissioned officer in charge of A Division's small Security Service unit. Sweeny told him that A Division's last function in the case was to see that Gideon got it and to have him waiting at a telephone booth on St. Catherine Street in downtown Montreal at a pre-arranged time. Sweeny would meet Gideon and if their dollar halves matched he would know he had the correct man. The next day Sweeny phoned the telephone booth and instructed the man who answered to move to a phone booth on Sherbrooke Street where the telephone rang again with instructions to meet him in front of the elevator on the fifth floor of the Mount Royal Hotel.

The two men arrived within thirty seconds of each other at the hotel. "That bellhop downstairs is something," said Sweeny pulling out his half of the dollar bill. "I wanted to tip him but he grabbed so fast he tore it in half."

"That's funny," replied Gideon, pulling out his half of the matched bill, "the same thing happened to me."

They walked down the stairs to Sweeny's room on the fourth floor where Sweeny introduced himself as Eugene Walker from the Canadian Security Agency which, he explained, was an elite organization responsible for protecting the country from foreign espionage. (Neither Eugene Walker nor the Canadian Secret Agency actually existed.) Gideon had never heard of the Canadian Security Agency and thought it odd his thorough briefing in Moscow never mentioned this organization. In fact he was sure the KGB told him the RCMP was Canada's only security organization.

"I thought the RCMP was in charge of security," said Gideon.

"Oh, those flat footed Mounties couldn't catch a cold," scoffed Sweeny. "They play on the edge of security, haunt the Communist party and think they're in the game. But they don't know what a spy is. They're a bunch of policemen and anybody who knows anything doesn't deal with them."

Sweeny explained how much difficulty he had rescuing him from the RCMP's crude clutches and within minutes convinced him that this mythical organization was Canada's real security service. For somebody who wanted out of spying, Gideon agreed quickly to stay on and work as a double agent. Sweeny arranged to visit him regularly in his shop as a photographic supply salesman and to legitimize his cover would register in the province of Quebec as a supplier. If Gideon required quick help, he need only go to a pay telephone and call a dentist in Ottawa and ask for Mr. Walker. The dentist, called a "cutout" in the spy business, would phone Sweeny who fifteen minutes later would phone Gideon at a different pay phone.

As Sweeny talked, Gideon grew warm, confident and optimistic. Finally somebody understood what was happening and could help him and before long came to believe that defecting was almost a privilege. Without receiving a single promise, Gideon felt working as a double agent would earn him entitlement to a life in Canada. It sounded ideal. The work requirements of a double agent were minimal and in the meantime his secret role protected him from Soviet revenge because the KGB would not know he had defected. Later, when Sweeny was gone, doubts surfaced in Gideon's mind. He did not like keeping his love affair hidden, but he had given his word and it was now too late for second thoughts, so he let his doubts slide. Besides, it was too late to turn back. He had compromised himself and his fate now rested with his Canadian case officer.

Gideon soon proved he could be emotional, impatient, self indulgent and volatile. Handling him, as the KGB already knew, was a challenge under the best circumstances and now that he was in love, became almost impossible. Sometimes Sweeny subtly had to intimidate him into line. He would confound Gideon by arriving in Montreal an hour after an emergency signal had been sent although car travel would take two hours. "Don't you think we have planes?" replied Sweeny to his bewildered agent. He wanted Gideon to respect the Canadian Security Agency as much as he did the KGB. Such tactics usually kept him submissive enough for Sweeny to maintain authority although his romantic infatuation was so jeopardizing the case, Guernsey felt forced to take action to move her out of the picture. Guernsey asked the military to transfer the woman's husband out of Montreal's reach.

The transfer had hardly been issued when the dentist relayed to Sweeny another emergency signal from Montreal. Sweeny arrived in Montreal to witness Gideon strutting about in alternating fits of anger and remorse. His lover's husband was being moved to the Yukon which was about as far as he could be sent and, he charged, it was no accident. He accused Sweeny of conspiring to destroy his wonderful relationship. Sweeny claimed the transfer had to be innocent because it had nothing to do with him or his agency, explaining that transfers represented the luck of the draw and come with military life. People in the military are always being moved, he said. Gideon, neither consoled nor convinced, said he defected for his woman and was now being denied her so was quitting his double agent life and nothing could change his mind. Indeed, Sweeny's efforts to dissuade him failed and his only consolation was to persuade Gideon to carry out his dead letter box drop in Ottawa the following week and then visit his superior in the Canadian Security Agency.

Guernsey was introduced by Sweeny to Gideon as Mr. Henderson, the chief of the agency, but Gideon was no more pliable to his influence. In fact, time seemed to harden his resistance and raise his scepticism while he poured out his grievance. Guernsey made no effort to defend himself and only occasionally, during a pause, asked in quiet, methodical slowness an antiseptic question. Guernsey's pace did not deter or slow Gideon whose own talking kept fuelling his tension as if revved by a self-generating battery. His tirade came in outbursts and each outburst roused his temperature a little more like a volcano ready to blow the one big eruption. The coming explosion did not ruffle the unflappable Guernsey whose passive face seemed oblivious to the danger signals. Self control slipping away and each volley landing further off target, Gideon's impotence further aggravated him and pushed his temper beyond his own reach. Gideon collapsed onto the floor, lying full out on his side, hands covering his face, and sobbing.

With Gideon broken and amenable to suggestion, Guernsey started to act. How was his wife in Moscow, Guernsey asked. The memory of his lover had to be erased from his mind. The question pricked his memory for he still loved his wife and missed her. Guernsey expanded the subject to include his parents and as attention shifted from Canada to Russia, Gideon began to appreciate the stability and happiness of his wife and family. Everything else he sought was illusory except his loved ones in Moscow. The KGB did not care about his welfare, neither did the Canadian government, nor his lover who had followed her husband to the Yukon. His wife still waited for him and so did his parents. He started thinking romantically about bringing his wife to Canada and talked wistfully about experiences in Russia. Without saying so he was agreeing to continue on as a double agent. Nobody spelled it out but Gideon was back on board.

Gideon hated broadcast transmissions. They forced him to sit up late into the night to take advantage of atmospheric conditions and even then the messages from Moscow were hard to read. The broadcasts came in Morse code and were a long series of five-digit number combinations. After copying the numbers, he pulled out his gummed set of one-time cipher pads which also were a series of five-digit numbers neatly printed in columns and rows. By subtracting the first block of numbers on his cipher pad from the first block of numbers in the message, he got a number ranging from one to twenty-six, with one representing A and twenty-six representing Z. He now had the first letter of The Centre's message. To decipher the second letter he subtracted the second block of numbers on his cipher pad from the second block on his message and again converted the resulting number to a letter. He repeated this procedure for each letter in the message. Upon reaching the bottom of the cipher sheet he ripped off the page from the pad and destroyed it and continued on the next page. His cipher pad was never used twice, which made the system unbreakable because identical letters were randomly enciphered by different banks of numbers. Code breakers had no repetition to guide them.

Security had its price, namely in the laborious deciphering process. A broadcast could take four or five hours to copy and decipher and sometimes the message only wished Gideon happy birthday, noted his wedding anniversary or trumpeted the annual celebration of the Russian revolution.

Bad atmospheric interference during the spring equinox often wiped out the messages, making them almost impossible to hear. When he missed, Gideon mailed an innocuous letter to an electronic and appliance store on Rideau Street in Ottawa and upon receiving it, the owner placed a card in his top-floor window. He acted as a "live letter box." Bourdine walked past the store regularly and the card told him Gideon had missed the latest broadcast. Bourdine relayed the news to The Centre in Moscow, which repeated the message the following week.

Bennett, as a jack of all trades, set up the observation post on the store by convincing a merchant across the street to give the RCMP one of his upper floor rooms for a drug investigation and through monitor-

ing, documented the card in the window as the owner's signal. Guernsey liked Bennett, especially his initiative, dedication, hard work and
inclination to accept responsibility, and started to bring him along in
the Security Service with heavier assignments.

Gideon was instructed to post his letters to the store on Saturday
morning. Once he put it off until Sunday morning and searched the
empty streets of downtown Montreal for a post office. His KGB
briefing had taught him that North American policemen could be
asked reasonable questions without fear.

"Where can I buy a stamp?" Gideon asked a policeman.

"It's Sunday," shot back the surprised cop. "The post office is
closed. Where do you come from anyway?"

Thinking his identity was being challenged, Gideon, without saying
a word, turned around and fled. Such moments subdued his growing
cockiness.

Gideon felt he could skip a few broadcasts and blame the weather
conditions. It saved him hours of copying and deciphering time not to
mention the assignment work, which was often unreasonable and
always overburdening.

Gideon wanted Sweeny to help him with his assignments but
Guernsey ruled against it in the belief that enhancing the status of a
double agent jeopardized the case and the double agent. Ironically, an
agent who becomes too successful incurs the suspicion of his superiors
who wonder whether he is getting help. If Gideon encounters a
problem, Guernsey decided, then the KGB has to resolve it—he is the
KGB's agent. Sweeny cheated slightly and advised him how to proceed, but on the basis of Gideon's record of achievement the KGB had
no reason to suspect outside assistance.

Only one thing aggravated Gideon more than receiving short wave
messages and that was meeting Bourdine who became more demanding
and domineering on each occasion. The Centre stepped up the number
of these encounters. In addition to his standard twice-yearly meets,
broadcasts directed him to attend special meets with Bourdine and
arranged pay-phone-to-pay-phone telephone encounters. Gideon
fretted over each encounter. He went into a quiet panic when he
missed the bus to Ottawa and discovered the next bus would deliver
him late. When he arrived in Ottawa Gideon jumped into a taxi for the
three-mile ride to the pre-arranged spot at the south end of Bank

Street, arriving as Bourdine was leaving. It was dark and raining and his tardiness put Bourdine into a worse than usual disposition.

Bourdine had never unloaded on Gideon as viciously as he did this time. He first attacked him for missing the meet and then handed him a stack of short wave messages he had missed and demanded to know why. Gideon fell back on the excuse that atmospheric conditions ruined the broadcasts but Bourdine did not believe him. Gideon protested but Bourdine thundered back that they knew he had not tried, implying something that worried Gideon. Was Bourdine merely guessing or had the embassy been monitoring the transmissions to satisfy itself that the broadcasts were clear and readable? Or could it be worse? Did Bourdine know he was working for the other side? The prospect that the KGB no longer trusted him and was checking up terrified him.

Bourdine was not finished. He demanded to know why he had not fulfilled his assignments. Gideon replied that the demands were too high and that completing everything was humanly impossible. It was true The Centre overloaded its agents in the belief that pressure kept them subservient and tested their mettle. Bourdine understood the policy and knew the limitations of an individual agent, especially one working alone in a foreign environment, but his performance was still unsatisfactory and Gideon's complaints failed to soften him. He berated him for a slothfulness and shirking duty to the motherland and socialism and then chided him for growing soft and suggested maybe he was being seduced by the comforts of materialistic capitalism. "Are you still with us?" Bourdine asked. Gideon mustered a persuasive reply but was shaken. Now for sure, he thought, The Centre was doubting his loyalty.

On the late bus back to Montreal Gideon, exhausted, defeated and afraid, leaned back in his chair and closed his eyes to a replay of the meet. He saw Bourdine insisting the short wave messages were readable because, he implied, somebody else had read them. By this stage Gideon was too rattled to think that the somebody was the radio officer in the Soviet embassy. Ever since he loaned Sweeny his cipher pads and described the pattern of his signal plan, Gideon knew the west was listening because once Sweeny helped him out by giving him a fully deciphered message from one of the broadcasts he had missed. Gideon's agitated mind concluded Bourdine's "somebody" meant not the Soviet embassy but the Canadian government and if Bourdine knew that much, his secret role must surely be exposed. He wondered how far the Canadian government would stand behind him and whether he would be discarded once his usefulness to Canada was over. By the time the bus reached Montreal he had conjured up the fear that maybe the KGB and Canada were in this together. He vowed to terminate his double life and forsake this crazy and treacherous business.

Sweeny had grown accustomed to racing out to Montreal and quenching fires but sensed the special gravity of this crisis and doubted that Gideon could be won back. He quickly talked Gideon out of the notion that Canada and Russia were partners and convinced him his cooperation was a tightly-held secret that Bourdine could not know, but his other arguments got nowhere. "I've had it," cried Gideon. "These bastards are driving me up the wall. I'm losing my sanity." Even pulling him to Ottawa for another session with Guernsey proved impossible. Gideon proclaimed the case closed and cut off further communication. Sweeny returned to Ottawa thinking Gideon was irretrievably lost.

As a last-ditch effort, Guernsey drove to Montreal and in his car confronted Gideon. Guernsey's unhurried voice and worry-free style camouflaged the desperate nature of the mission. He quickly realized that Gideon was not budging and after a few attempts declared in a quiet monotone that his attitude was killing the operation and rendering him valueless to Canada. With calm finality Guernsey revealed he would not be needing his services any longer and said good-bye. Gideon said nothing and made no effort to leave the car. Guernsey politely told him to leave but Gideon stayed frozen. What would happen to him now, Gideon asked. Guernsey told him that it was his problem. Gideon tried to fathom the consequences of Guernsey's discharge: playing a double role frightened him but being turned out in the cold frightened him more. If he left the car uncooperative, Canada might imprison and execute him as the KGB did back home to uncooperative foreign agents. If Canada did nothing he would return home eventually and did not cherish that thought either, especially undergoing debriefing in Moscow when he thought his own organization suspected him. The inquisition at The Centre would make Bourdine's sessions seem a picnic. Even if he was not under suspicion he had to account for his performance. A day of reckoning was coming and he doubted he could withstand the judgement. Stepping out of Guernsey's car opened a series of scenarios he did not like.

"Get out, get out," erupted Guernsey. "I never want to see you again."

Gideon quaked but still did not move. Guernsey lost his temper so rarely it could jolt anybody, and was forcing a response out of Gideon. Struggling with two undesirable options, Gideon stayed put. Guernsey lowered his voice and said: "Okay." Gideon uttered no sound but his presence confirmed he would carry on his role.

Gideon did not know it at the time but he would never again meet Bourdine and his life as a double agent was about to become tolerable. Waiting at the next rendezvous was a new man with a strikingly pale face who introduced himself as Nicolai Ostrovsky. Bourdine, he explained, had returned to Moscow and from now on he would be his contact. Unlike Bourdine, Ostrovsky was relaxed and easy going and Gideon had no trouble relating to him. He was at least fifteen years older than Bourdine and in comparison an untidy bundle of hay. Although not obese, Ostrovsky carried a beer belly on his short frame. Gideon sometimes felt Ostrovsky was a little too nonchalant, especially the time he invited him for a beer at a nearby tavern. Gideon declined and thought his offer a shocking breach of security but nevertheless liked the fellow.

Ostrovsky informed him The Centre had an important new task for him unlike anything he had been assigned before. He was being given responsibility for handling Green[1], a Canadian working as a KGB agent in Toronto with access to confidential information on the Canadian aircraft the Avro Arrow. Ostrovsky held out the hope he would be given more agents to run and could take charge of a stable of agents if he impressed The Centre with his handling of Green. He expressed confidence he could do the job. Gideon felt he could happily live such a life and for the first time as a double agent left a meet with his Soviet contact not wanting to quit.

The development delighted the Security Service because it represented the biggest break since the defection. Each agent Gideon received exposed another KGB operator in Canada. It indicated

[1] RCMP code name

Gideon's training stage had ended and that he was showing signs of fulfilling his earlier promise of developing into a genuine illegal resident. Transferring Green to Gideon made perfect sense for the KGB. If Green was valuable The Centre would want him cut off from the embassy where RCMP surveillance might expose him. Transferring Green from the legal residency (the embassy) to an illegal resident (Gideon) was a way of minimizing the risk of discovery and giving Gideon experience. Entrusted with Green, Gideon stopped worrying about being suspected by his own organization.

Nearly two decades older than Gideon, Green was easy to control because of his dedication. He was an old-line ideological communist talent-spotted by Grif[2], a ranking member of the Communist Party of Canada based in Toronto and introduced to Bourdine who recruited him. He took no money, followed instructions carefully and worked hard while Gideon revelled in his role as a spy master. If Gideon had a problem with Green, it was clearing the time to meet him in Toronto. As a factory worker, Green's access was not classic but through planning and sleuthing he produced two sets of plans for the Arrow, one of the fuselage and another for a portion of the engine.

Green's spying proposed a dilemma for Guernsey because the Green-Gideon connection was putting secret information into Soviet hands. The fundamental purpose of the Security Service was to stop espionage. Do you stop the leak or keep the case running? Was it worth sacrificing Operation Keystone and foregoing possible future benefits to secure the confidentiality of the Arrow project? Some of the classified information belonged to the United States and an agreement of confidentiality required that Canada keep it safe. Neither the United States nor the Avro company knew about the leak or about Operation Keystone. The official owner of the information was the Canadian government. Finally, Guernsey decided that since there was no war and the information would become obsolete in a few years, he would let it go.

Gideon's success with Green gave him a sense of accomplishment and seemed to rub off on The Centre which congratulated and encouraged him. He was passing the test as an illegal resident. At the next meeting Ostrovsky handed Gideon simplified technical sketches for

---

[2] RCMP code name

installing "Omega"—the Soviet name for a short wave broadcast transmitter—and told him to study them and determine whether Omega could be introduced clandestinely at his home. What The Centre specifically wanted to know was whether he could erect an antenna-type device discreetly enough so the neighbours would not know. Omega would give him direct two-way communications with The Centre. The plans represented further evidence that his role as a spymaster was expanding. Traditional transmitters were one thing. A state-of-the-art Omega meant Moscow was serious because their signals would be almost impossible to trace.

An ordinary transmitter using handspeed Morse kept operators on the air a long time which made it vulnerable to enemy intercept operators whose direction-finding equipment would sooner or later pinpoint the source. A simple intercept located the city, then mobile units with revolving antennas on the roof rolled into action and whittled the zone to several blocks. From here inspectors with hand held equipment set out on foot and zeroed in on the target. With enough time, or enough transmissions, every clandestine transmitter in the country would be ferretted out. The Soviets were only too aware of this weakness and retaliated with Omega, which cut transmission length to a fraction of the old time. The agent prepared the message ahead of time on a tape and when ready to transmit, fed the tape into Omega at four to fifteen times handspeed Morse. The Centre in Moscow tape recorded the broadcast and later replayed the tape at a slower speed to copy down the message. Some transmissions flashed by so quickly the dots and dashes sounded like crackling and enemy interceptors had trouble distinguishing them from static. Omega proved to be virtually an insuperable barrier. Interceptors with a little luck might catch the signal but could never trace the source.

The Security Service savoured the prospect of Gideon acquiring Omega. It wanted to be among the first in the west to gain physical possession of this prize. Gideon also relished the prospect because he saw it giving him greater freedom. Although Omega would draw him closer to The Centre, it promised to cut him virtually free from the embassy and the face-to-face meets with his handler. Bulky material would still move through dead letter boxes but microdots, hidden in letters or on postcards, could cut even that tenuous link.

Then one day, after seeing a picture of a large oil tank in a national magazine, Gideon decided to scout Montreal's East End refinery area to see if he could take a similar shot and post the portrait in his shop as an example of his work. It had nothing to do with the KGB. He was intrigued by the light and shadow effect of the stairs as they spiralled up and around the walls of the tank. He had finished setting up his equipment near a tank when an oil company security guard challenged him.

"What the hell are you doing here?" hollered the guard. "Let's see some identification."

"Identification?" responded Gideon. "I'm a Russian spy and this stuff is going straight back to Moscow. What do you think I'm doing?"

"Get out of here," barked the chagrined guard never thinking the little guy was a Russian spy.

Gideon was no longer the frightened agent fearful of restaurants, streetcars and policemen's rhetorical questions. He no longer feared the KGB the way he once did and stopped worrying about his status with the organization. His life was settling down and only one doubt gnawed away: the realization that soon The Centre would recall him to Moscow on furlough.

Each illegal returned for a few months every two or three years for debriefing, training, family reunion and vacation. It was the spring of 1955 and his third anniversary would arrive before the year was out. Whether talking to Bourdine or Ostrovsky, Gideon had always carefully left the impression he looked forward to returning. Now, he figured, he would go a step further and claim homesickness and request a furlough. It would help legitimize his status with The Centre as a loyal Soviet. The recall was inevitable anyway and he was doing nothing irrevocable until the journey back actually started which would give him plenty of time to defect openly if he changed his mind. The Centre replied that events were being set in motion for his return that fall. This would give him nearly six months to ponder whether or not he should chance it.

Deciding intellectually to return and following through with action were different matters. He wanted to go back, yet he did not. As the deadline approached the risks loomed larger in his mind and despite his earlier confidence he started re-examining everything and wondering how risky the venture really was. Returning required him to fool the KGB and once back in Canada continue as a double agent a few more years. Staying would fetch him Canadian citizenship, resettlement under a new identity and the freedom finally to lead his own life. Sweeny told him the decision was his to make.

He felt confident of outwitting the KGB. He knew they would examine him closely but figured himself to be a little smarter than they. Inwardly he thought he could survive an interrogation and nothing could give him more satisfaction than closing off his espionage career by strolling into KGB headquarters and pulling off this one last great deception. But adopting a new life in Canada appealed to him too. He was sobered by the Canadian offer and the fact he was being given the freedom to decide even though Sweeny and Guernsey dearly wanted him to carry on as a double agent at least long enough to return from Moscow with Omega and maybe some new agents. He was no longer a defector who switched sides over a woman. The last few years had opened his eyes about Soviet propaganda and turned around his allegiance. He now cheered for the west and wanted to contribute to the cause and earn his citizenship.

Gideon worried about his wife and family. They were hostages and would suffer when he openly traded sides. Continuing as a double agent would keep his new allegiance secret a while longer and give them a few more years of peace. Gideon was influenced by Sweeny's perverse argument that his family would not be hostages if he returned to Moscow and was exposed there. He missed his wife and wondered how she had changed after three years and still entertained hopes of somehow getting her to Canada. Seeing her was worth the risk. He told Sweeny he would go provided he was given an emergency escape plan to spring him out of Russia in case things turned sour.

Gideon's resoluteness lasted two weeks. "You're not going to be there with me," he told Sweeny. "You'll be sitting safely over here." Sweeny promised a meeting with the man drawing up the escape plan for a detailed briefing. The escape scheme was being engineered by the British since the RCMP possessed no intelligence assets inside the Soviet Union. Gideon exploded with anger when he saw the plan and realized how little help his flight from Moscow was getting. British personnel would spirit him out of Moscow and head him north to Leningrad at which point he would essentially be on his own and use public transportation in a police state employing an internal passport system. His final escape would come on foot through open countryside at the point where the borders of Finland, Norway and the Soviet Union meet.

"This is ridiculous," pronounced Gideon. "Do you expect me to do that? No way can I escape over the ice to Norway."

The border crossing lay 200 miles north of the Arctic Circle and he would be negotiating it during winter when he would surely freeze to death well inside Soviet borders. Gideon announced he would require a better plan before putting his life into jeopardy and was awarded a revised scheme that looked more reasonable. On Gideon's insistence, Sweeny made a special trip to Montreal to show him the hand gun he would get during an escape.

En route to Moscow that October, Gideon, as instructed by The Centre, stopped off in Paris for a meet in a park with a KGB officer from the embassy in France. RCMP surveillance was not on because parks were difficult to surveil discreetly. Nobody wanted to endanger Gideon at the eleventh hour.

Paris represented Gideon's last opportunity to back out. After the meet he was supposed to send Sweeny a typical tourist's post card addressed to Eugene Walker in Canada with a coded signal to indicate how things were going. Two weeks later a post card arrived in Canada signalling distress but since Gideon carried on with the journey, everybody worried only a little and then assumed he had suffered merely some last-minute jitters.

5

Agent Hector

EVERYBODY IN B BRANCH refused to admit trouble when Gideon failed to return after twelve weeks. Nobody knew for sure how long the Soviets were planning to keep him in Moscow, whether four weeks, eight, or more. Such detail was one of the many things Keystone was supposed to teach the West. The common guess was six weeks based on Ostrovsky's pre-return briefing to Gideon and the feeling the Soviets would not take an entrenched agent out of his cover for too long.

Ears pricked up whenever somebody mentioned Gideon's name. Were there any developments? Suddenly, with the dawning of 1956, fledgling B Branch had several Russian counterespionage cases running but Keystone remained special. It was B Branch's original big case, the one where the Security Service sent its agent behind enemy lines. Nobody wanted to face the prospect of making a mistake.

The RCMP arranged to beam short wave messages into the Soviet Union at pre-arranged times and frequencies. If Gideon could somehow get access to a short wave set he would know when and where to listen. If he was all right he was supposed to return a non-radio signal. None came. Maybe Gideon was not hearing the broadcasts. Short wave radios were hard to get in the Soviet Union. Thought was also given in the planning stages to dropping off a short wave radio in a Moscow dead letter box, but this was vetoed as too dangerous; Gideon's game was up if he was caught picking up or transporting a short wave radio in Moscow. And in any case, Gideon could not receive the broadcasts if he had cracked during debriefing and now occupied a cell in the KGB's prison at Lubyanka. The British and the RCMP worked on the possibility he could be safe but unable to secure a short wave radio or return another type of signal.

The signal everyone awaited was Gideon taking a five P.M. stroll past a pre-arranged point in Moscow while carrying a phonograph album and hesitating briefly to pull out his handkerchief to blow his nose. This sequence of actions was the safety signal. The British waited each day at the appointed hour but Gideon never appeared. The longer they waited the more Guernsey feared Gideon was being forcefully confined by the KGB.

Several months later, as western hopes faded, Gideon let fly his signal that was supposed to say everything was fine. Gideon walked past the check point with a phonograph record in hand at the correct time but failed to pull out a hankerchief and blow his nose. It was half a signal, whatever that meant. Had he merely forgotten to blow his nose? Had he forgotten a hankie? With him was a woman who was assumed to be his wife. If his failure to complete the signal was perplexing, the presence of the woman was alarming for he had been instructed to come alone. Gideon understood that and possessed enough sense not to bring along somebody frivolously. Was Gideon trying to tip them off he was under control? If Gideon had broken under interrogation the KGB would likely know about the signal system and be forcing him to go through with it. Maybe Gideon broke only partially on this point, telling them about the five P.M. stroll with a record album under his arm but purposely withholding the nose-blowing element and adding the presence of his wife, figuring these two significant deviations would alert the RCMP to what was really happening.

Gideon's stroll was witnessed by more than the British. As he disappeared around the corner it was clear he had been under heavy surveillance, so he must at least have been under suspicion. The evidence suggested the KGB had broken the case and, for a reason not yet established, wanted to deceive the west into thinking Gideon was undiscovered.

As far as the Security Service was concerned, the case was dead and Gideon would never emerge from the Soviet Union alive. Invoking the escape plan was not considered because it never existed. It was drawn up to satisfy Gideon and give him courage and confidence. Once he crossed the Soviet border nobody in the West could save him. Soviet spies Kim Philby, Guy Burgess and Donald Maclean fled with the assistance of emergency escape plans because they saw the suspicion against them unfold and had a jump on the authorities. They vanished from countries whose open borders let them pick their routes to Moscow. The KGB was the Soviet Union's intelligence agency, security service and border patrol and would not be giving Gideon any of these advantages. After it was too late Gideon probably understood the realities too, because he never took steps to trigger off the phantom escape plan.

Sweeny, Gideon's only close Canadian friend, talked about going to Moscow and rescuing him but he came to accept the hopelessness of Gideon's fate.

When Gideon had left Canada, The Centre continued to broadcast weekly as if he was still in Montreal and these continued to be monitored and deciphered. Then, a month after Gideon's suspicious appearance in Moscow, a dramatic development breathed new life into Operation Keystone. Apparently a new illegal had arrived in Canada to replace Gideon. Suddenly The Centre's broadcasts were addressed not to Gideon but to an agent named Hector and the first transmission sent a message confirming receipt of his previous message and revealing his safe arrival from Rio de Janeiro. The Centre's message told Hector to dispatch his next communication through the pre-arranged dead letter box.

The appearance of the mysterious Hector raised new hope for Gideon because if Gideon had been unmasked in Moscow the KGB would not use his signal plan to communicate to Hector. Gideon's signal plan would be considered compromised and abandoned. So the possibility arose that maybe the KGB trusted Gideon's loyalty but doubted his personal suitability for the role of an agent and assigned him a desk job in Moscow. Or maybe he was given a different assignment and would surface in a year or two in another part of the world in which case the West would be hearing from him. While the Security Service waited for more clues about Gideon it went to work on identifying Hector.

The job of searching for Hector fell to Bennett. At the outset he believed Hector did not exist and that The Centre was sending the broadcasts to delude and disrupt the RCMP. If Hector was real The Centre would never have mentioned Rio de Janeiro since that piece of information, if intercepted, gave a clue about Hector's identity. The Centre protected its agents better than that. The clue smelled wrong, as if planted to lure the Security Service into a long and fruitless investigation. Rio de Janeiro was just specific enough to start the hunt but general enough to waste a lot of RCMP time. Furthermore, as long as the case lived the RCMP would not roll up the ring connected to Gideon for fear of endangering his safety. So short of sending Gideon back to Canada the KGB had an incentive to keep the case alive to protect from arrest agents such as Green, the Avro spy; Grif, the talent spotter; and the Ottawa appliance-store owner, the live letter box.

The more Bennett thought about it the more he became convinced Hector was a phony operation. Even if the KGB trusted Gideon, signal plans were easy to devise so why re-use them unless you want the other side to know about Hector.

The Centre did something else that violated security so fundamentally and represented such a basic departure from normal tradecraft that it convinced Bennett irrevocably the Russians were manipulating the case. The broadcasts to Hector were transmitted in Gideon's private code. The broadcasts to Gideon had always been protected by one-time cipher pads, which are unbreakable because each cipher substitution gets used only once. However the pads do have one weakness: the agent cannot memorize the cipher system so pads always have to be kept on hand which means the pads can run out before a new supply arrives, or they can become destroyed accidentally and leave the agent stranded or they can even fall into enemy hands. To protect against such misfortune the agent always keeps in his head for emergency use a simple cipher system known only to him and The Centre. Since the code is custom made for a single agent it is called the agent's private code and under no conditions will any other agent use it.

Transmitting to Hector in Gideon's private cipher made no sense except when viewed as deception. If Hector was receiving broadcasts with unbreakable one-time pads, the West would not be able to read the messages and would be unable to launch an investigation into him. So to carry out this hoax The Centre had to transmit in a cipher system the West already knew and on an existing signal plan to ensure the

West was listening. If the tiny Security Service was busy investigating a phony agent it would have fewer resources left for genuine counter-espionage cases and the KGB had greater freedom to operate in Canada. Clearly the KGB had broken Gideon and now was wringing out the final drop of advantage and revenge.

The weekly broadcasts lasted only three weeks with the final transmission announcing that one-time cipher pads and a new signal plan schedule had been sent. Presumably this material went through one of the officers in the Ottawa embassy and the most likely figure was Ostrovsky. Surveillance concentrated on him for the next few weeks hoping his movements would lead the Security Service to Hector. Ostrovsky kept the Watcher Service active but produced no meets and the manner of his activity suggested he might be acting as a decoy whose purpose was to attract and consume surveillance.

The search for Hector's new signal plan and for Hector continued. The Security Service might not have chased a phony operation like Hector but usually cool, analytical officers clutched straws on Gideon's behalf. Humanitarianism was creeping into Guernsey's thinking. He felt partly responsible for Gideon's predicament and wanted to exhaust every hope.

Although Bennett doubted the authenticity of Hector, he pursued every lead diligently. From Moscow's broadcasts Bennett knew the alleged Hector was a White Russian who came from China and entered Canada through Brazil and that he had a wife who seemed to help out on his espionage operations. Bennett handchecked Immigration Department files for details of all recent immigrants who matched the description. Several days later his net pulled in two suspects. One had settled in Toronto and the other in Montreal. A field investigation quickly cleared the Toronto immigrant but the other suspect opened possibilities as he duplicated Gideon's pattern of developing a business in Montreal while cultivating many more social and business contacts than Gideon had. The Security Service wiretapped, bugged, surveilled, and investigated him for a year before accepting his innocence.

No longer was there any doubt that the KGB back in Moscow had tried to manipulate Gideon into giving a false signal for the purpose of fooling the RCMP. But even at this late stage, the Security Service had only begun to uncover the truth behind the failure of Operation Keystone.

6

Long Knife

IT TOOK ONLY one look to notice that Long Knife[1] stood apart from other Mounties. He wore flawlessly tailored doublebreasted flannel pinstripes and parted his hair in the middle—he resembled the movie star Richard Dix. He drove a Buick, smoked cigars, married the daughter of a British naval commander, sailed his father-in-law's yacht and spoke impeccable French. He walked into every building as if he owned it. Outsiders assumed he was an officer on his way to becoming Commissioner; he was too cosmopolitan and too handsome to be only a lowly corporal going nowhere in the Calvinistic RCMP.

Long Knife joined the RCMP while Hitler's troops were invading Poland and instead of going to boot camp in Regina went overseas to fight in World War Two as part of the RCMP contingent in the Provost Corps. Starting as Lance Corporal at a dollar and a half a day he rose by the time of his discharge in 1946 to the rank of captain, only to be bounced back to the bottom rank of constable upon returning to the RCMP. But even after being sent back to boot camp and dispatched to police duties in small towns in Saskatchewan and Manitoba, he was not forgotten. His commanding officer during the war, Assistant Commissioner Len Nicholson, was back in Ottawa promoting Moun-

---

[1] Long Knife is the code name given this Mountie by the RCMP. His real name has been withheld in exchange for contributing his version of what happened. Why a Mountie was assigned a code name will become clear in the next two chapters.

ties who served under him in the Provost Corps and one day in 1950 a telegram from Nicholson beckoned Long Knife to Ottawa for a chat.

Nicholson introduced him to Superintendent George McClellan, the head of the Security Service, who told him he was being transferred into the Security Service for a particularly secret and sensitive assignment requiring him from now on to stay clear of RCMP headquarters. He would be told more later about his undercover work. As Long Knife waited on a park bench behind Parliament Hill's Center Block, McClellan, pretending to be out for a mid-day stroll, sauntered along with instructions. After four anxious summer months his task emerged: he was to form part of a three-member special surveillance unit responsible for following intelligence officers attached to the Soviet embassy in Ottawa. The surveillance group would be headquartered out of a separate building and wear civilian clothing to avoid identification with the RCMP.

It did not take long for Long Knife's main target, Leonid Abramov, to realize he was being followed and to identify Long Knife and his partner, Constable Hank Robichaud. Sometimes Long Knife and Robichaud were assisted by their supervisor, Sergeant Phil Keeler, but even a three-car surveillance posed no problem for Abramov, who was trained in countersurveillance, especially when the three cars had no radios. Abramov let himself be followed; he could lose them in five minutes anytime he wanted to make a meet. Later Bourdine replaced Abramov and inherited the role as principal object of scrutiny. Long Knife sometimes broke a cardinal rule of surveillance and allowed himself to be introduced to Bourdine at cocktail parties and exchange pleasantries. By this time McClellan's security precautions had worn off and Long Knife was freely visiting headquarters.

Guernsey, as head of B Branch, regarded the surveillance unit as worse than useless and tried to replace it with a proper Watcher Service of professional civilians. But he was frustrated by higher Mounties whose police minds failed to grasp the need for establishing a first-class surveillance team because they did not understand that KGB officers, unlike common criminals, always looked for surveillance and could usually spot it. The RCMP officers also feared losing Mountie positions to civilians. They still believed there was nothing a Mountie could not do better than a civilian. Besides, none of the senior officers wanted to challenge Long Knife now that Nicholson had become Commissioner.

Even Guernsey's immediate superior, Jimmy Lemieux, who had replaced McClellan as Director of the Security Service, held little enthusiasm for a civilian Watcher Service. Lemieux, an old-line policeman dropped into the post for a promotion, had small interest in security work and operated in the aristocratic style. For him, Long Knife was a dandy errand runner whom he pressed into service when he could not justify an official driver. Consequently Long Knife was pulled off surveillance from time to time to pick up Lemieux's family at the train station, deliver his laundry and drive to Montreal to pick up his favourite comics. Long Knife was perfect for such errands because his movements were not accountable. Guernsey frequently needed Long Knife for a task only to discover his boss Lemieux had made him unavailable with a duty of his own. Finally, an arrangement was made quietly with Lemieux's secretary to let B Branch know when Long Knife was undertaking a "director's assignment." Whether the surveillance unit was effective or not, Lemieux liked it just as it was.

Lacking confidence in the surveillance unit but unable to change it, Guernsey isolated it from vital operations, and secluded it particularly from Operation Keystone. Consequently Long Knife and his surveillance colleagues knew nothing about the big double-agent case in Montreal consuming B Branch's attention.

In the days when Gideon was still an unhappy double agent, he once bought two bottles of Old Tom gin and went home to drown his frustrations. He had consumed half the second bottle when he picked up the telephone and dialed the Montreal *Gazette* and proclaimed with a drunken slur: "I'm a Russian spy. Do you want a story?" He bragged about how he was an undercover Soviet citizen posing as a Canadian photographer in Montreal and had secretly defected and now worked as a double agent for the Canadian government. Gideon babbled drunkenly without a Russian accent and the *Gazette* reporter dismissed him as a kook.

The RCMP monitored Gideon's telephone and his harangue to the *Gazette* that night set off an alarm. Hardly had he hung up when a pair of Montreal Mounties descended on his home and without saying a word dragged him into a car heading for Ottawa. Each protest from Gideon received a belt in the mouth so he quickly learned to be quiet. For three days Gideon languished in solitary confinement with no communications and without knowing what was happening or how long his detention would last. Food was quietly slipped through the door. Finally Sweeny emerged to accuse him of blowing the case so badly the RCMP were onto him and seeking a criminal prosecution. Sweeny in resigned sorrow said he had tried his best to protect him from the police but he had lost control and the matter was in official hands. Two Mounties followed and accused him of breaking Canadian law. The Mounties started an interrogation and told him he might as well confess because he was on the way to prison for a long time. As the axe was about to fall Sweeny re-appeared triumphantly exclaiming he had wielded all his influence and exhausted his last IOUs in managing to wrench him free of the RCMP. In fact, the arrest and interrogation was a ruse designed to bully the rambunctious Gideon into staying in line and to teach him a lesson about pulling such stunts again. The interrogators were real Mounties but played their role on Sweeny's orders. Gideon did not understand Canada's criminal justice system and was frightened into believing he had committed a serious offence and had barely escaped.

Now "free," Gideon needed a ride back to Montreal. Lemieux usually did not involve himself in operations but this time intervened and called Long Knife to give Gideon a lift. After Lemieux briefed him about the importance of the case and warned him never to discuss it, Long Knife drove Gideon in his Buick and dropped him in the north end of Montreal some distance from his photo studio. Both Guernsey and Sweeny learned about Long Knife's chauffeuring and regretted that it was done, not because Long Knife was disloyal, but because it widened the circle of knowledge by one more person, a person who was known to the Soviet embassy. It was too late and nothing could be done except to ensure Long Knife and his surveillance colleagues never again had contact with the case.

Long Knife struggled to preserve appearances and maintain the social standing he achieved as a captain in the army. His Buick belonged to his mother-in-law who did not drive. The boat was his father-in-law's. His fashionable house was affordable because his parents-in-law lived with them. Still it was difficult raising two children and maintaining his lifestyle on a corporal's salary. Long Knife complained that the Force's mileage allowance for his car was too stingy and that he was operating his Buick on behalf of the RCMP at a loss but his superiors viewed him as a big spender and dismissed his grumbling. Meanwhile his personal unsecured debt reached the equivalent of nearly a year's salary and was growing, forcing him to borrow to meet his debt payments and putting him further into debt. One of the first pieces of informal advice new people got when they joined the Security Service was not to loan him money.

He cashed a personal cheque with Trans Canada Airlines and when it bounced the RCMP investigated and learned officially how far he was in debt. Guernsey dispatched a memo to Lemieux saying his financial instability made him unsuitable for sensitive work and recommended his transfer out of the Security Service. Nothing was done. As control over his financial affairs slipped away, Long Knife resorted to paying off his debts through kiting—making payments with worthless cheques and covering them with still more worthless cheques, and so on. Long Knife was getting desperate and in his own words, the days were getting long and the nights short. One last source of cash remained. It was the forbidden fruit so appealing and so easy, yet so sensitive and fraught with consequences that temptation had not beckoned before. But in desperation Long Knife bit the apple.

Every month Long Knife picked up a sealed envelope from Guernsey's office and hand delivered it to the president's office at the Bell Telephone Company. The envelope contained over $1,000 in cash to compensate Bell for its facilities and services for helping the RCMP wiretap. The payment had nothing to do with the RCMP's regular telephone bill. It was separate and Guernsey maintained delivery should be made personally by a trusted member of the force and be transacted in cash. He wanted no unnecessary records. Guernsey himself used to deliver the payments but necessity forced him to delegate the duty. But to whom? Virtually everybody around him wore a uniform which would advertise the RCMP's presence in the Bell office. Long Knife wore no uniform and did not look like a Mountie, had a car and was handy. At the time Guernsey did not know about his debts.

When Bell reported non-payment of two consecutive bills, Guernsey had a good idea what happened. He knew the payments had been forwarded because he had personally signed out the cash and sealed the envelope. Only one person handled the transaction between his office and Bell and that was Long Knife. Tied up in the office all day running the B Branch and planning Gideon's return to Moscow, Guernsey called Long Knife to his home that evening and sitting in his backyard neatly extracted a confession. Long Knife proved easy to break. He admitted readily to having twice opened the envelopes and removed the money and forged receipts. "Well, that's a hell of a mess to get in," said Guernsey quietly. "Now we've got to figure how to straighten matters out."

By this time Lemieux had moved on to a different corner of the RCMP bureaucracy and was replaced by Cliff Harvison, another policeman passing through the post as Director of the Security Service. Nicknamed Slim, Harvison was tall and thin and seized attention through aggressiveness and a show of authority. During World War Two, before there was a real Security Service, he had tried to run a defecting Nazi spy as a double agent through his short wave broadcasts from Quebec. When Harvison discovered that the spy's transmitter lacked power to reach German headquarters in Hamburg he boosted the wattage to twice the output. As the signal boomed across the ocean the Nazis knew the case was compromised. Harvison had not realized the transmitter was not intended for Germany but an intermediate location which would relay the message.

Harvison remained calm when told about Long Knife's theft. He considered dismissing him from the force and laying criminal charges. By now Guernsey had managed to develop a modest Watcher Service of half a dozen civilians so if Long Knife left quickly he would be unmissed. But laying charges against a Mountie would attract publicity, damage the RCMP image and possibly compromise operations so, through Guernsey, Harvison ordered Long Knife to replace the money within a week. Missing the deadline could cause dismissal from the Force and a criminal prosecution. Where Long Knife would find the money is one thing Harvison did not consider. He was deeply in debt and had no credit left. No bank, friend or colleague would spare him a dollar and his ingenuity for raising cash had run out.

Since Bourdine had returned to Moscow most of Long Knife's surveillance time concentrated on Ostrovsky whose slower pace made his job easier. Ostrovsky usually left the embassy around nine-thirty A.M. and parked downtown to check if he was being followed. Sometimes he took in a movie. At noon, as the pubs opened, he headed for the Grand Hotel across the street from the railway station and leisurely sipped a few beers. He invested a lot of effort in killing time. Long

Knife sometimes waited outside the hotel and other times followed him inside and had a beer himself. By doing so he breached standard security procedures but for practical purposes it did not matter since Ostrovsky long ago knew who his 'tail' was and how to shake him.

Ostrovsky betrayed no sign of reaction when one day, according to what Long Knife later told the RCMP, he stopped by Ostrovsky's table for a talk. Long Knife did not hide the fact he was advancing a business proposition so Ostrovsky suggested they meet in a more discreet location. Conducting business in a pub where both were known was not prudent. Long Knife followed Ostrovsky's car to a secluded spot underneath a downtown bridge crossing the Ottawa River to the province of Quebec. They parked their cars side by side and got out and leaned against their respective front fenders while interprovincial traffic rumbled overhead.

Long Knife lost no time coming to the point. He told Ostrovsky he had information of extreme importance to him and he could have it, but he needed money quickly. Long Knife was nervous but Ostrovsky remained relaxed, quiet and almost detached, knowing and enjoying the fact he had control. His deadpan expression never flickered. He quickly sized up Long Knife as a desperate man who could be manipulated. What kind of information did he have, Ostrovsky wanted to know. Was it a case, he asked. Yes, replied Long Knife. Was it happening in Canada? Yes. Was there an agent? Yes. Was the agent cooperating with the RCMP? Yes again. Long Knife in his desperation felt clues were bolstering his bargaining position but Ostrovsky through deft questioning and without any promise of reward quickly extracted the information that the double-dealing agent was a photographer in Montreal. Long Knife realized instantly he had divulged the case and surrendered his bargaining power. Ostrovsky remained expressionless. "I'll see what I can do," he said and arranged to meet at a different location the following day.

On the night of the following day Ostrovsky hid his car on the Quebec side of the river behind some bush at the back of the parking lot of the Royal Ottawa Golf Club and climbed into Long Knife's waiting Buick. Following Ostrovsky's instructions, Long Knife drove west into the historic village of Aylmer, headed north, and stopped at the side of a forgotten country road a mile out of town. Ostrovsky was much warmer this time and treated him like a comrade. "I can give you some money to help out," he said laying an envelope on the car seat. He told him the envelope contained close to $5,000 and made it clear his government was prepared to spend more money for additional information. Ostrovsky wanted to know everything possible about Keystone and then asked about the RCMP's surveillance capability. Long Knife told him about the emerging Watcher Service, how big it was and how it operated. Ostrovsky instructed him to get a notebook and write down what information about the Security Service he had to offer and present it at their next get-together the following week.

Long Knife returned Ostrovsky to his car, sped away, and once safely out of sight pulled off the road to check the inside of the envelope. It was packed with used $20 bills of which he counted $4,200 worth. Long Knife sold his mother-in-law's car and although he was now a surveillance man without a car, the sale provided an explanation of how he raised the money to reimburse the RCMP.

Long Knife trembled visibly when he appeared at headquarters to replace the Bell money. His loud self confidence had never flagged before, even when facing his most persistent creditors, but as he stepped into Guernsey's office he could not conceal tortured nervousness. The change in personality struck Guernsey at the time but he ascribed it to shame over the theft and worry about the punishment Harvison would be meting out. Long Knife handed over the cash and left. The Soviets' twenty-dollar bills were covering in part the RCMP's wiretap operations against the Soviet embassy but Long Knife was in no frame of mind to see the irony.

At his next meet with Ostrovsky Long Knife produced a pocket-sized notebook with handwritten notes containing the names of everybody in the Security Service, starting with Harvison at the top and working through Guernsey on the way down to the new civilians in the Watcher Service. Long Knife had jotted down the information the previous weekend while relaxing at the RCMP camp on Long Island. Ostrovsky flipped the pages curiously for a few minutes. He asked about the addresses of the civilian watchers but Long Knife said he did not know that. "That's fine," said Ostrovsky as he slipped the book into his inside breast pocket. The notebook·in Long Knife's handwriting constituted physical evidence of treason and pulled him into what the Soviets call "the net." He could no longer change his mind without fear of exposing himself.

At the previous meet Long Knife had asked for an emergency escape plan out of Canada in case his treachery was discovered and now raised the subject again. Ostrovsky replied that a plan was being drawn up which would send him through New York City. The answer, rather than soothing him, made him more nervous because he figured his Soviet friends could spirit him to Moscow a little more safely than that.

Ostrovsky told Long Knife $3,000 was available to cover his expenses for a trip to Mexico for debriefing with comrades from Moscow. A signal system in Mexico City would put him in touch with the right people. Long Knife recoiled at the thought. If discovered, how could a man in his financial condition explain a trip to Mexico? The passport factor made the trip even riskier. Ostrovsky pressed the idea, saying the trip would last only a few days and his absence could be covered by claiming a visit to his father in Montreal. Long Knife promised to think it over but remained dubious.

Before the Mexico proposal developed further Harvison issued his punishment for theft: a transfer to Winnipeg where he would be taken out of the Security Service and put back on police duties. The new posting put a short horizon on his productivity as a KGB mole since he lost access to the very stuff the Russians wanted. With 1,200 miles separating him from Ottawa and Ostrovsky's unrestricted travel limited to a radius of seventy-five miles, Long Knife's new source of revenue looked like it was shrivelling up.

Nobody in the RCMP was sorrier to see Long Knife leave Ottawa than Bennett. Long Knife was one of his best friends. Other Mounties were friendly and helpful but still saw him as a civilian and did not invite him into their homes. Long Knife never showed such snobbishness and invited his civilian colleague not only into his home but took the Bennetts to the RCMP's Long Island camp for weekends. Their wives, both foreigners to Canada, became close friends too.

Bennett found Long Knife not only a good friend but a competent colleague and selected him to help out on special assignments like X-raying Soviet shipments into Canada under diplomatic seal. They wanted to know what equipment the embassy was importing and the project worked until the Soviets started lining certain boxes with lead. Long Knife was also Bennett's pick whenever a clandestine observation post had to be established. They usually set out as a pair looking for a convenient shop, office or home and when they sought the permission of the owner, always under a pretext, Long Knife did the talking and never encountered a rejection.

Before leaving, Long Knife invited Bennett duck hunting in Manitoba, so when fall arrived a few months later Bennett's first annual vacation with the RCMP started with a motor trip through northern Ontario with a non-RCMP friend of Long Knife's while Shev worked at her job with the British High Commission. From Winnipeg, Long Knife and his two Ottawa friends travelled south to Manitou and spent two cold days splashing through streams in search of ducks. On the third day they found a lake-like slough and brought down dozens but most landed in the water too far from shore to be reached. Their recoverable harvest was only fifteen.

As Bennett and Long Knife shot ducks in Manitoba marshes, Gideon was leaving for Moscow unaware he had already been betrayed.

7

Operation Dew Worm

SMOKE SEEPED OUT of the upper windows of the Russian Embassy on Charlotte Street on New Year's Day, 1956. Neighbours at first thought the cook had burned dinner. When flames broke through the tar roof at four fifteen P.M., they started phoning the fire department but diplomatic immunity blocked firemen from reacting as unaided embassy staffers tried to extinguish the fire. Finally, at four fifty-five P.M., the embassy officially called for help but barred access to the embassy's secret area containing its communication centre and cipher room. While firemen stood back, embassy officials tackled smoke so thick in the restricted area they had to feel their way along walls, returning with arms full of documents delivered into two black limousines which, when loaded, rolled over fire hoses and patches of ice and snow and out of the embassy compound en route to the safety of the Soviet trade mission several blocks away. When all the documents were cleared an hour later the whole building was opened to fire fighters but by that time the blaze had gained such an advantage that the stately three-storey mansion overlooking the Rideau River was irretrievably lost.

The Russians suspected the motives of the firemen from the outset and indeed a few Mounties dressed as fire fighters did appear on the scene to retrieve a hollow log which held metal containers used as a dead letter box. With it the RCMP found a sheet of carbon paper with seven typings that the Security Service were able to reconstruct into a nearly complete document.

From the day of the fire there was never any doubt that when the Russians built a new embassy, B Branch would try to penetrate it with listening devices. The embers still glowed as Guernsey opened Operation Dew Worm and turned his attention toward exploiting this opportunity. Constructing a new building put the Soviets into the hands of Canadian builders and gave the Security Service rare access. By happenstance Guernsey was in the process of hiring a young engineer named Howie Jones to undertake wiretapping, bugging and related technical operations; his hiring gave hope to the success of Dew Worm. The Security Service still lacked state-of-the-art listening devices and required guidance on where to put them, so they called in the British. The new Soviet embassy would have a secret section as its communication centre and within the section a KGB room, a GRU room and an embassy room with separate cipher machines and cipher staffs for each. A security guard at the entrance to the secret section would block access to unauthorized staff and screen documents coming out. Short of securing a defector the only way to penetrate this area was through bugging. The British had sophisticated bugs that could elude the Russian electronic sweepers.

The challenge was to spot the bugs in the correct places. The Security Service figured it could penetrate only one area otherwise so much cable and so many workmen would become involved that the Russians would inevitably find out. B Branch would have to guess the location of the embassy's secret section and concentrate its attack there. After consulting with Peter Wright of the British Security Service (MI5), Guernsey, with Bennett's help, selected the north-east corner of the second floor as the likely spot. It provided handy access for laying underground cable since RCMP facilities were nearby and, being the back of the building, sheltered the installers from prying eyes on the street. The corner would be filled with six microphones numbered randomly from one to twenty so that if discovered the Soviets might think there were more than six.

Planning had hardly started when George McManus, the CIA's Liaison Officer in Canada, volunteered the CIA's help in bugging the embassy. The CIA had not been cut into the operation but must have assumed the Canadians were up to something. McManus was never fully trusted since he had been stationed in Europe a few years earlier and incensed the RCMP by trying to slip burned-out European agents into Canada's immigration stream behind the Force's back. His offer was declined delicately, on the one hand not leaving the impression the Security Service already had something going while on the other hand mildly discouraging the CIA from trying something independently.

The Security Service clandestinely laid underground coaxial cables as soon as construction chewed up the grounds and as the walls went up Mounties snuck onto the site each night and pulled the cables up a little further between the stone work and the inside wall to keep pace with construction. Along the way the Security Service noticed a fault in the wall the contractor had overlooked. The wall had been started in such a way that it would not meet the windows and could cause the company to demolish its work and start over, tearing out the secret cables in the process. The Security Service kept quiet and hoped the contractor could somehow rectify the problem. But when the error was discovered the contractor tore down the wall, forcing the Security Service to patch its cable and patiently start again.

The Russians, sometimes carrying walkie-talkies, dropped by the site at odd and unpredictable times for impromptu inspections, particularly during the critical days when the microphones were being implanted into the window cutouts. The Russians disrupted Dew Worm just enough to leave time for only five microphone installations instead of six.

If the Soviets had ever considered the north-east corner of the second floor as their secret section they changed plans and moved to the centre of the building and well out of microphone reach. The Security Service had guessed wrong although the bugging attempt was doomed to failure even if the location had been right because the Soviets were starting a world wide policy of quarantining their secret sections. Once Canadian workmen were finished Russian carpenters moved in to build a segregated and soundproof shell with a separate electrical system to house the secret section. Even properly located bugs could not penetrate the sealed shell. The failure seemed straight forward: the Soviet's desire to protect themselves from technical intrusion had simply outdistanced the RCMP attack.

Guernsey had been hoping the Russian sweepers lacked the wherewithal to find the bugs because the moving-coil microphones emitted an electro-magnetic field so small that the dampening effect of the metal window frames drowned their emissions. The sweepers spent nearly a week searching the north-east corner and, as RCMP head-quarters was listening, passed over and repeatedly missed the micro-phones. The Russians tapped and banged the walls but the devices stayed in place. Why did the sweepers spend so long and try so hard? It seemed strange they would spend such an inordinate amount of time in one corner.

The new embassy building gave the Soviets surprisingly little work-ing space. The building itself was not big. The top floor was devoted to residences for clerical staff and much of the main floor was set aside for reception purposes, leaving the crowded second floor as the main working area. But when the Russians occupied the building, the north-east corner of the second floor remained empty. This surprising development, along with the strange behaviour of the sweepers, sug-gested the Soviets knew the area was wired. If the Soviets knew bugs were there but couldn't find them, leaving the area vacant made perfect sense. Or possibly they felt they could not "afford" to let the Security Service know that it knew. Either way, the evidence suggested that somebody told the Russians. Who told was another question.

The microphones passed along noises and echoes but few voices and almost no intelligence. Soviet consular officials once briefly occupied the empty space to write an annual report and the bugs recorded their discussions on the nature and size of ethnic groups in Canada. Occa-sionally officials entered and discussed plans for using the room and the Security Service became hopeful but nothing ever developed. A few years later, when Soviet sweeping technology had improved, the microphones were discovered and removed. By this time the Mounties had virtually stopped listening.

Winnipeg cut Long Knife off from Security Service happenings every bit as much as he had feared. His personal debts continued to accumu-late and again Ostrovsky represented his only source for an injection of capital. From earlier briefings, Long Knife knew if ever he wanted a meet with Ostrovsky he could arrange it by writing a letter to a fellow code-named Lambert in East Berlin. The letter's purported message was meaningless. The sending of the letter itself requested a meet and a simple code number stipulated the date Long Knife would show up in Ottawa at a pre-arranged location.

Arranging a meet was not without risk. As a Mountie, Long Knife needed permission to leave his duty district so a meet forced him to slip out of town on a weekend and be careful. Otherwise, if caught, an RCMP service court would make him explain his actions and the purpose of his departure and, more vexingly, ask how a man in his financial condition could afford travel to Ottawa. But Long Knife needed money and had to take risks.

Meeting Ostrovsky in itself did not resolve his money problems. First he needed marketable intelligence to sell and at the moment he had none. He devised a plan to look up old Security Service colleagues in Ottawa and talk some shop to see what nuggets he could find.

One evening Bennett and Shev were returning from St. Patrick's Church when they noticed a light burning in the living room of their Somerset Street apartment. Bennett thought he had turned off all lights and hurried inside to discover Long Knife in the apartment. Long Knife apologized profusely for the intrusion, explaining that he was visiting Ottawa and had dropped by for a visit and found nobody home so, being cold and in need of a washroom, slipped the lock with a piece of celluloid.

"Don't do it again," sighed Bennett. "You nearly gave us a heart attack."

As Shev made coffee, Long Knife asked Bennett which radio frequencies the Watcher Service was now using. Bennett said he did not know.

"Is there any sign of our friend coming back?" asked Long Knife, referring to Gideon who was seriously overdue.

"No," replied Bennett. "Nothing so far."

Long Knife gulped down the coffee and left. He had come to Bennett's house for a secret document or some piece of intelligence but had so far failed to get any information and he would have to meet with Ostrovsky soon. When Ostrovsky and Long Knife finally met they greeted each other warmly; this was their first meet in more than six months. Ostrovsky realized quickly that his Canadian comrade had nothing substantial to offer but did not seem to mind since the Mountie had already made his contribution to the KGB. Ostrovsky asked what kind of technical attack the security service was planning on the new embassy. Long Knife did not know but said he would find out. He was hardly aware that the embassy had burned down. The weather was cold so Ostrovsky did nothing to prolong the encounter. After twenty minutes they parted.

Before he left, Ostrovsky handed him an envelope containing cash. The amount disappointed Long Knife later when he checked because it did not solve his financial problems. In keeping with the KGB's policy of paying agents, the money covered his expenses generously with a little extra for his trouble, but gave him no windfall. The Russians from now on compensated him as an ideological agent when his interest was strictly monetary.

Long Knife's plans for milking the KGB suffered another setback when he was transferred out of Winnipeg to a small-town detachment where he and a junior Mountie resided as town cops. If Winnipeg put him out of touch, his new country post isolated him entirely. Now the mechanics of travelling to Ottawa were an exercise, but they were not impossible and several months later he made another visit. This time he stayed the weekend in Bennett's apartment.

Shev was washing dishes while Long Knife was relaxing with Bennett in the spacious apartment.

"Let's visit your sun room," said Long Knife moving out of Shev's earshot to the back room. Here Long Knife asked whether R. A. Crain, the contractor, was obstructing the Security Service's plans to bug the Soviet embassy.

"They are a problem but don't worry, we'll get around it," replied Bennett.

"Well, if you do have a problem," said Long Knife, "let me know. I know R. A. Crain quite well. What sort of plans do you have?"

Top level secrecy surrounded Operation Dew Worm and the direction of the conversation made Bennett uncomfortable. An outsider like Long Knife was not supposed to know anything, but evidently he knew something. Or did he? The fact that R. A. Crain was working on the embassy was not secret and Long Knife, with his experience, could have guessed bugs were going in. We have great plans for the Russian embassy, replied Bennett. Then he started describing a grandiose but improbable scheme for installing close-circuit television cameras inside the walls. Long Knife, showing no sign of being put down, said it sounded tremendous. He was so desperate for intelligence, he evidently did not care if the information was accurate or credible.

Long Knife rented a car and met Ostrovsky over a few beers in a Quebec pub alongside the Ottawa River near the town of Buckingham. They were unlikely to be recognized in this low-income French-Canadian milieu half an hour northeast of Ottawa. Long Knife offered Ostrovsky what information he could but Ostrovsky was not impressed. Long Knife conceivably had been discovered and turned into a triple agent disseminating false information. In the end Ostrovsky must have assessed him as a desperate man willing to manufacture information for money and this made him unreliable as an agent.

Back home Long Knife's financial predicament worsened and threatened again to reach the crisis proportion that had propelled him to court Ostrovsky in the first place. He sensed the KGB's welcome was wearing thin but felt compelled to signal another rendezvous. Once again he wrote Lambert in East Berlin only this time before leaving for Ottawa he wrote a cheque for $2,850 at a bank in a neighbouring town and covered it with a cheque for $3,000 at a local bank days later while telling the manager the cheque represented government funds coming from an Ottawa bank account for secret service work he was performing. The bank manager knew him and accepted implicitly the word of the town's senior police officer. Long Knife figured he could cover the cheque during his Ottawa visit with money from Ostrovsky. He slipped quietly out of town and flew to Montreal where he could claim to be visiting his father and brother and at Montreal he borrowed his brother's car and drove into the Gatineau Hills northeast of Ottawa and parked on the main street in Buckingham.

The night was chilly and Long Knife received a surprise when he slipped into the Soviet car. Inside waiting for him was not his friend Ostrovsky but a tall and thin Soviet Third Secretary who identified himself as Rem Krassilnikov. In his early thirties, Krassilnikov was younger than Ostrovsky and unfriendly. There was no warm introduction and small talk and not even a vague attempt to flatter Long Knife. He came directly to the point. What information do you have, he asked. Long Knife produced nothing and Krassilnikov flew into a rage.

"What are you here for?" he demanded. "Why did you ask us to meet you here?"

Long Knife replied he needed money.

"That's not my department," snorted Krassilnikov. "I don't deal with that."

Long Knife protested that he had come to see Ostrovsky and resented such treatment. Anything he had to say would be said to Ostrovsky and with that got out of the car. The entire exchange lasted only minutes.

His finances were in tatters and the KGB well had run dry. Krassilnikov had not even covered his travel expenses so the trip to Ottawa merely enlarged his debt and hastened the inevitable day of financial reckoning.

Driving off, Long Knife spotted a single car parked a block from his meeting place. As he motored past it the momentary light from his headlights caught, he thought, a single figure sitting inside. He looked back in his mirror but the car did not move and he wondered why on a chilly fall night would somebody sit alone in cold darkness. He feared the Watcher Service had surveilled the meet and now the RCMP was onto him. The thirty-minute drive to Ottawa aggravated his fears and as he wondered about the suspicious car and the consequences of discovery by the RCMP, his financial problems paled into insignificance. If discovered, he faced serious trouble, trouble that would make his chafing money worries a picnic. He wondered what to do and started mulling over the idea of short-circuiting events by reporting the encounter and attempting to remove the stench of treason. That way he would have a defence when the Force confronted him with its evidence. He took a room for the night at the Chateau Laurier and as he brooded in the bar his desperate mind hatched a plot. He would offer himself to the Security Service as a triple agent and secure a multiple purpose: pre-empt suspicion, acquire money, get back into the Security Service and at the same time wreak revenge on the ungrateful KGB. The more he pondered it the more sense it made.

Long Knife had always blamed Sweeny for his plight because he believed Sweeny's dismissal of his claims for more generous mileage allowances created the indebtedness that ultimately drove him to Ostrovsky. Long Knife had more seniority with the Force and had outranked him in the army but now in the RCMP he was stuck at corporal and Sweeny was the officer. Long Knife returned to his room, picked up the telephone and tried to peddle his story to the person he disliked most and who would be least sympathetic to his tale.

The telephone awakened Sweeny at two A.M. and on the other end of the line an excited Long Knife, whom he had not seen for two years, announced he had gone AWOL from his detachment to make contact with the Soviet embassy and now was in a position to penetrate the Russian espionage service. The phone call itself was surprising and the message stunning. If he had been in contact with a Russian why had he not reported the development fifteen minutes after he first knew it was coming, Sweeny wanted to know. Long Knife babbled an answer, saying he knew more about Soviet intelligence than the Security Service did. Nothing he said made sense to Sweeny. "Stay where you are," said Sweeny. "We'll be over."

Long Knife's story upon closer examination sounded to Sweeny and others even more nefarious and untrue. Sweeny suspected he was flying a brazen scheme either to raise money, get back into the Security Service or get revenge on the RCMP. After his discovered theft of funds and related disciplinary transfer he possessed the financial need and the motive for vengeance to try such a scheme. Sweeny worried that maybe Long Knife had approached the Russians and used his Security Service connection to sucker money out of them but found it difficult to believe he would have deliberately betrayed secrets. Such a spectacle required a horrendous leap and no one, even Sweeny, at this point thought that Long Knife was a traitor.

Long Knife at first claimed Ostrovsky was trying to recruit him but later said his encounter that evening was with Krassilnikov. He denied having given them anything but acknowledged accepting money. The story was becoming more suspicious and Sweeny started worrying over the extent of his contacts and the kinds of secrets that might have been compromised. Sweeny and his colleagues started patching the scenario together and grew alarmed. Two years had passed since Gideon went to Moscow and disappeared. By now most observers of the case agreed the Russians had broken the case but nobody knew how. It had been assumed that Gideon cracked under interrogation and confessed. The possibility Gideon had been betrayed from the inside had never been considered. But now as they reviewed Long

Knife's indebtedness, his access to Ostrovsky, the Bell theft and his ability to replace the money quickly and, finally, his own acknowledgement of meeting clandestinely with the Soviets—the pieces fell into place.

"Sweeny wants to see you," growled Corporal Henry Tadeson the next morning. "You better just tell the truth because he's got a lot of stuff to go on."

The news from Sweeny was that he was under arrest. An apartment suite inside RCMP headquarters was converted into a comfortable jail after glass, mirrors and sharp objects were removed. Two Mounties, one by the door and the other next to the window, watched every move.

Staff Sergeant John Dean and Tadeson opened the interrogation and at first counselled him it was in his best interest to come clean but their efforts failed to extract a confession. They used logic, parading before him the inconsistencies and contradictions in his story but could not persuade their stubborn subject to talk. "I have nothing to say," he replied. Long Knife realized they had no evidence against him. The Force could not subpoena the Russians so keeping quiet represented his only chance for survival. Sweeny and Len Higgitt, the new head of B Branch, joined the interrogation and advised him with triumphant glee that the RCMP Act authorized the Commissioner to imprison any Mountie for up to a year without laying charges or bringing him to court. The Commissioner did not need his confession so they urged him to tell his story while people were still prepared to listen and believe him. Long Knife remained unmoved.

While the interrogators bristled over their impotence, Long Knife silently cursed himself for phoning Sweeny in the first place, realizing now that the Force had no inkling of his dealings and would never have caught on if not for his own stupidity.

Each morning at nine, with an hour break for lunch, Dean and Tadeson alternating with Sweeny and Higgitt pressed on with few resources except for two things—Long Knife's isolation from his family and the outside world. Their threat to lock him up for a year on the whim of the Commissioner was true. It was permitted under the RCMP Act, so they could now keep him interned and wait until he broke. Long Knife wanted to telephone his wife who was back home with their two sons wondering what happened to him. They told him there would be no phone call until he talked. After his second weekend from home—nine days after the interrogation started—his stubbornness cracked and he agreed to divulge everything for a talk with his wife.

The story unfolded piece by piece: his meetings with Ostrovsky, the pay-off and his trips to Ottawa. By the time the account with all the details was out, the statement grew so long the stenographer needed a full day to type out the finished draft.

"Sign this," ordered Dean, thrusting the typed confession at Long Knife.

"I want to read it," protested Long Knife.

"I haven't got time to let you read the damn thing," shot back Dean. "We're going to throw it in the drawer anyway. We're not going to prosecute. The Force just doesn't want this kind of stink associated with her name."

Long Knife signed when Dean promised to get him to Winnipeg the next day. The following morning he was paraded before the Adjutant and reduced from corporal to constable and then flown to Winnipeg on the RCMP plane.

Winnipeg stuck him into a dank jail cell in the basement of the RCMP building on Portage Avenue but this offended Sam Bullard, the commanding officer, who proclaimed: "This man is a member of the Force and a veteran. Until he's proven guilty nobody is going to treat him this way." Long Knife was moved upstairs into a self-contained room with a guard outside and permitted visits each night from his wife. Bullard knew nothing about the real reason for Long Knife's detention. The Security Service was keeping his treachery secret and, like everybody else in Winnipeg, Bullard thought his misdeeds were financial transgressions.

Long Knife waited in jail while the Force investigated his financial history for some criminal violation to punish him legally without sullying the RCMP reputation too much. The Force wanted revenge without admitting it had a money-inspired traitor within its ranks. The investigation quickly uncovered the last kited cheque which bounced during his interrogation while Long Knife was helpless to cover it. Kiting constituted intent to defraud and as far as the RCMP was concerned served as a pretext to charge Long Knife in open court.

The Manitoba Attorney-General's office saw matters differently and wanted the RCMP to handle it internally but the Force maintained Long Knife had violated his trust as a police officer and deserved court punishment. The Manitoba authorities could not understand the RCMP fuss. The Royal Bank of Canada, the victim, had never pressed a complaint and wanted Long Knife free so he could make compensation. A background check by the provincial authorities revealed that Long Knife was a popular policeman and lacking in criminal disposition but the RCMP persisted and a few weeks later Manitoba relented and charged him with fraud.

Once charged, Long Knife went free on bail with money from a friendly medical doctor. He expected a prison sentence of five years, maybe three years with luck, and toyed briefly with the thought of defecting to Russia, but rejected it.

Long Knife stood in court with his head bowed while his lawyer pleaded for a suspended sentence that would spare him from imprisonment. Long Knife, his lawyer said, had already suffered public humiliation and financial loss because dismissal from the RCMP two years before qualifying for a lifetime pension of $160 a month would cost him nearly $50,000 over 25 years. The judge delivered a two-year suspended sentence and ordered him to pay restitution at the rate of $100 a month. The judge said his leniency was based on his past good character, his exemplary record with the RCMP, his military service and the suffering his family would experience from losing nearly nineteen years service.

Had the defendant anything to say, asked the judge.

"No," whispered Long Knife, head still bowed. "I have nothing to say."

8

The Russian Desk

BENNETT WATCHED THE unfolding of Operation Keystone from a special vantage point as Guernsey's de facto assistant. Although in the background, Bennett made an impact of sorts on the running of the case. Sweeny returned from his meets with Gideon to discuss each move with Guernsey, who in turn confided in the British. Very little went onto paper and was available for cold inspection. The best documentation came out of Sweeny's diaries and they carried only highlights. Bennett maintained this major double agent case had to be documented meticulously if the Security Service hoped to avoid the sophisticated traps the KGB would surely be setting along the way.

It was because of Bennett's intervention that details such as the date Gideon posted each letter to the live letter box in Ottawa to signal a missed broadcast were recorded. Such information allowed the Security Service to observe more precisely how the live letter box passed on letters to the Soviet embassy.

One of Bourdine's last acts before returning to Moscow was an attempt to recruit a woman who had recently immigrated to Canada. The woman, telling Bourdine she wanted to think it over, nervously reported the approach to an immigration officer who contacted the Security Service. In her forties, the lady was not classic double-agent material. She lacked confidence and had no access to classified material. But aside from Keystone, the case represented the Security Service's only Russian operation and she had potential as a live letter box, so despite her misgivings, the Force talked her into becoming a double agent. With a little luck the woman might uncover for the Security Service the identity of a functioning agent.

In early 1954 the Russian Desk had only one Mountie, Hank Tadeson, although Guernsey, then still head of B Branch, operated as effective chief. When Guernsey needed somebody to run Gideon he would borrow Sweeny from the Satellite Desk instead of going to Tadeson, and when he needed research he would use Bennett. None of this enhanced Tadeson's status. Choosing a civilian like Bennett over a Mountie like Tadeson violated tradition but Guernsey justified it on grounds that Keystone was an extraordinary case and Tadeson was a young corporal with limited counterespionage experience.

Eyebrows were raised when Guernsey selected Bennett over Tadeson to run the female double agent because this case was not special. Now Guernsey clearly valued Bennett's skills over Tadeson's. Tadeson and some other Mounties grumbled at the time because civilians were ancillary staff whose function was to support regular members, not pre-empt them.

Soon after the case started, Bourdine left Canada and handed control to Ostrovsky but neither the woman nor Ostrovsky displayed much enthusiasm and Ostrovsky stopped calling meets within a few months. At the time the Security Service assumed that the case failed because of the woman's ineptitude, which would have made sense had not Long Knife been betraying the operation as it went along. Long Knife knew about the operation because he helped Bennett set up observation posts on the woman's meets with Ostrovsky.

Bennett seemed to be handy whenever work was needed. Civilians, the untouchables, floated in a semi-no-man's land and this lack of place provoked them either to quit—as McClung and his group would do eventually—or bear down and conquer the adverse atmosphere. Bennett followed the latter course, which meant he needed to show he was twice as good and this required exploiting every asset and pulling every trick and sometimes stretching his counterespionage experience a bit.

Each morning B Branch members would arrive in the office to find Bennett already sitting behind his desk bent over files. He left the office last at the end of the day. Almost everybody in B Branch was dedicated and overworked but Bennett was compulsive. He always appeared on the spot to solve problems or at least articulate a thoughtful solution.

He was brighter and quicker and more adaptable than the police minds around him and parlayed his British experience tracking clandestine radio transmitters into a perceived expertise on all counterespionage matters. Almost everybody thought he came from MI6, Britain's legendary intelligence service, and Bennett did nothing to deflate the "six myth." In off hours he bolstered his knowledge by blitzing bookstores and libraries for anything they had on the history and technique of spying.

The Security Service viewed this aggressive oncomer with respect and more amusement and fondness than rivalry. His rumpled greyish green tweed sports jacket, which he wore with grey slacks, came with him from Britain and each year attracted more good natured wisecracks that the suede elbow patches and cuff linings served a functional and not a decorative purpose. Cigarette ashes were always falling on the lapels. His other outfit, a brown suit of equal vintage, became a sports jacket when the pants wore out. These two garments became his trademark for more than a decade and were discarded only when the material itself wore out. He wore imported ankle high brown suede shoes dubbed brothel creepers because their translucent white sponge soles created a silent walk. Later he kept a pair of moccasins in his office. In a sea of Mountie uniforms he stood out as a slightly comical unkempt professor who didn't realize what he was wearing. Everybody's hair was short and slick. Bennett's hung long and perpetually out of place, not to make a statement, but because he did not get to the barber as often as others. If he appeared in the office with his hair shorn to Mountie length he would receive funny looks for several weeks. He was fondly known as "Jiminy Cricket" and while not a man of ecumenical interest his intellectual scope outdistanced that of most Mountie colleagues.

Bennett's pre-eminence evaporated when he walked down the corridor into the environment of the civilian researchers in D Branch, the countersubversion section. Here a little pocket of intellectuals led by Mark McClung, a Rhodes Scholar, Don Wall and Bill Rodney held informal esoteric chats that seemed incongruous in a police building. Although he too was a civilian, Bennett had few compatible interests with this group and rarely fraternized. Five people here had overseas degrees and their presence reminded him of his lack of university education. When the conversation turned to outside subjects like art, music or world events, Bennett would remain quiet for a while and drift off.

He scarcely talked to anyone about his past or his family background. Sometimes he would mention one of his foreign postings without divulging why he had been there, and most people learned only peripherally that he had experienced places like Turkey and Hong Kong. The one exception was Australia, the home of his wife, about which he talked freely, especially about retiring one day in Perth because it had the perfect climate, scenery and way of life. When asked what brought him to Canada, he said opportunity.

Almost as though someone had turned on the tap, the Russian Desk was swamped with half a dozen routine counterespionage cases against the Soviet embassy. Through the RA Club, the civil service recreation association, the Security Service spotted Gennadi Popov, nominally a Second Secretary at the embassy, meet and recruit James Staples, a thirty-year-old civilian clerk with the Royal Canadian Air Force and intervened as Staples was about to hand over plans of the CF-105 airplane. Staples was fired and Popov declared persona non grata for "activities incompatible with his continued presence in Canada."

The onslaught of Russian cases forced the Security Service to beef up the Russian Desk and break it down into KGB and GRU sub-desks. Like the Popov case, most of the cases originated in the RA Club. Clause four of the RA charter offered foreign diplomats associate membership status and the Soviet embassy exploited this channel as an opportunity to meet, assess and recruit civil servants with access to classified material. All eight Soviet members of the chess club were identified as intelligence officers belonging to the KGB. The GRU moved into the stamp club. The three Soviets there were GRU officers.

The Security Service wanted the Soviets barred from participating in any RA Club and, as usual, Bennett devised the plan. He talked to Roy Baxter on the RA Board of Directors and explained the problem. Baxter, who Bennett knew from his job as chief of security for the Department of Transport, was won over immediately and persuaded the other directors to repeal Clause Four. The Watcher Service soon discovered that the manager of the sailing club was quietly disregarding the new policy and Bennett passed the word to Baxter who had the sailing manager pulled into line.

The government's Social Relations Reporting Program required civil servants to report each contact with somebody from a communist bloc embassy. Guernsey proposed the policy and, after an initial failure, the Security Service persuaded the government to accept it. Consequently an account of each reported incident of Soviet contact landed on Guernsey's desk the next day. This stream opened the door a bit on the scope of Soviet activity and revealed something about their patterns and areas of interest. If the Soviets followed up any particular contact, the civil servant became a double agent prospect.

When Guernsey lobbied the Department of External Affairs about cutting back the size of the Soviet presence in Ottawa, Bennett again jumped in. No ceiling limited the number of officials posted in the embassy. In those days about sixty percent of the personnel had intelligence functions, which meant that the Soviet establishment of fifty-eight translated into about thirty-five people involved in some form of espionage activity. Guernsey wanted everything cut down because a smaller staff meant fewer intelligence officers and probably fewer recruitments. External Affairs hesitated to create problems with the Soviet government—its job was to solve problems, not create them. But the Security Service campaign worked and External Affairs not only imposed a ceiling but reduced the Soviet establishment to fifty-one.

Word soon came that Guernsey was being transferred to London as liaison officer to MI5 and MI6. The posting was logical because Guernsey had worked well with the British and enjoyed their confidence and he had been ill a lot so he needed a less demanding post. Despite the logic of the post, many people felt he was being exiled. Ever since he returned from training with MI6 with a non-police approach to his work, Guernsey was considered tainted by the British concept of civilian security. Each internal battle made his officer colleagues a little uneasier about him. They worried that his belief that the Security Service should be separated from the RCMP undermined the entire Force. An inside report prepared by civilian Mark McClung revealed that virtually everyone in B Branch believed the counter-espionage function should be moved out of the national police force. The Mountie officers saw their empire threatened by such sentiment and felt posting Guernsey across the Atlantic might banish this philosophical sedition. Commissioner Nicholson had given Guernsey a year's grace for fear of jeopardizing Operation Keystone but now that it was indisputably dead, Guernsey was leaving.

The RCMP replaced Guernsey with a safe and reliable pick. Len Higgitt believed in the RCMP paramilitary system because he was oblivious to any alternative. The career minded officer from Saskatchewan never contemplated the system; he accepted it and operated within it to best advantage. He befriended everyone and threatened no vested faction and a decade later his diplomacy would land him in the Commissioner's chair. If Guernsey went home at the end of the day concerned about the fate of Gideon, Higgitt left the office wondering how he could lower his golf score.

Higgitt did not delve into the operations of the Russian Desk the way Guernsey had. He ceded control to whomever was at hand, which meant nominally to Tadeson but really to Bennett. Bennett's dedication, experience and hard work impressed Higgitt and, in fact, made life easy for him. Whenever a major decision arose, Bennett assembled the material and laid out the options for him, sparing him the drudgery of doing it himself. In fact Bennett went further and effectively prepared the work load and set the priorities of the Russian Desk, which represented an outright invasion of Higgitt's executive responsibilities. Rather than feel threatened, he valued the service and viewed Bennett, despite his civilian status, as a good candidate to head the Russian Desk. Higgitt was happy, too, with the straight-forward Tadeson and wanted to appoint him head of the Russian Desk because he was a real Mountie and really next in line. Higgitt resolved the dilemma by promoting Tadeson from corporal to sergeant and giving him the Watcher Service and raising Bennett from a Research Analyst 3 to a Research Analyst 4, making him equivalent to a sergeant, and officially putting him in control of the Russian Desk in 1958.

The physical positioning of Bennett's new office demonstrated his enhanced authority. He was in the corner of the back wing on the fourth floor of RCMP headquarters, immediately next to the office of the head of B Branch. Others were scattered down the hallway. The Russian Desk was virtually integrated into Higgitt's office which provided Bennett good access to the boss.

Bennett's pace did not falter now that he ran the Russian Desk. He showed no inclination to relax while his underlings did the work. If anything, he worked harder since now he possessed the authority to act on his own impulses and had staff to help carry them out. His aspirations for the desk put demands on his staff but he also liked to get along with people and rather than rely on the paramilitary practice of issuing orders he employed humour and encouragement. He accepted good-natured ribbing and dished it out. Although his men sometimes struggled to maintain the pace, he remained popular with them.

He held direct responsibility for the KGB sub-desk, the GRU sub-desk and the Travel Desk, which processed Soviet embassy applications to send their officials on journeys outside Ottawa. And because the Russian Desk required surveillance services more than any other department, he influenced Tadeson's Watcher Service. Howie Jones, the civilian electronic genius in charge of bugging, was Bennett's best friend. The only uncertain area was the bullpen which housed B Branch's special investigators.

The bullpen had been born out of Operation Keystone. Logistically, A Division personnel should have handled Keystone under Headquarters' direction, but Guernsey lacked confidence in A Division, so assembled a group of investigators in Headquarters who worked in a single room down the hallway. They were called in for special assignments the way a relief pitcher in baseball is pulled in, so the name bullpen stuck. Bennett got on well with John Dean, the head of the bullpen, but lacked authority over him. Actually, Sweeny, Bennett's counterpart on the Satellite Desk, held more influence here.

Two Mounties manned the observation post on the Soviet Embassy and dictated onto tape every arrival and departure, whether it was the ambassador, the cleaning staff or an unidentified visitor. The tape went to headquarters and joined the lineup at the transcription section which stretched from two days to three months. The lethargic pace drained much of the value out of the observation post because its information was often outdated by the time it finally reached the Russian Desk.

Bennett's technical mind believed the information should be gathered, transcribed and processed in a continuous assembly-line drive and he proposed setting up an on-line cipher relay between the observation post and the Russian Deak at headquarters. The benefits were clear and simple. Details of Soviets comings and goings would stream onto his desk immediately and two civilian transcribers would be freed for other duties. The Mounties in the observation post complained about having to learn to type and use ciphers but the system was installed the way Bennett wanted it.

The Watcher Service on any day could cover only one or two of the suspected Soviet intelligence officers. From time to time off-duty Security Service personnel by happenstance would spot one of the Russians in a strange location and report it. Although sporadic, these reports offered further glimpses into Soviet movements. Bennett got the idea that if the Security Service could not squeeze extra money out of the RCMP for more surveillance, why not turn everybody into an informal Watcher. He called it the Vehicle Sighting Program and started distributing wallet-sized cards listing Soviet licence plate numbers to all RCMP personnel—not only those in the Security Service—and local police forces. The card asked them to report from the nearest telephone twenty-four hours a day any vehicle bearing a licence plate listed on the card. The system held the potential for confounding even the shrewdest KGB officer for he could spend hours successfully cleaning himself prior to an agent meet only to be spotted and reported by an off duty civil servant. The twenty-four-hour phone number belonged to the observation post across from the Russian Embassy and it would punch the sighting into the teletype that fed the Russian Desk. If the sighting looked promising the Watcher Service would converge on the area immediately and start surveillance.

The Vehicle Sighting Program started inauspiciously. Hundreds of cards went out but few phone tips came back. The Soviet licence plate numbers were scattered without sequence all over the place giving the cardholders little incentive to check the card each time a diplomatic plate drove by. There was another problem. The KGB and GRU cars in the embassy usually avoided the highly identifiable red diplomatic plates in favour of regular Ontario plates for better cover. Since they looked no different than any other car with an Ontario licence plate, they had effective immunity from the sighting program. Bennett, undaunted, lobbied for block numbers and distinctive plates for all foreign diplomats. External Affairs agreed quickly enough but the Ontario Department of Transport needed pushing before assigning block-numbered F-plates. It meant that sighters needed to remember only numbers F1151-F1200 to identify Soviet cars and put the program back in business.

Behind the modernized observation post, the Vehicle Sighting Program and the easily identified licence plates lay a master plan called Movements Analysis. The observation post on the embassy recorded an intelligence officer's schedule at the embassy. Bugs and wiretaps registered his comings and goings at home. The Social Relations Reporting Program noted his contacts with the civil service. The Watcher Service, when available, chronicled comprehensively his movement through the city. The Vehicle Sighting Program pinpointed observed random movement. The bullpen conducted investigations and dug up specific information. Every piece of intelligence from each of these sources filled a gap in the jigsaw puzzle on the activities of Soviet Intelligence in Ottawa. One could never accumulate all the pieces but might discern enough to make out the picture.

Movements Analysis looked for patterns in the activities of Soviet intelligence officers. KGB officers, like all humans, fall into habitual routines and once Movements Analysis plotted them the breaks in the pattern might divulge when the officer was setting out on a mission. If KGB officer Rem Krassilnikov left the embassy when Movements Analysis said he should be in his office working at his cover job as Third Secretary, he might be leaving for a twice-yearly meet with an illegal and the Watcher Service could be called in to cover him. On the other hand, he might be merely going out for a haircut. The system had its shortcomings but rather than stabbing in the dark the Russian Desk had a scientific technique for deciding each day which Soviets to follow. Furthermore, if the target was heading toward a meet, Movements Analysis might some day reach the stage of anticipating his counter surveillance routine so well as to be able to let him go free while he cleans himself and know where to pick him up later.

Movements Analysis did not bring the KGB to its knees. Information trickled in but no clear cut patterns emerged. Different Mounties looking at the same material detected different patterns while others discovered no patterns at all. This setback fazed Bennett not a bit. The approach, he maintained, was good, although the system had a few deficiencies. The data base was small and needed to be built up further and, he felt, Mountie minds lacked the mathematical background to comprehend the material. The Russians moved in patterns, he insisted, and Movements Analysis, with the help of trained analysts, would spot them eventually.

Bennett maintained something else too—the Security Service was probably penetrated by the KGB. He urged his case officers to study their operations for evidence of compromise. The Long Knife disclosure strengthened his conviction the Mounted Police was vulnerable to penetration and that a mole already flourished in place on a long-term basis. His obsession was curious because at that time the penetration of other western services had not been uncovered, yet he preached his mole theory in the office, at lectures and in the officers' mess.

At the time the Russian Desk's most promising case was a GRU operation run by Nicolai Ranov who worked under the cover as Soviet Commercial Attache. Through the RA Stamp Club he had recruited a historian from the Department of National Defence who reported Ranov's approach and acted as a double agent. While Ranov was still developing the friendship he hinted he was unhappy with Soviet life and raised the RCMP's hopes of a defection.

As with most double agent cases, the operation reached the stage where the requirements to authenticate the double agent by passing documents exceeded the return; the intelligence given to the Russians outstripped the intelligence the Russian Desk was learning about Soviet personnel, techniques and objectives so the Security Service decided to terminate the case. At the next scheduled meet Mounties would jump out from hidden corners and arrest Ranov in the act of accepting a classified document and hold him while the Security Service went through the official charade of confirming with External Affairs that he enjoyed diplomatic status and was immune from arrest. During these hours the Security Service had Ranov all to itself and would try to lure him into defecting with the offer of a new and prosperous life in Canada. If successful, the RCMP would have its first defector in fifteen years and enjoy the applause and envy of friendly security and intelligence organizations throughout the western world. If it failed Ranov would be declared persona non grata and given forty-eight hours to leave the country.

The tête-à-tête with the GRU officer never happened because for the first time Ranov failed to appear for a meet. Without apparent reason the Soviets cut off the case when they should have been expecting a classified document.

What went wrong? It was generally agreed that somehow the Russians must have known what was coming. An autopsy revealed two possible mistakes. The stodgy Department of National Defence had earlier dithered for several weeks before allowing the double agent to pass along the plans of a World War Two army tank thus forcing him to stall. Stalling would automatically raise Soviet suspicions. Yet the Soviets stayed with the case and finally got the tank plans. The other mistake might have been made by the Watcher Service which hours before the aborted meet had conducted a surveillance dress rehearsal through the area. Routine advance countersurveillance on the part of the Soviets might have picked it up.

While fingers pointed in these directions, Bennett offered a different interpretation. He claimed the operation was betrayed at the outset by a mole and that the Soviets, rather than accept the public humiliation of an expulsion and maybe a defection, and realizing no more classified material was coming, decided to kill the case.

9

Operation
Apple Cider

THE NAME JOHN WEITZ was obviously phony but everything else about the correspondence looked genuine. The mysterious Weitz had written a letter in 1959 to a live letter box in Lausanne, Switzerland, saying he had arrived safely in Vancouver and was setting up a business. The live letter box's role was to pass on the sealed envelope to his Soviet contact from the GRU. But the live letter box was a double agent working for the Swiss and before reaching the Russians the letter was carefully opened and copied. The Swiss showed it to the CIA, which passed it along to the RCMP. It was a good lead but at that stage all the Security Service knew was that a GRU agent had entered Canada and was establishing a business in Vancouver as a cover.

Only a handful of Soviet illegals had ever come to the attention of the west and the Security Service already had its quota with Gideon. Bennett could hardly contain his excitement and started pushing the investigation, which was given the code name Operation Apple Cider. The unidentified agent was called Fuzzy. As was custom, Bennett directed all Russian cases from his post in headquarters and the local Security Service division did the legwork. Vancouver had no B Branch and, in fact, had never run a counterespionage case before, having directed its entire effort at the Communist Party of Canada and associated groups. Occasionally, on instructions from headquarters, it had surveilled members of the Soviet embassy visiting town and followed-up local counterespionage leads from Ottawa investigations.

To get Apple Cider going, Sergeant Reg McKernan, Vancouver's non-commissioned officer in charge of the Security Service, pulled himself and a few men off the Communist party and formed an instant B Branch. Aside from knowing Fuzzy had recently settled in Vancouver to open a business, the Security Service had one other lead—the handwriting from his short note to the live letter box. Using these slim clues, Operation Apple Cider set out to find Fuzzy. It checked every recent business licence application in the Vancouver area in hope of matching handwriting samples but the search found nothing positive. The search spread to birth certificate applications on the assumption that one of Fuzzy's first acts would be to legitimize his legend by acquiring a birth certificate. That too failed. As a long shot the investigators tried screening driver's licence applications and the thousands of handwritten forms so overwhelmed them that Mounties from other sections were brought in but sheer volume ultimately defeated them.

Apple Cider turned to immigration records in case Fuzzy had legally entered the country and applied for official status. Classic illegals like Gideon by-passed immigration processing by arriving as a visitor under one name and, once inside the country, picking up a new identity and leaving no record of entry for the new identity. But Apple Cider searched immigration records in case Fuzzy was not a model illegal and more closely resembled an immigrant acting as an agent. More than 100,000 people immigrated to Canada in 1959 and investigators did not know his point of entry. Immigration forms contained no handwriting except a signature which was no sample. The investigators cut down the size of the field by assuming he entered at Vancouver and further narrowed the number by looking only at applicants who were single and had backgrounds hard to verify since these characterized most Soviet illegals.

The screening pruned the number of suspects down to a few dozen and simplified the investigation. The CIA shortened the list further by checking overseas the backgrounds of these suspects. Traces of suspicion came back on several suspects, including one immigrant from Brazil who listed as referees two people the CIA believed had contacts with Russians from the Soviet embassy in Brazil. The suspect was Rudolph Kneschke, a middle-aged bachelor whose seemingly intertwined ethnic background made his personal history difficult to trace.

His background claimed German heritage and his family had fled revolutionary Russia when he was a child and settled in China. He had been living in the Manchurian city of Harbin when the Chinese expelled the white colony in the early 1950s forcing him to Sao Paulo, Brazil, where he worked as a clerk in a clothing store. Naturally his background betrayed no evidence of communist ideology or Soviet bias. A refugee of two communist countries, he seemed an unlikely recruit for Soviet intelligence. But was his background real? If he was a GRU agent his background would be concocted to make him appear something he was not. His roots in the Soviet Union could not be checked and neither could the majority of his life in China. But Brazil could and while Brazil claimed only five of his fifty years and in itself was not reliable, it was here that a possible link with the Soviets emerged through the CIA.

Kneschke was not the prime suspect and his link to Fuzzy was hypothesized on circumstantial intelligence. Kneschke passed through the immigration stream and applied legitimately for immigrant status. He had not assumed a dead Canadian's identity and no evidence disputed his claim as the real Rudolph Kneschke. The fact he once lived in China had been confirmed by British Intelligence's processing center in Hong Kong which had debriefed refugees from Harbin. Fuzzy's letter to the live letter box in Switzerland claimed he was setting himself up in business but Kneschke was not opening a shop— hence the failure to find him through searching business licence applications—and instead had enrolled in radio-TV repair school. Kneschke could be a genuine immigrant who came to Canada for a new life and was undertaking a new trade to improve himself.

An investigator checking out Kneschke's rooming house on Burnaby Street in Vancouver's West End peered through his window and saw a long plain strand of wire resembling a radio aerial strung along the ceiling. As a Soviet agent, Kneschke might be picking up Moscow's transmissions on short wave. However many people listened to short wave and a new immigrant might want to keep in touch with the old world.

While his radio-TV training was finishing, Kneschke moved out of his downtown rooming house and into the back of a small shop on Alma Street deep into Vancouver's west side and opened a business under the shingle, Ray's Radio & TV Service. His tiny quarters did not accommodate a live-in owner willingly but the one-storey, wood frame row unit had a tiny washroom at the back and space for a cot, hot plate and refrigerator so he moved in. Kneschke had set up a business after all and seemed to be following an undercover agent's customary practice of living in his store. Suddenly Kneschke loomed a more suspicious prospect.

The investigators got a sample of his handwriting from the radio-TV school and it convinced them they had found Fuzzy. The two hand styles seemed to match and were sent to Ottawa for expert handwriting analysis. Ottawa disagreed and sent back word they did not necessarily compare. Vancouver refused to believe it and requested Ottawa to check again. Bennett viewed Kneschke as a secondary suspect and instructed McKernan to interview him for an explanation about his contacts in Brazil.

The unkempt appearance of Kneschke's tiny shop told every passerby it did lousy business. Had not a handwritten cardboard sign in the window proclaimed it a radio-TV repair shop, people might mistake it for a junk store. A couple of used radios, a broken TV, a work bench and soldering iron littered the interior. The whole shop had an uninviting smell of neglect that kept customers away. Either Kneschke was a very bad businessman with no marketing sense or other preoccupations pulled his attention away from the store.

As he walked into the shop for the interview, McKernan told himself he would never entrust any set of his to such a workshop. Kneschke was only a suspect but McKernan could not believe Ray's Radio & TV Service was a genuine enterprise and before introducing himself suspected he had found Fuzzy. A rough looking, yet feeble chap about 5' 10" and 175 pounds, balding with a dark complexion, a square frame and a German accent acknowledged that he was Kneschke. McKernan in business fashion said he had come from the Immigration Department and wanted to ask a few questions about his application and after querying his personal history asked about his contacts in Brazil. The Brazil contacts struck a chord. Kneschke's face and neck muscles tightened and his eyes bulged and his expression could not hide his surprise that the Canadian authorities had discovered his friends' connections with the Soviets. Rather than bury McKernan with explanations as most immigrants in a similar situation would do, he became brittle and elusive and yielded as little information as possible. McKernan stayed only a few minutes and left the store convinced Kneschke was Fuzzy.

McKernan's revealing encounter had not grown a day old when Vancouver received a telex from Ottawa to cancel the interview because Kneschke's handwriting had turned out positive after all. Although the telex did not mention it, headquarters had passed the sample to the CIA for a second opinion and the CIA offered the firm opinion they were written by the same person. Now that headquarters viewed Kneschke as the prime suspect it did not want to tip him off but the telex arrived too late so the Security Service could only wonder whether the interview had blown the case. McKernan's probe had disturbed Kneschke and the fact Canadian authorities had uncovered the link and were asking questions had to provoke his suspicions. If Kneschke concluded the RCMP was onto him the case was effectively dead. Yet maybe not. McKernan had posed as an immigration official and there was no hard information except for the matched handwriting samples which Kneschke had no idea the RCMP knew about. Under Bennett, the Security Service, eager to run the case, assumed Apple Cider remained viable and started mounting a clandestine attack against Kneschke.

Alma Street between West Tenth and West Eleventh Avenues is so short that a strong arm can throw a baseball from one end to another. Within that compressed block sat two government-issue 1960 Fords, one green and one white, each containing two husky men and displaying special aerials at the back. When Kneschke moved the two Fords moved too and not always circumspectly. A woman area resident reported the two suspicious cars to Vancouver City police who were quickly advised it was an RCMP stakeout. The Mounties never said they were surveilling a suspected Russian agent but if they caught the attention of a local woman chances were they attracted Kneschke's notice as well.

Vancouver in those days never used concealed observation posts and had no feel for discreet surveillance. The Watcher Service had not yet arrived on the west coast so surveillance became a sideline for some Mounties. Whenever B Branch needed surveillance on a visiting Soviet it raided the Countersubversion Branch for bodies, pulling investigators away from their pet projects on the Communist party and throwing them into a makeshift crew of surveillers whose broad shoulders, closely cropped hair and shiny shoes often exposed their identity. One Mountie recalls following a Soviet in Eaton's Department Store and discovering too late the escalator was delivering him into the staring eyes of his target who had stopped at the top and turned around and waited. "We got a half hour lecture and were expected to be surveillance experts," said one Mountie in hindsight. "My number one concern was the professional (communist front) clubs and I wasn't happy about being taken off my work to do surveillance and help somebody else look good. We made goons of ourselves. The Russians used to spot us immediately and wave at us. We didn't have sufficient manpower to change once we were spotted. The surveillance was horrible. There was only one way to go and that was up."

The two Fords were waiting in place on an otherwise empty street one Sunday morning when Kneschke came out his front door and walked south on Alma and into a little park at West Twelfth Avenue and disappeared along a footpath into a small bush. Kneschke always walked extraordinarily quickly and the cars responded by moving into position. One Mountie got out and followed into the bush on foot while the other car drove around to observe him emerge on the other side. Midway through Kneschke stopped and reversed his steps and on his return encountered his Mountie pursuer face to face. Each man hesitated slightly and after a flash of eye contact diverted glances, stepping politely to the side of the path to make passing room. A man with a police build wearing a shirt and tie had no innocent reason for walking in the bush. If Kneschke had not spotted surveillance before, he had then.

Even crack surveillers get burned occasionally. Had skilled surveillance experts been compromised so blatantly their professionalism would have compelled them to report it within the hour and a telex to Ottawa would alert headquarters and ask for instructions. Bennett would have hurried to the office and convened an emergency meeting. Headquarters would want to "hit" Kneschke quickly and put an intimidating interrogator on the next flight to Vancouver. Kneschke would be living in crisis not knowing what to do while expecting at any minute Mounties 10 feet tall breaking through his door. Help from the Soviets would be days or weeks away. The case was ruined so headquarters would want to exploit this moment of fear and helplessness to extract a confession and, more importantly, his contacts.

In Vancouver the four Mountie surveillers huddled together to assess the significance of the incident. They agreed that Kneschke had set a trap and successfully lured them into the bush. But the possibility existed it was no trap and that Kneschke suspected nothing, so the incident was "down played." The official report noted that Kneschke acted in a peculiar manner and that he may have suspected surveillance. It was not an unusual observation in a surveillance report, so headquarters had no reason to suspect the case had been blown.

Kneschke pulled up stakes on Alma Street and moved across town into a slightly larger shop on Commercial Drive at East Third Avenue under the name Radel TV Service. The shift was not linked to the exposure or viewed with any suspicion because Alma Street had almost no business and Kneschke had been previously looking for a new site. Vancouver's blue-collar East End offered better potential for a poor man's store.

Having learned a lesson on Alma Street, Vancouver this time mounted a proper observation post by renting a third-floor apartment on the other side of Commercial Drive. The observation post, down the street 100 yards, witnessed everybody going through his front door although Kneschke could slip out the back and disappear along East Third Avenue unseen. Everybody walking through the front door was photographed and, as a potential espionage accomplice, open to investigation. Two Mounties at a time manned the post virtually around the clock. To avoid attracting attention from neighbours they changed shifts one at a time and took care to park their cars at different spots several blocks away. Their attitude this time was more professional. And although off-duty Mounties dropped by for visits and to drop off football tickets they were certain neither Kneschke nor anybody else suspected their presence. When Kneschke left his shop, Vancouver's newly-arrived Watcher Service took control and mounted professional moving surveillance. Kneschke would never again see a suspicious Mountie.

Even in his new location Kneschke seemed almost not to want customers. Grime covered his windows so thickly it clogged the observation post's view and the interior was just as unappealing. Days often passed between visits from a patron. A woman once brought in an electric iron and Kneschke put it in the window untouched for weeks. Sometimes he walked down the street to another radio-TV store for technical assistance. During summer hours he stood on the sidewalk in the shade outside his front door swinging the keychain attached to his belt.

Once a week or so, Kneschke visited an independent radio-TV shop in downtown Vancouver owned by Carl Mumphrey.[1] Mumphrey operated as a sort of broker of used TV sets and Kneschke dropped by to pick up used parts and occasionally a fifteen dollar broken TV set to fix up for resale. Kneschke developed into a semi-regular at Mumphrey's store although he spent very little money. His connection with Mumphrey intrigued the Security Service as a potential key to the Apple Cider mystery. Kneschke had never been observed collecting information the way Gideon did but by this stage nobody viewed him as a mainline spy because he lacked drive and talent. But he could be a support agent for the local illegal resident, whoever he was. Perhaps he was the communications officer who handled radio messages with Moscow, thus drawing the risks of exposure away from the illegal resident whose safety was more important than his. Or he could be a courier running errands for the illegal resident. The Soviets needed low-level support agents and Kneschke fit the description. If Kneschke was a support agent somebody nearby was giving him orders, which meant somewhere along the line he would attend regular meets. In the interest of security the meets would be protected by a cover appearing innocent and natural. What could be more natural than for a second-hand TV repairman like Kneschke to rendezvous with his superior under the guise of buying used parts?

An investigation into Mumphrey unveiled a few clues that seemed to fit. Mumphrey himself was an immigrant and his past revealed socialist views. He possessed the intelligence and drive of a top flight agent, the kind the Soviets would want to protect by assigning an expendable type like Kneschke for the higher-risk role of communications. Further investigations uncovered more. Mumphrey's repairman was a Russian immigrant via Harbin. The similarity was striking. Both Kneschke and Mumphrey's mechanic were middle-aged, lower-class and loners who rarely talked about themselves. Maybe the repairman was the contact or maybe both. Classic illegal operations ran as trios

---

[1] Carl Mumphrey is a pseudonym. He was interviewed during the research of this book and requested anonymity.

with the agent having separate support agents for radio communications and courier work. Possibly Mumphrey was the illegal resident; the repairman the courier and Kneschke had come to complete the ring as the radioman. The investigation intensified.

Mail scrutiny picked up the fact that Kneschke sent a letter to an Ottawa businessman named Syd Frankman.[2] The Security Service did not know what the letter said because it merely examined the cover of Kneschke's outgoing and incoming mail and was not opening it. It was soon learned that Frankman, seven years earlier, had operated a textile store in Harbin which had been kind of a community meeting spot and that he had left the city in the same emigration wave with Kneschke. Since Frankman was prominent in Harbin's white community they probably knew each other yet it seemed strange that Kneschke was rekindling an old friendship because he was not a social animal and had looked up no other Harbin refugees and avoided Vancouver's ethnic German and Russian organizations. Moreover Kneschke's tongue was German and Frankman was a Jew who fled Poland to escape Hitler. Further probing revealed that Kneschke had deposited $50,000 into an Ottawa bank account belonging to Frankman's wife. At a time when salaries ran about $5,000 a year and $50,000 represented a genuine fortune, such an amount was surprising if for no other reason than it violated Kneschke's cover as a marginal businessman scratching out a living. Maybe Kneschke was a courier and Frankman one of his contacts. The Soviets had recruited many agents when fascism was engulfing Europe in the 1930s and Frankman had reason to oppose Hitler.

The bank on the Security Service's instructions put a red flag on the $50,000 account which would notify the manager the minute the funds were touched and when he phoned a special number at the Security Service instant surveillance would follow Mrs. Frankman and the money.

Kneschke had another curious friend who seemed to defy explanation. His friend was a carefree barber about half his age who drifted from job to job in remote areas of British Columbia and looked up Kneschke when passing through Vancouver. The itinerant barber also

---

[2] Frankman is a pseudonym since he is still an active businessman in Ottawa.

was an immigrant, having arrived from Austria a year before Kneschke and possessing some of the visible characteristics of an agent. He was single, without a regular girlfriend and kept to himself. As a barber he could contact almost anybody without raising suspicion and his movements took him across the province.

One of his trips attracted special curiosity. After visiting Kneschke in Vancouver he travelled south to Mexico, which is a notorioius meeting spot for Soviet intelligence. Because Mexican security was lax, the Soviets used Mexico as its North American debriefing and meeting headquarters. The barber travelled to Mexico for a long visit.

Nobody doubted that Kneschke was a dispatched agent. There was his handwriting, his lifestyle, his fear of surveillance, the Frankman money transaction, his unusual relationships and his discreet behaviour on the telephone. The circumstantial evidence pointed to him as a spy, yet thousands of hours of investigation failed to uncover hard evidence. And his espionage role—communications man, courier or what— remained a mystery. Kneschke never travelled outside the city and had no car—this lack of movement seemed to exclude him as a courier. He had already been effectively eliminated as an illegal resident or intelligence-gathering agent, so if active he must be the radioman who keeps in touch with Moscow. His cover as owner of a radio-TV shop provided perfect communications cover but locked up in the back of his shop the Security Service could not tell what radio work, if any, he was up to. The bug inside his shop told the observation post he was listening to his short wave radio but it could not determine if his listening included Soviet transmissions. This particular suspicion appeared unsolvable until the British brought word to Canada of a new secret technique for monitoring short wave communications that would absolutely resolve the uncertainty.

Tracking down illegals was almost impossible through traditional investigation. Without leads to work from, the only technique was searching official records and hoping for a lucky break which never seemed to come. An investigator could invest his career in the random study of immigration records, birth certificates, passports and driver's licences and never find an illegal. The odds worked against it. Existing techniques fell so far short of success that western agencies largely gave up trying because the prospects of a defection were better than the hope of a hit. The British developed a new investigative technique that could change the whole approach and, if the technique worked, give the west a crack at ferreting out every illegal in the country. Western agencies knew already where Moscow's broadcasts to illegals were coming from. The trick was to find out where they were going.

Bourdine's behaviour during Operation Keystone led observers to believe the Soviet embassy was monitoring Moscow's broadcasts to Gideon. Mulling over the implications of this discovery, the British figured that if the Soviets were doing it for Gideon they could be doing it for all their illegals. If one could somehow monitor the embassy's monitoring, one could discover how many illegals operated in the country and even learn their signal plans. GCHQ seized upon the idea of tuning in on a short wave radio's IF value and from that calculating the frequency it was tuned to. It was widely known that most short wave receivers had a characteristic called the IF value which, in effect, gave off a muted signal whose frequency changed as the operator turned the dial. Careful tuning was needed but GCHQ performed tests showing that on a minute by minute basis it could calculate almost the precise frequency of another short wave set from IF monitoring alone and that it could be done from several city blocks away. It meant GCHQ could set up clandestine monitoring posts near Soviet embassies around the world and overhear their listening activity. At last the west would finally know roughly how many illegals were being serviced by radio. The potential was even greater. If authorities could dissect where broadcasts were being listened to, mobile monitoring units could fan across the country listening to IF values and one by one like a vacuum cleaner suck up the illegals in the act of receiving instructions from Moscow. One clean sweep could purge each western country of this wily menace. Nothing remotely equivalent had been developed before. The technique's potential was truly breathtaking.

The British did not need to sell the Security Service on the importance of its breakthrough because Bennett, with his background in communications, grasped its significance immediately and moved to exploit the opportunity. Since the potential outstripped existing practices for discovering illegals by a hundredfold, Bennett enthusiastically launched with CBNRC a country-wide receiver hunt. CBNRC provided the operators, the machinery and the technical expertise while the Security Service came up with investigators, the operational back up and set the targets. The attack consumed resources and gave no guarantee of success, but Bennett figured the risk was worth the investment since the discovery of a single illegal would pay for itself. Besides, he argued, nothing else worked.

With all its potential the technique still had to overcome technical problems. The decibel level of the IF value was usually so low, and the tuning process so tricky, that the prospect of wildcatting from the back of a moving van was not feasible in the foreseeable future. IF monitoring needed a specific target within a range of a few blocks to be effective at ground level. But higher up the signal strength grew and the coverage area widened. So Bennett got a Beech aircraft and outfitted it with special equipment for the purpose of sweeping an entire city from the air at night during the hours Moscow would be transmitting. Once the airborne equipment found a receiver tuning into a Moscow broadcast the mobility of the Beech allowed it quickly to get several bearings that could place the IF signal in a particular locality so that the mobile ground crew could get close enough to have a shot at pinpointing the receiver.

The Beech spent many nights over Montreal, Ottawa and Toronto but needed a depth of at least several broadcasts to secure a bearing precise enough for the ground crew. Broadcasts from Moscow were picked up and the Beech thought it detected responding IF values but the fickle signals disappeared into a storm of static and never reappeared in a detectable pattern. The ground crew could not confirm the few possibilities that emerged and everybody wondered whether the signals were real. Bennett and CBNRC waded through the mass of monitoring data and detected no coherent signal plan but after six months the Beech was scrapped in favour of a stationary monitoring unit atop Mount Royal in Montreal. It also produced no suspects and eventually the program was dropped. The British and CBNRC disagreed with the Security Service's decision but Bennett concluded the program's effectiveness as a basic technique for tracking down illegals was unproven and should be abandoned as a general searching device. Henceforth, he decided, the Security Service would no longer use IF value monitoring as a technique for finding suspects and would limit its role to monitoring already known suspects from close ground range to determine if they were listening to Moscow.

As a suspected agent who listened to short wave into the early hours of the morning, when Moscow was broadcasting, Kneschke was precisely the kind of specific target IF monitoring had been set aside for and was to become its first defined target. If the monitoring showed he was pulling in coded Soviet transmissions then it would not only resolve the nagging question of whether he was acting as an agent but would go a long way toward identifying him as a radioman. With such an identification the Security Service could focus its investigation into more specific areas and possibly get a better fix on this elusive target.

Bennett and fellow civilian Jack Douglas went undercover for nearly a month in a ramshackle house around the corner from Kneschke's store. Bennett and Douglas could not see his shop but were briefed on his activities by the observation post and could easily pick up his IF signal. They monitored his shop for twenty hours a day and received nothing for almost a week. Then the observation post phoned Bennett in the middle of the night to report that the bug had picked up the ring of Kneschke's alarm clock and a minute later reported he had switched on his lights. Kneschke had set the alarm for two-fifteen A.M. which was two-and-a-half hours after he had gone to bed. Within fifteen minutes Bennett and Douglas picked up Kneschke twirling his short wave dial. At the same time on the same frequency an enciphered message in Morse code came over the air waves.

The Security Service never cracked the cipher so the message remained a mystery. But the fact that Kneschke woke up in the middle of the night to catch a secret message firmly identified him as an agent. His alarm next rang eight days later and again drew him from bed in the early hours to copy a transmission. He overslept his alarm on a third occasion and his angry mutterings seemed to confirm that he had missed a broadcast. With the knowledge he was an agent, the Security Service halted the monitorings with Kneschke's signal plan undefined. There were six or seven signal plan possibilities and more if as a west coast agent he was served from Vladivostok rather than Moscow.

Without warning, Kneschke several weeks later taped a temporary paper sign in his window saying his shop was closed for the weekend. He then boarded the bus for the airport. Kneschke had previously given no sign of planning a trip and the Security Service learned of this one only by following him to the airport and watching him buy a ticket for Toronto. It was his first known trip out of the city and appeared to represent one of the bigger breaks so far, possibly the one that would bring about the long-awaited meet with his control officer. A check with Ottawa revealed that several Soviets from the embassy were visiting Toronto that weekend.

While Toronto was putting together a surveillance team to meet him at the airport a snowstorm diverted the flight to Montreal. The Toronto surveillance team waited for him to make up the missed connection. Maybe it was already too late for the suspected Toronto meet because he stayed the weekend in Montreal where surveillance reported nothing suspicious. On Sunday night he flew directly back to Vancouver without stopping at Toronto and without having contacted anybody. Kneschke never returned to Toronto and the purpose of the trip remained a mystery. It seemed the more clues the investigation followed, the more confused the trail became.

Kneschke had occupied his Commercial Drive store about a year when he liquidated his meager stock of used radios and television sets and put three boxes of personal belongings into commercial storage. He was closing shop. Unlike his hush-hush aborted trip to Toronto, Kneschke this time did not conceal his plans to travel abroad. His ticket to Amsterdam was purchased in advance and his conversation with acquaintances told of a European vacation. Presumably Kneschke would be getting instructions and maybe new assignments. The Force could hardly wait to see what Kneschke would do on his return. It also wanted to keep track of him in Europe and asked the CIA to surveil him.

The CIA reported that Kneschke had duly arrived in Amsterdam and boarded a flight to Rome and promptly disappeared. Subsequent efforts to trace him failed. Rome was a famous disappearing place for agents and speculation had him picking up new documentation and travelling on, but nobody knew. The Security Service had lost Kneschke and now could only keep watch for his return by monitoring his goods in storage and keeping tabs on his few acquaintances in Vancouver. Months later a letter signed by Kneschke and posted in Switzerland advised the storage company to ship his belongings to an international forwarding house in Helsinki. The Security Service had already searched his meagre belongings and found nothing suspicious, only an old typewriter and some other items of little value. The Security Service had no contacts in Finland and merely as a check, a Mountie in Vancouver bought a tourist map of Helsinki and placed the forwarding address in a dock area. It was the only form of scrutiny the shipment of Kneschke's goods received. The Russians had pulled the same trick on the Security Service with Kneschke it had with Gideon—dressing up the withdrawal as temporary leave and, once gone, keeping the agent out.

After waiting to ensure that the case was irrevocably dead, the Security Service started interviewing some of his contacts who had previously been untouched for fear of tipping him off. The suspicious $50,000 bank deposit in Ottawa turned out to be innocent of any espionage connotation. Currency restrictions abroad tied up some of the Ottawa businessman's money and, having met Kneschke in Harbin, he hired him for a fee to bring money to Canada. Kneschke's freelance money-running must have been a private affair with Frankman, handled on the side without Moscow's knowledge because the Soviets would have vetoed it for jeopardizing his cover and risking his safety.

The itinerant barber was interviewed too and quickly convinced the Security Service his connection with Kneschke was straight forward and innocent. Kneschke and the barber met at the West End rooming house when both were new immigrants. A friendship developed despite their age difference because they found with each other the only German conversation in town. The barber provided a credible explanation for his travelling. He said he enjoyed Canada except for its winters. He made good money working up north and quit in late fall to spend the winter in Mexico. En route there and back he stopped in Vancouver for some big city life and while there looked up Kneschke to speak a little German. The implications of his friendship with Kneschke so awed the barber that for the next five years he reported all his movements until the Security Service told him to stop.

Mumphrey, Kneschke's television parts supplier, was never interviewed because by this time the investigation had cleared him. The fact his repairman was a Russian from Harbin was coincidence.

"He was a cantankerous old bugger," recalls Mumphrey about Kneschke. "Even if you were looking to make a friend he would be the last person on your list. As far as I know he had no friends. He was very temperamental and had no self control. You could say something and he would blow up. He never talked politics. He wasn't left or right, just a knothead. I wouldn't remember him at all except he was so opinionated. That's why we didn't encourage him coming around. I think the RCMP is suffering from excess imagination to think he was a spy."

The full dimension of Operation Apple Cider's failure emerged during the mop up. Only after Kneschke disappeared did the Security Service realize how little it knew about him. Except for determining that he twice listened to Soviet transmissions, the Security Service had learned nothing. It was inconceivable that the Soviets could send Kneschke to Canada and in more than two years never be caught making a meet, filling a dead letter box or flying a signal. Kneschke did none of the nice little things support agents are supposed to do. The Security Service had not realized Operation Apple Cider was fizzling until it was fizzled out.

The autopsy produced several plausible scenarios about how the Soviets had found out.

First, the Soviets knew from the start the case was compromised— even before the Security Service was notified—through the live letter box. Live letter boxes merely pass along letters and never open them. Kneschke's letter to the live letter box in Switzerland was opened. If the Russians set a trap in the letter not even the most professional handling could conceal the tampering. The Soviets curiously used the live letter box for more than one case, a deviation in procedure and possibly an indicator they already knew he was a double agent. If the Russians knew, they would want to play back the live letter box as an unwitting triple agent by feeding him phony cases and tying down western agencies with useless work. By observing their responses, they could expose the west's techniques and investigators. To inflict maximum damage, the Russians might feed the live letter box several cases.

Apple Cider exhausted thousands of man hours of Security Service resources on observation posts, moving surveillance, investigations into the hundreds of dead end leads, record checking, transcribing bugged conversations and so on. Sacrificing a low grade agent like Kneschke would be worth it and might explain the seeming carelessness of his immigration application.

If the Swiss Live Letter Box did not compromise the case the Security Service's initial clumsy investigation probably did. First, the Security Service tipped its hand with the interview and then surveilled Kneschke so amateurishly he could not help but spot it. When a legitimate agent suspects surveillance the Soviets freeze him for a couple of years and tell him to watch for further signs of scrutiny. Once convinced Kneschke was compromised, Moscow would order him out of the country to guard against arrest and the possibility of an induced confession.

Another scenario suggested that Apple Cider died at the outset through betrayal by a Soviet mole inside the Swiss Service, the CIA or the RCMP. The Soviets took more than two years to kill the case. Besides clogging up the Security Service with false work, the Soviets would need a slow death to avoid jeopardizing its mole by ensuring the case dragged out long enough for several possibilities to explain the failure. If the Soviets had pulled up stakes at the beginning the Security Service's autopsy could, for instance, eliminate bad surveillance and narrow down the possibilities. Indeed, the Security Service had several credible explanations to choose from and the least credible seemed to be the mole theory.

10

Operation
Moby Dick

"ARE THEY HERE already?" asked the tiny, half bald man bolting upright into his chair. "Are they here already?"

His compressed frame turned itself toward the living room window through which a flashing red light shimmered against a wall, each pulse spreading a little more terror across his thin, wrinkled 61-year-old face. The flashing light pulled into the driveway and stopped directly in front of his jalopy, which he had positioned facing outward for instant escape. The light blocked his car only for a second, then backed out and left. It was merely a municipal works truck turning around in the driveway.

George Victor Spencer, wearing his usual rag clothing, issued a sigh of relief and turned back to the task that brought him to the home of Jervis Bloomfield, who was once a fellow worker in the Vancouver post office and now one of his few remaining friends in his time of flight. Weeks earlier Spencer had snuck over to Bloomfield's home in the evening and asked him to care for his most prized possession, his British Empire Medal from World War Two, awarded for inventing a mechanical device to detonate mines in front of tanks. The proudest moment of his troubled life came at Buckingham Palace when King George VI pinned the decoration on his chest. Now a refugee from his own home in Vancouver's East End, Spencer spent part of his hiding time at Bloomfield's isolated suburban home overlooking Burrard Inlet. Spencer needed companionship to interrupt the hours of loneliness, and after checking to make sure the driveway was clear, appeared unannounced at Bloomfield's door. Looking beaten and sick, and obsessed by fear, Spencer still carried his old zeal for righting society's wrongs, as he saw them, and now had Bloomfield, a writer of sorts, collaborating on a booklet to be called *The Red Tape Jungle*,[1] which would tell his story of woe and expose the bureaucratic government which for more than two decades had made his life miserable.

"Where do you start to tell of a nightmare?" *The Red Tape Jungle* began.

Spencer wanted Bloomfield to start it during World War Two at the time of his father's death when Spencer was already forty, because that is when his life started being "twisted and warped by any nincompoop with a rubber stamp or by some alcoholic or incompetent." He had not planned on describing his early years growing up the only child of a small-town hotel keeper, moving from community to community in British Columbia until being sent to a Catholic convent by Anglican parents for no apparent reason; or the time he was shuttled off to live with two aunts while finishing public school. Nor would he describe his early years of adulthood when he drifted from job to job until he established himself in the early 1930s as a machinist but left that trade to move to the Vancouver Island community of Cumberland to help his parents run their hotel. Then partial paralysis struck his father. During those years he was married to a local girl. Already a perpetual misfit, Spencer championed firm but sometimes unorthodox views on many subjects and during the ferment of the depression started reading the works of Russian sociologists and economists while working as a part-time mechanic, and from there he grew into a disciple of Marx and Lenin. Communism and the leftist labour movement consumed his energy so completely—among other things, he mimeographed political tracts in a secluded forest cabin at night and impelled workers to rise up against the ruling class—that his father, now recovered, renounced him loudly, kicking him out of the hotel. After a string of odd jobs the frail Spencer tried twice to join the war effort in 1939 (when most communists opposed the war) but was rejected both times, making it only in 1942 when the army raised the age limit and lowered

---

[1] Portions of *The Red Tape Jungle* were published in the Toronto *Star*, March 30-April 1, 1966.

the physical requirements. But in spite of his varied and tempestuous life, Spencer saw none of this information as germaine to his saga.

Spencer wanted *The Red Tape Jungle* to begin during his war service when government bureaucracy and soulless officials started descending upon him. Word came in April, 1944, that his father had died leaving his mother, Ammie Eliza Spencer, to operate a twenty-six-room rooming house alone in downtown Vancouver. Spencer wanted to apply for compassionate leave to comfort his mother and help her carry on but felt the war needed him in England. "I should have applied for leave right then," his book said. Spencer could sense from his mother's letters that she was deeply despondent but only months later learned she had turned on the gas in her room and only prompt action from tenants saved her. "I applied for compassionate leave at once and we entered the red tape jungle," said Spencer. "A twenty-year nightmare had begun. It was to cost me thousands of dollars, years of mental anguish, my mother's health as well as my own." The leave was granted in August 1944 but was misplaced and Spencer did not get out until normally discharged from active service more than a year later.

"I entered the old family door on Burrard Street with misgivings," chronicled Spencer's saga about landing in Vancouver on July 1, 1945. "An atmosphere of decay, of death, seemed to permeate the place. The place was filthy, the windows opaque with grime. I knocked on our door. No answer. Walking in I was horrified to find Mother in her bed, half covered with dirty linen. She didn't recognize me. She looked ready for the grave.

"A look around the apartment confirmed my worst fears, the nightmares that had haunted me through those harrowing twelve months in the red tape jungles of England. The place looked as though it had been ransacked—as, indeed, it had been. Not a sign of anything belonging to my father. Nothing of mine. And Mother, now semi-conscious on the bed, had fared no better. As I stood there, a great bitterness welled up in me for all those petty minions of authority who had done this to me. Looking down at the emaciated wreck of the woman who was my mother, I did not see how she could ever survive. I was home—one year too late. July the first, Dominion Day. God save the King."

Gritting his teeth and cursing unknown stooges in London, Spencer spent the next two years nursing his mother back to health and repairing the rooming house for potential sale. Eventually he moved with his mother into a small gray stucco home in the East End and began drifting between odd jobs and unemployment before catching on as Christmas help in the Vancouver Post Office where he graduated to full-time employment as a mail sorter in the city room. During the day he made dinner, washed the dishes and then tucked his mother into bed. At night he went to work dreaming of the time seniority would advance him to dayshift. "Often when I came home mother would be awake, upset and nervous from some noise she had heard or thought she had heard. There had been a thumping in the basement, the pipes were going to burst. She had heard a latch being pried open. Thieves were breaking in to rob her as she lay trembling and helpless in her bed. The scars of that hell on Burrard Street lay deep. Of that year when—but for the red tape—I should have been home. Sometimes a second cousin stayed with us, sometimes another friend. But the irregularity was unsatisfactory. On a postal clerk's wages I couldn't afford a housekeeper. Putting mother in a nursing home would have killed her. She wanted me."

A batch of appointments from Ottawa in 1955 gave everybody in the group that started in 1949 his permanent status except Spencer. He felt discriminated against and retaliated with a one-man war against the civil service that eventually alienated his union colleagues. He sent letters to his member of parliament, the Conservative party and his permanent status finally arrived but was dated one year after the others in his group and deprived him of the seniority he felt he deserved.

"At first I guess I was just too stunned to realize the enormity of the situation, or, indeed, to credit its actuality. Some terrible mistake must have been made. I started to make inquiries...[some] pipsqueak of a bureaucrat at Ottawa lounging smugly in his air conditioned office, who had disregarded the recommendation of our Vancouver post-master. I knew his ilk. Sadists. The kind who would kick a man in the teeth when he was down." Spencer grew to know "each excuse, each meaningless stereotype of words, each spineless evasion of the call of a fellow human for help. It was vitally important that this further injustice be corrected. There were still far too many men ahead of me on the seniority list. It still wasn't good enough."

Spencer's tale never mentioned his longest single clash with officialdom—his expulsion from the Communist Party of Canada.

Nor did it disclose even an association with the party or his belief in Marxism. The Communist party, called the Labour Progressive party during part of the 1950s and 1960s, adhered loyally to the Moscow line, faithfully following Mother Russia through each ideological shift, seemingly oblivious to the consequences to its credibility and popularity. Such sacrifices did not sufficiently satisfy a super Soviet stalwart like Spencer who revered Moscow as the messiah. Spencer saw the Russian experiment in equality as the most noble and ambitious undertaking in human history and worked diligently as a minor party functionary who, if not given a task, created one, which once included lecturing middle-aged women about birth control. He harangued overworked comrades to work still harder and paralyzed party meetings with arguments over ideological detail until, after several warnings, the party expelled him as a disruptive influence. The banishment did not diminish his convictions or sour him on the party and merely caused him to re-direct his fanaticism toward lobbying for reinstatement. The party was determined to keep him out and the lonely man with few friends and no girlfriend maintained his futile campaign for the rest of his life. "In twenty years my friends and relatives never came to see me once," Spencer would later say.

As Russian freighters docked in Vancouver in the 1950s to pick up wheat, the Soviet government proudly gave guided tours to members of the Canadian-Soviet Friendship Society. As a member, Spencer would not miss the opportunity to admire Soviet technology, but more importantly wanted to appeal his expulsion from the Communist party. The Soviet host greeting Spencer was Youri Afanasiev, the Commercial Attache in the Russian embassy in Ottawa and Spencer lost no time describing his plight. They talked until visiting hours expired when Spencer drove Afanasiev to his lodging spot at the Hotel Vancouver. Security Service surveillance picked up Afanasiev giving Spencer something—it later turned out to be his business card—and saying good-bye outside the hotel. Spencer disappeared into a snack bar. The Watcher Service had not yet started in Vancouver and to the Mountie surveillers Spencer was an unidentified semi-bum in his fifties and not worth pursuing, so they forgot about him in the snack bar and did not mention the incident in their report.

Spencer was tending his mother at home in the fall of 1960 when a phone call from a man with a Russian accent asked him to appear in front of the Broadway Theatre near Broadway and Main. Spencer did not know it but the man who met him there was Rem Krassilnikov, the Soviet Third Secretary who a couple of years earlier severed relations with Long Knife. Krassilnikov did not give his name and identified himself only as a member of the Soviet embassy in Ottawa. Krassilnikov said he understood he believed Canada should draw closer politically and culturally to the Soviet Union and asked whether he would like to help realize this objective by coming, at Soviet expense, to Ottawa and meeting one of his colleagues. With cash from Krassilnikov and elaborate instructions on when to come and where to stay, Spencer booked a flight with Trans Canada Airlines under the name McNeil.

Krassilnikov showed up at Spencer's modest motel in suburban Ottawa at precisely the correct time, bringing with him a colleague introduced as George. "George" was Lev Burdiukov, a KGB officer listed as Second Secretary at the embassy. Burdiukov spoke with a thick Russian accent and did most of the talking as Krassilnikov watched silently like an old professor overseeing a student. Burdiukov chatted pleasantly and showed patient interest in Spencer's background in Canada and his involvement with the party. He listened too, but with slightly less interest, when Spencer gave his views on bringing together a closer cultural exchange between their two countries. Burdiukov expressed interest in learning more about ethnic groups in Canada, particularly Russian, Ukrainian, German and Chinese and why they left their home country. He also wanted to know about their political beliefs and whether they had their own schools and inquired about Russian prisoners of war who had chosen to stay in Canada. He said it would be helpful if Spencer could gather this information for the next meet and explained he would be receiving in about six months a letter advising him when a film was available for showing. If he could come to Ottawa on that date he was supposed to send a reply to the film editor at the embassy saying he could show the film on that date. Spencer received mail under three different names to hide his communist subscriptions from postal security checks but the embassy's letters would always arrive under his real name and the meets in Ottawa always fell at seven P.M. on a Saturday.

Unknown to Spencer, Burdiukov and Krassilnikov, the Ottawa Watcher Service waited quietly outside the motel room. Surveillance had picked up Burdiukov and Krassilnikov and followed them to the motel. The Security Service called the case Operation Moby Dick and assigned Spencer the code name Leaf. Although Spencer was only a postal clerk, Bennett felt Moby Dick carried potential and told Vancouver to conduct a full operation. From now on, Spencer could do little without the Security Service knowing about it. A wiretap recorded all telephone conversations at home; a member of the newly-formed Vancouver Watcher Service moved into a house behind his and could see into his kitchen and observe him leave home; surveillance shadowed his movements around Vancouver; one of his fellow workers on the city floor at the post office kept out a discreet eye.

Burdiukov arrived at Spencer's motel room for the next meet alone and seemed surprised at Spencer's productiveness. Spencer had produced information on all the requested ethnic groups and had it neatly categorized. As directed, he had taken pictures of Vancouver life— mostly of poor housing areas in the East End—and supplemented his own work by buying some. He had fulfilled every assignment. All of the material came from open sources, much of it from the public library, but that did not matter because the KGB was not so much interested in the information as it was in Spencer. The KGB needed reliable and meticulous people who did as they were told without second guessing. The Soviets knew already from the Communist Party of Canada that Spencer was committed ideologically to the Soviet Union and now was testing him for suitability as an agent. His first assignment showed he was conscientious but the careful KGB wanted to ensure he was competent.

This time when Burdiukov gave Spencer his new assignments there was little pretense of cultural interest. He handed him a detailed list of tasks and discussed each one until convinced Spencer had absorbed everything. The biggest undertaking was gathering information on the Trans Mountain oil pipeline that carried petroleum from Edmonton to Vancouver. Like an eager student, Spencer said he would be taking his annual vacation in a few months and could drive the route of the pipeline and take photographs. Burdiukov liked the idea and told him to pay his expenses en route by cash and keep receipts for reimbursement.

Bennett wondered whether the pipeline assignment was another test or if the information was wanted for sabotage purposes in case of war. Any useful information Spencer could observe by wandering through the interior of British Columbia the embassy could get off a detailed pipeline map available from official sources in Ottawa. The suspicious Soviets, coming from a closed society which manufactures information for propaganda purposes, did not trust official sources and would want to confirm that the pumping stations were located where the official maps said they were. So in that context the Spencer trip would contribute to KGB knowledge and make Canadian interests more vulnerable to Soviet plans.

The Security Service knew exactly when Spencer was leaving on his pipeline trip. Without divulging his real purpose, Spencer talked Gus Hasselstrom, a retired friend, into motoring with him and from the planning discussions over the phone the surveillance team of two cars and four Mounties knew the pair was departing on May 31, 1961. Spencer's green 1952 Chevrolet got off to a late start, leaving Vancouver eastbound on the Trans Canada Highway around two P.M. and stopping in the Fraser Valley town of Clearbrook ninety minutes later when the radiator boiled over. As usual he had no inkling he was being followed and took no measures to look for it. The Soviets had instructed him to watch for it and during the preceding weeks he had undertaken some countersurveillance exercises in a romantic way but never suspected or detected surveillance. This time, with the innocent Hasselstrom in his car, he did not look at all.

The arrival of darkness in British Columbia's Fraser Canyon made him an especially easy target because the red covering of one tail light was broken and the bare bulb set him apart from other nighttime traffic. Spencer drove north into the central British Columbian town of Lac La Hache where he stopped for a few late beers, and retired for the night in a budget motel. The next day he continued driving north, stopping near Quesnel to take pictures of general scenery and then carrying on to Prince George where after cruising the city for hours he settled into a pub. It seemed he would stay overnight in Prince George but as darkness approached he set out northeasterly along the partly gravel Hart Highway and kept driving until midnight bedded him down at a rundown motel in the middle of the Rocky Mountains. The surveillance team had no choice but to book into the same motel. It did not matter because Spencer remained oblivious to any possible scrutiny. The Mounties were up at six the next morning to ensure their erratic target did not slip away.

Each time Spencer snapped a picture a Mountie positioned himself in the same spot a little later and took a similar shot. So as Spencer started up the Alaska Highway the surveillers had almost a duplicate photo of every refinery, natural gas scrubbing plant, compressor station and pumping unit Spencer managed to get between beer stops. He had already veered off the Trans Mountain pipeline and was following another oil pipeline up the Alaska Highway and when the pavement ran out north of Fort St. John his surveillers thought he was going all the way to the Yukon and phoned Vancouver for authorization to continue the surveillance that far. But as soon as permission was granted he stopped for pictures of a pipeline station and turned south again and, after a few beers in Dawson Creek, headed east into Alberta where he stayed the night in Grande Prairie.

Spencer arrived in Edmonton the next evening and it seemed logical he would start following the pipeline directly to Vancouver the next morning since he had missed most of it on his trip out. Edmonton surveillance took over while the Vancouver Mounties took the evening off for their first decent meal. Their dinner was only half eaten when word arrived that Spencer, after making a phone call and downing a few beers, had headed back west. Spencer stopped for the night an hour later and the Edmonton crew returned home after blowing an engine.

Spencer drove only about fifty miles the next morning before stopping at a pub in Edson. By this time Hasselstrom, his easy-going Finnish friend, had had enough. He complained that Spencer would not stop for a proper meal and with his mad rush from one point to another never took time to enjoy the trip. "What kind of a holiday is this," he demanded. "We are always on the go." The two argued noisily until the big Finn picked up the tiny Spencer, slapped him twice and walked out in the direction of the local train station where he bought a ticket to Vancouver and waited for the next departure. Spencer hung around the pub until four P.M. and then searched for a second hand store to sell Hasselstrom's goods before starting to patrol the backroads of Edson for several hours, and crawled on his stomach under fences so he could photograph pipelines and installations. If Spencer had been alert he would have spotted surveillance along the gravel backroads of Edson, but he did not.

It was evening when Spencer took to the highway again and dark by the time he reached Hinton and the surveillance team guessed he was stopping for the night and ordered chicken. But before it could be eaten he was moving again, this time to Jasper where for the first time during the trip he booked a decent motel. Another surveillance team had positioned itself in Kamloops further along the pipeline route to spell off the worn down Mounties but the next morning, after taking a few pictures, Spencer confounded everybody again by turning south-easterly through the national parks straddling the Alberta-British Columbia border and forcing the original crew to stick with him while pondering the meaning of this diversion miles off the pipeline route.

Spencer pulled off the road to sleep a few times but otherwise kept driving until nearly midnight when he reached Fernie in the southeast tip of British Columbia. Surveillance lost sight of him for about ten minutes as he entered the bus depot. Nobody knew what he did inside but upon emerging he checked into a seedy establishment called the Northern Hotel. Incongruously a fashionable man and woman parked their late-model Oldsmobile behind Spencer's old Chevrolet a few minutes later and registered in the same hotel causing the surveillers to wonder what attracted them to such a rundown place. The Mounties themselves took a room in another seedy hotel across the street to serve as an observation post but otherwise booked rooms for sleeping in a comfortable motel elsewhere in town.

From the observation post the next morning, before the pub opened, the Mounties saw Spencer loiter in the lobby. For a while he seemed to be in conversation with somebody but the reflection of the lobby's window screened their view. Nevertheless one of the two attending Mounties felt he had made contact with the stylish couple as they passed through the lobby. Spencer left the hotel to discover his car had a flat tire and as he was pulling the jack out of the trunk the couple strolled by without a nod. It was strange behaviour for people who had talked to him only minutes earlier. The trip had produced its first break.

Through checking his Alberta licence plates, the Security Service quickly discovered the man lived in Edmonton and held an executive position with the Alberta Government Telephone System which made them wonder even more why he stayed in such an hotel. Further checking revealed he previously took leaves of absence from his job and was currently on leave on short notice. Maybe he had received

Spencer's telephone call in Edmonton. It seemed strange the two, who had both been in Edmonton two days earlier, would drive 600 miles to meet in an inaccessible mining town. Conceivably the KGB was using the pipeline trip to cover Spencer's meet with his illegal resident. If Spencer had passed the test as an agent, the KGB would want to cut off contact with the embassy and assign him to an illegal. Spencer probably knew nothing about the Fernie meet until his phone call in Edmonton. It was only a theory but explained his sudden abandonment of the pipeline.

As Spencer started heading back toward Vancouver via the United States the office stopped surveillance figuring it had spotted its man making his meet. That evening, unsurveilled, Spencer slept in his car in Idaho and the following day spent most of his time in a hotel pub in Keremeos, British Columbia. The surveillance team, meanwhile, took the weekend off in the Okanagan Valley and during the return to Vancouver bumped into Spencer on the Hope-Princeton Highway. Since they were going in the same direction they resumed surveillance. The conscientious Spencer must have been tired that evening for he drove through Abbotsford without stopping, putting off until several weeks later an expedition to photograph nearby natural gas facilities for his next meeting with Burdiukov about two months later.

The Security Service always had to scramble to bug Spencer's motel room in Ottawa. It would know in advance when he was coming but would learn where he would be staying only when he checked in, which, late Saturday afternoon, would leave only a few hours before Burdiukov's arrival at seven P.M., to install listening devices. A mobile technical squad led by Howie Jones and Bruce Crosby would wait anxiously for Spencer to go for a walk or a sandwich—he did not drink immediately before a meet—and when he did, the squad would rush into the empty room and plant a hidden microphone. Spencer was a perfect person to bug. He talked to himself and answered himself so the Security Service usually knew what he was thinking. The bugs could pick up the little man rehearsing what he would tell Burdiukov and, when the meet was over, recapitulate the conversation, even mimicking Burdiukov's Russian accent. Although he was not derogatory, Spencer enjoyed histrionics and had a private sense of humour.

Burdiukov's appetite for information grew with every meet. At the next meeting he wanted the names of as many bankrupt firms as

Spencer could supply plus the names of torn down apartment buildings and defunct slaughter houses that operated between 1912 and 1921 and logging camps and machinery shops in business between 1943 and 1952. He wanted to know all Vancouver public schools shut down and destroyed since 1941. Obediently, Spencer handed over his British Columbia driver's licence and Burdiukov told him to claim he lost it and apply for a duplicate. Then Burdiukov advised him that at some time before the next meet he might receive a phone call in Vancouver requesting him to appear in front of the Broadway Theatre the next day at seven P.M. He gave no details about who would phone and where it would lead but it sounded important.

The turn of events excited Bennett. The Moby Dick investigators studied carefully the transcripts of the meet. The evidence suggested the Soviets were gathering documentation through Spencer for an illegal who, if not coming to Canada, was at least anchoring part of his legend in British Columbia. The Soviet interest in defunct schools and businesses offered no other reasonable explanation. Spencer's driver's licence gave the KGB a current British Columbia specimen with which to create a forgery. It looked increasingly hopeful that Spencer would be turned over to the illegal network and it was that tantalizing prospect which made the meet in front of the Broadway Theatre so intriguing.

Bennett felt the Security Service could not afford to miss this mysterious meet. The mystery man could be the illegal resident himself assuming control over Spencer, the Alberta phone company executive from Edmonton, a KGB officer off a docked Soviet ship or several other possibilities. It could represent an emergency command technique for activating Spencer on a moment's notice. Whatever it was it had to be covered. The wiretap in Spencer's home should alert the Security Service in time to set up coverage but the contact man might phone at the post office where the lines were difficult to tap or at Spencer's drinking spot at the Waldorf Hotel or slip him a note to wait at a pay telephone. The only certain way to ensure coverage was to monitor the Broadway Theatre each night at seven P.M. So Vancouver set up an observation post in a fourth-floor dentist's office at Broadway and Main.

Each night two Mounties with a camera peeped out the dentist's window from seven to eight P.M. hoping for Spencer to appear.

Summer stretched into autumn and rain seemed to fall every night but no meet took place. As the months wore on, the Broadway Theatre shut down and was demolished but the Mounties kept their lookout. Surveillance was not dropped until early 1962 when Spencer flew to Ottawa for his next meet.

Despite the no-show in front of the Broadway Theatre, Operation Moby Dick progressed well. Burdiukov now wanted information on farms for sale in Surrey and an outline of legal steps required to buy one, suggesting that possibly the Soviets were planning to settle an illegal on a farm south of Vancouver close to the American border. He also asked Spencer to acquire the proper forms for emigrating to the United States. Although nothing suggested Spencer would be emigrating, the assignment resembled Gideon's assignment for moving south. Furthermore, Burdiukov wanted Spencer to survey tombstones of out-of-the-way graveyards for names of one Japanese male and one occidental male who had died in infancy and then secure precise birth details from the provincial bureau of vital statistics. Another promising development concerned the KGB's experiment to test the security of Spencer's mail. Burdiukov informed him he would be getting letters with a corner of the stamp missing. These letters, he said, should be returned unopened and experts in Moscow would determine if the letters had been touched. Also Spencer was told to take steps to increase the volume of his normal mail delivery. Bennett waited with anticipation. Maybe the Soviets were establishing Spencer as a live letter box. The test letters would assure the Soviets that his mail was safe and the higher volume would not make his live letter box flow seem suspious later on. Bennett believed that Spencer as a live letter box would lead the Security Service to other KGB agents.

The first disturbing sign about Moby Dick emerged at the following meet six months later when Soviet Commercial Attache, Anatoli Bytchkov patrolled the chosen vicinity of the meet. Spencer knew nothing about his neighborhood appearance but the Watcher Service observation post spotted him conducting countersurveillance. The development suggested that maybe the Soviets had doubts about the integrity of this operation.

Inside Burdiukov quietly explained he was returning to Moscow and had enjoyed meeting with him but would not see him again. He told Spencer he had performed a valuable service in bridging cultural and political gaps and had served the cause of socialism well. Burdiukov did not expressly say that no other Soviet would carry on the meets, he was giving his agent the golden handshake as diplomatically as he could. But Spencer was not prepared to go and protested he was not finished making contributions. Burdiukov soothed him temporarily by suggesting that maybe his services would someday again be needed.

Spencer later brooded over his "firing" and decided to fight the termination just as he had fought the Canadian government over his postal seniority. Burdiukov always had compensated him generously for his expenses and even left him a little extra, but money was not the issue. The Soviets had not given him a trip to Russia or reinstated him into the Communist party and, furthermore, were making a mistake, not using his services. He felt he needed to meet them and explain the circumstances. He was a delegate to the postal union's national convention in Windsor and already travelling East, so before leaving, he sent a letter to the film editor at the embassy saying he could show a film on September 22, 1962. He ducked out of the Windsor convention early and travelled to Ottawa at his own expense to argue his case for remaining an agent.

Showing up at his motel room was Bytchkov, who explained that Burdiukov had returned to Moscow. Spencer said he understood that but explained he still had some photographs and information to provide and could continue to pass on more in the future. Spencer did not act as tough to Bytchkov as he had when he rehearsed his complaint earlier to the television set. He mumbled rather than snarled and showed self pity rather than anger. Bytchkov consoled him in a fatherly way without delving into substance and subdued Spencer but did not satisfy him.

Like swelling after an injury, Spencer's bitterness grew later on. The injustice sunk in only when he re-enacted the conversation and fully realized that Bytchkov had really done nothing. Since the Soviets were not levelling with him Spencer felt another trip to Ottawa might set things straight. Almost on impulse he flew to Ottawa unannounced at his own cost and walked through the main door of the Soviet embassy and asked for Bytchkov. He was told abruptly Bytchkov would meet him at the normal time and to leave the premises at once and not to loiter in the vicinity. When Bytchkov appeared at his motel room at seven P.M. he did not enter but suggested they take a ride in Spencer's car. Bytchkov felt Spencer may have compromised himself by appearing at the embassy and evidently figured Spencer's room might now be bugged. Bytchkov took the wheel and started reprimanding Spencer for coming to the embassy in violations of firm instructions from Comrade Burdiukov. Spencer mumbled an excuse about Burdiukov not explaining the matter in definite terms. With Spencer already on the defensive, Bytchkov drove into the Ottawa Valley and talked about the theory of communism, always asking Spencer questions and pulling off to the side of the road when the discussion grew weighty. Bytchkov seemed to like the troubled little man and held out vague hope that some day he might be rewarded for his services with a trip to Russia. However, he added, there were other priorities and the time was not right. Before returning to the motel, Bytchkov reimbursed him for his travel expenses and told him not to do anything foolish again.

Spencer never again visited the embassy but it was not too long before he phoned the embassy from Vancouver to ask what was going on. And not long after that he sent a letter saying he could show a film on February 16. His persistence which had so long dogged the Communist Party of Canada was now annoying the Soviet embassy.

Bytchkov again showed up at the appointed time and again went for a ride with the determined agent. Although he had been given no assignments Spencer produced an assortment of information including a list of Vancouver area firms that went bankrupt in the previous three months. Bytchkov took the information but this time was not gracious or patient. He told him he had again violated instructions by phoning the embassy and now had certainly compromised his security and usefulness and that his own safety demanded he freeze all activity and realize his imprudence was damaging the cause of international socialism. Furthermore, he said, good soldiers know how to take orders and it had been decided he must return to Vancouver and not return unless summoned. The fact he had been dropped sank through when Bytchkov gave him no expense money. A lowly postal clerk could not routinely afford to travel 3,000 miles at his own expense.

The last two meets in the car went unbugged but the bugs in his room picked up the replay as Spencer sadly recounted the conversation. Moby Dick had officially died but nobody could predict what Spencer would do next so the Security Service kept monitoring him. Bennett could have had Spencer interrogated but the Soviets had dropped agents in the past and then re-activated them. If asked, Spencer certainly would oblige the KGB.

The unresolved lead was the Alberta telephone executive suspected of having rendezvoused in Fernie nearly two years earlier. An exhaustive investigation had uncovered some bizarre behaviour but produced nothing of a subversive nature. With little left to lose, Bennett had him pulled in for an interview and during his talk with the Mounties he recalled seeing the old man fixing the flat tire in front of his car but denied having met him or having anything to do with him. The explanation sounded plausible. His disregard for Spencer on the street was perfectly normal if they had not met before. The Mounties in the observation post could not positively say there had been an encounter. As for staying in a cheap hotel in a mining town, he explained that the woman wearing the polka dot dress was not his wife. He had taken time off from his job and left Alberta to avoid being seen by other employees and had chosen an offbeat hotel to ensure privacy. The investigation had probed deeply and his explanations satisfied the suspicions, so the matter was dropped.

In January, 1964, almost a year after his final meet with Bytchkov, Spencer developed a deep, harsh cough which doctors diagnosed as a lung condition. Treatment relieved the symptoms but nine months later, around the time of his mother's death, the cough returned and more intensive tests eventually uncovered lung cancer. Doctors surgically removed his left lung but cancer had already spread to the bronchial tube leading to the other lung. The most optimistic prediction gave him a ten percent hope of surviving another five years if cobalt treatment worked and even then paralysis may numb his brain at any time. On the other hand, doctors concluded, he could die in two or three months. Either way it looked like the chain-smoking Spencer would escape his worldly miseries before too long, in spite of his claim that his invented technique of "brain discipline" had cured his cancer by controlling his mental and physical state. Before he slipped from its grasp, the Security Service wanted a crack at Spencer to see exactly what he had done and who he had worked with. At that point Bennett did not know the intercepted meet of October 1960 was his first trip to Ottawa. The Security Service had to assume he had been working for some time before that. Only Spencer could supply the missing knowledge and Bennett did not want to repeat the mistake on Kneschke by waiting too long and losing the only vulnerable target with the answers.

Spencer agreed to see the men from the Security Service and a low-key interrogation in his home went on between radiation treatments at the hospital. The sessions went badly for the Security Service. His home territory fortified his resolve to stonewall when an effective interrogation needed to intimidate. The poor man was dying and looked like such a harmless loser that ultimately the Security Service was more intimidated than Spencer. The questions remained polite and Spencer volunteered nothing. He acknowledged his activity piecemeal only when confronted with facts and revealed nothing his questioners did not know. The only revelations came from the investigators' questions and they told Spencer how much the Security Service knew, so rather than waste all its bullets the Mounties terminated the interrogation early.

Bennett as head of the Russian Desk had authorized Spencer's interrogation but when the authorizing telex went out to Vancouver it was Hank Tadeson, the head of B Branch, who signed it. When William Kelly, then the Director of the Security Service, heard that Spencer had been interviewed he turned angry and reprimanded both Tadeson and Bennett. Kelly wanted Spencer interviewed for prosecution purposes which meant that the police side of the RCMP, who had the powers of a peace officer, had to do it. Otherwise the results were inadmissible as evidence in court. The Security Service had interviewed merely to pull as much information as possible out of a dying man. Among other things, its failure to warn Spencer his statements may later be used against him may have irrevocably undermined future efforts to prosecute him. Kelly called the Security Service off Spencer and turned the case over to the RCMP's Criminal Investigation Branch to investigate and see if Spencer was now prosecutable.

Even before the Criminal Investigation Branch conducted its investigation, Kelly suspected that prosecution was hopeless and decided to salvage something by convincing the Department of External Affairs to kick a few Russians out of the country. Public diplomatic expulsions embarrassed the Soviets and ridded the Security Service of certain Soviet intelligence officers. The problem was whom to expel. Burdiukov, Spencer's main handler, had already left the country on his own.

So had Krassilnikov, the recruiter. Only Bytchkov remained. So on May 8, 1965, the Department of External Affairs issued a press release saying it had informed the Soviet ambassador that Bytchkov and an embassy colleague, V. N. Poluchkin, "had engaged in activities incompatible with their official status and had, therefore, found it necessary to declare them persona non grata." The Poluchkin expulsion had nothing to do with Moby Dick. Poluchkin had been buying defence-related information from an unnamed double agent who was supposed to seduce female civil servants for the purpose of securing information.

Spencer also remained unidentified in the press release which referred to him as a Canadian civil servant who "was paid thousands of dollars to gather information and documentation in Canada, the purpose of which was to assist in the establishment of espionage activities in Canada and in other countries, and to perform economic intelligence tasks, including the provision of detailed information on the Trans Mountain Pipe Line system in Western Canada."

Sergeant Maurice Low and Constable Keith Dane of the Criminal Investigation Branch proceeded more judiciously than their Security Service counterparts in approaching Spencer. First they checked with Dr. Coy, Spencer's surgeon, to see whether his medical condition could withstand an interview. Dr. Coy, after consulting Spencer, who was now shrivelled down to 115 pounds, assured the Mounties an interrogation would not retard recovery and scheduled Spencer's cobalt treatments for the morning to open up afternoons for the RCMP. Low and Dane picked up Spencer in the cancer clinic at Vancouver General Hospital and each day brought him to the RCMP barracks in South Vancouver. As he switched on the tape recorder, Low formally advised Spencer that whatever he said could be used as evidence in court.

At first Spencer admitted nothing. He denied having any contacts with Soviets and denied having travelled to Ottawa under a false name. In fact he denied visiting Ottawa at all. The session lasted only an hour because the Mounties did not want to strain him. That evening Low and Dane picked up Spencer at the hospital and took him to his home on Adanac Street to search his premises with a warrant. Among other things they found and seized the business card of Youri A. Afanasiev, the Soviet Commercial Attache aboard the Russian grain freighter; a map with a heavy black line outlining his pipeline trip four summers earlier; a purchase contract under a false name for a movie camera; and pictures and negatives of various scenes along the pipeline. There was also a February 14, 1963, letter from the Vancouver School Board enclosing a list of schools and their dates of opening. Spencer had requested the information for Burdiukov a long time before. A covering letter apologized for the delay, explaining his request had been mislaid. Spencer had received the letter a couple of days after his last meet with Bytchkov, too late to give it to the KGB. The red tape jungle had struck again.

When questioning resumed he next day Spencer acknowledged that he had been in touch with some Soviets, saying he had approached them to gain a trip to Russia. He felt he could help mentally disturbed people and wanted to study Soviet methods of psychoanalysis. He still would not admit to performing any tasks or having anything to do with espionage. Spencer said he would probably lose his property if charged for dealing with the Soviets but Low assured him that would be very unlikely. Despite his lack of cooperation, Low and Dane remained polite, which confused Spencer's view of the police as the running dogs of the bourgeoisie who stopped at nothing to smother the working class and uphold the unjust status quo. These Mounties showed no anger and made no threats and seemed sympathetic. While being taken back to the hospital, Spencer saw an Indian ceremony outside the barracks and asked what it was about. He was told the Squamish Indian Band was making an RCMP corporal an honorary chief of the tribe. Spencer wondered how it could be that even Indians liked the Mounties.

The next afternoon Spencer accepted a cup of coffee for the first time. "I didn't trust you guys," he said, explaining why he had declined previous offers. "I was afraid you would be doctoring it." After that he started to talk.

"I have been warned," began Spencer's official statement, "that I am not obliged to say anything but anything I say may be given in evidence." The statement then covered his early life growing up in British Columbia, his service in the war, his expulsion from the Communist party and his meeting with Afanasiev aboard the freighter. Spencer described each of his seven meets in Ottawa and told of the assignments he was given and the type of information he supplied and the effort he expended getting it. He detailed his pipeline journey through British Columbia and Alberta. Spencer, neither in his statement nor in discussion with the Mounties, complained about the red tape jungle or showed any bitterness about bureaucratic bungling ruining his life. Those complaints would spew forth later to a different audience.

Spencer's "confession" recalled facts such as meeting places and dates that were mostly accurate and he was forthright in describing the various tasks carried out for the Soviets. But when interpreting events and explaining motivation for doing certain things, Spencer still held back and always would. He stuck to his story that it was his desire to travel to Russia and not re-admittance to the Communist party that brought him to Afanasiev in the first place. He also claimed that at first he never suspected the Soviets had ulterior motives in inviting him to Ottawa and explained travelling under a phony name as a precaution against alarming his mother in case of a plane crash. That way, he explained, the authorities would not phone his mother with news he had perished. He said that after his third trip he suspected something was wrong and that maybe he was being used as an agent but wanted to keep on the good side of the Soviets in hopes of getting his desired trip to Russia. He acknowledged that at the end he travelled to Ottawa on his own initiative and that he had phoned the embassy contrary to their wishes. He said he was not getting satisfaction regarding his trip and wanted to discover what was happening but found them not prepared to sit down and talk so he, not the Russians, cut off the relationship. He said the Russians requested another meeting but he refused to answer it.

"During all my trips to Ottawa," concluded his fifteen-page statement, "I would only get my actual expenses reimbursed to me. I never did get a bonus. When I first made contact with these people I did not think that there was any ulterior motive but after the third trip I suspected there was something wrong and I was maybe being used as an agent." The statement had been prepared by Low. Spencer read it and initialled the bottom of each page and suggested a couple of minor corrections which Low made. When Spencer finished the document he signed the final page.

The RCMP and the Department of Justice agreed they could not successfully prosecute Spencer. The Security Service interview had indeed jeopardized the case and, besides, he had violated no law.

Spencer in his beaver-like industriousness had given away no classified information. He had merely gathered together public information which, for practical purposes, even the powerful Official Secrets Act could not challenge. Spencer could be arraigned for giving away his driver's licence and falsely claiming he lost it and for travelling and signing documents under a false identity but these infractions fell under the Criminal Code of Canada and would have to be prosecuted by the British Columbia government since law enforcement is a provincial responsibility. The federal government did not especially want to involve the British Columbia Attorney General on a national security issue when the prosecution rewards were so small. Furthermore, the Security Service did not want to get tied up with the demands of court evidence and wanted even less to divulge its secret investigative techniques knowing the defence would demand to know them. Spencer was such a feeble specimen and not likely to impress the public about the awesomeness of the KGB. In fact prosecution would probably make him a victim in the public mind. So the authorities decided to leave matter be. Spencer's fate would soon resolve itself and even the Mounties did not particularly want to beat up on a dying man.

However, there was the matter of Spencer's employment at the post office. When Spencer started working full-time in 1949 he swore an oath of allegiance and secrecy promising not without authority to "disclose or make known any matter or thing which comes to my knowledge by reason of such employment. So help me God." In fact Spencer told Burdiukov everything he knew about post office security and procedure. He divulged how often postal security officers opened mail bags for inspection and what prompted these searches and how the post office kept a continuing watch on an individual suspect's mail and how, with knowledge, the suspect could circumvent such scrutiny. The information was not crucial but could benefit an organization like the KGB, which used the Canadian mail for espionage. Spencer betrayed his oath of employment and the government felt justice demanded his firing so dismissed him without a hearing as permitted under Section thirty of the Civil Service Act. Since Spencer had not built up sufficient pensionable time he got back $4,283.16 in pension contributions. The little scrapper who had once declared war over two years of seniority and had even fought a speeding ticket by claiming in court (unsuccessfully) he could tell the speed of his car by the sound of his engine accepted the judgement meekly.

The diplomatic expulsions created a one-day sensation in the Parliamentary Press Gallery and died when reporters failed to squeeze further details out of the press release. Tom Hazlitt, a reporter for the Vancouver Province, kept digging and with the help of RCMP sources wrote a story later that year suggesting the unknown civil servant was a low-level person stationed in Vancouver. Hazlitt received a phone call from a man who refused to identify himself asking if he had more information. Suspecting that the mysterious caller was the man in question and spurred on, Hazlitt started checking Vancouver hospitals giving cancer treatment to junior government employees and narrowed a list of suspects down to Spencer. He confronted Spencer and obtained a confession and a scoop.

Now that the civil servant had a name and face the political opposition in the House of Commons protested Spencer's firing because its arbitrariness denied him a hearing and stripped him of a pension. Both the Conservatives and the New Democratic party demanded an inquiry but Prime Minister Lester Pearson and his cabinet ministers said an inquiry would expose secret RCMP techniques. When the opposition persisted, Pearson replied Spencer was not complaining about mistreatment.

For a few fleeting days Spencer, the perpetually unwanted man, enjoyed national attention but soon discovered reporters asked questions less politely than the RCMP and did not accept contradictory statements like his claim he had spied but had not engaged in espionage. The press demanded satisfactory answers and Spencer started avoiding reporters but found them waiting on his doorstep, at the Waldorf Hotel pub and wherever else he might appear. Once he tackled a much bigger news photographer taking his picture and wound up on his back. He started suffering anxiety about outraged erratic citizens searching the city for him so they could beat him up. A student of Pavlovian psychology, Spencer experienced moments of grandeur followed by bouts of depression and persecution and sought out a psychiatrist but disputed his approach and withdrew. Besieged and alone, Spencer turned for support to the RCMP who hid him in various small motels and checked twice a day to ensure he was safe. He filled time going on aimless drives, watching movies and drinking in pubs. He sometimes violated the honour system by disappearing on drinking sprees and the Mounties went out looking for him. When the media's hunt abated, the Security Service moved him back into his house with a temporary guard. Spencer, humbly grateful, returned his thanks with a note:

TO WHOM IT MAY CONCERN

When the first news releases were made early in May last year, about my contact with a Russian Embassy official, it was reported that the R.C.M.P. were *grilling* me when I undergone a major chest operation and was under Cobalt radiation treatment for cancer.

I emphatically deny that any officers of the R.C.M.P. grilled me, or used any type of third degree methods to gather information about my contacts.

It was also reported that I was dying and was too sick to be brought to trial. Yes, I was very low at that time, having lost close to forty pounds in weight, which is quite normal for that type of operation plus the radiation treatment, but at no time was I close to death because of the magnificent work of the Doctors and Nurses in the Heather Pavilion and later in the cancer division of the Vancouver General Hospital.

The officers of the R.C.M.P. were more than co-operative with me when we discussed my actions, and at no time interfered with the rutine (sic) of my treatment as prescribed by the Doctors.

If the least tired, or in need of pills or nurishment (sic), I returned to bed, leaving unfinished business until a later date, sometimes a few days or a week if necessary.

Because knowledge of medicine and treatment is only in its infancy, we have to depend on doctors and nurses who are too few. More and more must all people train themselves to take care of the sick and injured. To give first aid, and especially study what are good human relationships.

The officers who spoke to me would qualify as nurses. If they had more schooling, they could be doctors, and contrary to what we often see on T.V. they did not grill, shout or get mad, but treated me as a human being whose first job is to get well, as I eventually will due to the care and attention given by the nurses, doctors and many, many others, such as the social workers who arranged rest home care when I was able to leave the hospital, and those who taught me about diet, bodily movements to compensate for the loss of a lung, that is, how to breathe correctly and make the one lung do the work of two.

To all, officers, doctors, everyone. THANK YOU

> Sincerely,
> G.V. Spencer (signed)
> Jan. 15th, 1966[2]

Through the months with the RCMP as his guardian cum babysitter, Spencer never complained about his post office firing and told the Mounties he had done better receiving his pension contributions back instead of a pension because he thought he had not long to live. He acted as if the last thing he wanted was an inquiry that would open to the public his relations with the KGB. Spencer wanted to fight battles of old rather than join the chorus in Ottawa demanding an investigation into his dismissal. The compassionate leave he did not get in World War Two and the short-changing of his post office seniority suited him better as issues on which to claim a wrong so he recruited Jervis Bloomfield to detail his travails through the red tape jungle. "One of these days I expect to retire to England," he told Bloomfield. "I want my friends to know what has happened to me and why I have acted in certain ways." Sneaking up to Bloomfield's home in the evening, Spencer laid out his plight for the manuscript but omitted mention of his recent dismissal from the post office among the woes and usually remained silent about the controversy swirling over him.

The politicians in Ottawa, exercising no such restraint, kept agitating for an inquiry until Pearson suddenly announced he would telephone Spencer and ask him if he wanted one. That evening with the Prime Minister on the line and the country awaiting his response, Spencer mouthed an unenthusiastic yes to a hearing. Pearson appointed Mr. Justice Dalton Wells as a one-man "commission of inquiry into complaints made by George Victor Spencer."

The Wells Commission had scheduled its first open hearing for Wednesday but the preceding Sunday, Eugenio Barazzuol, a shop foreman with a fireplace company and a neighbour of Spencer's for eleven years, started wondering about the light that had burned

---

[2] Later published by the Wells Commission in July 1966.

continuously for several days in Spencer's bedroom. Spencer's Chevrolet had not left the garage for days. He usually spent most days away from home as a security precaution. When Barazzuol returned from church he decided to investigate and after receiving no answer found the back door unlocked. Stench poured out of the house as he opened the door and saw before him two bottles of beer on the kitchen table and a patch of dried blood on the floor. In the centre Spencer, black and bloated, sat slumped on a chair with his head hanging between his legs six inches from the ground. He had been dead about a week. The bottles of beer on the table could not account for his .24 blood alcohol level so the city coroner concluded he had started drinking elsewhere first. A box of matches in one hand and a nearby cigarette on the floor suggested he was about to light one of his perpetual cigarettes when he collapsed.

After a postponement the Wells Commission carried on the inquiry and issued a report condemning Spencer's spying and concluding that the government had treated him fairly. A loser to the end, Spencer lived long enough to get the inquiry he never wanted but not long enough to finish his book denouncing the red tape jungle.

11

Operation
Top Hat

WHY DID THE KGB cut off Spencer?

The KGB would normally grab all the Spencers it could get, especially in a centre like Vancouver, which had no Soviet consulate. The nearest legal base for the KGB was the Ottawa embassy. The KGB needed somebody in Vancouver to fill and clear dead letter boxes, service local agents, act as a live letter box, conduct routine countersurveillance, dig up background information to document the legends of illegals and run errands. The embassy handled these chores in the Ottawa-Toronto-Montreal triangle but Vancouver on the other edge of the continent lay out of the reach of the KGB Legal Residency.

Spencer fit the circumstances almost perfectly. The KGB would have had trouble inventing a more ideal agent for doing dog work. He looked so weak and harmless that nobody paid him any attention, which made him unlikely to arouse suspicion as shown during his first meeting with Afanasiev when the RCMP surveillers did not bother reporting the derelict. When the KGB talent spots somebody in a local communist party, the individual severs all links with the party before becoming an agent. Spencer, although not willingly, had already been cleansed. He had been out of the party so long the Security Service had no file on him. Yet the KGB knew his background well enough not to worry about his authenticity as an ideological disciple. He fulfilled his KGB assignments conscientiously and never once complained about the demands placed upon him. Burdiukov discovered he could not impose too much work. Spencer always acted discreetly and, despite everyday disdain from peers, never boasted about his special work that took him to Ottawa regularly, or gave any hint he was wrapped up in clandestine matters. He carefully covered his trail when collecting information and often used false names to ensure protection. What more could the KGB want from a low level agent? Spencer did violate security with his visit and phone call to the embassy but that occurred only after he had been dropped, so evidently the Soviets cut him loose for another reason.

The KGB does not forego opportunities frivolously. Maybe KGB countersurveillance had exposed the RCMP surveillance. It is possible but not likely. Because the Security Service knew his schedule in advance, Spencer's meets in Ottawa received only light surveillance from the Watcher Service. Vancouver followed him closely but the days of the very clumsy surveillance from Operation Apple Cider had mostly passed and Vancouver's new Watcher Service did most of the monitoring around town. Besides, the surveillers could tell Spencer never suspected he was under observation. Maybe the KGB carried out countersurveillance without Spencer's knowledge. That was not likely because with its embassy 3,000 miles away the KGB lacked the facilities in Vancouver for professional countersurveillance. However it was possible Spencer's first meet in Ottawa, which was surveilled intensively, could have been picked up by KGB countersurveillance. In that case, the Soviets were playing back the unwitting Spencer to the Security Service all along.

Maybe the mail test convinced the Soviets to drop Spencer. He inadvertently opened two of the three letters he was supposed to return unopened and the KGB could have written him off as an aging incompetent unable to carry out a simple exercise. If Spencer forgot about the letters he could not be relied on for other tasks and was therefore useless to the KGB. The Russians were always fussy on detail and sought, above all else, agents who were dependable.

Maybe the British betrayed the case. The Security Service told MI5 about Operation Moby Dick once the KGB had established the practice of meeting Spencer in his motel room. Such tradecraft deviated from established routine so clearly the Security Service felt it had to pass on this new development to its chummy cousin across the Atlantic. Sir Roger Hollis, then head of MI5 and later a mole suspect, could routinely learn about it. Hollis may have been loyal but the secret could have been leaked by somebody else in MI5 who was a mole. Possibly Moby Dick had leaked to the Russians from the RCMP itself. A mole almost anywhere in the Security Service would know enough to compromise the case. Considering all the Security Service personnel who knew about the Spencer case from the watchers to the people who listen to the wiretaps, to the investigators and support staff in Vancouver, Ottawa and Edmonton, and the tendency around headquarters to gossip about cases, even a poorly-placed mole could trip across enough of a tidbit to do the damage. The mole would only have to know that the transcribers were giggling at this weird postal employee who talked to himself.

With Apple Cider and Moby Dick, Vancouver had seen two potentially good cases evaporate within a couple of years. But Vancouver had another counterespionage case unfolding at the same time that was progressing so well that nobody could suggest it was not genuine. From the start, Operation Top Hat showed signs of eclipsing Apple Cider and Moby Dick. It had the feel of a winner and for once a case with potential was taking off the way it should. Top Hat represented the Russian Desk's best case in the country. Bennett felt if Top Hat did not move from the legal to the illegal residency then no Soviet agent would ever switch over. The agent was no Spencer or Kneschke destined to a role as errand runner. He was educated, bright and could think on his feet and possessed all the personal qualities to make him a top-flight agent. A couple of other things made this a dandy operation. The agent was a double agent reporting back to the RCMP, which meant the Security Service learned about everything through his debriefing and without tying up thousands of hours listening to bugs and watching from observation posts. It hardly required any work from the Watcher Service, thus saving resources and removing a major risk of exposure. In fact, the need for surveillance was so minimal that if Top Hat went wrong, the Watcher Service could not be blamed.

The international cold war in the post-war world broke out in Berlin first and no part of the world was thicker with agents than divided Germany. Whenever the Russian Army moved, people got the jitters. It happened the Russians were just on maneuvers but the maneuvers always rolled west and nobody knew their intentions. The American Army thirsted for reliable intelligence about the Soviets' activities and among its spy rings recruited a rowing team in the East German city of Potsdam. One of the youngest rowers was Aquavit[1], a twenty-one-year-old son of a state railway employee in East Germany. Aquavit did not blindly jump into either ideological camp in the global dispute between the west and the Soviet Union. He spied for the Americans mainly because the Russians had taken over his homeland and he was determined to do what he could to help kick out the occupying forces. When talking to the Americans he never informed about East Germany, only about the Soviets and their military installations. Whenever he saw something Russian, he reported it.

Riding his bicycle on a spying mission through the East German countryside, Aquavit stopped to rummage through the off-limits refuse pile of a major artillery exercise ground southeast of Berlin. The camp had a history going back to the Prussian Army but in 1950 was being used by the Soviets who quickly spotted him sifting through discarded Russian documents. Under arrest, Aquavit invented a story that he had cycled to the next village to visit his girlfriend but she was still working in the field. While waiting for her he was searching through the refuse for metals, which were in short supply. The Russians accepted his story and released him but the close call convinced him to abandon spying at least for the moment. He moved to Frankfurt and stuck to his safe professional work in medical supplies.

Aquavit returned to espionage a year later working under cover as a translator for the United States Army in West Berlin. His new duties put him behind a desk but he frequently crossed quietly into East Germany on reconnaisance missions and soon the Russians became wise to his activities. Twice the East Germans, under Russian leadership, hatched plans to kidnap him and drag him into the eastern sector, only to have an informer within their ranks foil the plot. On one occasion, one of the plotters had a fight with his girlfriend who revenged her lover by telling West Berlin police of his scheme to spike Aquavit's brandy.

About six months later Aquavit's father, who knew nothing of his son's secret work, failed to return from work in Potsdam. His wife correctly assumed the East German authorities were holding him incommunicado for some reason. He reappeared two days later and

---

[1] Aquavit is the man's RCMP code name. In return for his story I have agreed to withhold his identity. As a further precaution his line of work is referred to loosely as "medical supplies."

visited his son in West Berlin urging him to write the Russians confirming he would cooperate with them. One of Aquavit's former spy colleagues from the rowing team had come to accept the new order in East Germany so the Russians had reason to believe he would too. Aquavit sent the Russians a letter agreeing to collaborate on condition his parents would be left alone and then secretly he gave a copy to the Americans. In a secret meeting in East Berlin the Russians told him to keep his position with the United States Army and remain in place as a double agent. The Americans had a chance to play along and use Aquavit as a triple agent but vetoed it and put him out of his job.

Aquavit met the KGB several more times in East Berlin and kept being pressed to supply inside information. He was sure the Russians had already partly infiltrated his army office so he told the Soviets generally what he thought they probably knew. Aquavit insisted he no longer worked for the Americans and when the Russians realized the truth they told him to train his attention on West German targets. He bluntly refused. He said he had spied on the Russians for the Americans and now on the Americans for the Russians but he would no more spy on West Germany for the Russians than he had on East Germany for the Americans. Spying on anything German was out, he announced with finality. His streak of loyalty failed to soften the KGB which warned him to cooperate. By cooperating he was betraying his country. By refusing he was jeopardizing his parents' security. Facing a choice of violating one of two sacrosanct allegiances, Aquavit sought to escape the dilemma by running away. The American Army offered to fly him to the United States and smooth out visa difficulties but the smell of American McCarthyism in the mid-1950s repelled him. Instead Aquavit took a chance on Canada and joined the immigration stream as a normal applicant. The United States Army gave him free air passage but otherwise pulled no strings. He landed in Montreal with the Canadian authorities ignorant about his intelligence background.

Settling in far-away Vancouver, Aquavit picked strawberries in nearby Langley for sixty-four cents an hour and took jobs in ditch digging and construction and later in his old profession in medical supplies to raise money to bring over his wife and young son.

Hardly two years had passed when a stranger with a Russian accent phoned his East Vancouver home asking for a meet in Stanley Park. Aquavit knew what was happening, especially when the stranger instructed him to carry a magazine under one arm and use code phrases as recognition signals. Waiting at the foot of Comox Street on the edge of Stanley Park was a man in his early thirties about six feet tall with dark wavy hair who said he was visiting off a freighter docked in the harbour. The fact that the Russians had tracked him down worried Aquavit but he quickly realized the Russian was more nervous than he. As they walked slowly along Second Beach further into the park, the Russian expressed disappointment that he had disappeared so suddenly from Berlin. He said he hoped they could still be friends. With his parents still in Potsdam, Aquavit agreed there was no reason they should not remain friendly. The Russian did not scold him, describe the virtues of communism or try directly to re-enlist his services as an agent. But he did ask Aquavit to meet another Soviet representative. It was a feeler, only an arrangement to meet somebody else, yet Aquavit knew he was being asked to do more than just meet. By agreeing to meet he would in effect be agreeing to work for the Russians. He did not know what to do. The Russian mentioned nothing about his parents but did not have to. It was an unstated given. Aquavit could not understand what intelligence interest the Russians could have in a recent immigrant who spoke English badly and was having trouble adjusting to his new environment. "Well okay," replied Aquavit. "We'll see." He thought maybe he could play along long enough to get his parents out of East Germany and free himself from this persistent blackmail.

The nervous Russian told him to appear at the corner of Robson and Burrard at noon the next day with a newspaper under his arm in case he had further questions. Aquavit had no questions but was curious so showed up and waited but the Russian failed to appear. It did not matter because he had already told him what he wanted to say.

Contact from the next Russian did not take long. A man identifying himself as Peter invited him into Stanley Park close to the earlier meet. Peter said he worked in the Soviet embassy in Ottawa and his style showed the professional confidence missing in the first Russian. About forty, solidly built and a little short, Peter, with his jowls, had a bulldog-look. As well as being relaxed and confident, he was friendly and likeable. He was also patient and chatted leisurely before raising the issue that brought them secretly together. Peter wanted him to write a letter offering to spy for his old outfit, United States Army

Intelligence, and instructed him on how to approach the army and what the letter should say.

Aquavit wrote the letter thinking the army this time might accept him as a triple agent and waited but the army was not replying. He did not know it but the letter got lost in the army's paper labyrinth and would never elicit a response. In the meantime, as Peter had told him, a letter had arrived with instructions to come to Ottawa and check into the Peter Pan Motel and at one forty A.M., following the late movie on television, wait for a phone call about where and when to meet. Peter's letter set the Ottawa rendezvous in three weeks, forcing Aquavit to make a decision on whether to meet it. With no word from the United States Army, he called on the RCMP.

From RCMP pictures Aquavit identified Peter as Petr Borisov, a counsellor in the Soviet embassy. Bennett was very familiar with Borisov and assessed him as the KGB resident. Certainly he was one of the most active intelligence officers in the mission. Bennett gave Aquavit full freedom to play along with the KGB. Aquavit's Security Service handler, Reg McKernan—"Red" according to Aquavit's rudimentary English—told him to use his common sense and keep him informed about every meet and each request.

Aquavit waited in his rented car outside the Peter Pan Motel near the south end of Bank Street where, six years earlier, Bourdine had humbled Gideon. The location was perfect for a meet: wide open with little traffic and few secondary roads to shelter the Watcher Service. It was the kind of spot the Russians would probably spot moving surveillance. While waiting, Aquavit noticed a car in which Borisov was a passenger drive by twice without stopping. He quickly realized Borisov was looking for surveillance. The third time around the car parked and Borisov got out and slipped behind the wheel of another car. For the next twenty minutes both cars drove around in maneuvres together looking for evidence of the Watcher Service and, when satisfied they were clean, rendezvoused. Borisov parked and then entered Aquavit's car with a picnic basket.

Borisov initiated small talk during the drive out of the city and into the Rideau Lakes countryside giving no hint of the business at hand. After thirty minutes they stopped at a resort and rented a rowboat and upon reaching the middle of the lake Borisov began to talk.

"How are your parents?" he asked.

"They are fine," replied Aquavit.

Is there anything we can do, Borisov inquired. Do they need more coals?

Aquavit repeated his original condition for cooperating back in Germany and that was to have his parents kept out. They were not supposed to be contacted and should have nothing done to them or for them. Borisov seemed agreeable but pressed Aquavit on why he had fled Germany. Aquavit said his parents had become involved and that he could not work against Germany. Besides, he added, he had wanted to emigrate for some time. Aquavit's bluntness and undisguised loyalty to Germany seemed to impress Borisov who made no effort to lecture him. Let bygones be bygones seemed to be his attitude as he started inquiring about what he had done in Canada so far. Aquavit told him he was working mostly as a labourer on construction projects because the money was better than in medical supplies but, once established, he planned to return to his profession. Borisov's interest picked up when Aquavit said he would like to open his own medical supply shop some day. Borisov had no assignment for Aquavit that day and spent most of the "picnic" extracting promises of cooperation and patiently explaining the procedures for future meets and bragging quietly about the amount of money he would receive for his expenses and effort. He promised to pay for any work, lost time and expenses.

Several meets later Borisov introduced a new chauffeur, Ivan, whom he called his colleague. Borisov was more forthright with Aquavit than the Soviet Union was with the Canadian government because the Department of External Affairs knew Ivan Baranov strictly as Borisov's chauffeur. Although Baranov did chauffeur Borisov around, he was actually a junior KGB officer who, while driving, assisted Borisov on intelligence operations. Baranov's shortness and thin reddish blond hair with a big bald spot in the middle reminded Aquavit of a weasel, although, at about thirty, a youthful, enthusiastic, friendly and likeable weasel. The enlistment of Baranov into the operation puzzled the Security Service because, designated as a chauffeur, he lacked diplomatic immunity and could be prosecuted and jailed by the Canadian government for violating the Official Secrets Act. The KGB usually put vulnerable personnel such as agent-running officers into cover positions offering diplomatic protection.

Borisov truly needed a chauffeur. He was running several other agents known to the Security Service, developing a score of other possible recruits and perpetually attending social functions and sizing up potential targets. Not surprisingly, Borisov received the heaviest attention from the Watcher Service and his constant maneuvring revealed he was aware of that fact. Borisov needed a skilled countersurveillance expert to help him out and the Watcher Service quickly learned why Baranov had joined him. Baranov, the Watchers discovered, was a good "counter" man and contributed much to Borisov's effectiveness and to the Watchers' frustrations. The Borisov-Baranov team set up "trap" operations designed to funnel Watcher Service cars into certain routes where they could be identified. They usually failed but Baranov's henpecking forced the Watchers to lay back so much that Borisov usually broke away and got free to go out unsurveilled, presumably to make a meet. On occasion they completely fooled the Watcher Service by posing as husband and wife. The small Baranov disguised his identity and played the husband behind the wheel while the husky Borisov, dressed as a woman from the shoulders up, acted as the wife. When their car left the embassy gates the Watcher service thought they were a Soviet couple from the diplomatic side and waited for a more rewarding target to surveil.

The Watcher Service did not have to surveil Aquavit's meets in Ottawa. A pattern soon developed. Every three or four months Aquavit flew to Ottawa on a Friday pretending to look for a job, visiting his sister in Buffalo or just examining the prospect of relocating in the East. Upon arriving in Ottawa he checked into a suburban motel and the following morning went for a drive with Borisov and Baranov in his rented car. Usually both Russians came but occasionally one failed to show. Procedure inevitably captured the Russians and they always started discussions inquiring whether the instructions had been clear and if he encountered any problems. They asked whether he had at any point been followed and then checked up on his cover story. Coming from a country with internal passports, where inside travel is not assumed, Borisov stressed the importance of having a ready pretext in case somebody stopped him on the street for an explanation. Then they inquired about his wife, his children and, finally, his parents. The two Russians always mentioned his parents but never dwelled on it.

They greeted Aquavit as an old friend and always socialized with him and after the camaraderie ended Aquavit handed over the results of his work.

They took Aquavit's information and put it aside without a look or comment. Any comment usually came at the next meet. Borisov systematically and slowly explained his new assignments for the next get together. Most of the meet was consumed with elaborate instructions. Safety and format dominated their counsel. Procedures had to be followed. Aquavit got the feeling Borisov was not so interested in good results as he was in predictability. Before they parted they gave him details about the next meet, telling him which flight to take, which motel to use, which car rental company to patronize and precisely where and when to appear for the rendezvous. As they were parting Borisov pulled out of his suit coat an envelope full of used twenty-dollar bills. The reimbursement earned Aquavit no windfall but more than covered his costs. Later in the day, less than twenty-four hours after arriving he boarded an airplane for his return flight. At some point during the next few days he slipped into downtown Vancouver's Georgia Hotel for debriefing with the Security Service.

Aquavit had no access to secret information but with an effort to see things, an observant eye and an inquiring mind could assimilate a lot of information. Many of Aquavit's assignments almost copied those given Spencer. Like Spencer had done six months earlier, Aquavit checked out the procedures on immigration and gathered together information about Vancouver's power supply, food supply and water supply. Like Spencer, Aquavit took pictures with a camera purchased with Soviet money and travelled up the Trans Mountain Oil Pipeline and Westcoast Transmission Natural Gas Pipeline on photography expeditions. The Soviets also ran the same mail test on Aquavit to check whether his letters were being opened.

Aquavit did some things Spencer had not done such as investigate travel opportunities to Eastern Europe. And the Soviets paid not only for his still and movie cameras but for his basement darkroom so he could avoid commercial photo processing. The KGB wanted names of German Canadians with relatives in East Germany; as a victim of blackmail, Aquavit knew the purpose of that request. The Security Service helped him acquire none of his information but neither did they hold anything back. He was on his own and merely had to report to the Security Service everything he passed on. On one occasion, Aquavit mistakenly described the natural gas pipeline at Rosedale, British Columbia, as an oil pipeline. Borisov at the next meet cautioned him not to make up things. The odd lapse aside, Aquavit, with his German efficiency, proved to be a productive agent and evidently the KGB thought so too because soon the assignments took on a different nature.

Operation Top Hat started taking off when Borisov assigned him work helping document the legends of illegals. The new turn could be false, as it was in the Spencer case, but at this stage the Spencer case was still developing and nobody suspected it would fail. Spencer's illegal documentation work was general, the kind one could later, in hindsight, pick apart as not genuine. Aquavit did general work too, compiling data on dead people by searching through cemeteries and checking the obituaries of old newspapers. But the KGB gave him specific assignments, ones with a genuine feel that Spencer's never had. For instance, Borisov showed particular interest in a German immigrant who owned a Vancouver travel agency, and wanted to know his life story, especially his activity during World War Two. Borisov seemed to think he had been an officer in the panzer tank corps.

He also wanted to know the history of a private residence at 151 Government Street in Victoria. Aquavit investigated and reported: "Two-storey, colonial style, wood construction building with basement in it. Is located on a corner lot east of Government Street and south of Simcoe Street. The house is about fifty years old and still in excellent condition. The whole area west of Beacon Hill area and south of the Parliament Buildings has always been a residential area, except the waterfront. Since 1943 the house had been owned by Mrs. Batchelor who operated it as a boarding house during World War Two, giving board and room to single men for about thirty-five dollars a month. In 1947 Mrs. Batchelor sold the house to a Mrs. Vaughn (not positive of name because the word didn't come out clearly) who up to 1950 occupied the house together with her two daughters alone. In 1950 the house was bought by Mr. and Mrs. Gidney (also not too clear), the present owner, who again converted it into a rooming house." With Mrs. Batchelor gone, nobody could refute an illegal's claim to having lived in her boarding house for a spell during World War Two.

Operation Top Hat kept growing and the KGB showed signs of wanting to transfer Aquavit to the illegal residency—not merely as a support agent but as an intelligence officer. Preliminary signs emerged during one of his pipeline trips when he scouted out a hiding and lookout place west of Kamloops from where saboteurs could watch an oil pumping station blow up. During the excursion he located, for future communication with the KGB, a dead letter box in the Coqui-halla area north of Hope, British Columbia, and later another one outside the gates of Fort Langley. In case the link with his handler was severed, through war, a break in Canadian-Soviet diplomatic relations or whatever, they would maintain contact through these dead letter boxes.

Borisov asked him if he would move to Ottawa and open a medical supplies shop but Aquavit flatly ruled out relocating in such a cold climate and the compliant Borisov never forced things. Since Aquavit had been an active rower in Germany, Borisov later casually broached the idea of opening up a sports club in Vancouver. It would provide cover for meeting people. But all of this was nothing compared to the big development Borisov had in mind for Aquavit.

At one of the meets Borisov suggested he start thinking about setting aside a few months to visit Moscow for some training. All the travel details would be taken care of and he would be reimbursed for lost income. Borisov counselled he would need time off from work under proper cover and would have to hide the real purpose of the disappearance—even from his wife. He warned that such a trip was still in the future but that he should start thinking about it. If the offer from Borisov was genuine, and time would eventually determine that, Aquavit would be the Security Service's most successful double agent ever against the KGB. Since the spectacular failure of Gideon, none of its other agents had come close to such an undertaking. The KGB was proposing a bureaucratic investment in Aquavit it reserved for its most promising agents; Soviet Intelligence did not spend its technical resources frivolously. It was the best sign that Aquavit was passing the tests. More importantly, it signalled the KGB's trust.

Now that Aquavit had proven his ability to gather information, the KGB wanted to teach him how to send that information to Moscow without relying on the embassy and that required the technical skills of short wave radio, Morse code, secret writing and one-time pads.

Training in Moscow would pull Aquavit one step closer to the illegal residency.

The Soviets had dangled carrots before and not delivered. They had waved a high-speed transmitter in front of Gideon and successfully induced him to return to his doom. They had teased with the embassy bugs and flirted with agent Hector. They had sent Kneschke back East and never followed it up and seemed to be playing with the prospect of moving Spencer to the illegal residency, then dropping him. Maybe the Soviets were playing with Aquavit too. Both Borisov and Baranov gleamed when describing the trip and showed more excitement over the prospect than even Aquavit. Baranov in particular treated the trip as the ultimate mission. It also excited Aquavit who announced he would quit his job to get the time off work. In his usual frankness he told them one does not get a chance to visit Moscow every day. By this time they had become friends and both Borisov and Baranov talked freely about their wives and children, which was uncharacteristic for KGB officers. Two meets later the excitable Baranov clasped Aquavit in his arms and gave him a true Russian bear hug and kiss. He could hardly contain himself because Moscow had approved the trip. Baranov treated it as a personal triumph.

Aquavit knew nothing about Gideon's experience so his excitement over going to Moscow was not tempered by that disaster. The Moscow prospect both excited and disturbed the Security Service as it balanced off the anticipation of professional success against the possibility of human tragedy. Not going would spoil its best case but nobody could forget what happened to poor Gideon. The ghosts of Gideon and Long Knife haunted the organization so profoundly that it would sacrifice Operation Top Hat to avoid jeopardizing the personal safety of Aquavit. It was a chess game between Moscow and Ottawa with each move spaced out by several months. So far the choices had been easy, but now the Security Service faced an irreversible decision and feared being outmanoeuvred another time. Back in 1955 Bennett, as a junior worker, had witnessed Gideon going to his doom. Now, in 1963, he had to shape the Security Service's decision.

Bennett and his colleagues mulled over the matter and after some hard thinking concluded Aquavit could go safely. For starters, the case smelled genuine and as long as the Soviets believed Aquavit was a genuine agent working for their side they had no reason to harm him.

Even if the Soviets knew or suspected the truth, they would not likely touch him. Unlike Gideon, Aquavit was not a Soviet citizen who betrayed his country by defecting to the other side. Gideon was theirs, and the Soviets knew the Canadian government could not and probably would not lift a finger once he was back on Russian soil. Aquavit was different. As a Canadian citizen with a family in Vancouver, his failure to return would spring the Canadian government into diplomatic action. The Security Service figured the Soviets would never risk a diplomatic incident over an issue that exposed KGB spying in Canada. Besides, if the KGB was onto Aquavit's double dealing and wanted vengeance it could torment him at will through his parents in Potsdam. So Bennett, with backing from both senior and junior colleagues, approved the trip with only slight misgivings and high hopes of retrieving valuable intelligence. In the end the decision rested with Aquavit. The Security Service advised him of the dangers and said the decision was his to make. Aquavit never wavered. He felt the Soviets had nothing to gain by detaining him and affirmed he was going.

At the next meet Borisov told Aquavit he would enter the Soviet Union by way of an excursion boat cruise from Copenhagen to Leningrad but at the last minute told him to fly to Paris and book a spot on a Russian ship sailing out of Marseille for Odessa. Before sailing, Aquavit visited relatives in West Berlin but refused the Soviet offer to arrange a visit with his parents a few miles across the wall on the principle they were not to interfere with anything relating to his family. Once aboard at Marseille, a Russian named Gregory introduced himself and said he would be accompanying him while in Moscow. Aquavit was allowed ashore at Genoa, Napoli and Athens but had to stay on ship at Istanbul, Bulgaria and Romania. At Odessa, Gregory informally sneaked him past the officials by disguising him as a disembarking sailor. The next day he was flown to Moscow and put into the fifth-floor suite of an eight-storey concrete slab pre-fabricated apartment building a mile from the Kremlin. Young and old everyday working-people and their families filled the other apartments. Aquavit could stroll the streets in his spare time but, not speaking Russian, he carried a little card with a phone number in case somebody challenged his presence. There were no problems. His neighbours in Moscow had learned to mind their business.

The next morning his first instructor arrived at his apartment and started teaching Morse code. Each day he would practice sending and receiving but the instructor emphasized receiving over sending. Clearly the Soviets felt it more important for Aquavit to understand the incoming message than to be able to reply. On another day a different instructor arrived to teach short wave radio. The following day somebody else came to give instruction on secret coding and invisible writing, showing him how two people with identical copies of any book could devise a simple yet practically unbreakable cipher system by setting down their messages in numbers corresponding to individual letters in the book's text. The following week Gregory and a colleague took him on a field trip to teach techniques for spotting surveillance and showed him how to choose places for dead letter boxes and how to recognize other peoples' dead letter boxes from written instructions, as well as illustrating techniques for physically concealing messages. They ran tests by giving him a note with instructions for finding a dead letter box in a city park. Later he selected a dead letter box and wrote out the instructions for his teachers to discover.

Each day the instructors stopped teaching their technical crafts around lunch time and, with Gregory present, started an informal conversation lasting through the afternoon. Sometimes they showed a film but generally talked political theory and world events. They knew Aquavit was no communist—he never pretended to be one, even to Borisov in Ottawa—and delivered their sales pitch softly in contrast to normal Russian bravado. They did not so much sell him on the Soviet Union as say "here is another view." One of the favourite themes was Germany versus Russia and somehow the talk always slipped back to what happened to him in Berlin. Why had he worked for the Americans? Why had he left? Gregory and his companions could not untrack this preoccupation and checked and double checked his replies. Aquavit retorted bluntly, but not antagonistically, that he worked for the Americans because the Soviets had occupied his country. "What would you do?" he asked. "You are in my country and we don't want you there. It's natural to try to do something about it." Aquavit laid out his real political views, saying he favored socialism on the scale practiced in West Germany but thought communism was the wrong policy. He felt the Soviets could spot phoniness and in any case would suspect him for changing sides so completely. The Soviet instructors showed no chagrin over his views, if anything they seemed to appreciate his honesty. They never directly asked him why he was cooperating with their side but Aquavit left the impression that after working against them so long he was balancing the scale by working on their side. The KGB had hundreds of non-communists who for a variety of reasons worked loyally for Soviet intelligence. As far as the Soviets were concerned, Aquavit could be a Nazi as long as he suited their purposes.

After four weeks of lessons, during which he worked on his Morse code speed most of the time, the time had come to leave. The night before his departure a couple of senior KGB officers dropped by his apartment with vodka and big glasses for a farewell party. The celebration moved along smoothly as Aquavit and the two KGB men started discussing the role of intelligence in the cold war. "Well, it's too bad," Aquavit said about espionage. "Let's drink to the time when all these things are not necessary anymore." Everything stopped for a second. Surveying their disapproving expressions, Aquavit realized he had said something wrong. The KGB men did not reply but their one-track minds perceived intelligence as an integral part of Soviet foreign policy and suggesting its demise was recommending destruction of one of the fibres supporting Soviet world power. The thought was more subversive than silly. Soviet agents did not have to be communists but neither should they mouth anti-Soviet sentiments.

The Soviets never did anything simply and that included getting Aquavit back to the west. After changing plans a few times, they assigned him a phony name and passport for the first time and put him on an airplane to Budapest where Gregory said good-bye and turned him over to an escort from the Hungarian secret police who boarded him with a private family while he waited for a flight to Zurich. The family, led by a former officer in the Hungarian army, occupied a big apartment but had been forced by the police to give up a room for Aquavit who, after two days, was happy to escape the unpleasant atmosphere. After arriving in Zurich under his fictitious identity, he took the train to Lausanne and taped the phony passport underneath the cover of the toilet tank in a downtown public restroom. Aquavit turned around outside and watched a man, about fifty, enter the washroom a minute later. After he had gone, Aquavit returned inside to find the passport gone. In the darkness of night he had not gotten a good look at the support agent.

When the Security Service met Aquavit in Toronto en route home, he carried with him a nice little haul. Moscow had awarded him $5,000 to buy a car and replace lost income while creating the impression the future would bring more. Aquavit handed over to the Mounties a seven-inch spool of reel-to-reel recording tape full of Morse code signals for practicing reading skill, a gummed pad of large note-writing paper that appeared to come from a drugstore but was chemically treated for invisible writing, and a small vial of pills for making solution to make the invisible writing reappear. The Security Service took the materials because it wanted to radiofingerprint the tape and run tests on the notepaper.

With neither a short wave radio nor sufficient Morse code, Aquavit was not yet ready to enter the illegal residency phase. Bennett figured the Russians would take up to five years completing the transfer. On operations like these the KGB had the patience of Job.

Before the Moscow trip, Borisov and Baranov had suggested moving east but each time dropped the idea when Aquavit objected. Now they raised it again and while remaining gentle seemed more determined. They explained the province of Ontario had better espionage targets and would bring him close to them. They wanted him to open a medical supplies shop in Toronto and immerse himself in the local German community. Aquavit still resisted but was prepared to be convinced.

Aquavit's next trip east took him to the Ontario town of Perth about fifty miles southwest of Ottawa. There he met Baranov who was driving his new Pontiac to Oshawa for servicing.

"How are your parents?" Baranov asked routinely.

"Oh, they are quite well," replied Aquavit. "They are in West Germany."

The emotional little Russian could not hide his surprise as Aquavit told him his father had retired and crossed the border to draw a West German pension. Despite the Berlin Wall, East Germany permitted— in fact encouraged—pensioners to emigrate because non-workers drained the state treasury. Aquavit did not know whether Baranov was surprised because the parents were beyond blackmail's reach or because the KGB did not know about the move. The eager Baranov recovered and with the shadow of his superior, Borisov, missing, began talking more openly about himself and especially his son, who was taking grade three in the Moscow school system.

Since Moscow, the meets started falling increasingly outside Ottawa, and Aquavit's handlers grew more wary about exposure. At first Aquavit had always booked into suburban motels and rendezvoused nearby. Now the Soviets directed him into perimeter towns an hour's drive from the city and sometimes near the edge of their seventy-five-mile unrestricted travel zone. Aquavit met Borisov several times in Montreal, and once visited New York as a pretext for returning through Ottawa. Borisov and Baranov started worrying more about surveillance and grew nervous when unknown cars came too close. They seemed preoccupied about matters going wrong. They coached him how to signal danger by sending the embassy a letter with a crooked stamp and a phony name and gave him elaborate instructions on how to summon an emergency meet in Mexico. Aquavit assumed the new timidity reflected his more sensitive status as an agent and that maybe it presaged more advanced and riskier assignments in the future. Maybe, he thought, it was connected with their desire to establish him in Toronto as a businessman with an antiseptic background. The whole atmosphere was changing with each meet but not as much as it would change at his next encounter outside tiny Alexandria, halfway between Montreal and Ottawa in the eastern tip of Ontario.

Aquavit flew into Montreal and as usual rented a car and followed the impeccably detailed sketch map the Soviets always provided. On this occasion the map took him to a crossroad at Highway 43 near Apple Hill, west of Alexandria. But instead of meeting Baranov's familiar Pontiac he encountered a white Corvair with an F-licence. A young man he did not recognize got out and slid into his car. He wore black casual shoes, black pants, a black stepped-up ski jacket and a black turtleneck sweater. It seemed the only thing not black was the gold wristwatch on his left arm, a cheap pair of green sunglasses and his straight brown hair. He introduced himself as Mike and said Peter and Ivan had returned to Moscow. Mike spoke with detachment and kept the relationship formal. Aquavit sensed Mike was ambitious and out to make a name for himself in the KGB and figured the days of the buddy-buddy relationship were over. Whereas Borisov and Baranov spent the first half hour inquiring how things were going, Mike went straight to business and adhered to the KGB procedures manual.

From now on, Mike said, the meet days were moving from Saturdays to Sundays except the emergency meet in Mexico, which would stay unchanged. He told him to check the dead letter box in Fort Langley the last Sunday of months with an uneven number of days for the next three times. New agent-running officers liked to put their personal stamp on the cases they inherited, so none of this was cause for concern. Mike told him to apply for a business loan to help him learn the procedures for establishing a medical supplies store. Mike expected him to open shop in Toronto at some point in the near future. Mike's next meeting lasted only about fifty minutes. He gave Aquavit seed money for opening the business and told him to be prepared to move to Toronto. He also told him to return the training tape, secret writing pad and bottle of pills he had gotten in Moscow.

The KGB could hardly have done anything to upset the Security Service more than ask for its materials back. At this point, the Security Service dreaded no other development as much. The simple fact was the Security Service could not send back the writing pad because the lab at N Division in Rockcliffe had accidentally spilled acid on it which disfigured the entire pad. The technicians had tried desperately to salvage the pad with an antidote but only damaged it further. Now a freak accident threatened the life of a gold star counterespionage case. Operation Top Hat was in deep trouble the minute the KGB realized the pad was not being returned. The only recourse, unacceptable as it was, was for Aquavit to stall and hope the Soviets would forget, as unlikely a prospect as that was. Not surprisingly the matter at the next meet had not slipped Mike's mind so Aquavit played for time claiming he had forgotten. Later when he could stall no longer he said his kids had scribbled on the pad and had thrown it away. Mike made no comment but such an explanation in a profession built on suspicion was not reassuring. The KGB was in the wrong business if it did not wonder about the loyalty of its agent.

Aquavit still disliked the thought of moving to Toronto but by now planning had progressed too far and he could not pull out. He left his family in Vancouver and moved into a small apartment. He signalled his safe arrival in Toronto by phoning the embassy and asking for Richard Burton. Had he encountered trouble he would have mailed newspaper clippings about China and shown up at noon at the Green Acres Motel near Ottawa one week after the date of the envelope's postmark.

Aquavit could have driven from Toronto to Ottawa for his next meet but instead was instructed to fly to Montreal and motor back halfway to Ottawa. The meets were getting more remote and this one was scheduled in the bush in rural Quebec. When he reached the town of Papineauville, Quebec, he turned north off the main highway for five and eight-tenth miles and after crossing the bridge over the Petite Nation River turned right onto a secluded gravel road for another two miles. He got out of his car and walked to the correct spot along a trail inside a large bush. It was a mysterious setting and was the first meet happening wholly outside a car. The Russians always appeared at precisely the correct time but now Mike was late. He finally showed up on foot along the trail from the opposite direction and in contrast to the cool professional image built from previous meets looked obviously nervous. He had no assignments and told Aquavit to hold everything and move back to Vancouver and await further direction. Mike usually had an envelope with cash in his pocket. The Soviets enjoyed the procedure of doling out money and liked to make sure the agent knew he was getting it and where it came from. This time Mike motioned that the money was in some brush, pointing in the direction but keeping both heels planted on the ground seemingly afraid to take even a step in the direction of the money. After a few words, he turned and walked away as though he could not leave too fast.

After he had left, Aquavit picked the envelope of cash out of the root works of a tree stump. Mike had told him to leave by driving the long way out while he would exit through the direct route. But Aquavit missed a fork and got lost and turned around. While coming back he passed Mike from the rear while he was walking along the road. It was the last time he ever saw Mike because the Soviets never again contacted him. After nurturing Aquavit as an agent for seven years the KGB let him wither on the vine.

12

The Klochko Defection

NOBODY DOUBTED THAT Operation Top Hat had died. Mike openly feared Aquavit's presence and abandoned him crudely. In hindsight, the Security Service could detect unhealthy signs shortly after the trip to Moscow, but in the end the KGB killed the case overtly. It did not keep the Security Service guessing the way it had in Apple Cider and Keystone, nor did it strike back with active deception as it had in Dew Worm and with the phony Hector. In fact, the KGB did the RCMP a favour by dropping out so neatly, and saving the Security Service from wasting resources. The organization could now at least conduct a post mortem knowing one was needed, except that this time the Security Service could not blame the British or the Americans or any other foreign agency, not even U.S. Army Intelligence, which recruited and originally ran Aquavit, because nobody outside B Branch knew about Top Hat. Neither could it use the old standby excuse that the Watcher Service had probably slipped up. The Watcher Service had not been used.

Yet perfectly innocent factors could explain the failure—maybe. Aquavit's Moscow trip might have tripped the suspicions of the KGB. His peacenik statement longing for the demise of espionage surprised the KGB and probably caused it to wonder. Spying on the "cutout" who picked up the phony passport in Lausanne might have been observed and made the KGB doubt him. Yet both these actions were plausible and not grave enough to kill a case, not even by Soviet

159

standards, or the KGB would not have carried on another two and a half years. Maybe the Soviets decided to terminate the case when Aquavit's parents moved beyond blackmail's reach to West Germany. Aquavit started cooperating under duress so theoretically he should have stopped once the duress had passed. Sometimes hostages join their captors. It had happened before with blackmailed KGB agents. If the KGB thought Aquavit had defected philosophically, it would not worry about his parents. Even if Aquavit had not switched allegiances to the Soviet side, he had by this time travelled too far down the KGB road to back out innocently. If blackmail over his parents no longer did the trick, blackmail over his years of service to the Soviet cause probably would. Sending Aquavit to Toronto could nicely deceive the Security Service into thinking he was heading toward bigger things, but it made sense only if the KGB followed through with real deception. The KGB never did. Almost as soon as he arrived in Toronto he was sent back. One had to assume the KGB's misgivings arose after the move to Toronto, which happened two years after his parents left East Germany.

Then there was the matter of the ruined secret writing pad. The KGB would undoubtedly wonder about Aquavit's failure to return the material and question his loyalty, but not necessarily conclude he was a phony agent. Agents bungle from time to time and the practical KGB does not drop a good operator for an occasional slip. Experience told the Security Service the Soviets always changed agent-running officers before killing a case. Ostrovsky took over from Bourdine in Keystone; Krassilnikov took over from Ostrovsky in Long Knife; and Bytchkov took over from Burdiukov in Moby Dick. So precedence suggested the KGB brought in Mike to kill off Top Hat, except Mike took over before the KGB asked for the materials back and presumably before the KGB knew that Aquavit could not supply the pad. In this case, Mike's entry could have been legitimate because the KGB also changed officers for reasons other than killing a case; Borisov, whom Mike replaced, had been in Ottawa a long time and probably had legitimately come to the end of his Ottawa posting. On the other hand, if the KGB knew the pad was ruined it could kill the case unsuspiciously by asking for it back. The only practical way the KGB could know about the ruined pad was through a mole—even Aquavit did not know it had been ruined until after he was asked for it. By waiting a few years and introducing a new officer with different tradecraft the KGB could innocently ask for the pad and kill the case without jeopardizing the mole when Aquavit failed to deliver.

Maybe the failure did not hinge on any of these factors by themselves but together—Aquavit's behaviour in Moscow, the transfer of his parents and the missing materials—they frightened off the Soviets. The spy world cannot afford to be uncertain about an agent. Doubt destroys his usefulness. Like the other failures, the more Top Hat was analyzed the more conclusions one could think up.

Carton[1] was an examiner in the Mechanical Branch of the Patent Office in Ottawa and in September 1963, as Aquavit was leaving for Moscow, he sat in the bar at the Talisman Hotel in the West End of town when a short, somewhat stocky blond man with a Russian accent sitting a few feet away started talking to him. The Russian introduced himself as Vasily Tarasov, the Canadian correspondent for the Soviet newspaper *Izvestia*. The engaging Tarasov knew the art of conversation and smiled a lot and after learning that Carton worked in the Patent Office casually secured his name and approximate address.

Two days later Tarasov, unannounced, appeared on Carton's doorstep and took him for a ninety-minute drive for some friendly conversation. When Tarasov took him for a second drive the following week and started asking about the Patent Office, Carton realized what was happening and called the RCMP who told him to play along. Tarasov dined Carton every week or two and splurged on drinks and wine. The next day Carton would walk into the front door of the Ottawa Civic Hospital and promptly duck out a side door precisely as a Security Service car drove by to whisk him to nearby Webb's Motel for debriefing. Other times he was debriefed in a rented room at the Chateau Laurier.

Tarasov gave Carton a few miniscule payments and a Russian-made wristwatch which broke down, but later he produced a lump sum of $200 as a demonstration of what the Soviets were willing to pay. Tarasov called it an advance on future services and implied more would be coming once Carton produced. Eventually Carton agreed to pass him a couple of classified documents at their next meet in the Peter Pan Motel, the same place Aquavit stayed on his first trip to Ottawa.

---

[1] RCMP code name.

Tarasov did not know which material he would be getting and did not seem to care—as long as it was classified. Neither did Carton know what he would be giving.

The documents Carton would pass to Tarasov carried a secret classification but their release hardly jeopardized the security of Canada. In fact the classification would expire in another month at which time the Russians could get them by walking into the Patent Office, and since the Soviet Union violated western patents anyway, Tarasov's espionage gave them merely one month's jump on patent infringement. Before the meet the Security Service wired a small microphone under Carton's lapel and packed a tiny transmitter underneath the back of his jacket. When he passed the documents, hidden Mounties jumped from all corners to arrest Tarasov. The room filled so quickly with Security Service officers that even Carton, who knew what to expect, was surprised. Front page news stories told the world that Tarasov had been caught spying and was expelled from the country.

Bennett usually squeezed every ounce of life out of his counter-espionage cases by letting them run as long as he could. Occasionally somebody mumbled that he let them run too long because he was consumed by the process at the expense of the objective. But the Tarasov operation was young and had plenty of life left when the Security Service arbitrarily cut it short. The aggressive William Kelly was Director at the time and liked to punish and embarrass the Soviets with public expulsions. With a minor case like Tarasov, Kelly felt he could disrupt and embarrass the KGB with a loud expulsion. The Tarasov declaration carried another purpose as well. The Soviet Embassy had launched a campaign to convince the Department of External Affairs to exempt Soviet journalists from being counted part of the diplomatic staff for determining the size of its establishment in Canada. Exempting journalists allowed the embassy to bring in more officers without exceeding the designated limit. In fact the Soviets were trying to raise the ceiling on the size of their establishment, arguing that journalists were not diplomats so should not be counted part of the diplomatic ranks. The Soviet argument seemed to be swaying External Affairs. The Security Service contended that journalistic positions had to be counted because the KGB abused journalistic cover for espionage purposes as much as it did diplomatic cover.

Allowing more journalists in means admitting more spies, the Mounties said. The Security Service rolled up the Tarasov operation early to provide External Affairs an example. Whether the Tarasov expulsion played a role or not, External Affairs held firm and turned down the Soviet request.

The Tarasov incident represented an innocuous—almost innocent—case that the Security Service handles routinely. But a few things did not feel right. Most intelligence officers approach unknown targets gingerly. They develop a friendship over many months and only after securing the target's trust do they slowly begin recruitment, starting with a simple request of public information for a niece writing a school paper in Moscow. As a favour the target goes to the public library and gets the information and his grateful Soviet friend insists on giving a token gift of appreciation to cover the Canadian's car fare. The requests grow and the payments get larger and before the civil servant realizes it he is caught in the KGB net supplying confidential information. By that time it is too late to turn back or call the RCMP.

Tarasov made no effort to follow such a charade. He barely hid his ultimate intentions and hurried the pace so much he aroused Carton's suspicion before he could be ensnared. Carton was a husky military type often mistaken as a Mountie. Six months earlier he had worked in the army on a top-secret radar system but Tarasov never probed deeply enough to discover that. KGB officers are human and often buckle under the burdening KGB system. Moscow demands results and officers in the field sometimes falsify reports to comply. They say a poor prospect looks good and then must falsify further to keep "developing" the case. Tarasov's crude approach showed signs of such desperation.

If a highly placed mole lurked inside the Security Service the KGB would know Carton was a phony agent and decide at the outset whether to kill the case or play along for deception purposes. To protect its precious mole, the KGB would let it develop slowly to string it out. Tarasov's unseemly haste in recruiting Carton did not fit the pattern of a deception operation. If the KGB had a pipeline into the Security Service why did it allow Tarasov to walk into the last meet? The Soviets loathed the adverse publicity of an expulsion and, like it had done with Nicolai Ranov five years earlier, would want to duck out of the meet and deny External Affairs an expulsion. But the Soviets could not afford to skip such meets too often because eventually somebody in the Security Service would add things up. So Soviet Intelligence might have decided to let Tarasov walk into the trap and hope External Affairs would keep the expulsion private.

KGB officers posing as journalists had virtually a licence to poke around Ottawa asking questions they could not pose under diplomatic cover. As well the KGB "journalist" could move in the Parliamentary Press Gallery, cultivate ministers' aides and ostensibly interview civil servants while actually talent-spotting for the KGB. However, journalistic cover had one big drawback: it denied them diplomatic immunity and if caught spying, a "journalist" could be arrested and prosecuted under Canadian law like anybody else—at least in theory. In fact, External Affairs never prosecutes Soviet officials lacking diplomatic protection because the Soviet government would arbitrarily retaliate against a non-protected Canadian in Moscow. So the two countries meticulously honoured an unofficial truce. As a so-called journalist, Tarasov had no diplomatic immunity but the KGB could be confident Tarasov would not be thrown into prison.

Although External Affairs never considered prosecuting Tarasov, the Security Service, for whatever it was worth, did. Canada had the legal right to do so and the RCMP kicked around the idea, although not for long because the idea was not fundamentally sound. Prosecution would require the Security Service to identify Carton so he could testify at the trial. The documents were not sensitive and losing in court would embarrass the government and, in the propaganda war, vindicate the inevitable Soviet claim that Tarasov had been framed. Besides, prosecution would require political approval up to the Prime Minister, which almost certainly would be denied. So in the end the Security Service abandoned the idea on its own.

Above almost everything else, the Soviets fear losing their personnel. The KGB takes Machiavellian measures to guard against defections but imprisonment worries it too. The KGB officer in a western jail could change his thinking and eventually return to Moscow as a double agent. If the KGB knew the Security Service was considering prosecution it would not have sent Tarasov to that final meet. Since it did, the Soviets either had no mole who knew the latest events or the mole lacked time to send out a warning. Maybe it was coincidence, but after the discussion on whether to prosecute Tarasov, Ivan Baranov, the chauffeur without diplomatic immunity in Operation Top Hat, never met Aquavit again.

While Top Hat ran its course in Vancouver a similar double agent case unfolded in Toronto. Bruno[2] was a German, with parents in East Germany, who moved to Canada with his wife during the post-war years. He took a blue collar job with Fruehauf Trailers while his wife worked as a hairdresser in a small beauty salon on Broadview Avenue. While visiting his parents back in East Berlin during the late 1950's, the Soviet GRU blackmailed him into working as an agent. Upon returning to Toronto he called the RCMP and was set up as a double agent. Normally headquarters assigned code names randomly from a prepared list of approved names but this time a local officer in Toronto looked out the window and called the case Operation Blue Skies.

Blue Skies at first glance showed the same potential as Top Hat and the Security Service hoped it would lead to the illegal residency, but Bruno as a double agent did not measure up to Aquavit. Bruno lacked Aquavit's intelligence, cunning and motivation. The GRU wanted Bruno and his wife to buy a hairdressing salon but the money never arrived. The case seemed to take off when the GRU sent Bruno to East Berlin for training while ostensibly visiting his parents. The Security Service hoped he would return with new tradecraft and a big assignment. East Berlin taught him some techniques of observation intelligence and a little photography but nothing about countersurveillance, radio or Morse code. The trip seemed purposeless and ultimately became wasted because after Bruno returned to Canada the quality of his assignments deteriorated, gradually withering away.

Bruno usually drove to Ottawa for his meets and at one rendezvous in a field near the end of Alta Vista Drive, protested that he did not get enough money. The Soviets paid him adequately and his complaints failed to loosen the GRU's purse strings so Bruno loudly tore up the bills, threw them to the ground and stormed off. Later, after the Russians had left, Bruno snuck back to retrieve the wind scattered bills. Double agents were counselled to act naturally and vent their anger, but Bruno acted like an agent out to make a buck, which he was. The GRU had no qualms dealing with mercenary agents, but if he had

---

[2] RCMP code name.

been acting like a blackmailed agent a few years ago, why had he suddenly changed? Evidently he did not feel blackmailed.

The Russians were not the only ones with reason to distrust Bruno. Bennett had misgivings and pegged him as a reluctant and lazy agent with mixed motives who might be sabotaging the operation or possibly cooperating with the Soviets more than he was disclosing. Bennett asked the CIA to surveil the East Berlin safehouse where Bruno received his training. He wanted to know whether Bruno showed up. The CIA did conduct the surveillance and reported that Bruno did appear at the right place and time. The wisdom of surveilling a GRU installation in a communist country was later questioned because the Soviets could have picked it up which may explain why they failed to properly exploit Bruno after East Berlin.

Bennett stuck low-key surveillance on Bruno's meets in Ottawa to ensure he carried them out. Although non-intensive surveillance like this was difficult to spot, neither was it detection-proof and maybe the Soviets discovered it. Bruno usually drove to Ottawa on weekends and returned home the same day but sometimes they told him to stay overnight. On one of his first overnight stays, the GRU directed him to book into the Beacon Arms Hotel in the downtown area and Bennett decided to bug his room. So when Bruno checked into the hotel the Security Service took the next room.

The Security Service routinely plants bugs and acts so prudently it rarely gets caught, but each operation carries a margin of risk and over hundreds of attempts the odds catch up. A chambermaid using her pass key opened the door, apologized for her intrusion and left, but not before seeing the Security Service's bugging expert, Bruce Crosby, wearing a headset and sitting next to the wall of the adjoining room with wires attached.

Few things ruffle a counterespionage operation more than raw exposure. It not only threatens the operation but attacks the organization's pride. If it cannot hide from harmless citizens how is it supposed to fool the professionals in Soviet intelligence? An emergency meeting reconstructs the exposure, analyzes the implications and looks for an antidote. In this case the Security Service knew the manager of the Beacon Arms who told the chambermaid she had seen nothing and would never discuss it. The Security Service felt no harm had come out of the incident.

When news of the exposure reached headquarters, Sergeant Murray Sexsmith stormed into Bennett's office with a brash "I told you so." He had opposed the bugging from the start and now was letting Bennett know he was right. And he was. As he had predicted, the operation secured no results and now jeopardized the case. Sexsmith was one of Bennett's non-commissioned officers on the Russian Desk but he never felt restrained by his junior status. The bugging, insisted Bennett, was a calculated risk worth taking and the lack of positive information itself was information about Bruno. The risk was not worth it, shot back Sexsmith, because it could resolve the suspicion of Bruno only if the meet took place in the hotel room and the Soviets did not do that. Why not, proclaimed Bennett, Spencer had been successfully bugged meeting his Soviet control officer repeatedly in his motel room. That was different, snapped Sexsmith. The acrimony grew louder and carried through Bennett's open door and down the hallway where a captivated audience marvelled at Sexsmith's audacity. Bennett almost never admitted an error. He rarely lost his temper and usually subdued his opponent through argument, but nobody in B Branch was so opinionated and inflexible as Sexsmith. When logic failed, Bennett resorted to cutting humour or outright sarcasm but such barbs merely ricocheted off Sexsmith. Bennett turned white when he lost his temper and now he was shouting as loudly as Sexsmith but the Sergeant cut him off. "Don't you raise your voice to me," shouted Sexsmith. Ordering a senior officer to simmer down showed defiance but Sexsmith often did nervy things and usually got away with them. He did this time too because Bennett pulled himself together and turned quiet.

Sexsmith never looked healthy. He was tall but not robust. His leanness carried a tinge of sickness. The upper half of his face looked like putty and his skin had a tint of yellow jaundice. The illusion of weakness vanished the minute he opened his mouth for he was loud, opinionated, dogmatic, forceful, inflexible, defiant and famously right wing. He could smile and operate diplomatically but one always saw him reach for the switch. Given the choice between diplomacy and brute power, he preferred the latter although later in life he realized the value of switching on the smile more often. Sexsmith was intelligent and well read, but not broadly read, and one of the few Mounties in B Branch who refused to buy the prevailing view of Bennett's counterespionage wisdom. One Mountie put it bluntly: "Murray was the only guy who occasionally told Bennett he was full of shit." Bennett on the other hand manipulated Sexsmith and used him as a stalking horse to crack the whip when the divisions needed discipline. "It's lucky we have a hatchet man," Bennett was once overheard saying.

Sexsmith hardly read files and could not return them to Central Registry fast enough. His desk lay bare and shiny clean. Nothing, not even an out basket, cluttered it up. Next door stacks of reports drowned Bennett's desk as he diligently plodded through everything. Bennett was a researcher who picked his leads from patterns in the files. Sexsmith came from the police, where one made snap decisions based on instinct. Sexsmith had great instincts. Another reason, besides his quick temperament and police background, explained his decision making. Sexsmith was lazy and openly admitted it. He showed little initiative during quiet periods in his early days on the Czech Desk and waited for a file to land on his desk. If none did he would sit and wait. One day Security Service Director Jimmy Lemieux rattled Sexsmith's spine with a tongue lashing for sitting back with his feet on the desk. Sexsmith had a rebel's impulse and always seemed to operate on the edge of trouble. Lemieux's rebuke did not faze him because when Lemieux turned his back he propped his feet back onto the desk, this time taking more care not to get caught. Yet if something piqued his fancy, Sexsmith worked hard. He could not be bothered combing the files for potential defectors, but if somebody else did the work and pulled together a case, Sexsmith's interest was immediate. He had good imagination and an undeniable flair for counterespionage work that could be dynamite as long as somebody did the groundwork first.

Bennett savoured conterespionage cases the way a food connoisseur relished a feast. He studied modus operandi—MO became a catchword under Bennett—and noticed every detail. Bennett believed a case was more than the sum of its parts; more than the KGB desk man in Moscow, the Soviet officer in the Ottawa embassy, the agent, the Security Service handler, or even Bennett himself directing the Canadian side from his cubby hole in headquarters. The case lived its own life and had a feel. Bennett studied the cases not only for their tradecraft but their artistry, and enjoyed playing with them, sometimes pausing to scrutinize their characterisitics when others only wanted to execute the next step.

For Sexsmith a case was not an art form but a tool of battle whose sole function was to defeat or frustrate the other side. Sexsmith did not think in abstract terms. What he could not see, hear or smell did not exist and neither did the life of a case. Whereas Bennett saw a case as a skirmish in the wider war against Soviet Intelligence, Sexsmith saw each case as the war itself and prosecuted it for its own ends. He sought only to win the immediate encounter.

Bennett felt the Soviets dominated the various Satellite intelligence services and wanted to pool experiences and look for common practices. A bigger data sample would help sift out deception MO from genuine MO but the suggestion was turned down because each desk guarded its autonomy. Sexsmith on the Czech Desk, among others, wanted no interference in his bailiwick.

Sexsmith's career at headquarters had moved along normally until 1961 when a Russian scientist wanted to defect and Sexsmith seized the initiative to help him. That year a Soviet science delegation visited Canada and while passing through Ottawa Dr. Mikhail Klochko, a fifty-nine-year-old chemist who had won the Red Banner, the second highest award next to the Order of Lenin, told one of his contacts at the National Research Council he wanted to defect. The NRC had warned its employees not to encourage defections because they antagonized the Soviet Academy of Sciences and jeopardized future scientific exchanges. However, Klochko had planned his defection for five years and needed help at this critical moment, so the NRC scientist called the RCMP.

As soon as he received the tip, Charles Sweeny called an emergency meeting at his home on the late afternoon of August 15, 1961. In Sweeny's living room were Ross Booth of B Branch's Travel Desk, with the known information on all visiting Soviets; Don Atkinson, acting head of the Russian Desk while Bennett was on vacation; and Sexsmith, who had recently moved to the Russian Desk as a case officer. Bennett, called in from his holiday, joined the meeting late. The Soviet delegation of scientists, freshly arrived from Montreal, had booked into the Lord Elgin Hotel and would move next to Toronto. The Security Service had to act quickly and could not consult the pussyfooters at External Affairs for whom a defection only caused problems since the Soviets would inevitably protest with outlandish allegations. The meeting hesitated over what to do. It knew only that

Klochko reportedly wanted to defect. It did not know whether he shared a room and where the delegation's dreaded KGB SK (security) man was located. Bennett said he had a source in the NRC and phoned one of the interpreters who knew about the Klochko feeler. So did the senior officials at the NRC who had already warned the interpreter not to help the RCMP. Bennett persuaded the interpreter to drop by Sweeny's house where he explained the restrictions imposed on him. "Fair enough," said Sweeny, "but can you give us some idea of how he behaves and what room he is staying in? Can you give us any information at all?" The interpreter provided the room number and a physical description of Klochko and the important news that he spoke nearly perfect English, which simplified matters. For the next couple of hours he would be resting in his room, which he shared with another Soviet. The interpreter withdrew while Sweeny's group formulated an attack.

Sexsmith said they had to act immediately. Klochko's desire to defect had already spread to NRC officials and the ever-vigilant Soviets could soon find out, if they had not already. The presence of Klochko's roommate prevented the Security Service from simply knocking on his door. Sexsmith proposed walking into the hotel lobby and phoning Klochko's room, posing as an External Affairs' officer who needed to clear up a routine passport matter. He would invite him down to the lobby, spirit him away and then put him up in his own home. It was a bold attempt fraught with risks. The sophisticated Sweeny disliked the rawness of the plan but Bennett supported Sexsmith. Time was short and nobody had a better plan, so Sweeny approved it.

Klochko sighed with relief in the lobby when Sexsmith offered him asylum but said he first had to return to his room for some things. A few minutes later he appeared with a Trans Canada Airlines flight bag containing personal documents.

Klochko was a pure scientist with little information of interest to the Security Service. He represented a passing propaganda victory in the Cold War. After a few debriefing hours with the RCMP he was passed over to the scientific community for thorough questioning. Four months later another Soviet defected to the West, only this time one who came from the KGB itself, had carefully stored up secrets, which he now gave to the CIA. His cache of intelligence changed the course of the global espionage war and over the next decade made an impact on both the Security Service and Leslie James Bennett.

13

Operation Rock Bottom

A SHORT, STUNTED, rotund man in his thirties, with a moon face and heavy Russian jowls, appeared uninvited on the doorstep of the home of the CIA's Helsinki Station Chief in December, 1961. He brought documents and carried the name Klimov but that evening identified himself really to be Anatoli Golitsin, a KGB Major working out of the local Soviet Embassy. He wanted to defect.

The CIA reckoned that Golitsin could be a provocation agent passing false information to deceive and disrupt the KGB's biggest adversary, so at first it treated him warily. But soon his documents, phenomenal memory and knowledge of events behind the secret veil in Moscow convinced the Americans that he was genuine. Once in the United States, Golitsin's debriefing tied up CIA officers with details about the KGB for months. The wealth of material astounded everyone. Among many things, he alleged a Soviet agent code named Sasha had penetrated the CIA's operations in Germany and the ensuing investigation led to the dismissal of a contract employee named Igor Orlov. He warned of the "Ring of Five" in Britain and a year later the infamous mole Kim Philby fled to the Soviet Union. He pointed at the British Admiralty as a victim of KGB espionage and his clues started an investigation eventually unveiling John Vassall, a homosexual clerk acting as a Soviet agent ever since KGB blackmail had ensnared him during a posting in Moscow. Golitsin alleged KGB moles had penetrated France and Germany. He also had revelations about Canada.

Golitsin defected shortly before Christmas and around Easter two trusted representatives from Britain came to Ottawa and briefed the Security Service on a hush-hush eyes-only basis. Everything in counterespionage is automatically top secret but this message exceeded the normal strict standards. To avoid regular channels, the CIA tapped the services of the MI5 and MI6 officers helping debrief Golitsin since they were already travelling to Ottawa. With excitement, the two British officers revealed how Golitsin defected and had lifted the cover off the KGB. They explained that Golitsin had worked mostly in the KGB's Second Chief Directorate which, responsible for internal security, operated inside the Soviet Union against foreign missions, tourists and other visitors. The Second Chief Directorate had engineered some outstanding successes during the 1950s in blackmailing and co-opting foreigners to spy on their country. Meanwhile the First Chief Directorate, which conducted espionage abroad, had fallen short of its targets. The KGB had carried out a fullscale review of the techniques and records of all its directorates and transferred personnel from the successful Second Chief Directorate into the flagging First Chief Directorate. Golitsin, one of the officers parachuted in, had worked on the review and learned about many operations in many countries.

Golitsin, the British representatives said, brought with him a collection of assorted leads to Second Chief Directorate operations against the Canadian Embassy in Moscow, including a blackmail operation against a homosexual Canadian ambassador who had fallen into a sex trap. Golitsin could not identify the ambassador or pinpoint the time other than during the 1950s, or say whether he had succumbed, but he could say the trap had been planted. Suddenly, the Security Service had a major investigation to mount and Sweeny and Bennett wanted to flesh out further details from Golitsin himself. They were told they had to wait their turn, and that once the Americans and British were done with Golitsin, the French, Germans and Dutch waited in line. It was August 1962 before Sweeny and Bennett got their crack at Golitsin. Nevertheless, the delay didn't hold up Operation Rock Bottom, as the hunt for the unknown ambassador was called, because investigators first had to comb through nearly 500 files at External Affais to match up clues. By the time Sweeny and Bennett finally questioned Golitsin in a Washington D.C. safehouse, they fleshed out no additional leads.

Rock Bottom quickly focussed its suspicion on David Johnson,

Canada's ambassador to the Soviet Union from 1956 to 1960, since he had already been identified as a homosexual. Two years earlier he had been recalled from Moscow and summarily dismissed. Ironically, Johnson had precipitated his own exposure by the above-board manner in which he had handled one of his embassy clerks who had fallen into a KGB homosexual trap. The clerk voluntarily approached Johnson and confessed that he had been photographed in a compromising encounter with a Soviet male and was now being blackmailed. In 1960 homosexuality would see anyone promptly fired from the Canadian Civil Service but, rather than betray his country, the clerk reported everything to Ambassador Johnson. The clerk suspected the ambassador was a homosexual and thought he might react compassionately, but Johnson followed the book by returning the clerk to Canada for interrogation.

External Affairs did fire the clerk. The fact that he had been honest and loyal did not matter and neither did the fact that his voluntary disclosure had freed him from future blackmail, thus making him a good security risk—the department blindly fired all homosexuals. Yet despite his firing the clerk talked about his past, produced an address book and divulged every one of his many relationships stretching back to his years in Ottawa. Most of his partners were Ottawa civil servants, including some holding sensitive positions involving secret information that the KGB would want.

B Branch followed his leads and started interviewing his old lovers who in turn talked; soon the Security Service's investigation swept through the civil service like an epidemic. Homosexuals in government quivered about the prospect of discovery but, curiously, when interviewed, they never denied their homosexuality nor fought dismissal. They resigned meekly to save public exposure and during their confessions tattled on their lovers, producing more suspects, more interviews, more resignations, more confessions and yet more leads. One Security Service investigator says they could hardly stop their victims from talking. The investigation spilled into the local universities and out into the community at large. All government departments lost good servants but the major victims were External Affairs, the navy, and the top-secret CBNRC. The homosexual hunt soon grew administratively out of control as the number of files expanded into the thousands. By about 1962 B Branch could no longer afford the manhours and gave the investigation to a special homosexual investigation team in A Branch which in future informed B Branch of the cases with a counterespionage interest.

The External Affairs clerk who had ignited this purge also told the Security Service about his suspicions of Ambassador Johnson. The clerk said he had never had an affair with the ambassador but had heard his name through the network. So Johnson, who a week earlier had sent the clerk home, suddenly found himself flying back for interrogation. The ambassador admitted an ongoing relationship with one of his senior embassy officials, who was subsequently recalled and questioned, but said he had no relationships outside the embassy and had never been entrapped or blackmailed by the KGB. Both he and his lover promptly resigned.

When Rock Bottom reopened the Johnson file two years later, it was thought that Golitsin's leads belonged to him. But other than the fact that Johnson had been a homosexual ambassador to Moscow during the 1950s, the clues did not match up well. Further investigation suggested that the unidentified ambassador might be Johnson's predecessor, John Watkins, who was posted to Moscow from 1954 to 1956. If Watkins was the man it meant homosexuality had put two consecutive Canadian ambassadors to Moscow in trouble. Watkins had returned to become Assistant Undersecretary with External Affairs and now, as Rock Bottom was getting underway, was retiring to Paris. With two suspects and firm evidence against neither, the investigation soon stalled and seemed unresolvable until another defector fled to the west in the Fall of 1963.

Yuri Krotkov, touring Britain with a delegation of Soviet writers and artists, slipped out of his London hotel room and presented himself to British intelligence. A strikingly handsome man, Krotkov did not belong to the KGB staff. He was a writer who cooperated with the KGB as an agent mainly because his good looks and sophistication opened doors. The KGB used Krotkov's services in an intricate plot to strike up a friendship with Madame Dejean and seduce her into illicit love affair while a pair of inviting Soviet women did the same to her husband, Maurice Dejean, the ambassador from France. Although Krotkov failed to ensnare Madame Dejean, the women successfully enticed the ambassador. While working on Madame Dejean, Krotkov learned from KGB cohorts that they had another entrapment operation proceeding against the homosexual Canadian ambassador. Krotkov's story confirmed Golitsin's disclosure but Krotkov also had not been told the ambassador's name and did not know how the operation ended. But Krotkov could say the operation had been run directly from the top echelons of the KGB and that the ambassador had fallen into the trap. Furthermore, Krotkov placed the timing closer to Watkin's tour of duty than Johnson. So Krotkov had nudged the suspicion closer to Watkins but had not produced enough evidence for the Security Service to roust him out of retirement for an interrogation, especially since Watkins suffered from a heart condition.

Rock Bottom had run out of leads and it again appeared the mystery would go unresolved when the following year, 1964, produced a third defector bearing relevant information. Yuri Nosenko, a KGB captain, had been secretly passing information to the CIA from Moscow for nearly two years but while visiting Geneva as part of a delegation in February 1964 he suddenly skipped to the west. Like Golitsin, Nosenko had also spent time in the KGB's Second Chief Directorate and during the debriefing positively pinned down the elusive ambassador as Watkins. Nosenko said Nikita Khrushchev had half-openly mocked Watkins' homosexuality at a freewheeling dinner party at his Crimean dacha held in honour of External Affairs Minister Lester Pearson's visit in 1955. After many toasts the exuberant Khrushchev proposed a toast to women while noting that not everyone present loved women. Years later the incident was backed up by Pearson's posthumous memoirs which said: "As the evening went on the atmosphere became mellower and mellower. John Watkins, however, looked less and less happy." The CIA withheld Nosenko's identification of Watkins because it suspected the defector was a KGB plant dispatched to undermine Golitsin. The CIA did not pass along the lead until August and even then did not let anybody from Canada interview Nosenko.

By this time the Security Service had already ransacked External Affairs' filing system and read every dispatch Watkins ever wrote from Moscow and afterward, looking for evidence that he had been trying to steer Canadian policy toward a more pro-Soviet line. Rock Bottom wanted to compare his policy positions before and after he had been allegedly entrapped. The mass of the files overwhelmed the RCMP and really provided no firm evidence. The Security Service could resolve the matter only by going to Paris and confronting Watkins.

There was never any question that Bennett, the counterespionage guru, would lead the interrogation. The intrigue centred on the number-two interrogator backing up Bennett. Precedence demanded Lloyd Libke but a lot of people felt Sexsmith's experience and no-nonsense style suited him for this plum. Sexsmith a few years earlier seemed in line for the position as non-commissioned officer in charge of B Branch but had been pushed aside when the RCMP brought in Libke who had been working as the Commissioner's orderly. This time events upstaged Libke. Higgitt selected a junior and ambitious corporal named Harry Brandes who was a traditional conservative with a keen mind for counterespionage work.

Once in Paris, Bennett and Brandes headed directly to the Canadian Embassy and met Ambassador Jules Leger who, a decade later, would become Canada's twenty-first Govenor-General. Bennett and Brandes briefed him as head of the Canadian Mission but also sought him out because he was Watkin's friend and frequently invited him to the embassy and his home. Madame Leger was in some ways even closer. As Bennett outlined the reason for their trip and the allegations against Watkins, he tried to enlist Leger's help in urging Watkins to cooperate. The ambassador listened attentively and then said he could not believe Watkins would act disloyally.

"You've got no evidence he was recruited," said Leger.

"No, we haven't," acknowledged Bennett. "We just want to talk to him and find out what really happened and do a damage assessment. You can appreciate this."

Leger said that three months earlier Watkins had suffered a heart attack, still took medication and neither looked nor felt healthy. Bennett assured him they knew about his medical condition and would question him civilly and gently with due regard for his condition. Leger acted as though the matter should be dropped and Bennett reminded him the matter had to be investigated and, without his cooperation, he had no alternative but to approach Watkins on his own.

"Let me think about it," replied Leger. "It's a question of principle."

The next day Leger met Bennett and Brandes in a sidewalk cafe.

"Okay," he said, "I'm prepared to cooperate with what you have in mind."

Bennett said they could approach Watkins anywhere they wanted but felt the embassy made the best site.

"We want to do it with your full cooperation," said Bennett. "He at least then knows he can fall back on you if he needs some counsel and guidance."

By coincidence, Watkins had been invited that evening to a private dinner party at the embassy, and as he arrived Leger ushered him into his office where Bennett and Brandes waited. At sixty-two years, he looked frail.

"Look John," Leger told him, "we have some business from Canada. We have two people who want to talk to you and it would be appreciated if you would cooperate with them fully because they have a matter of national importance to discuss with you."

With that said, Leger stood up and left the office. Watkins recognized the purpose of their trip even before Bennett officially explained the reason. Only one thing could bring the RCMP all the way to Paris to see him. His face froze with a gaze of startled incredulity and his cheeks and forehead coloured slightly.

"If there's anything I can do to help," he replied weakly, "I will be only too happy to do so." They agreed to start discussions in the morning. Bennett suggested a location away from the embassy.

"It might be very embarrassing to be identified with us," he said. "We want to keep this private." Bennett told him he could consult Ambassador Leger or anybody else during the proceedings.

"No, I don't want to do that," Watkins replied. "It would really hurt them. It would really hurt them to know the details."

The next morning a car picked up Watkins at his apartment on the Left Bank and took him to a safehouse provided by the CIA. The proceedings started slowly; shame more than anything else seemed to hold Watkins back. His homosexuality embarrassed him deeply. Bennett gently led him through events and he acknowledged that he had engaged in liaisons with somebody evidently under KGB control and that he had failed to report them, but denied being blackmailed or having done anything to damage Canada's interest. The interrogators paced the questioning. Rushing things might produce pressure and incite a heart attack or provoke suicide. The Security Service needed him alive. If Watkins died, so would his account of events in Moscow. Still, they mounted a subtle form of pressure beneath the relaxed pace. Stacks of documents, piled conspicuously high, stared at Watkins. Watkins wondered how the RCMP found out and how much it knew, but the interrogators were not telling. They phrased the questions to suggest they knew a lot.

"It's very difficult for us to conduct this interview because it's going to be a long time before we're through," said Bennett, motioning toward the pile of documents. "We're not too happy about doing it here in France because the last thing we really want is to have the French Security Service find out what's really going on."

Bennett said the Canadian government would pay his travelling costs if he came to Ottawa but Watkins feared running into old friends, so declined. Bennett then suggested London and after thinking about it for a day he agreed.

London started off with a soccer match. The three, with the help of tickets from MI5, watched Arsenal play at Highbury Stadium. Watkins seemed to relax and enjoy the game. When questioning resumed in an MI5 safehouse, the growing bond between Bennett and Watkins put the former ambassador still more at ease. Bennett played the role of the nice guy while Brandes took the heavier part. When Brandes overreached, Bennett pulled him back and said, "Harry, let's slow down." With Brandes ready to pounce Watkins had an incentive to cooperate with Bennett.

Bennett and Brandes, one by one, reviewed the approximately 600 dispatches sent under Watkin's name from Moscow to Ottawa, putting each document under the microscope for evidence that he had acted as a Soviet agent of influence. They queried anything that could be interpreted as being soft on Russia. The process inched along slowly, Bennett insisting on preparing a precise damage-assessment report. Watkins needed to refresh his memory and often had to provide additional background to defend his actions. Sometimes a single document took an hour or more.

The interrogation was a trauma for Watkins but no picnic for Bennett and Brandes either. Each night they worked into the morning hours writing their daily report and feeding it to headquarters through a special communication link, and then they would prepare for another day. Headquarters expected a quick confession and had little understanding of the reams of material. Both Bennett and Brandes felt the pressure and wanted to continue the probe in Ottawa. Watkins still refused but after a week they convinced him to come to Montreal where he would encounter no old homosexual acquaintances. Watkins wrote relatives saying he was coming to Canada for some temporary consulting work with External Affairs.

Shortly after, the interrogation settled into a large suite at the Holiday Inn Chateaubriand in suburban Montreal, and the questioning focussed onto greater detail about homosexuality in Moscow. With Watkins relaxing more each day, details came out and when these were combined with those from Paris and London, the story emerged. Watkins, a most pleasant and erudite man, was a compulsive homosexual who never had a regular lover, even in Ottawa, despised his homosexuality but could not contain his lusts. He cruised Ottawa's gathering spots and sometimes made a wrong approach and got beaten up. He knew about KGB tactics and once posted to Moscow realized he could not cruise. Once, while walking in a park, he encountered a good opportunity for a liaison but sensed provocation and resisted.

His resolve weakened in the fall of 1954 during an extended trip through the Soviet Union's southern republics when in a Muslim area he met a young man, hardly in his twenties, named Kamahl. A clerk who worked on a farming cooperative, Kamahl's boyishness and innocence appealed to Watkins and, so far from Moscow, he thought it would be safe. After a sumptuous meal in the hotel dining room, he invited young Kamahl to his room. Evidently the hotel staff spotted the pair entering the room and a few months later Watkins received a letter from Kamahl saying he would be visiting Moscow for his first time and would appreciate being shown the city. Kamahl's visit had been staged by the KGB and by the time the kindly Watkins had entertained him and liaised with him—each time in Kamahl's hotel room—the KGB had all the photographs it needed. Kamahl returned home and Watkins never saw him again.

Now that the KGB had the goods, it had to exploit the situation carefully because at Watkin's level overreaching blackmail usually backfired. The KGB could afford to threaten a clerk or a security guard because failure would attract only a pro forma diplomatic rebuke from External Affairs. Moving upscale increased the rewards but dramatically boosted the risks and the penalty of failure. If Watkins reported the incident, the failed blackmail would disrupt every phase of Canadian-Soviet relations. Worse still, Watkins might take his life, leave a note that would devastate relations for years and focus world attention onto the unsavoury KGB. So the KGB had to blackmail

Watkins without being seen to blackmail him, which required gentleness. Rather than threaten Watkins, the KGB sought to envelope him in a debt of gratitude.

Bureaucratic Moscow suddenly opened its doors to Watkins. He enjoyed unparelleled access to top officials in the Soviet Foreign Ministry and received invitations to exclusive social functions that other western ambassadors could not get. The meetings and events were all choreographed by the KGB and many of the friendly officials were disguised KGB officers. Watkins did not know it but Oleg Gorbunov, his new senior contact in the Foreign Office was really Oleg Gribanov, a KGB man who held the number-two position in the Second Chief Directorate and was the mastermind of the operation against him. Anatoli Gromov, whom Watkins knew as a professor of International Relations, was Anatoli Gorsky, one of Gribanov's senior officials. While posted in London during the 1940s, Gorsky for a time had the dream assignment of directing Kim Philby for the KGB.

More than a year later, shortly before Watkins was scheduled to return to Ottawa in a senior post, the friendly Gribanov, still posing as the foreign office official Gorbunov, invited Watkins into his office and pretended to be troubled when Watkins arrived. Motioning to a closed file on his desk, he said the KGB had dug up an unpleasant and most unfortunate matter which he wished could be forgotten. Gribanov, who engineered the entrapment with Kamahl, cursed the KGB and expressed shock it could stoop to such base tactics. The matter now, he said, was causing him difficulty because the KGB wanted to exploit the situation. Gribanov told Watkins that fortunately he had managed to gain custody of the file and forced the KGB to back off. He promised that as long as he had anything to do with it, he would keep the KGB out.

The charade put Watkins into Gribanov's debt for the purpose of manipulation, while at the same time allowing the Soviets to finish his career anytime they wished, all orchestrated in such a delicate and positive manner that the Soviets could never be accused of blackmail. Khrushchev, at the famous dacha dinner party, had already gone to the brink with Watkins by announcing to his minister, Lester Pearson, that not everyone present loved women. Watkins realized his career depended on the goodwill of the Soviets. Even a drunken slip of the tongue could finish him.

Bennett grew up in a company-owned house near the top of Aberdare Valley in poverty-stricken Penrhiwceiber. His house (third from the left, between the two chimney stacks) overlooked a deep quarry and a set of railway tracks leading to the mine on the valley floor. (Photo taken in 1982 by Mark Budgen.)

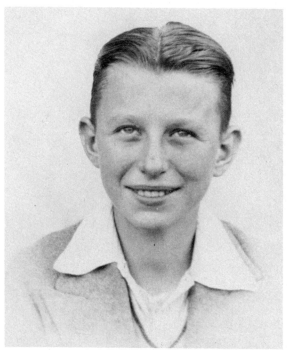

At the age of twelve, during the depth of the Depression, Bennett was a normal youngster in South Wales who played sports and routinely supported the Labour party. With the urging of his father, a mine worker, Bennett sought to escape life in the mines.

When World War Two broke out, Bennett volunteered for the Royal Corps of Engineers in hope of gaining professional experience but was rebuffed twice and later drafted and assigned to the Royal Corps of Signals. He learned Morse code and was sent to Malta as a radioman intercepting enemy wireless communications. This photo shows Bennett in 1942 at the age of 22.

Cedric Homer was Bennett's best friend during the Malta posting. Thirty years later, Bennett's interrogators would try to make a case that Homer had recruited him as a Soviet spy.

Malta gave Bennett his first promotion, rising from the bottom rank of signalman to Lance Corporal. It also transferred him from interception to intelligence. Bennett was transferred to Egypt shortly after this photo was taken.

Bennett in 1951 as an officer with Britain's civilian organization responsible for intercepting communications in the communist world. The previous year he had married a young caligraphist from the Australian intercept organization.

The RCMP Security Service in July 1953, one year before Bennett joined the organization. Sitting on the left end of the front row is Mark McClung, the civilian Research Director who first interviewed Bennett when he applied for a job. Terry Guernsey, the legendary head of B Branch (counterespionage), sitting next to McClung, hired Bennett as a research analyst. The man in the middle of the front row is George McClellan, the director of the organization. Second from the left in the second row is Phil Keeler, the RCMP's first watcher. Next to him is Charles Sweeny who ran double agent Gideon. In the middle of the row, fifth person from the right, is Henry Tadeson, one of the first Mounties on the Russian Desk and later head of B Branch.

Charles Sweeny in later years as an Assistant Commissioner in the police side of the RCMP. He was head of the Satellite Desk in 1958 when he played a pivotal role in discovering Mountie traitor Long Knife and inducing him to confess. Sweeny was head of B Branch in 1964 when he transferred out of the Security Service.

J. R. Lemieux was one of many policemen parachuted in as head of the Security Service. Lemieux realized he lacked counterespionage experience and usually kept hands off operations. However, he intervened once to introduce Long Knife to Operation Keystone and thereby set in motion an event that eventually led to betrayal and the death of the Security Service's top double agent. (Canapress photo, 1965.)

Cliff Harvison ran the Security Service less than a year but his ultimatum to Long Knife in 1955 played a key role in causing the indebted Long Knife to betray Operation Keystone to the KGB for money. Harvison became RCMP Commissioner in April, 1960. (RCMP photo.)

Fire completely gutted the Soviet Embassy on January 1, 1956. The building may have been saved but the Soviets waited nearly an hour before calling the fire department and even then barred access to the cipher room until secret documents were cleared away. (Ottawa *Citizen* photo.)

The following year the Russians built a new embassy on the same site which the Security Service tried to bug by placing microphones into the window frames at the back left corner. Most of the microphones worked well but the Soviets left the room empty which later caused suspicion that somebody inside the RCMP tipped them off. (Ottawa *Citizen* photo.)

A 1956 class from a security and intelligence course posing with the Security Service's senior officers. Dressed in a uniform in the middle of the front row is Joseph Brunet, who briefly headed up the Security Service. Next to him, from left to right, are Terry Guernsey, Charles Sweeny, and Bennett. Murray Sexsmith is standing at the right end of the second row. Sandy McCallum, the long-time head of the watcher service who eventually suspected a mole in the Service, is third from the left in the top row. (RCMP photo.)

W. L. "Len" Higgitt at the time that he succeeded Guernsey as head of B Branch in 1958. Higgitt made Bennett the head of the Russian Desk. He became Commissioner in 1969 and presided over the Force in 1972 when Bennett was interrogated as a suspected mole. (RCMP photo.)

This is one of the few photographs of Soviet scientist Mikhail Klochko who defected to Canada in August 1961. Klochko used this photo to help prove his importance to the Security Service. He is standing beside an unidentified woman and Premier Chou En Lai of China. Klochko's defection was a feather in the cap of Murray Sexsmith. (Ottawa *Citizen* photo.)

A June 1963 training class that Bennett lectured to. In the middle of the front row are the Security Service's four most senior officers: Charles Sweeny (fourth from left); William Kelly, the Director; Bing Miller; and (wearing glasses) Henry Tadeson. Second from the right is Reg McKernan who handled agent Aquavit in Operation Top Hat and who in Operation Apple Cider suspected Soviet agent Rudolph Kneschke in his Vancouver radio–TV repair shop. Next to McKernan, at the end of the row, is Henry Robichaud, Long Knife's surveillance partner in the 1950s. (RCMP photo.)

George Victor Spencer was a pathetic, disturbed, and maligned old man and exactly the type the KGB could use and trust as an errand runner. The Vancouver postal clerk worked tirelessly and never complained about his assignments yet the Soviets dropped him soon after the RCMP secretly discovered his activity. (Canapress photo.)

Vasily Tarasov, a KGB officer posing as an Izvesetia correspondent being escorted by three Mounties into RCMP's A Division headquarters. Tarasov had recruited a civil servant in the patent office who reported everything to the Security Service. Tarasov was arrested on April 27, 1954, in the act of accepting classified documents. He was expelled from Canada. (RCMP photo.)

John Watkins, Canada's ambassador to Moscow, was ensnared in the KGB homosexual sex plot. Watkins kept the incident secret for eight years until he was gradually exposed in the early 1960s by three Soviet defectors. He was interrogated by Bennett and died of a heart attack as the questioning was ending. (CP photo.)

William Kelly, the aggressive director of the Security Service in the mid-1960s. His policy of publicly expelling Soviet embassy staff members caught in acts of espionage is believed to have made Soviet Intelligence officers jumpy. (Jon Joosten photo.)

Bower Featherstone sitting in an Ottawa courtroom awaiting a jury verdict in April 1967 for violating the Official Secrets Act. The 27-year-old civil servant was convicted for one count and sent to prison. (Ottawa *Citizen* photo.)

The Watcher Service discovered Featherstone by setting a surveillance trap on Soviet Military Attache Eugeni Kourianov in Operation Gold Dust. Kourianov led the Security Service to a clandestine meet with Featherstone near Ottawa's Elmvale Shopping Centre. Kourianov soon returned to Moscow and the Soviets never again contacted Featherstone which caused some insiders to wonder whether somebody had betrayed the case.

Anatoli Golitsin defected from the Soviet embassy in Helsinki in December 1961. A Major in the KGB, he brought with him a wealth of information. He also claimed the Sino-Soviet split was a KGB hoax designed to fool the West and that a KGB mole had penetrated the CIA. The Americans virtually tore apart the CIA but found nobody. An artist drew this sketch in 1981 from a description of Golitsin as he was in the 1960s. (Artist: Gordon Suckling, Australian Broadcasting Commission.)

John Starnes, the civilian Director-General of the Security Service who for two years presided over an intensive internal investigation into Bennett. Although the investigation found no proof of disloyalty, Starnes decreed that Bennett could not remain in the Security Service. (Ottawa *Citizen* photo.)

Murray Sexsmith never hesitated to express his opinions, even when he was junior to Bennett. Later he was promoted above his old boss and led the hunt for the KGB mole. Sexsmith interrogated Bennett for five days and came to believe he was innocent. Sexsmith is shown here in 1978 shortly after he was transferred out of the Security Service. (RCMP photo.)

After his departure from the Security Service in 1972, Bennett eventually settled in Perth Australia and went into semi-retirement. It would be only a matter of time before public exposure disturbed his peaceful existence. For a while he maintained he had retired for medical reasons but eventually acknowledged that he had been investigated as a mole suspect. He insisted vehemently that he was loyal and the victim of a KGB frame-up. (Canapress photo.)

Gribanov sought Watkins not as an espionage agent but as an agent of influence. Any clerk, security guard or cipher clerk would betray secrets. Somebody like Watkins could use his high post to nudge Canadian policy away from the United States and toward the Soviet Union. After Gribanov had finished bragging about keeping the KGB away from him, he implied Watkins could return the friendship back in Ottawa. He said Dimitri Chuvakhin, the Soviet Ambassador to Canada, had a difficult job and needed help. "Be friendly to Chuvakhin," counselled Gribanov. "Be friendly to Chuvakhin" became the code phrase warning Watkins to cooperate.

During the interrogation Watkins acknowledged the Soviets had tried to squeeze him and admitted he had withheld it from his superiors. He described Gribanov's and Gorsky's soft recruitment tactics in detail but denied succumbing to them. Bennett and Brandes studied Watkins's record as Assistant Undersecretary and found no pattern favouring the Soviet Union. In fact, it was during Watkins's tenure that External Affairs imposed a ceiling on the size of the Russian Embassy, and arbitrarily cut back, by seven, the number of Russians in the establishment. Watkins also turned down requests for more liberal diplomatic travel restrictions. He could have cut out visa processing for Soviet diplomats but did not. The Soviets pushed for a consulate in Toronto but that too was shot down. His record showed no sign of favouritism either to Soviet diplomats or to Soviet foreign policy. If he was an agent of influence he failed to deliver when the Russian needed him the most.

Watkins realized his predicament and upon returning to Ottawa protected himself by cutting all ties with Soviet diplomats. He felt the Soviets could not pressure him if they could not meet him. He attended none of their social functions and sent underlings to conduct business with them. He could not "be friendly to Chuvakhin" because Chuvakhin found him impossible to see.

It was conceivable that Watkins could be lying or exaggerating the extent of his resolution. Maybe more had happened than he acknowledged. Bennett and Brandes wondered about that and tried to trip him up but eventually they were convinced that he told the truth on all the important matters, and Watkins's accumulated dispatches from three years in Moscow verified his statements. At the time Watkins's dispatches had delighted his superiors for their literary beauty and perceptions of Soviet society. He would have excelled as a high-class travel writer, and his dispatches, which were often twenty pages long, captured the workings of the Soviet system. Now nearly a decade later, pulled out of a filing cabinet and subjected to hard-nosed scrutiny, his reports impressed the interrogators as well. But the dispatches' completeness rather than their beauty impressed Bennett and Brandes more. Watkins had written prolifically, almost compulsively, and reported everything. He had described every encounter in Moscow, including each meeting with Gribanov and Gorsky, and recounted the discussion. The only thing he had withheld was the homosexuality and its resulting complications. Watkins had even reported his encounters with Kamahl and described him as a young man with certain reservations about the Soviet system, omitting only the sexual aspect of their relationship. The interrogators used this mass of detail as a reference guide to check the claims Watkins now made ten years later and found they held up. They concluded that the KGB blackmail attempt had failed.

"John, you don't seem to be taking as many tablets as you should," said Bennett referring to his heart condition.

"Oh," he replied, "I don't really need them. I have been taking the ones that matter."

The interrogation was winding down. During one of their strategy sessions Brandes told Bennett he had a hunch more lay behind Watkins's page-and-a-half description of his encounter with a lyric poet he visited at a vineyard on a festive occasion in the Soviet Republic of Uzbek on that fateful southern tour in 1954. They had already questioned Watkins twice about the poet and Watkins had discussed him reluctantly so Brandes wanted one more try. "Okay," said Bennett, "fling it at him again." On the morning of October 12, 1964, under some prodding, Watkins admitted engaging in buggery with the Uzbek poet as a result of overdrinking and curiosity about the region's homosexual customs. He said he had withheld the affair from them because their meeting had been a one-shot encounter which the KGB never exploited and maybe did not even know about. Watkins viewed his homosexuality as a sickness and tried to minimize it whenever he could.

Divulging the truth about the Uzbek poet lifted his spirits and he behaved as if rescued from his last secret. After finishing a light lunch he complained of slight pain in his upper arms and chest. This had often plagued him after meals so it did not worry his interrogators, but as a precaution they advised him to rest in his room. After a nap he returned at mid-afternoon for another two hours of questioning. The trio then broke for a leisurely dinner together in the hotel dining room. After finishing his filet mignon, Watkins again felt the same pains and on advice returned to his room for more rest but he returned an hour later. For practical purposes the interrogation had exhausted itself with Watkins's admission that morning about the Uzbek poet. Virtually no lead had remained unprobed and the two interrogators felt satisfied that they had extracted almost everything. They were merely reworking a few questions while waiting for the CIA to relay Golitsin's final assessment. If the CIA had no more questions the interrogation was finished.

Watkins sat in a quiet reflective mood in the room's single cushioned chair while Bennett and Brandes sat before him in hard chairs. Watkins was reminiscing about his diplomatic career and talking about some of the people he met and while reaching for a cigarette gasped suddenly and froze with his chin pointing slightly up. The interrogators instantly suspected the calamity they feared most: a heart attack. It struck so quietly and with such swiftness it seemed anticlimatic. They jumped up. Bennett grabbed his pulse, feeling nothing, while Brandes pumped his chest. They next telephoned for help and two plainclothes St. Laurent detectives arrived, followed by two police ambulance attendants who told them it was too late. Watkins had died instantly.

The Security Service could take small solace in the fact that the heart attack had felled him after the story had come out and not struck in France or Britain where official explanations would have complicated the affair. As it was, Gus Begalki, the senior non-commissioned officer in the Security Service's Montreal office, visited the St. Laurent police station and convinced the chief to hush up the incident on the grounds that the dead man had exposed some KGB operating methods and publicity about his death would alert the KGB which could take countermeasures to nullify the intelligence. The coroner treated it as a routine heart attack and performed no autopsy. The coroner's report listed Brandes as the only witness and described him as a friend.

The attack on Canadian embassy personnel in Moscow did not concentrate wholly on homosexuals. Operation Broken Arrow in the late 1950s revealed that heterosexuals made good targets too, as long as they could be induced into doing something they had reason to hide. Roy Guindon worked as a security guard and through the KGB's manipulation met seductress Larissa Dubanova and fell deeply in love. Lara satisfied his desires and then broke the news she was pregnant. Now Guindon was in trouble with Soviet law and had no diplomatic immunity to fall back on, but the KGB came to his rescue by arranging a marriage. The marriage had to be kept secret from the Canadian embassy, which promptly recalled personnel who married Soviet citizens. Guindon did not want to risk losing Lara. A few months later Lara suffered a "miscarriage." Guindon did not know it but Lara had never been pregnant. Under KGB control, she fabricated the claim to push him into the secret marriage which was as phony as the pregnancy but which, in Guindon's eyes, made him subject to blackmail. Guindon apparently felt at first he could ride it out and satisfy the KGB without harming his country, but soon found himself fulfilling the KGB's demands.

As night security guard, Guindon could open virtually every embassy safe and as relief cipher clerk, knew the codes and had access to the cable traffic with Ottawa. While on duty alone he planted bugs in the embassy walls and carried on unhampered until posted to Warsaw where he continued his work. The Soviets sent Lara on visits and Guindon continued acting as an agent in Warsaw and in his next posting to Tel Aviv. However, surveillance by the Israeli service intercepted a meet with his Soviet controller. Responsible for External Affairs' worst known security breach, Guindon suffered a fate no worse than the honest homosexual clerk who confessed his entrapment and remained loyal. He was allowed to resign because the Department of Justice felt it could not get a conviction. To diminish his treachery, Guindon at first claimed he had recently been recruited in Tel Aviv and the interrogators had to drag the truth out of him. The Department of Justice concluded the duress and the interrogators' failure to take standard police precautions killed the chance for a conviction. When Golitsin defected in 1961 he brought with him the story of Broken Arrow and the CIA passed it along, but by this time the Security Service had already rolled up Guindon.

Golitsin knew more Canadian cases than Rock Bottom and Broken Arrow. He revealed that an operation had been mounted against two female embassy staffers in the mid-1950s. While the Canadian women had been picnicking within the travel-free zone outside Moscow, two handsome young Russians invited them to their dacha and entertained them well and wholesomely. However the young women got suspicious when they later tried to parlay the encounter into friendship. The ambassador instructed them to stay clear of the Russians and consequently the KGB operation died. Since it had been reported at the time, the Security Service knew about this incident years before Golitsin told of it.

Golitsin passed along word that a Communist Party of Canada official had visited Moscow in 1952 and while there was rewarded with a wristwatch for services rendered the Soviet Union. He did not know the Canadian's name or what services earned him the reward, but through investigation the Security Service concluded the official was Grif, the Toronto talent spotter in Operation Keystone who set up Green, the Avro employee, for his recruitment as an agent. The KGB awarded Grif his watch prior to Operation Keystone so it must have been thanking him for earlier favours. By the time Golitsin made his disclosure, Grif had long been exposed as an agent through Keystone. So he too was not new.

Golitsin had one last lead for Canada and this time the Security Service knew nothing about it. Golitsin alleged somebody in External Affairs had been recruited by the KGB while posted in Moscow during the 1950s and for all he knew still operated within the Canadian foreign service as a functioning agent. It sounded ominous but he knew no more. He had no name or time of recruitment and could not say whether he had been recruited through a sexual relationship. All Golitsin could offer was the KGB's Russian-language code name for the case. Try as it did, the Security Service could not flesh out the alleged agent. The lead was simply too slim.

For all the sensation caused in other countries, Golitsin's revelations had affected Canada very little. He had initiated Rock Bottom but his fragments could not resolve the case—he could not even provide the KGB's code name for the case—and finally other defectors broke it open. He revealed Broken Arrow (and gave a wrong lead that could have misdirected an investigation) but after it was already rolled up. He told about the homosexual clerk and also the two women out on the picnic, but the Security Service already knew about both. His story about the wristwatch reward in Moscow was new to the Security Service but the agent had already been identified. The External Affairs' recruitment was new in all respects but practically meaningless since Golitsin did not provide enough information to uncover the agent—if he existed. Golitsin revealed a mine of valuable information about general KGB policy and tradecraft which taught the Security Service many things, yet, when put together, Golitsin's disclosures about the KGB's Canadian operations told the Security Service relatively little. But Golitsin had not yet finished with Canada. He would have more to say...at a later date.

14

Gathering Suspicion

EVER SINCE IT was established in the mid-1950s, the observation post covering the Soviet embassy had complained about the big maple tree blocking its view. The obstructing tree stood behind the wrought iron fence squarely on the embassy's diplomatically protected property so not a soul—not the Security Service, the Canadian government nor the City of Ottawa—could legally touch it. The Watcher Service, which ran the observation post, concluded that the tree had to come down in the interest of national security and in early 1960s started searching for ways to kill it clandestinely. Through the CBNRC and its connection with the National Research Council, the Watcher Service discovered chemical tablets that thrown on the ground during a rainstorm would poison the nuisance tree to death. The tablets worked brilliantly during a trial operation in the Gatineau Hills, killing the intended target and several surrounding maples, so during the following spring thaw the Watchers tossed tablets into the snow beneath the Soviet tree at night and waited for results. But rather than die, the tree flourished and grew leaves as big and plentiful as the previous year.

At first the Watcher Service felt that perhaps the water from the spring thaw had diluted the poison, so they tried again, but still the stubborn maple refused to succumb. Then they furtively drilled liquid poison directly into the stump until it finally worked. A windstorm eventually blew the three over.

From the beginning the Security Service realized that the Soviets would suspect foul play and plant a new tree but still it expected to have an unimpeded view at least while the young tree matured. On cue, the Soviets replaced the dead tree but to the Watcher Service's disappointment they planted one just large enough to block the observation post's line of sight. All the conniving had gone for naught and the tree incident became a symbol for the Security Service's seeming impotence against the KGB. Like the coyote flubbing his attacks on the defiant roadrunner, whatever the Security Service did failed to defeat, much less faze, the Soviets.

Alarmed gossip swept through the fourth-floor hallways at headquarters when Kim Philby defected to Russia in 1963. Philby originally fell under suspicion in 1951 when his partners, Guy Burgess and Donald Maclean, dashed madly for Moscow. But nobody could prove anything against Philby, so after an interrogation, MI6's liaison officer to the CIA and FBI was allowed to resign. Twelve years later, the British investigation closed in on him and, one step before arrest, Philby also fled to Moscow. A non-commissioned officer sitting in one of the many little groups discussing the news burst forth with the observation that Bennett was British and probably a spy too. The speculation slipped through offhandedly in a tone of resignation and nobody, not even the maker, really believed it. Neither did it shock anyone. And nobody challenged or reprimanded him for questioning the loyalty of his boss.

The Security Service's counterespionage cases had not fared well but few Mounties in B Branch knew enough to realize it, and nobody had the feeling an insider might be betraying the organization. When a case fell apart the men reacted not with alarm but with puzzlement about the operation's ultimate purpose. Cases moved slowly so people never knew whether operations had failed or merely slowed down.

Philby's defection showed proof that the KGB had penetrated the top ranks of one of the world's premier espionage services and the experience seeped into the Security Service's consciousness and started Mounties thinking that maybe it could happen in Canada too. Over the next few years pockets of Mounties questioning the reasons for the RCMP's lack of success formed across the country. Vancouver, which always distrusted headquarters and had been the loser of several major cases as well as some minor ones, started wondering first. Everything that went to headquarters went wrong, they concluded. After visiting

Ottawa, some investigators returned saying the fault must be Bennett. Vancouver, which took orders from 3,000 miles away, was alienated and Bennett, the non-Mountie who gave the orders, made a good target. Even Mounties in Montreal and Toronto occasionally vented their frustration: "It must be Bennett"—not differentiating between Bennett the suspect and Bennett the whipping-boy. Sometimes the Ottawa division, not much more than a long shadow from head-quarters, grumbled about the uselessness of their efforts. "Are we really that bad?" they murmured over a beer, "Or is something else happening?" They realized they were semi-amateurs with half-baked resources and half-hearted government support fighting trained and equipped professionals backed by the determination of a totalitarian state. So the odds conspired against them, and plausible explanations could account for their failures: lack of skill, experience and manpower, as well as rigid police thinking. Still the results seemed too lopsided. Even last-place teams win a few games. The Security Service seemed to win nothing. They acknowledged they were bad, but not that bad. Besides, the KGB bungled too and that alone should give them the odd success.

At first it was only a minority who did the questioning. Most Mounties plugged along oblivious to the failures, which were hard to notice for a single non-commissioned officer following orders. And regional separation made it difficult to get a complete picture; Van-couver did not know what Toronto was doing and could not compare its Apple Cider or Moby Dick failures with Toronto's Blue Skies. Even within a division the high standard of security within the secret service suppressed knowledge of the failures. So with only slivers of evidence, suspicion formed slowly and collected mainly in the minds of brighter, well-positioned Mounties and, the RCMP being a para-military organization, never filtered up to the commissioned ranks in the beginning years. But gathering suspicion could not remain static forever. As it accumulated, somebody eventually had to move it upstairs and in the mid-1960's it happened, coming, ironically, not from a hawkish outpost like Vancouver but from one of Bennett's lieutenants at headquarters.

Staff Sergeant Don Atkinson joined B Branch the same year Bennett did and worked continuously on the Russian Desk. He started out in charge of the GRU sub-desk and transferred to the KGB side and by the mid-1960s became the non-commissioned officer in charge of B Branch and in some ways operated as Bennett's righthand man. A thoughtful person who avoided the pranks and inane banter of the bullpen, Atkinson mulled over problems quietly and shed his police background quickly. Everybody realized the Security Service's biggest cases had not developed but they also thought that some of the smaller cases had worked out successfully. Indeed the Security Service over the years had uncovered espionage operations and had investigated them and expelled Soviet Intelligence Officers. But Atkinson realized the Security Service could win an expulsion and lose the case. The Security Service sometimes resorted to expulsions as a last resort to salvage something out of a case that otherwise produced nothing. According to Atkinson, success required fooling the Soviets long enough to discover their objectives and possibly uncover other agents. None of the Security Service's cases could make such a claim.

From his vantage point on the Russian Desk, Atkinson saw more than the other NCOs did and noticed that when small, mundane cases were excluded, the Security Service's record against Soviet intelligence amounted to consistent failure featuring a disturbing pattern. All the failures followed a similar course. The Russian Desk would discover a case bursting with promise and under Bennett's direction let it run, hoping to follow it into the KGB's illegal residency. The case at first met expectations but soon slowed down and eventually dragged and sputtered and then fizzled out entirely. Even the fizzling deceived the Security Service into holding back until the death grew so cold it complicated the eventual post mortem. Why had the KGB killed the cases so tenderly? The KGB seemed reluctant, almost afraid, to let the Security Service know. If a well-placed mole was telling Moscow everything, the KGB had to protect the mole. It could not cut off a case without first assessing the impact on the safety of the mole. So the KGB would have to fool the Security Service by deceitfully running cases it knew were decoys. The KGB could not afford to chop operations, it had to phase them out slowly and let time mask the failure. Viewed in this light, the KGB's behaviour made perfect sense.

A decade of observation from elbow's length had taught Atkinson a few things about Bennett. When Bennett rambled about his childhood, especially over a drink, he kept returning to the theme of how his leftist background could have recruited him to the other side. His reminiscences carried the tone of "there but for the grace of God go I." As Bennett recapitulated his record of anti-communist service Atkinson wondered why he felt compelled to justify his background.

Atkinson wondered about the incredibly long hours that Bennett worked. Members of the Security Service believed their functions carried a special responsibility and contributed free time when the RCMP paid no overtime, but Bennett's performance far exceeded even this heightened call of duty. An eight-hour day could not handle Bennett's self-imposed work load so he expanded his daily office schedule to ten and, when necessary, twelve hours or more. He often returned to the office in the evenings and frequently popped in on weekends. Work overburdened Bennett because he insisted on knowing everything. Each detail and telex flowed across his desk and he did not go home until he read them all. Bennett almost seemed afraid something might slip past without his knowledge. A conscientious mole would want to know everything for his own survival and in the early days when the organization had no internal security system his evening and weekend forays into the office opened the filing system to him.

Atkinson could not understand Bennett's passion about penetration, and in fact regarded it an obsession that did not feel right. It made no sense unless he had an axe to grind. Bennett preached penetration when the major penetrations of the western services had not been uncovered—except for France—and when few people were thinking in those terms. He figured that Bennett, if a mole, would realize that consistent betrayal, no matter how carefully done, would over the years leave an inevitable trail and eventually arouse suspicion. A mole would constantly worry about leaving evidence and probably perceive a bigger threat than existed and try in advance to deflect suspicion by warning lethargic colleagues about the perils of Soviet infiltration so that when the suspicion finally arrived his roused colleagues would say: "He was right." The organization would fall into line behind his efforts to root out the mole. If the mole led the mole hunt, he could, with the help of KGB deception, manipulate the investigation in the wrong direction, thus not only prolonging treachery, but tying up the organization in knots and allowing the hunt to uproot some of the best people.

The theory fit, except for one thing. Atkinson could not reconcile Operation Keystone with the rest of his evidence. Keystone's demise held no mystery. The case had succumbed to simple betrayal which had been exposed. The failure defied the pattern. Atkinson grappled with the inconsistency, and then, *Eureka*, the answer flashed out. Bennett had betrayed Gideon at the outset and later fingered Long Knife to take the rap. It made perfect sense, especially for somebody as bright as Bennett. If Bennett was a mole he would be looking for somebody to shoulder the suspicion for Keystone's failure and who better than Long Knife who was vulnerable?

According to Atkinson's theory, once the KGB discovered Gideon's defection to the RCMP, it would deperately want to recall him to Moscow but could not do so without jeopardizing Bennett. Only a handful of people worked in B Branch in the mid-1950s and a rash move could precipitate an internal investigation that could root out Bennett in days. The KGB could not risk losing a mole with such access. But neither could it leave Gideon alone, for the KGB was vengeful and insisted on punishing its own traitors. It had to find a way of terminating the case and recovering Gideon without endangering Bennett, so it had to contrive circumstances to shift the blame away from Bennett and onto a straw man. The KGB had done this sort of thing before. With his problems, Long Knife made a perfect scapegoat, but first he had to be talent-spotted and only the real mole could do that. Who was Bennett's best friend in the Security Service? — Long Knife. Who would know about Long Knife's financial vulnerability? — Bennett. When Long Knife's indebtedness grew desperate and he had nowhere to turn, Bennett could tell the KGB to recruit him and Ostrovsky could offer Long Knife a bundle of cash with a virtual guarantee of success. Once Long Knife had been recruited, the KGB would wait for his debts to accumulate and expose his treachery. If Long Knife was a fall guy, it explained why Keystone broke the pattern.

Atkinson jotted onto a notepad the reasons he thought Bennett was a spy: radical youth, his obsession with penetration, his penchant for hard work, the case failures and the Long Knife set-up theory. Staff Sergeant Sandy McCallum walked into Atkinson's office to tell him the Soviets seemed to be anticipating the tactics of his Watcher Service. McCallum ran the Watcher Service and helped devise some innovative techniques which the Soviets now seemed to foresee. Something was wrong, McCallum said. "I think our problem is that we've got a god damn spy," shot back Atkinson, "and I think that spy is Jim

Bennett." McCallum, standing, leaned over with both hands on Atkinson's desk: "You've now voiced what's been on my mind for a long time." The words had been spoken—in headquarters—and by two of the most capable and senior NCOs in the branch. McCallum sat down to pursue the matter but such discussion was so unusual and explosive that neither said very much.

NCOs could do little by themselves so Atkinson decided to test his theory on Murray Sexsmith who had been freshly made a commissioned officer. Sexsmith listened carefully and had only one comment: Long Knife's confession said he approached Ostrovsky and not the other way around. If Long Knife took the initiative, Bennett could not have set him up. It was the one big flaw in Atkinson's theory and caused him so much trouble he tore up his piece of paper. Gut feelings alone could not carry the case and it was not something one advanced frivolously, so Atkinson dropped the matter and retired a few years later not knowing that Long Knife would ultimately change his confession to say that Ostrovsky had indeed approached him.

As Atkinson tore up his list in 1966 another counterespionage case against the KGB was failing in a manner nobody could call subtle.

15

Operation
Gold Dust

ON FEBRUARY 13, 1966, a cold Sunday, an on-duty Watcher dropped
by Sandy McCallum's home in Ottawa's Alta Vista area and announced
excitedly, "We've got a live one." McCallum jumped into the Watcher's
car to see for himself. McCallum normally ran the Watcher Service
from behind a desk but the organization had scored a hit five minutes
from his home and was parading its triumph to the boss. He arrived at
the Elmvale Shopping Centre and captured a brief glimpse of Eugeni
Kourianov, a GRU agent-running officer listed as an Attaché, strolling
in the cold with an unidentified young man. The two talked earnestly
and the Watchers earlier saw them pass a white piece of paper back and
forth. After forty minutes they parted. Kourianov boarded a west-
bound city bus and the unidentified male hitchhiked north along St.
Laurent Boulevard. The Watchers dropped Kourianov who now held
little interest for them and followed the hitchhiker home, identifying
him as Bower Featherstone, a 26-year-old printer in the mapping
section of the Department of Mines and Technical Resources.

The Watcher Service got to know Featherstone well over the next
few months and under the code name Operation Gold Dust followed
him everywhere while bugs from the CIA recorded even arguments
with his wife. The Security Service surreptitiously searched Featherstone's locker at work each Sunday but found nothing suspicious and
after several defeats rummaged through all the lockers before discovering inside another locker a handwritten note within a plastic jar placing

194

the next meet on Sunday, March 27, at the corner of Shillington Avenue and King Street on the west side of town. The locker, according to department records, belonged to nobody but the investigators assumed Featherstone was using it to store his espionage-related material and that the note with the instructions was the piece of paper Kourianov had exchanged with him that Sunday morning.

Operation Gold Dust dug into Featherstone's background and pieced together evidence of how a seemingly normal civil servant had turned into a Soviet agent. Before long the investigation uncovered information that Featherstone enjoyed wagering at the race track and lost more than he won. When the horses did not race in Ottawa he sometimes took his money to Montreal. He supplemented his civil service income by working as part-time caretaker in his small apartment building. Featherstone lived in suite number one. Occupying suite number five was a Soviet embassy employee named Vladimir Barteniev who befriended him, sensed his financial plight and offered thirty-five dollars each time he collected a letter on his behalf. Whenever Featherstone received an envelope addressed to him with the words "Ottawa, Ontario" underlined in red ink he passed it along unopened and collected his reward. For a financially strapped man it represented a minor stroke of luck. Barteniev soon moved out of the building and turned him over to Kourianov. Featherstone, who did not know what a live letter box was, much less suspect he was being made into one, suspected nothing at first and realized he had become an agent only after it was too late. By this time he was meeting Kourianov clandestinely.

In the following weeks Featherstone received two mail drop letters with a Cornwall, Ontario postmark and later checks of the second locker turned up two identical copies of a confidential marine chart showing shipwrecks off the coast of Newfoundland and a non-classified geo-chemical map of the district surrounding Keno Hill in central Yukon. William Kelly, the Director of the Security Service, decided not to let the case run further and ordered Featherstone arrested on the spot at the next meet if he passed classified material to Kourianov. Kelly thought there was no point in letting the case continue if he was passing secrets.

As anticipated, Featherstone left his apartment on March 27 and took evasive action on route to Shillington and King. Security Service investigators in a nearby house watched him arrive and pace up and down the blocks a few times while waiting for Kourianov. But Kourianov failed to appear and after forty minutes Featherstone gave up and left. Although the Soviets usually adhered scrupulously to their meets, Kourianov's absence did not alarm the investigators at the time. Later Featherstone filled a dead letter box near Riverside Drive and Brookfield and signalled the loading by turning sideways a triangular step on a wood telephone pole at Gilmour and Metcalfe several miles away. The Watcher Service waited for a chance to identify the Soviet embassy official unloading the dead letter box but nobody went near it. The material sat there untouched. It seemed the Soviets had abandoned Featherstone.

That summer, with his normal term in Ottawa less than half completed, Kourianov returned to Moscow for a holiday and did not return. The embassy never attempted to re-contact Featherstone. Hardly in the history of the Security Service had the Soviets dropped a compromised case so suddenly.

By the fall, with not a stir from the Soviets, and now no doubt in anybody's mind that the case had died prematurely, and with no operation left to run, Kelly turned the evidence over to the government for prosecution under the Official Secrets Act. The Security Service never doubted that Featherstone had passed information to the Soviets but lacked proof because there had been no more meets. Only one piece of evidence linked Featherstone to the second locker and it was the result of Featherstone's own carelessness. A bottle of Heet body linament with a unique stain on the cork, photographed earlier in Featherstone's assigned locker, showed up later in the other locker. This single strand tied Featherstone to a case, already weak. The prosecution sighed with relief when Featherstone's lawyer conceded the second locker belonged to his client. With that battle won the prosecution never needed to introduce as evidence the bottle of Heet. A jury of eleven men and one woman declared Featherstone not guilty of retaining two naval charts prejudicial to the safety of the state but convicted him for obtaining the two charts and the judge sentenced him to two and a half years in prison.

While the Security Service's cases usually withered away into gradual nothingness, Gold Dust had been chopped unabashedly. Maybe Kelly's decision to arrest Featherstone at the next meet forced the

GRU's hand. Kourianov had diplomatic immunity so he would be released within hours of the arrest but photographers would be snapping pictures and newspaper headlines would describe the GRU being caught redhanded. Later Featherstone's trial would rekindle the fire again. As it dragged through the courts, newspaper stories would remind the Canadian public each day of the evils of Soviet intelligence. Years earlier the GRU had chopped the Ranov operation on the day of the intended arrest. If the Soviets knew about Featherstone's arrest it did not seem to be the first time in recent months they had successfully anticipated the Security Service. As McCallum had told Atkinson, the Russians seemed to have an uncanny knack for knowing what the Watcher Service was doing.

Ever since 1954 when ordinary-looking civilians started replacing Mounties on the streets, the Watcher Service grew into a crack surveillance unit, although the change from the buckshot days of Long Knife did not occur like magic. Mountie heads such as Hank Tadeson and Robbie Robertson laboured with the civilians to hone their skills in the art of following a target clandestinely. Patrolling in radio-controlled teams of six cars with two watchers per car, the Watcher Service seemed to jump ahead of the Soviets for a time in the late 1950s but the advantage lasted only until the early 1960s when both the KGB and GRU rebounded with new forms of countersurveillance. Soviet countersurveillance had always used crude traps of some sort: the Soviets would stop at green lights to see who else stopped or boarded a subway train and jumped out seconds before the doors snapped shut. But by the 1960s the Soviets' new traps were so sophisticated that the watchers might fall into them and become exposed without ever knowing it.

A Soviet intelligence officer would set a trap by driving over bridges, through railway crossings, through greenbelts and any other traffic artery without secondary streets. If the surveillance target crossed a river on the only bridge for miles around, the Watcher Service had to come off side roads and onto the same bridge in order to maintain surveillance. As the watchers would be slipping across the bridge behind the target, a Soviet countersurveillance officer, parked at the other end, would be monitoring the traffic. Fifteen minutes later the countersurveillance officer would position his car in another trap at a different location and watch the intelligence officer lead the watchers through. After three or four times the Soviet lookout man could flush out the surveillance and expose the actual vehicles. Ottawa's gnarled street grid blessed the Soviets with scores of handy traps and the KGB and GRU used them routinely whether or not the traps were loaded with a countersurveillance vehicle. The watchers could hardly do a surveillance without confronting them. They could drive around the trap, lose the target and fan out in all directions in the hope of relocating him. Or they could drive through and take a chance on the trap being empty. Eventually the Watcher Service cultivated its trap-avoidance skills and, like a chess player thinking several moves ahead, learned to anticipate the movements and, before getting to the trap, shoot a watcher around in time to pick up the target on the other side. Still, such skills could only diminish the danger, not neutralize it.

When Sandy McCallum took over the Watcher Service in 1962 the battle had started to tilt decidedly in favour of the Russians. McCallum admired the watchers' strong technical skills but believed unimaginative strategy devalued their worth. So instead of stressing better individual skills, as his predecessors had done, McCallum and his civilian assistant, Harry Hurd, turned their attention to devising new surveillance techniques. As matters stood, one watcher team surveilled one target for one shift. Since each target needed at least two watcher teams for around-the-clock coverage and the number of targets vastly outnumbered the surveillance teams, no single intelligence officer got surveilled every day or even necessarily every month. Each morning the surveillance assignments were handed out and the targets of the day stayed under scrutiny until they went to bed. The practice had been used so long it was yellow with obsolescence.

McCallum felt that if the Soviets could set traps against the watchers, nothing should stop the watchers from setting traps against the Soviets. So he introduced a general trapping system called wolfpacking. Instead of waiting near the embassy or hanging around the target's home, as had been done before, the watchers retreated like a wolfpack into a designated quadrant of the city and lay in wait for a target to come to them. The entire area served as a primitive trap and when a vehicle with a Soviet licence plate passed through they started spontaneous surveillance. If the target was an intelligence officer on a mission, he may have already finished his countersurveillance exercises, thus sparing the watchers from running the gauntlet of the Soviet trapping system. Even so, the watchers could avoid the traps more easily because with the area saturated, a watcher car was inevitably stationed on the other side of the trap. Sometimes the wolfpackers staked out the major shopping centres—a favourite Soviet gathering spot—or monitored the bridges from Hull, Quebec. Sometimes they reacted to a promising siting from Bennett's random sighting programme.

Wolfpacking tempered some of the hazards of the Russian trapping system but the Soviets used other techniques too. The Russians knew the watchers had trouble in the country so shifted some of their meets out of town where open spaces and a lack of alternative routes exposed the watchers. Here an intelligence officer could clean himself without the help of a countersurveillance officer. On a lonely road he merely had to stop his car beyond the crest of a hill or park around a corner and watch cars drive by, or do a U-turn and pass his surveillers head on. Few watchers could defy such tactics for more than an hour or two. Soviet cars stayed in the country as much as eight hours and burned the watchers regularly. Each time a watcher became exposed the car had to be painted and some cars were painted twice in a week. The Watcher Service retaliated by following their targets from Cessna airplanes and seemed to conquer the problem except that they often lost the target while rushing to the airport and becoming airborne. The watchers picked up new on-ground skills too but could not master one-on-one coverage in the country.

McCallum introduced the country version of wolfpacking, patrolling the perimeter towns. Rather than following the Soviets into the country, the watchers sometimes abandoned the city en masse and flocked into the neighbouring towns taking up positions along the main street and waiting for the Soviets to drive through. Soviets motoring to the country invariably passed through some small towns clustered around the capital. McCallum believed if one or two watchers scouted the main street of each town the Soviets could not help but fall into their trap. When spotting a Soviet car, the watcher would follow discreetly and radio the next town to expect a visitor. If the target stopped or changed directions, the Watchers from nearby posts on all sides started to converge. Either way, the watchers maintained coverage without exposing themselves.

Wolfpacking and the perimeter-town technique should have swung the pendulum back toward the watchers, but it did not. In fact the Security Service's counterespionage operations produced evidence that the KGB changed its techniques with every innovation from the Watcher Service. The most dramatic Soviet adjustment came during Operation Top Hat following Aquavit's return from Moscow. Aquavit at first made his meets in Ottawa but after wolfpacking came along the KGB moved them outside the city. When the watchers started taking up positions in the perimeter towns the KGB moved beyond the perimeter towns and into villages beyond the watchers' normal coverage area. As the watchers responded again the KGB retreated further and, in the case of Aquavit's last meet with Mike, took to the bush. Whatever the Watcher Service did, the Soviets seemed to undo it with evasive countermeasures.

Watcher Service coverage, despite its advances, still had one big weakness. The Soviets could neatly outmanoeuvre the new surveillance techniques by cleaning themselves in the country and returning to the city for the meet. Driving into the country avoided the wolfpackers in the city and coming back shook off the country patrols. As long as they returned only to the edge of the city and did not venture into it, where the wolfpack would be waiting, they could split the seam of the Watchers' coverage.

The watchers in early 1966 tried to mend this seam with another new strategy that represented its most sophisticated trap yet. When doing traditional one-on-one surveillance, the watchers decided no longer to follow the target into the countryside even if nobody that day patrolled the perimeter towns. The Soviet target would drive into the country and perform his countersurveillance exercises unwatched. Meanwhile the watchers would mark off all re-entry points back to the city and monitor them. The target had to return sometime so the watchers waited for him to pass through one of their re-entry traps and resume surveillance. Since the Soviet had already cleaned himself he would not be looking hard for surveillance which made it easy for the watchers to follow him.

With the new trap technique only a few weeks old, Eugeni Kourianov, driving with F-plates, headed into the countryside. The watchers set their traps and hours later caught him returning along Richmond Road from the west. True to form, Kourianov stopped at the edge of town in the suburb of Bayshore and parked his car next to an apartment building. Evidently knowing the wolfpack looked for licence plates and not faces, and virtually safe from detection with his car, Kourianov hopped a city bus to the centre of town and strolled casually before boarding a couple more city buses eventually going to the Elmvale Shopping Centre in the East End. After walking leisurely for about an hour he met Featherstone. Kourianov had been ensnared by a technique so new most of the Security Service knew nothing about it and neither, apparently, did the Russians.

Featherstone was dropped too dramatically for the Security Service not to notice and worry. The circumstances forced everyone to acknowledge that somehow the Russians had known. The questioning focussed on surveillance since that was what started the case. Both Bennett and Hank Tadeson suspected the GRU had intercepted the watchers' radio communications. Tadeson worried that watchers had chatted on the air too much following Kourianov across town. Furthermore, he pointed out, Kourianov's meet with Featherstone happened two air miles from the Soviet embassy and within probable eavesdropping reach of the sophisticated antennas on its roof. Tadeson theorized that after the meet, Kourianov arrived back at the embassy to be told "you bugger, you were followed." According to Bennett, the Soviets could park an empty car near the meet with a radio tuned to the Watcher Service frequency and a tape machine recording any transmissions. The Soviets would recover the car after the meet and replay the tape with the watcher's chatter on it. Bennett's theory was plausible because in the mid-1960s the watchers stayed with one frequency all day long and had not yet acquired scramblers. The watchers clothed their talk in a code but one so simple the Russians could break it in five minutes. The Watcher Service was both the Security Service's most effective weapon and its weakest security link.

McCallum interviewed each watcher and, sometimes with a chalkboard, retraced the entire surveillance. He had done this sort of thing before and each time urged them to honestly disclose everything. The watchers revealed no "incidents" and each individual reported feeling clean. McCallum probed the use of radio and became convinced his organization had been discreet. Finding no evidence of compromise from surveillance, he felt the case had died for a different reason. But McCallum was merely the head of the Watchers while Tadeson and Bennett were head of B Branch and the Russian Desk respectively so their view prevailed.

Maybe Tadeson and Bennett were correct. McCallum had to back up his organization so his defence was not disinterested. Yet his case seemed stronger than Bennett's and Tadeson's because not a shred of evidence implicated the watchers and the theory blaming them hinged entirely on speculation and ignored the possibility that the Soviets had dropped Featherstone to avoid a redhanded arrest. The impending arrest gave the Soviets an incentive not to appear at the March 27 meet. If McCallum's defence of the watchers was correct and if the Soviets dropped out to avoid the arrest, then only one explanation remained: somebody inside had tipped off the Russians. But who?

Gold Dust and Top Hat both buttressed the mole possibility, but their fragmentary clues pointed in opposite directions. Top Hat indicated that the Soviets learned about the watchers' new techniques almost as they were introduced. Bennett or somebody on the Russian Desk could have told them. But Bennett knew the Security Service was not surveilling the Top Hat meets because he set the policy. That meant that if Bennett was the mole the KGB would know it could meet Aquavit without worrying about Watcher Service interception. Yet Aquavit's handlers trembled at any little sign of possible surveillance and kept moving the meets farther into the country to keep away from surveillance. With Bennett as a mole, the KGB would know that Aquavit was a double agent and that the Security Service was not surveilling his meets, which meant that Aquavit's handlers didn't need to worry or take evasive measures. So if KGB behaviour in Top Hat suggested a mole, it pointed to somebody other than Bennett—to somebody in the Security Service without knowledge of Top Hat. This single piece of circumstantial information alluded to somebody in the Watcher Service because the watchers knew about the new techniques from day one but did not know about Top Hat.

On the other hand, the evidence from the Featherstone failure in Gold Dust pointed more in the direction of the Russian Desk if one assumed the Soviets cut off Featherstone to escape arrest. The Security Service did not divulge to the watchers the fact it would be arresting Featherstone. The Russian Desk held that information tightly until the last moment.

The need-to-know principle served as a mixed blessing. It compartmentalized information and confined the damage a mole could do. But it also protected a mole from exposure by burying trends. Mounties working against the KGB wondered about the death of Top Hat while

Mounties working against the GRU wondered about the sudden demise of Gold Dust. Compartmentalization kept them from exchanging experiences, so life in the Security Service carried on as before. The Atkinsons and the McCallums, who had privileged access and saw the trends, felt no groundswell of doubt from their colleagues and remained silent. The Security Service needed a few more failures to shake top management out of its slumber.

16

The CIA
Mole Hunt

AFTER WRAPPING UP the Watkins interrogation in late 1964, Bennett proposed bringing defector Golitsin to Ottawa for some private lectures about the ways of the KGB. The Security Service could use his expertise, and some of the senior mandarins in the civil service needed education about the KGB and its tactics—nobody could talk about it better than Golitsin. The CIA seemed accommodating and so did Golitsin but the senior officers in the Security Service, despite Bennett's enthusiasm, had reservations about Golitsin because, since his defection, his views had become increasingly strident.

Golitsin had emigrated to Britain in April, 1963 to settle down, but did not stay long and, fearing KGB revenge, returned to the United States in August. Before Britain, Golitsin impressed everybody who debriefed him with his command of facts. Then, after Britain, Golitsin started giving out opinions as well. Golitsin said the widening gulf between Russia and China was a hoax concocted by the KGB to disguise the worldwide march of communism for the purpose of lulling the west into complacency. He said the KGB wanted the West to believe the Communist bloc was splitting into feuding factions.

The theory would have been laughed off except for two things. First, the proposer of the theory came from the KGB. Whatever he said had to be considered seriously. Also, Golitsin had backing him one of the CIA's most powerful officers, James Jesus Angleton, the Chief of Counterintelligence, who aside from Allen Dulles, the World War

One superspy who ran the CIA during most of the 1950s, was probably the CIA's most legendary figure. Angleton's gaunt frame shuffled through CIA corridors like a ghost. When people saw the man with the sculpted face and silver hair haunt headquarters they turned around and whispered. Nobody seemed to know what he did, but everybody knew it must be ultra secret and important.

Angleton believed in conspiracies. He brilliantly pulled seemingly innocuous events together and wove them into one giant Soviet plot. Years earlier a younger Angleton had argued that Stalin and Tito had manufactured a phony split to attract American investment into Yugoslavia and now had no trouble believing Golitsin's China theory. Angleton knew everything in the CIA and stood out as the one exception in an agency ruled by compartmentalization. A drop copy of every operation landed on his desk. In intelligence, knowledge is power. Angleton knew all the skeletons and the ring in his voice warned people of that fact. He was brilliant too. People might challenge Golitsin alone but not when Angleton stood behind him.

Golitsin argued his case with uncompromising force. With his fat face, heavy jowls and military haircut, the stocky defector, his frame so stunted it seemed almost round, overpowered his doubters more by force of personality than by his information. Golitsin based his theory largely upon claims that certain Soviet experts had not been withdrawn from China and that the two countries still continued to cooperate. But ultimately he viewed his case not as logic but as recognizing the truth. The Golitsin-Angleton team made such an impact, the CIA formed an in-house committee to assess the evidence. The committee produced credible evidence refuting the theory. "This is okay," responded Golitsin, "But now give me all the information, including sources." Sources were necessary, Golitsin claimed, because the KGB routinely concocted false sources of information, especially when pulling off major deception operations like this one. Golitsin, backed by Angleton, never retreated an inch from his "double think" theory and in the process recruited to his side some of the suspicious minds in the CIA.

The Security Service wavered for a period over Golitsin's theory. Bennett personally went to Montreal to re-interview defector Mikhail Klochko who had visited China in 1959 and who, during his debriefing to Canadian authorities, had described the growing hostility between the two communist giants. Now the Security Service wanted to question him again because if Golitsin was correct, then Klochko's information had to be false. Klochko, by nature a pleasant, reasonable man, held his ground with Bennett and insisted the political rift had already penetrated the scientific community in 1959.

A few Mounties sided with Golitsin's theories but Security Service Director William Kelly, a militant anti-communist, and most of his officers, rejected it, as did Bennett. Yet Bennett wanted to bring Golitsin to Ottawa because his knowledge of the KGB would be valuable. Bennett's seniors did not doubt his value but worried that Golitsin might spout forth his China views in front of some erudite deputy ministers and embarrass the organization, which in some circles already had a flat-earth reputation. Starting with Jimmy Lemieux in 1953, a long line of undistinguished policemen passed through the Director's office. Kelly in the mid-1960s, although sometimes too overpowering, stood out as the single exception. While his predecessors invariably relied on the advice of their officers, Kelly insisted on reading case files and, upon his command, Bennett bypassed the officer in charge of B Branch to report directly to him. Now Kelly had to decide whether to bring Golitsin to Canada, so he and Bennett flew to the United States to talk to the defector for an assessment. "This is incredible," Kelly muttered after the encounter. Golitsin was not invited and never would be as long as Kelly remained Director.

Upon returning from England in August 1963, Golitsin proclaimed another message: a well-entrenched Soviet mole was working to undermine the CIA from the inside. Golitsin had previously alleged KGB penetration of MI6, French intelligence, West German intelligence and NATO. Now, eighteen months later, he included the CIA. As evidence Golitsin cited a late 1957 trip to the United States by V. M. Kovshuk, a KGB officer of such high rank that his mission had to hold importance. Golitsin suggested Kovshuk, using the name Komarov, had come to activate a CIA officer who had been recruited by the KGB while stationed in Moscow, and put temporarily on ice. Golitsin offered no concrete clues to pinpoint his identity but said a study of the files would reveal patterns that might expose him and offered to help the agency in the search. Golitsin met Attorney General Robert Kennedy and asked for 30 million dollars for his own intelligence operation against the Soviets. He was turned down but did receive from the CIA much of a million dollar demand for his leads pointing to KGB penetration in France. As Director of Counterintelligence, Angleton held the responsibility for stopping hostile penetration of the CIA. Backed up with his own evidence compiled over a decade, Angleton bought Golitsin's mole theory as ardently as he had the China theory and arranged the transfer of four suspects out of the CIA's Soviet bloc division.

Angleton had cause for worry. His counterintelligence unit over the years compiled evidence that since World War Two the West held few secrets the Soviets had not managed to steal. Some of the leaks had been discovered and plugged but others remained unresolved. The U.S. Armed Forces Security Agency, after breaking the Japanese code during World War Two, turned its efforts against the Soviet Union at the end of hostilities and by 1949 had scored a dramatic breakthrough. When sending diplomatic messages to its embassies around the world, the Soviets used a dictionary-like book of 999 code words to convert each word into a five-digit number. For further protection, they then added to each code number another number yielding a new digit. Since these "additives" were random and non-repeating, two identical words in the message appeared as different numbers in the enciphered text. Thus the code breaks had no repetitions, or "depth," on which to crack the system. It was absolutely unbeatable.

The first break came during the war with the recovery in Finland of the burned remnants of the 999-entry Soviet code book. Since fire had damaged the book, the American cryptographers knew only part of the code and without the second part of the system they could not crack the double-enciphered code. To break the Soviet code, the Americans needed both the code book and the additives, so for a few years the charred code book seemed a futile benefit. Then the cryptographers uncovered a major Soviet blunder: during the crush of wartime the Soviets had repeated some of the additives when transmitting to different stations. So a set of additives used for the London channel might show up again in the Washington or New York traffic. The Soviets had started doing it in 1941 and let it continue beyond the war years, finally giving the code breakers some "depth" on which to try to pick apart the traffic.

The code-breaking effort crept forward painstakingly and by mid-1949 the cryptanalysts had opened a window on the New York-to-

Moscow channel for a brief period in 1945 and recognized a partial text of a top-secret telegram from Churchill to Truman complete with cable number.[1] Obviously the Soviets had a well-placed spy somewhere. Further breakouts uncovered more top-secret telegrams and pinned the leaks to an agent the Soviets code named Homer and soon it became apparent that Homer operated out of the British embassy in Washington. The investigation zeroed in on clerks and cleaning ladies and took almost two years to carefully reach the top diplomatic ranks. When it finally did, the investigators identified Homer as First Secretary Donald Maclean.

In 1948, shortly after the code breakers discovered the duplicated additives but before they could open the first window, the Soviets changed their system. The Russians could not undo the potential damage of the seven previous years but had stopped the enciphering mistake from continuing any longer. It seemed the American discovery had alerted the Soviets who responded with quick corrective action even though the Americans had guarded the discovery carefully. The pieces fell into place two years later when the Americans learned that William Weisband, an employee of the Armed Forces Security Agency, had given the secret to the Soviets. Before he was discovered, compartmentalization had already robbed Weisband of his access. So he knew about the cipher break but not its results, which meant the Russians did not know how many of their secrets the code breakers were uncovering. Unable to stop the Americans from progressively uncovering its agents during the 1941–48 period, the Soviets' only hope lay in monitoring developments to see how far the Americans got. Shortly after Weisband had been innocently cut off, Kim Philby moved to Washington as MI6's Liaison Officer and into a position overseeing, on behalf of the British, the unfolding cipher search. Whether Philby's transfer into the post had been coincidental or somehow arranged would be investigated later. Nevertheless it gave him inner access and the opportunity to see his own code name (Stanley) appear in the traffic. He watched the investigation work out the leads to the identity of Homer, his KGB colleague and friend, and

---

[1] My research on the breaking of the Soviet code has been supplemented by information from *Wilderness of Mirrors* by David C. Martin, Harper and Row, 1980, an excellent account of the cipher break and also the CIA's search for a mole. This chapter borrows from Martin's book for both stories.

did nothing as long as the investigation floundered. When the hunt veered in Maclean's direction and his colleague seemed doomed, Philby "uncovered" evidence on his own against Maclean and delivered one of the final blows. Having hastened Maclean's inevitable downfall, Philby sent Guy Burgess, another KGB colleague stationed in the British embassy in Washington, to London to warn Maclean to flee for safety. After receiving the tip-off, Maclean defected days before the authorities arrested him.

Philby's manipulation would have worked perfectly had not the mercurial Guy Burgess defected with Maclean on impulse and thus thrown suspicion on Philby. Years later, after Philby himself defected ahead of the closing net, Angleton concluded that the Soviets had managed to manoeuvre Philby into his Washington posting. How many more Soviet spies remained hidden? The code break ploddingly opened new windows on Soviet traffic and revealed that during the 1940s the Soviet Union had infiltrated western society with multiple spies. The traffic implicated atomic spy Klaus Fuchs (who in turn fingered Harry Gold), Julius and Ethel Rosenberg and provided circumstantial evidence against Alger Hiss, and others, some of whose agent code names were never broken.

The 1950s and 1960s brought one Soviet intelligence defector after another with secrets for the West. Had the West, after lagging behind, caught up and maybe overtaken the Soviets in the intelligence war? Or was the change of fortune too good to be real? Angleton thought the latter and carefully pulled together evidence to show that the KGB was manipulating events for the purpose of deceiving the CIA into thinking it was winning. The rush of defectors and moles looked impressive at first blush but a subculture of evidence revealed an ominous pattern that, depending on one's interpretation, seemed to support Angleton's suspicions. Just as the RCMP's counterespionage cases failed subtly over a period of time, the CIA's recruitments, when studied closely, seemed to go murky too. The pattern dated back to at least 1957 when, according to Golitsin, V. M. Kovshuk travelled to America to activate the CIA mole.

Colonel Peter Popov of the GRU had volunteered his services to the CIA from Vienna in 1953 and for the next six years fed valuable information from inside the GRU until hamhanded surveillance by the FBI of one of Popov's illegals in New York compromised Popov.

Everybody thought the operation perished for that reason. The CIA came across another explanation two years later when MI6 officer George Blake confessed to acting as a KGB mole inside British intelligence. Blake boasted he knew about the Popov case as early as 1955. Without a legitimate excuse to terminate Popov, the Soviets evidently let him continue his treachery until 1959 and took advantage of the misguided FBI surveillance to roll him up. If nothing else, the Popov experience demonstrated how far the Soviets would go in tolerating a hemorrhaging of secrets to protect a mole like Blake.

As the Soviets were snuffing out the unfortunate Popov, the U.S. Embassy in Bern, Switzerland received a letter from an iron curtain intelligence officer calling himself Sniper and offering to pass along intelligence. For nearly two years Sniper anonymously passed along intelligence through his letters and only when KGB suspicion forced him to defect in December, 1960, did the CIA learn Sniper was Michal Goleniewski, a high-ranking officer in Polish intelligence who, as liaison officer to the KGB, had become familiar with many KGB operations. Goleniewski exposed more high-grade KGB agents than any other defector in CIA history. His leads rolled up the infamous Portland spy ring in Britain including the capture and arrest of Soviet illegal "Gordon Lonsdale." His information also unmasked George Blake who, as a Soviet mole inside MI6, ranked second only to Philby; Heinz Felfe, Deputy Chief of Counterintelligence in West German intelligence; and Colonel Israel Beer, an adviser to Prime Minister David Ben-Gurion of Israel.

Despite Goleniewski's impressive record, Angleton declared him a KGB plant when the first letters arrived, and when Goleniewski defected he argued for turning him back. No number of exposures on the part of Goleniewski could shake Angleton's belief that he was under Soviet control. The KGB had to conceive a remarkably Machiavellian plot to inflict so much damage upon itself and possess an exceedingly high mole to protect. Later analysis of Goleniewski's fourteen letters from behind the iron curtain revealed signs of Soviet manipulation, so maybe Goleniewski started as a genuine mole yielding straight information and the Soviets found out and responded by quietly feeding him operational disinformation. Goleniewski's later letters had "corrected" parts of his earlier ones. If a mole had betrayed Goleniewski the KGB could not afford to extinguish him without jeopardizing the mole and may have found it expeditious to feed him deception material to unwittingly pass to the CIA. At the end, the KGB virtually frightened Goleniewski into defecting by telling him they suspected a leak in his department. Maybe the KGB felt it could no longer tolerate his activity but neither could it afford to roll him up, so induced him to defect, thereby getting rid of him. Goleniewski later said he had withheld his identity to protect himself from the mole inside the CIA and defected because the KGB were getting onto him. The CIA could not dismiss Goleniewski's mole claim because one of his early letters from Moscow alluded to a tightly held CIA attempt to recruit a Polish intelligence officer in Bern. Goleniewski had told the CIA before it could carry it out. How could the Soviets learn about a premature operation if not through a mole?

If Goleniewski was not the CIA's most valuable defector ever, then the honour belonged to Oleg Penkovsky, a trusted Colonel in the GRU who frequently visited the West. Penkovsky tried to offer his services as a mole for months but the CIA turned him down. After stopping Canadian and American tourists in the streets of Moscow he finally persuaded the British to accept him. The British and Americans jointly debriefed him for the first time on April 20, 1961, in a London hotel room. Over the following months Penkovsky worked devotedly and ultimately passed 10,000 pages of top-secret documents on Soviet missiles. Nobody could challenge his contribution. The following January, Penkovsky noticed surveillance in Moscow and that April his superiors postponed his scheduled trip to the United States. Formal arrest followed that fall. The Soviets had not taken long to plug a damaging leak.

Goleniewski planted the suspicion of a Soviet mole and Penkovsky's demise moved it along, so when Golitsin returned from Britain in August, 1963, Angleton needed no convincing. Golitsin said that at the time of his defection the KGB was putting the finishing touches on a multifaceted deception operation against the west, including phony defectors bearing disinformation. He went further and predicted the KGB would soon dispatch a phony defector to discredit him and divert the CIA's mole hunt. What Golitsin said made sense. The CIA could not infiltrate a closed society like the Soviet Union and therefore relied on defectors and secret dissenters with inside information. The KGB recognized the strategy and watched its personnel closely and mostly succeeded in snuffing out potential defectors and dissidents. Even the KGB's security measures could not achieve 100 percent efficiency. The odd Popov, Goleniewski, Penkovsky or Golitsin continued to slip through and do irreparable damage. If the KGB could not stop the flow it could at least poison the stream with false defectors.

Following Golitsin's défection in late 1961 three more Soviets quickly offered their services to the Americans. Scotch and Bourbon, the code names for KGB and GRU officers respectively, started passing information to the FBI from their posts at the United Nations in New York while staying in place. Angleton warned the FBI they were double agents but J. Edgar Hoover refused to believe him. As well, Yuri Nosenko, a KGB officer in the Soviet delegation to the disarmament talks in Geneva, offered to sell the CIA information so he could replace KGB money squandered in a drinking spree. Nosenko met the CIA several times in Geneva while passing material.

Nosenko showed no desire to defect and seemed prepared to remain in place as a mole until suddenly in February, 1964, while again visiting Geneva, he defected. Although Golitsin had talked of a KGB penetration of the British Admiralty his vague leads left the investigation unsolved. Nosenko supplied the details that led to the unmasking of John Vassall. Golitsin alleged that a Canadian ambassador had been blackmailed in Moscow but it required Nosenko's hard information to identify Watkins. Nosenko revealed that the U.S. embassy in Moscow was bugged and pinpointed the locations, which Golitsin could not do. In terms of results, Nosenko's disclosures rivalled and maybe surpassed Golitsin's.

Angleton saw Nosenko as the phony defector Golitsin had predicted would try to discredit him. His intelligence booty was valuable and had furthered Golitsin's leads but Angleton saw them as KGB giveaways to establish his authenticity to mislead the CIA on bigger matters. Nosenko did not allege CIA penetration by a KGB mole as Golitsin had done. If Nosenko's evidence was accepted at face value it tended to deflect Golitsin's clues and lead people to believe there was no mole inside the CIA. For example, Nosenko in effect contradicted Golitsin's claim that V. M. Kovshuk travelled to the United States to activate a mole in the CIA. Nosenko said he worked as Kovshuk's deputy and gave clues to the identity of the agent he came to meet. These lead to a Washington D.C. mechanic who had worked during the 1950s in the motor pool of the U.S. embassy in Moscow. The mechanic confessed to having been recruited while in Moscow, but since he had no access to classified material, and remained a low-level agent, it seemed unlikely that a senior official like Kovshuk would travel to the United States for a meeting. So it appeared that Nosenko might be deflecting the mole hunt by covering up the real purpose of Kovshuk's visit.

Nosenko, who defected only a few months after President Kennedy's shooting in Dallas, claimed that he had handled Lee Harvey Oswald's file while Oswald lived in the Soviet Union and, furthermore, had been called in later to review the file after the assassination. But Nosenko seemed to know little about the disaffected American and made two claims that conveniently served the Soviet interest: first, that the KGB did not recruit Oswald as an agent, and second, that the Soviet Union had nothing to do with the shooting of the president. While a marine, Oswald had worked in Japan as a radar operator at Atsugi Air Base which serviced the U-2 aircraft and the CIA could not believe the KGB did not at least debrief him about it. It seemed unlikely that of thousands of KGB officers, one who handled the Oswald file twice defected nicely in time to clear Russia before the Warren Commission.

Nosenko could not explain satisfactorily why he had defected when earlier he had said he would not. Nosenko at first claimed a telegram recalling him to Moscow made him suspicious and forced him to defect. However, when confronted with evidence that intercepts of Soviet cable traffic revealed that no telegram had been sent that day, he admitted that he had made up the story to increase his chances of acceptance from the CIA. Interrogation also got Nosenko to admit being merely a KGB captain and not the lieutenant colonel he originally claimed. He said he inflated his rank to enhance his attractiveness but his KGB travel documents described him as a lieutenant colonel. Nosenko's explanation that a clerk had made a mistake did not satisfy his interrogators. Furthermore, Golitsin flatly claimed that Nosenko had not worked in the KGB's Second Chief Directorate when he claimed he had or else he would have known about him. Then Nosenko failed a lie detector test. Before Nosenko admitted his lies, Scotch, the FBI "mole" in the KGB, backed up Nosenko's claim that he was a lieutenant colonel who had been recalled from Geneva. So not only did it appear Nosenko had help in getting phony travel documents, his falsehoods had been corroborated. Dozens of inaccuracies, contradictions, deficiencies and unexplained questions plagued Nosenko's credibility. The CIA advised that the Warren Commission into Kennedy's assassination disregard his information.

Nosenko would not confess so the CIA undertook to disorient him into talking. Incarcerated in a cell especially constructed to resemble a bank vault, he sweltered through the summers and nearly froze through the winters for three years. His guards underfed him bad food and refused to talk to him or let him read or occupy himself in any way. When he tried keeping track of time by fashioning a calendar out of lint, the guards swept it away as they did the chess set he fabricated. And the guards watched television with earphones to stop him from hearing it. He was constantly surveilled by closed circuit camera.

Angleton believed that phony defectors represented only the tip of the KGB iceberg and that most Soviet disinformation originated from other sources, including people posing as anti-communists. Angleton felt the KGB used anti-communist groups as fronts either by setting up phony groups or by secretly taking control of existing legitimate anti-communist groups and manipulating them for deception purposes. Angleton in particular suspected an Estonian emigre named Eerik Heine as a false anti-communist. Heine claimed he had escaped a Soviet prison, settled in Toronto in 1957 and applied for Canadian citizenship. He said he had been a war criminal in his Estonian homeland for serving in the Estonian unit of the German army during World War Two and wreaking sabotage against the Soviet Union in the 1950s. Now he travelled around North America lecturing against communism, supported Barry Goldwater and poured virtually all his money into an amateur anti-communist film called *Creators of Legend*.

Then Heine joined the Legion of Estonian Liberation and by the early 1960s seemed headed for an executive position. Angleton viewed this as further evidence of his Soviet-directed mission. Heine's activities irked the CIA particularly since the Legion operated as a CIA front group, and so it decided to stop him. In November 1963, Juri Raus, the Legion's National Commander and an active CIA agent, at a meeting in New York, denounced Heine as "a communist and an agent of the KGB." Back in Canada the Security Service had already screened Heine's citizenship application and had given him security approval but the CIA's intervention forced it to re-open the file. The CIA and the Security Service discussed the case for hours and reviewed each piece of evidence. In the end the CIA's claim rested on its assertion that Heine could not have escaped prison and snuck out of the Soviet Union as stated. After listening to the CIA, the Security Service interviewed Heine and scrutinized each step of his claimed escape, concluding that it could have been done and that he was genuine. The Security Service wrote off the CIA's suspicions as unfounded and Heine received his citizenship papers in the fall of 1964.[2]

In 1965 newspaperman Peter Worthington worked in Moscow for the Toronto *Telegram* and drew close to his official translator, Olga Farmakovsky who confessed being co-opted by the KGB to report his movements. While visiting Canada on Christmas furlough later that year, Worthington appeared at the RCMP's traditional New Year's levy in Ottawa and asked the Security Service to help Olga defect. The Security Service, not experienced in arranging defections from abroad, turned the matter over to the CIA, which arranged to have her jump ship in Beirut during a cruise for loyal Soviet workers.

Once she defected, Angleton became involved and dismissed her as a plant. The CIA considered abandoning her as the Russians pressured the Lebanese government for her return. The CIA barred her from the United States and Olga refused to submit to hostile questioning in the CIA's interrogation camp in West Germany so for several months she floated in limbo, eventually winding up in Brussels where local pro-CIA authorities questioned her suspiciously and agreed with their American colleagues that she was a plant.

The CIA warned the Security Service to have her barred from Canada, which the RCMP could do simply by submitting an adverse report to the Immigration Department. Again the CIA and Security Service huddled over the status of a Soviet citizen posing as a refugee. The CIA produced two pieces of evidence: she had produced little information and her husband worked as an intelligence officer for the GRU. How could an admitted KGB agent married to a GRU officer bring so little worthwhile information, the CIA asked. The Security Service replied that she had not belonged to the KGB and merely

---

[2] Heine, his public reputation ruined by Juri Raus' allegation, sued for slander. When the case reached court, Richard Helms, the Deputy Director of the CIA, intervened to admit that Raus was a CIA agent and claimed Raus could not be sued because his statement had been made on CIA instruction, which in effect made him a servant of the United States Government and thereby protected by government immunity. The court agreed reluctantly and dismissed Heine's claim.

worked as an Intourist translator who had been co-opted as an informer as have many other Soviet citizens. Her husband, as professional intelligence officers are supposed to do, apparently did not discuss his work at home and, besides, in the process of being divorced, they were not so close. The explanation did not mellow the CIA's suspicions. The two sides viewed her in different lights: the CIA saw her as a defector who should have information; the Security Service viewed her as a refugee escaping an authoritarian country. With neither side yielding, the Security Service asked the British for their opinion. A British interrogation team went to Brussels and grilled her exhaustively and concluded she was genuine.

With backing from the British, Canada decided to give her a temporary visa but at the eleventh hour Sid Stein, the CIA man in Ottawa, dropped into Len Higgitt's office. By this time Higgitt was very senior in the organization and could have swayed the Service's decision. Usually an impeccably polite individual, Stein painted Olga as a menace whose presence in Canada would jeopardize the security of both Canada and the United States. He repeated the CIA stand that she had been dispatched to the West and now added a new allegation: that she carried an assignment to penetrate high-government circles in Washington. Higgitt doubted the claim. A Soviet woman threatening the United States from Canada did not sound credible, but Stein insisted the information originated from a source. "Show us your source," replied Higgitt. The two organizations routinely exchanged sensitive information including, sometimes, source information, but this time Stein said the agency could not compromise the source. Higgitt, Kelly and Bennett all doubted there was a source, so Olga took up residence in Canada on a minister's visa and lived quietly, showing no inclination to recruit anybody for anything.

Years later, as information emerged, some individuals in the Security Service speculated that the sensitive CIA source was actually Golitsin. Golitsin made a lot of accusations. With Golitsin, the KGB authority, proposing conspiracies and Angleton, the CIA power, sanctioning them, the pair formed an awesome team. When Golitsin claimed he could spot trends by reviewing the CIA's files, Angleton served up some of the most sensitive documents. For a man who wrote off almost every defector as a plant, Angleton placed a lot of confidence in defector Golitsin. While Angleton and Golitsin rooted through the files in search of the mole, the head of the Soviet Bloc Division, under Angleton's influence, notified CIA stations around the world to stop recruiting Soviet agents. It was an unprecedented step for an agency dedicated to penetrating Soviet institutions, but since the KGB presumably knew everything, the CIA viewed each new agent only as more Soviet disinformation. Depending upon the observer's point of view, the CIA was either struggling to defend itself or rolling over dead.

The CIA's mole hunt focussed on the most senior officers in the Soviet Bloc Division. Angleton gave Golitsin the personnel files of all CIA officers who spoke Russian or had been posted to Moscow or had failures in their backgrounds. Golitsin compared the officer's personnel file with his case record and in some instances estimated where and when the recruitment had taken place. Without being told why, officers were transferred out of the Soviet Bloc Division and their careers irretrievably ruined. Only years later, when the word of the mole hunt spread, when it was too late to defend themselves, did they realize what had happened. Even the head of the division, who supported the Angleton-Golitsin enterprise, and who had issued the telegram stopping the recruitment of Soviet agents, fell under suspicion. He was transferred to Paris while an internal investigation probed him as he studied French. The investigation cleared him, but Angleton refused to accept the result and after the CIA man took up his post privately warned the head of French intelligence that the new man was a Russian mole, thus destroying the officer's effectiveness and undermining the CIA's relationship with the French. Adding speculation to flimsy evidence, Golitsin called Averell Harriman a Soviet spy and urged the CIA Director to warn the president. During the Prague spring of 1968, Golitsin predicted the rift between Czechoslovakia and the Soviet Union was another sham and confidently claimed the Soviets would never invade.

Nothing the CIA tried, whether transfers or internal investigation, uncovered the mole. Angleton's detractors claimed the mole did not exist. Angleton replied that more than one mole was on the loose. One mole in a senior position could promote and transfer other moles where the KGB needed them, thus the KGB penetration became a self-perpetuating phenomenon. Angleton looked not so much for an individual as a colony of moles.

The mole hunt more than brought the CIA to a standstill; it split the agency into two warring factions. A motionless CIA could always be restarted but a divided organization with individuals feuding over each other's loyalty did not mend easily. Golitsin's allegations practically severed the CIA's relations with France—French intelligence had been ripped apart over Golitsin and careers ruined; but no mole was found—and Norway and temporarily bruised its connection with organizations like the Security Service. Meanwhile the symbol of division, Yuri Nosenko, still languishing in solitary confinement, had defenders and detractors arguing over what to do with him. Golitsin said there was a mole; Nosenko's evidence suggested there was not. Whatever it did, the CIA could not find the mole but neither could it disprove the mole theory, or dissuade Angleton and Golitsin. As long as the controversy remained unsolved, the CIA could not decide what to do with Nosenko.[3]

The CIA might as well have had a mole because the search wreaked more destruction on the agency than the mole, if he existed, could do. A few years later people investigated the significance of that. Why was Golitsin the only defector the Soviets had not planted or manipulated? If one judged by the results, the circumstantial evidence of phony defectors pointed to Golitsin as much as anybody. Not only did he sow irreparable damage, many of his leads disintegrated or turned mushy under cold investigation. He made a lot of allegations but had not backed up many of them. In fact he provided less usable intelligence than some other defectors, including Nosenko, whom Golitsin called a plant. Nosenko gave some false leads that could deflect investigations, but so had Golitsin. He told the RCMP the KGB's co-opted agent in Operation Broken Arrow was a cipher clerk when he was a security guard, which might have sent the Security Service looking in the wrong direction. His crazy China theory could be deception. Curiously, Golitsin started proclaiming it in August 1963, a month after the Sino-Soviet talks broke down. The collapse upset the Soviets, so what message would they want the West to hear?

One could not challenge Golitsin's bona fides without questioning

---

[3] Forced to make a decision, the CIA in August 1968 administered another lie detector test and after failing in 1964 and 1966, Nosenko passed, was declared a genuine defector, given a new identity, a new home and a job as consultant to the CIA. Meanwhile the debate over him continues.

Angleton too. Clare Edward Petty, one of Angleton's counterintelligence officers and the man who identified Heinz Felfe as the Soviet mole in West German intelligence before Goleniewski's letters nailed him down, produced a voluminous report pointing to Angleton as the mole. If Golitsin's views were so disruptive they were so only because one man championed them. This was the same man who had written off defectors who later turned out valuable, and who blindly invested everything in Golitsin. He was the same man who gave top-secret files to a foreigner and had been responsible for a string of disrupting transfers. By Angleton's own logic, the mole could be Angleton. Petty submitted his report and retired.

Nearly a decade and a half passed before the CIA recruited another major defector or known mole. Some people blamed Angleton for frightening them off. Why would a KGB intelligence officer risk being interrogated as a plant and possibly worse. On the other hand, Angleton claimed the mole inside the CIA scared off defectors and that is why vigorous measures had to be taken to find him first. According to David Martin's book on the CIA mole hunt, John Hart, the CIA officer who reviewed the agency's treatment of defectors, said Golitsin was "diagnosed by a psychiatrist and separately by a clinical psychologist as a paranoid." Colleagues thought Angleton acted in an excessively furtive manner. Perhaps there was no mole and no false defector. Maybe the CIA had been victim of two overly suspicious minds living off each other's phobias. To this day CIA men privately debate the issue.

17

Operation Kit Bag

BY LATE 1965 the Watcher Service was already wolfpacking and patrolling the perimeter towns and the Soviets had already reacted with new evasive countersurveillance techniques. Also by this time, the watchers had started responding to the Soviet reactions. When the Soviets moved their country meets beyond the perimeter towns the watchers followed by posting their surveillance cars further out, so on Sunday morning, October 3, 1965, the Watcher Service was prepared for Victor Myznikov, a KGB officer in the Soviet embassy, as he arrived in Brockville, Ontario, about sixty-five miles south of Ottawa.

Myznikov got to Brockville using yet another new evasive tactic: hitchhiking. His thumb took him into the country and allowed him to slip through the watchers' traps in town after town. The waiting watcher teams monitored cars, not the people in them. Myznikov would have escaped surveillance entirely except that the watcher posted to Brockville that day had surveilled the handsome Soviet Attaché before and by chance recognized his face as he walked down the street.

"Holy Jesus," exclaimed the watcher. "We've got to look for licence plates, do we now have to watch for faces too?"

Myznikov strode briskly into the Brigadier Inn, poked around a little, entered the restaurant, and then sat down at the table of an unidentified male and ordered lunch. After eating, Myznikov and his companion walked out of town to the end of a dirt road where near a clump of trees Myznikov handed him two slips of paper. The two returned separately to Brockville and Myznikov hitched back to Ottawa.

Watchers' cars poured into Brockville to cover the new suspect who, they quickly discovered, travelled under the name of Jordan. He stopped in Toronto and scouted a neighbourhood in the west side of the city and then flew to Thunder Bay for a visit with an acquaintance before going home to Edmonton where the Security Service identified him as Mike Mihalcin, a thirty-four-year-old truck driver for a local dry cleaning company. Investigation revealed that Mihalcin had been born in Canada and raised in an immigrant Slovak colony but moved to his ancestral Czechoslovakia as a teenager and, using his Canadian birthright, returned to Canada in 1961 with his Czechoslovakian-born wife and young son. Settling in Canada legally under his real identity for a subversive purpose made him a semi-illegal like Kneschke in Operation Apple Cider. The roof of his house carried a radio antenna and a clandestine probe revealed a short wave radio inside his house. Evidently Mihalcin had been recruited in Czechoslovakia, trained as an agent and then dispatched to Canada on assignment.

Bennett ecstatically proclaimed Mihalcin a major discovery because he showed the early signs of a deep penetration agent. He assigned the young man the code name Elf, and mobilized the Security Service's resources for its newest case, Operation Kit Bag. Bennett wanted to know everything about Mihalcin and flesh out the details of his assignments. He threw everything at him—bugs, wiretaps, observations posts and moving surveillance.

Luck seemed to smile on the Security Service. Mihalcin lived near the home of a Security Service Mountie whose house immediately became an observation post. Setting up observation posts to cover a single meet was easy: Mounties merely searched the area for a reliable homeowner or landlord, told him and his wife they needed their place for a drug investigation and sent them expenses-paid to Florida for a week on the promise that they would tell nobody the reason. But long-term observations, like the kind Mihalcin required, presented a thorny problem, especially if there was no convenient home to rent. The Security Service could not send people away for months at a time, so with a Mountie already in the area, Kit Bag had gotten lucky. The good fortune had solved a problem but, as headquarters soon discovered, raised a new one. After a few months the Mounties' wife complained the virtual twenty-four-hour occupation of her home disrupted their routine and invaded their privacy. The Security Service had to withdraw and hunt for another observation post.

A bigger problem confounded the Kit Bag investigation. Despite intensive monitoring of Mihalcin's movements, the investigation had not caught him committing a single suspicious act. The setback worried some officers but not Bennett. Deep penetration agents acted subtly, Bennett said, and Mihalcin might still be settling in or, alternatively, establishing contacts in a way that eluded ordinary observation. So Operation Kit Bag, which had already followed Mihalcin making his daily laundry rounds, started checking the backgrounds of his customers on the assumption that he used his laundry deliveries as cover to pass messages. The investigation targeted regular customers or anybody with a subversive or criminal trace in the RCMP filing system. In some cases, investigators secretly searched the pockets of clothes he had delivered. "We were trying to discover his trapline," says one Security Service officer. "There was one hell of a pile of work done on that, I'll tell you." The Edmonton office lacked resources to surveil all his customers and the task proved massive and eventually fruitless. His customers' names rarely showed up in RCMP files. The Security Service would watch one customer and Mihalcin would never make another delivery.

Kneschke had stumped the Apple Cider investigation in Vancouver a few years earlier until IF-value monitoring of his short wave radio smoked him out listening to coded broadcasts from Moscow. It had worked on Kneschke so should work on Mihalcin too. So Bennett brought the IF value technique out of mothballs to pin down once again an elusive agent. But this time the monitoring revealed nothing suspicious. Mihalcin listened only rarely to his short wave radio and never to a broadcast from Moscow.

Operation Kit Bag dragged on for months and then a year without a break and the small battery of desk men, watchers and investigators urged Bennett to pull in Mihalcin to see what goodies he coughed up. A few hours of simple interrogation, they argued, might resolve the mystery and maybe create a dandy double agent operation. No, replied Bennett, Mihalcin is our only illegal and our only opportunity to collect KGB modus operandi for this kind of operation. The magic words modus operandi, MO, did not convince his men any more. In the early days Bennett let cases run long so that the fledgling Security Service could study Soviet MO and get to know the other side. Now people wondered if Bennett was overdoing MO a little bit. The Security Service had watched Soviet intelligence run dozens of cases and had picked up experience. Now, some of his men felt, the time had come to stop practicing and start acting. Bennett insisted that one never outgrew the need for MO because Soviet techniques constantly changed and, besides, MO was the most important counterintelligence technique for uncovering new cases. Bennett was correct. Without MO, there would be no debate over what to do with Mihalcin because he would not have been discovered. Through letting cases run the Security Service had learned enough about Soviet tactics to send the watchers into the country to wait for the intelligence officers to make their runs, which is how they spotted Myznikov meeting Mihalcin. Bennett's men did not argue the need to study and persue MO but argued that learning MO did not require every case to run forever. They suspected that Bennett so enjoyed the counterespionage game that he studied MO as an end in itself.

"Let's not spend ten years and hundreds of thousands of dollars for it to come out the way everything else has come out," argued Sandy McCallum, the veteran head of the Watcher Service who had seen enough cases evaporate after two or three years. "Let's hit him while it's still fresh in his mind."

"We can't pounce unless we've got the goods on him," replied Bennett. "He's not going to volunteer information."

What happens, asked Bennett, if Mihalcin denies everything and keeps his mouth shut? As far as we can show, said Bennett, he has done nothing subversive or illegal. We need something to hit him with and at the moment all we have is a single meeting with Myznikov. If he's a sleeper all we can do is look for his contacts. One false move spoils everything.

It does not matter, replied McCallum, the operation is already leading nowhere.

"She's going to boil down to nothing, Jim," warned McCallum. "By the time we're finished it's going to be zip."

Operation Kit Bag spotlighted within the secret service a creeping fundamental divergence in approach to the handling of a counteres-

pionage case. Did one sit back and wait, or move in and strike early?
Each course had pros and cons.

"Damn it, can't he be persuaded?" asked one of McCallum's
colleagues.

"No," replied McCallum. "You try."

Other Mounties argued with Bennett but failed too.

"I'm not aware of the identity of anybody who after a year or so
wanted to see the thing run any longer," says one Mountie. "The guys
who had been around for a time had seen this happen too damned
often. They didn't want to see it happen on this one because it was too
good. Nothing was developing so you could see the whole thing falling
into the same category: layers and layers and layers of paper until it gets
buried in a mass of paper and dissipates."

Circumstances had changed mightily since a hard pressed Bennett
landed at headquarters in 1954 as a support worker and confronted an
organization believing its own myth about Mountie superiority and
routinely discriminating against civilian employees. Bennett had managed to survive this inhospitable atmosphere and eventually prospered
and entrenched himself. He worked harder and longer, dug deeper and
read more, carried authority better and simply outperformed everybody until even the hidebound RCMP awarded him the Russian
Desk. Without stopping for breath, he built the desk from a handful of
semi-amateurs into a crisp bureaucracy of desk men, investigators,
watchers, researchers, technicians, translators and transcribers. Bennett's fortunes expanded along with the status of the Russian Desk and
the RCMP accepted him into the Mountie family by making him the
first civilian to reach the equivalent of a commissioned officer. Now,
after a decade of rule, he sat as an overlord and his innovations that
once so shook B Branch, had settled into tradition. Bits of gray flecked
the hair of the former insurgent as he presided over the status quo.

Chronic workaholism, as much as ambition, seemed to propel
Bennett. The intervening years had afforded plenty of opportunity to
slow down to a comfortable pace but his intensity never wavered. He
still reached the office first each morning and left last, and continued
popping back in the evenings a few times a week and sometimes on
weekends. As always, he read every piece of paper including the most
insignificant telegrams. Whenever something happened Bennett
showed up first on the scene and gave directions—nobody could
contain him. When a new case broke, he would excitedly issue step-by-

step instructions. "He completely controlled a case," says one of his investigators. "When I first went into B Branch I inherited a case. I had no input at all. Reports from A Division went straight into Bennett's office and he made notes in the margin as to what I was to do and I did it. Everything that was done was done not only at his sanction but at his instigation." The Russian Desk revolved around Bennett; when vacation or a business trip took him out of the office, people started pushing files.

Bennett in all his years on the Russian Desk never had a secretary. He typed his own reports. He was one of the few who could write one-draft copy. When perusing reports from his men he saved time by writing with nearly illegible handwriting notes into margins. Frequently he wrote, "See me." Investigators groaned when they saw it because it meant extra work. "Bennett wanted reports on everything," says one of his men. "Sometimes investigators delayed handing in their reports until Bennett had a day off so that somebody else would see it. Giving Bennett a report often resulted in more work since he had a tendency to ask to have the report correlated with something else."

Bennett's pace flooded his subordinates with paperwork and they felt not all of it was necessary. "When I joined the Russian Desk Bennett told me to research a file and prepare a brief on it," says one of his men. "I remember doing a lot of work and preparing drafts and making sure to get correct spelling and grammar. When I presented him with it he casually said: 'Now you know the file.'" Bennett did not often make such assignments but his men wondered why they had to trace money given by the Russians to a double agent back to the originating bank or determine in which mail box a certain letter had been posted. Such assignments absorbed time and work and even when successful usually produced a meaningless result. The Soviets could draw money from any bank or post letters anywhere. They were longshots and Bennett followed them without seeming to calculate whether the burden of work was worth the practical result.

Bennett made high demands on himself but also made high demands on his men.

"This is not good enough," Bennett would decree after reading a field report.

"It's impossible to get what you want," argued an NCO who had earlier sent out Bennett's original orders with embarrassment.

"They can find a way."

Said the NCO later, "Maybe his technique was to ask for the moon and settle for what you can get. But I think he actually expected what he demanded. He had no understanding of investigative techniques. He had no understanding of that whole area."

Bennett viewed the Security Service as an elite within the RCMP, and B Branch an elite within the Security Service. Not all men measured up and those found wanting would be moved to less demanding duties outside the branch.

"He got us to extract a lot more detail than we would have on our own," says one top aide. Bennett's supporters agreed he made tough demands but insisted he never demanded more of his men than of himself and claimed his high standards pushed individuals into pursuing objectives they thought unattainable but often that culminated in success beyond their expectations. His detractors called his demands not tough but unrealistic and a waste of resources. They said he had not the foggiest idea what an investigation was and had spent too many years behind a desk.

Few disputed that the personnel administration functioned well under Bennett. He was friendly, witty, decent and concerned for the welfare of his NCOs. If one of his men got promoted he made sure to attend the promotion party. His men worked for the sake of getting the job done and not so much for advancement, knowing their promotion would come in turn. (After Bennett left, the system reverted to favouritism with everybody bucking each other for the next promotion.) He always tried to keep relations light and amiable. He did not tell jokes but had a quick cut-and-thrust humour and would utter quick jabs which defused some of the heaviness of his assignments. If he scolded someone he did it once and let it drop. He did not hold grudges or push the offender to the bottom of the pile. So while he squeezed his men to their limits, they usually liked working for him.

The door to Bennett's office always stood open and he discouraged nobody, no matter how junior, from entering. He was always busy but found time for anybody who dropped by and made them feel welcome, although he was never too casual. The intensity of his response told his visitor he was listening. As he swivelled his chair and looked out the window, his intent profile would assure his guest that he was not thinking to himself, "I wish this guy would go away." Whenever he could, he helped out although such assistance burdened him further.

However, the ground rules were clear: the visitor had come to tell him something and not the other way around. Throughout the exchange, Bennett adopted the classic intelligence posture: get as much as you can, give as little as possible.

But was it a facade? Did he show affability merely for strategic reasons? When talking with other civilians, Bennett frequently disparaged Mounties and did not hide feelings that a lot of them were not particularly competent or bright. The Mounties never knew about these comments but gradually they started realizing over the years that despite his open door and willingness to talk, he took advice no better than some of the commissioned officers who paid no lip service to the process of dialogue. When confronted with an item for the first time, Bennett studied the facts carefully and arrived at a decision in a reasonable manner. But once made up, his mind rarely changed and from then on he would deliberate freely but usually hold his ground and invariably have the last word. He did not discuss so much as explain and if his men disagreed he sometimes talked down to them. As they grew into better counterespionage officers, his NCOs increasingly produced alternative proposals, which Bennett effectively brushed aside as the simple notions of babes. Bennett had been around the world whereas most Mounties had never travelled outside North America. One colleague said Bennett could be patronizing and maybe arrogant—he was not sure if Bennett was arrogant, but if he was, he was arrogant in a nice way.

Bennett never cut off disagreement by pulling rank and saying in effect, "I'm the boss and that's the way it is." He insisted on winning the argument and had the knowledge, intellect and debating tools to turn the questioner aside smoothly. "We have to look at objectives," he would start to say and irresistibly recite fact and logic that seduced the questioner into agreement. Ten minutes later the new convert would wonder what Bennett had said and why he had agreed with him. One of Bennett's brightest NCOs, the loser of many discussions, walked into Bennett's office one day determined to reverse one of Bennett's instructions he considered impractical. "It was like putting a child back into place," recalled the NCO. " 'Tut, tut, tut. You can't possibly do that. You know the Axhandle Case in Hong Kong of '51, don't you?' You'd admit you didn't. 'If you don't know that, what do you know?' It wasn't in an authoritarian way that he put you down but suddenly you were standing out in the hallway realizing you had been had again."

Such mastery did exact a price, namely that Bennett had gotten used to having his way. Bennett had so much become the sage that he could never admit to somebody else having superior knowledge. If somebody knew more, he bluffed. Ruling by virtue of his knowledge, he felt threatened when somebody topped him, and once an argument started he refused to admit intellectual defeat at any cost. People sometimes challenged him to test their own skills. "Jim and I used to have some pretty violent differences of opinion," says one NCO who admits to never having won one. "Jim never lacked an opinion nor was afraid to express it, at least to somebody who was equal or down in rank. Jim and I got into a discussion which ended up about the Labour Party of Great Britain. As my position hardened to the right, his hardened to the left, and became a defence of the Labour party. I remember feeling pretty satisfied walking out of there and thinking: 'At least I know he's a supporter of the Labour Party of Great Britain.'"

Only Henry Mendes, a fellow civilian, once stumped Bennett completely and pulled it off with effortless ease. Bennett assigned Mendes the task of plotting patterns from the mass of material Movements Analysis unearthed from the personal routines of suspected intelligence officers. Bennett wanted a "pattern" for every KGB and GRU officer on the theory that the officer would break the pattern to attend meets. Mendes seemed studious and academically inclined. And, indeed, Mendes worked diligently sorting out the various intelligence officers' movements and figuring out what sense came out of it.

"There is no pattern here," reported Mendes after exhausting himself.

"Henry," replied Bennett, "there is a pattern."

"Okay Jim, you're right," sighed Mendes, "there is a pattern."

The response stopped Bennett. He could thwart every debating tactic but that one.

Bennett, the father of Movements Analysis, treated his program of plotting the movement of intelligence officers as a special child and reacted like a parent seeing only what he wanted to see and taking personal offence to criticism. At first Bennett said Movements Analysis needed a bigger data base but later more data seemed only to muddy the water with detail. Then Bennett said more mathematically inclined minds needed to do the analysis and, better yet, computers. Since the Security Service at the time lacked the mathematical minds or the computers, the program floundered. Bennett, his enthusiasm never flagging, claimed the program still needed developing and said a pattern had caught Rem Krassilnikov meeting Victor Spencer in the meet that launched Operation Moby Dick and that it had uncovered other operations too. The argument did not impress the doubters who believed that even random surveillance turns up the occasional meet. The critics contended that more than processing held back Movements Analysis because the program carried basic flaws. For starters, Soviet intelligence officers deliberately varied their daily activities to give their movements little or no pattern, thus undermining the foundation of the program. Furthermore, they contended, even if there were patterns, a break did not necessarily mean anything. An intelligence officer leaving the embassy at an odd time might be going out to buy a birthday gift for his wife. He could break his pattern by driving his car to the garage for servicing or to the hardware store for a package of light bulbs. Movements Analysis tried to separate such routine breaks from intelligence-motivated breaks but how was that possible when intelligence officers covered their meets as personal errands? An intelligence officer could leave for a genuine meet and not break his pattern, according to Movements Analysis. In the view of the critics the high judgment quotient made Movements Analysis more subjective than scientific.

Bennett had sold Movements Analysis to MI5, which tackled the inflated size of the Soviet embassy in London with a dozen analysts and a computer and had come up with similarly disappointing results. MI5's Movements Analysis expert visited Ottawa in the mid-1960s to check his procedure and compare experiences and made the mistake of asking one of Bennett's men about the Security Service's experiences in front of Bennett. The Canadian felt he had to give, as he later described it, a "diplomatic answer."

In a curious way Bennett's stubbornness resembled the obstinacy of Jim Angleton of the CIA. Bennett did not take the extreme positions Angleton did but argued his points with a similar tenacity and usually refused to back down when confronted with mounting evidence to the contrary, although some argued that Angleton stuck to his views because he believed them, whereas Bennett held to his because he

could not accept being wrong. Something else likened Bennett to
Angleton, namely his view of the Russians as supermen who went to
conspiratorial lengths to deceive the West. Sometimes Bennett behaved
as if the tiniest Soviet action held an ulterior motive. For example, the
Russians patronized a small shoe repair store a few blocks from the
embassy, which Bennett had figured as a KGB live letter box because
the owner was Ukrainian, whereas most of his colleagues concluded
that Soviet shoes needed fixing and the Ukrainian shoe repairman had
the closest shop. The Russians also patronized Dain's Delicatessen a
few blocks further down the street where the owner spoke Russian.
Most Security Service officers thought the Russians enjoyed service in
their native language, especially the wives who spoke little English. But
Bennett suspected Dain's formed part of a signal system. If a Mountie
case officer reported that his target had gotten a haircut, Bennett
pointed to it as significant. "He's not getting a haircut," scoffed
Bennett. "It's probably a drop." If a suspect left oranges ripening on
his windowsill at home Bennett sent somebody out each day to check
the position and number of oranges. "With Bennett nothing was
straightforward," says a colleague. "Everything had a motive. He
became suspicious of everything." In retrospect he might have been
parading his expertise and training his men in the need for eternal
questioning yet his colleagues believed he took it all seriously.

Of all the speculative targets, the Towne Cobbler, a leather-goods
store frequented by the Soviets, piqued Bennett's suspicions the most.
He thought the owner's background made him susceptible to recruitment. Examination turned up the tidbit that the only Soviet customers
were KGB officers and that the Towne Cobbler changed its window
display following one of the visits. Every day somebody from the
Security Service visited the store on the Sparks Street Mall to check
the window display. The results showed nothing and the investigation
died off.

Bennett had no doubt the KGB fed the Security Service phony
counterespionage cases. "This is a deception operation," Bennett
would say as he read the reports.

"Bullshit, Jim," argued one of his men. "It's legitimate."

"It's deception," responded Bennett. "There's no way the Soviets
would be that stupid."

During the mid-to-late 1960s the Security Service hit upon case after case of low-level Soviet espionage in Canada and Bennett wrote off most of them as deception. Everybody agreed the KGB manufactured and fed phony cases for the mischievous purpose of making the Security Service chase its tail. The differences of opinion centred over how often. Bennett's men thought they did it sometimes; Bennett thought it was done a lot. So they frequently bickered over the cases as they came in. One NCO in the Ottawa division said every time they sent a new case to headquarters they waited for Bennett to send back word that it was deception.

Operation Carrot Top was one case Bennett quickly dismissed as deception. In Carrot Top an Ontario Department of Highways employee acting as a double agent for the Security Service made regular trips from Toronto to lonely country spots outside Ottawa to fill a KGB dead letter box with innocuous information about the Toronto water and sewer systems and the like. The tasking paralleled the assignments given Victor Spencer in Operation Moby Dick, and Aquavit in Operation Top Hat, which Bennett had defended as genuine. Only occasionally did the double agent meet his Soviet control officer. Bennett said the KGB modus operandi in Carrot Top exceeded the inherent worth of the case and therefore it had to be deception. The KGB kept introducing new dead letter boxes and changing the double agent's signal system. Sometimes he signalled the loading of the dead letter box by marking with chalk two bars on a telephone pole, or he would draw a circle with a dot in the middle, or stick a thumb tack into a pole or even use a wad of chewing gum. Bennett believed the KGB introduced all this activity to impress the Security Service.

Bennett's NCOs argued that Carrot Top smelled all right. The nature of agent assignments followed other cases almost classically and the switch to dead letter boxes for most exchanges merely reflected the KGB's growing fear of surveillance. The KGB had already moved other operations into the countryside and had shown increased nervousness about being caught. If the KGB feared discovery it might very well put new cases such as Carrot Top on dead letter boxes which were intrinsically more secure; switching locations enhanced security even more. So, the NCOs reasoned, the KGB behaved as might be expected under the circumstances. "Okay Jim," said one NCO, "let's get some mileage out of it. They're meeting out at Smith's Falls on a back road. Why don't we put on a film crew from the CBC and watch the Soviets clear the box live on television. They could jump out and interview the guy on the spot. If it's deception, let's get aggressive and shake them up a bit." The NCO who made the proposal later said, "They asked me to go for a medical checkup after I suggested that." The Carrot Top debate resolved itself shortly when the Russians dropped the case but the conflict between Bennett and his men grew.

The NCOs could have gone over Bennett's head at any time, even if only to sit down informally with a senior officer to outline their frustrations. Bennett held relatively junior rank among commissioned officers. Yet not a single dissenter toyed with the idea. Like a boy bending to an unpalatable decision from his father, they grumbled about him losing touch but always submitted to his judgement. Bennett may have been only the equivalent of an inspector but his authority outstripped his rank and, despite his official status, he wielded more effective power than anybody else. Nobody in the Security Service dominated any bailiwick as he did his. Other officers may have presided over him but when handling disagreements with his staff Bennett represented the Supreme Court. There was no seat of higher appeal. Bennett rarely argued with more senior officers even when they overruled him, because the upper echelons changed constantly and with few exceptions, such as Charles Sweeny, the men in charge of B Branch lacked Bennett's credentials and relied on his expertise. It was widely believed that Bennett really ran B Branch regardless of who sat in the Superintendent's office. If the NCOs wanted to commit the heresy of taking on a commissioned officer, Bennett respresented a strategically bad starting point. Furthermore, Bennett's frustrated NCOs were Mounties who had graduated through the paramilitary system and had learned to accept orders stoically no matter how much they disagreed with them. Old line Mounties did not buck the system.

Old line Mounties did not buck the system but young ambitious Mounties, products of the liberal post-war years, treated the structure with less reverence. They had not been around in the early days to witness Bennett molding the Russian Desk into its modern state and took for granted many of his achievements. What they noticed was the growing animosity and his growing curtness. The increasing arguments illustrated that he no longer deflected criticism the way he once did. The younger Mounties wondered why an English accent gave them orders. He had called the shots a long time and produced unimpressive results. They figured they could do as well. The fact was the old lion showed signs of slowness and the young cats hungered for opportunity and were prepared to take chances. People like Harry Brandes, the self-assured aggressive investigator who assisted Bennett in the John Watkins interrogation, Archie Barr, Ray Lees, Howard Gillard and Bruce James waited impatiently and would not retreat from a confrontation. None attached their stars to Bennett's coattails. Some mumbled their frustrations to Hank Tadeson, the assiduous head of B Branch, who assured them Bennett knew what he was doing even though his rationale sometimes seemed obscure from the trenches. "He's been at this a lot longer," counselled Tadeson.

Then in September, 1967, Mihalcin, the dormant suspect in Edmonton, boarded a flight to Montreal and nearly two years after Kit Bag had started, met inside the foyer of the magnificent St. Joseph's Oratory a Soviet citizen attached to the Russian pavillion at Expo 67 identified as Anatoli Shalnev. The next day the watchers followed Mihalcin to a park bench at Park Avenue near Mount Royal and observed Shalnev give him something. Soon after that Mihalcin started turning on his short wave receiver and pulling in Soviet broadcasts. The turn of events made people wonder whether Bennett had been right after all.

18

Operation Deep Root

HEADS TURNED WHEREVER Natasha Makhotin went. When she entered a room all eyes were mesmerized. At a reception she could glide gracefully into a small group and charge the atmosphere without a word. Whether it was raw beauty or unconscious elegance, nobody, man or woman, failed to marvel at her perfect union of looks and presence. Somehow she could be cool and vivacious at the same time. At thirty-two, she looked strikingly like Sophia Loren with cheekbones slightly more raised and a slightly broader face. She had once been a ballerina in Moscow, so the story went; her slenderness and flowing movements seemed to vouch for the gossip.

Natasha arrived in Canada in 1968 speaking excellent English and harmonizing with the upper levels of North American culture as though she was a member of the Eaton family. Her older husband, Vladimir, in his mid-forties, worked in the Soviet Embassy officially as a Second Secretary responsible for the press but within months answered nineteen of the twenty-one indicators on the Security Service's check-off list for identifying Soviet intelligence officers. Nevertheless the KGB did not seem to faze Natasha. She floated above it. She did not fit the party-faithful image of the embassy wife. While most wives carried a low profile in Canada and rarely strayed outside the Soviet colony, Natasha's first act in Ottawa was to take driving lessons to give her mobility. The briefings Soviets give their personnel about avoiding contact with foreigners and living a frugal and exemplary life had not stuck, for she dressed immaculately, enjoyed spending money, and quickly cut a wide swath around Ottawa.

As Natasha reached Ottawa another arrival to Canada preoccupied the attention of B Branch. Murray Sexsmith, the enigma who behaved as both a conservative and a rebel, the badboy establishment man, was returning from Hong Kong after two years as the RCMP's visa control officer and would be filling a position at headquarters. For years B Branch's tight establishment had held Sexsmith back from promotion. He had languished particularly long as a corporal. His commission finally arrived in 1966 and required him to leave B Branch and headquarters since there were no inspector openings. By all accounts, Sexsmith, buttressed by his counterespionage experience, performed well in Hong Kong and impressed the local police authorities. He could expect a more senior position back in Ottawa.

Although Sexsmith was returning, B Branch still had no Inspector openings. A Superintendent's slot as officer in Charge of B Branch had opened with Tadeson's transfer to Vancouver but Sexsmith was too junior for that. Sexsmith had been inspector only a few years and Bennett had been the civilian equivalent of inspector for eight. It seemed logical that Bennett would move up to fill the vacant superintendent's position overseeing B Branch while Sexsmith took over the inspector's spot as head of the Russian Desk. Bennett had always aspired to Head of B Branch and, as the Security Service's undisputed authority of counterespionage, seemed a logical choice. The post had been denied him twice previously, first when Sweeny took control in an appointment nobody could fault and later when Tadeson took over. Tadeson knew less about the job than Bennett but had been in the Security Service about as long and, more importantly, was a Mountie. This time nobody obstructed Bennett's path.

The promotion list arrived and finally rewarded Bennett his boost from a CM-14 to CM-15, which in civilian terms gave him his awaited Superintendent's status. However, his new job title listed him only as the Assistant Officer in Charge of B Branch, not Officer in Charge. B Branch had never before had an assistant officer. The title had been created specially for Bennett who stayed in charge of the Russian Desk with higher pay and an enhanced rank and would be filling in when the Officer in Charge of B Branch was away. The promotion list that had advanced Bennett had elevated Sexsmith from inspector to superintendent and appointed him officer in charge. After being junior all those years, Sexsmith suddenly vaulted over his old boss in one giant leap. The Security Service rationalized putting two superintendents in B Branch on the technicality that Bennett as a civilian was a CM-15 rather than a superintendent. B Branch might have two superintendents but the promotions left no doubt who reported to whom. As was his style, Bennett put the best face on the setback and pretended it did not matter.

Sexsmith had more going for him than his Hong Kong record and the fact he was a Mountie, while Bennett was not. Sexsmith had an attractive and supporting wife, which counted in the RCMP. Whenever somebody was considered for a commission, and each promotion thereafter, the Force examined whether the wife would enhance or impede her husband with the social appearance his new position brought on. If she did not measure up, neither did her husband. Bennett's wife had not integrated well into the RCMP community and by 1968 had mostly withdrawn from its social functions. Bennett often appeared alone at house parties. Promotions also required luck and Sexsmith was lucky when it counted. The most rapidly rising star in the entire RCMP happened to be Len Higgitt who was next in line as Commissioner. Sexsmith was one of Higgitt's boys. It did not hurt Sexsmith that his personable wife knew and worked in the SPCA with Mrs. Higgitt.

B Branch's two most senior officers felt out each other gingerly, moving cautiously, wary that a wrong move could detonate an explosion. Both sought to avoid confrontation. Bennett did not want to give up power but had never before directly confronted a more senior officer. He always used finesse on people above him. Bennett hid feelings while Sexsmith let everything out. Now Sexsmith, for the moment at least, seemed to borrow a page from Bennett's book. Sobered somewhat by his new responsibilities, Sexsmith feared an early run-in would confirm the skeptics' belief he could not handle people, so he did not gloat or impose himself. Bennett's deference gave him little cause to do so. Sexsmith supported Bennett on leaving Operation Kit Bag untouched. A year had passed since Mihalcin had met Shalnev in Montreal and since then he had listened to short wave broadcasts from Moscow but otherwise had done virtually nothing.

Sexsmith never had much patience for modus operandi but agreed to let Kit Bag run.

Although Sexsmith had eclipsed Bennett, the long-time head of the Russian Desk remained a powerful force. While Sexsmith made the big decisions, he still did not like drudgery and, now finding himself wrapped in paperwork and technicalities, he would unload a lot of work on his juniors of whom Bennett was the most important. So Sexsmith, willingly or not, relied on Bennett for the critical background work, which sometimes later tied his hands. Nothing about this experience was new to Bennett. He had influenced the heads of B Branch this way for years. To challenge Bennett required outworking him and nobody had the desire or energy to do that. So even with Sexsmith above him, Bennett continued to dominate all counterespionage work relating to the Soviet Union. How deeply Bennett dominated his empire surfaced each time his absence from the office kicked some of the decisions upstairs to Sexsmith.

Normally the Travel Desk came to Bennett twice a day for a decision on what level of coverage to assign Soviets travelling properly outside the 75-mile limit. Coverage ranged from Level One (full coverage) to Level Four (none). The Soviets had to submit detailed travel plans in advance and Bennett scrutinized each case before deciding. He systematically barred Soviets from certain routes of travel not because they contained any secrets but to intrigue the Soviets as to why they were being barred. He kept a map handy with coloured plastic dots overlaying certain localities to remind him of the restricted areas and whenever the Soviets proposed traversing these areas, as they repeatedly did, Bennett rerouted the travel. (Years later, after Bennett had left, the Security Service stopped the game and when somebody suggested reinstating the practice the plastic dots had fallen off the map and nobody could remember where they had been, and nobody much cared, so the Soviets travelled anywhere.) While Bennett was away, the Travel Desk took coverage instructions from Sexsmith who acted as if he should not be bothered with such detail and usually took the easiest decision by choosing Level Four, which gave no coverage.

With Sexsmith, Bennett found the decisions coming back faster and less predictably than before but otherwise the daily routine continued. Yet beneath the daily routine the circumstances had changed fundamentally. Bennett now worked in the shadow of somebody who might overrule him at any time. NCOs could now go over Bennett's head, which made him vulnerable to the growing resentment. Furthermore, if someone wanted to try on Bennett as a KGB mole he had somewhere to take the accusation.

Sexsmith had not sat in his new office long when a Watcher Service wolfpack patrolling the East End intercepted Natasha Makhotin pulling into the Elmvale Shopping Centre with a Soviet embassy car bearing diplomatic licence plates. She stopped in a corner of the parking lot and waited as the watchers staked her out. A few minutes later a handsome local man in his mid-thirties pulled up beside her. She slipped into his car, slid over and kissed him. The car started moving but before it cleared the parking lot the beautiful Natasha dropped below window level and out of sight. The watchers followed them across the Ottawa River and into the Quebec municipality of Gatineau where they entered a second-rate motel walled off in front by a fence, which hid the parking lot from passing traffic. Natasha and the unidentified Canadian seemed to be enjoying an old-fashioned secret love affair. Bennett called the affair deception and this time most people agreed. Soviet women never played around with Canadian men. Not only was she carrying off a clandestine affair but she had driven to the rendezvous with diplomatic plates.

With Natasha's love affair labelled deception, Operation Deep Root, as it was called, would not go far, although neither would B Branch drop scrutiny altogether. The Security Service could not ignore something merely because it looked phony. Natasha's lover happened to be an acquaintance of Security Service investigator Mel Deschenes who worked in B Branch in A Division and the fellow agreed to talk to Deschenes as long as his wife did not find out. Deschenes reported that the man drove a cab and moonlighted as a driving school instructor, which is how he met Natasha. A handsome specimen with beautiful facial features, curly hair, a flashy smile and gleaming white teeth, he was, as one Mountie put it, "full of bullshit." The Security Service assigned him the code name Joker. Joker might have wanted to pursue Natasha at the first driving lesson but it did not matter because she chased him first and never played coy or tried to hide her love, all of which made her look like a deception agent. But when Deschenes reported back to his superiors in the Ottawa Division they did a fast re-think: maybe she was not a deception agent after all. During the interview Joker revealed that Natasha had disappeared below window level at the shopping centre not to avoid being seen as had been thought. She had ducked down to perform fellatio on him. A little hanky panky prior to the motel was all in the line of duty, but fellatio before they left the parking lot exceeded the call of duty. Natasha was not promiscuous. Men often made passes and she invariably refused. She wanted only Joker, which suggested her love had no ulterior motive. If she sought to seduce in the interests of espionage she could do better than a local cab driver. The affair showed no sign of abating. Natasha and Joker went on joint picnics with their families. The Security Service's Ottawa Division concluded that it had struck lucky and tripped across a genuine case.

A Division felt that Natasha opened a rare opportunity to penetrate the closed Soviet community in Ottawa. Since she dressed and acted in the western style, seemed to enjoy Canada and had fallen in love with a Canadian she might be induced into defecting. A Division at first considered using Joker as the bait since he was her attraction, but A Division held too many reservations about his integrity to trust him. Although cooperating, Joker had not always been completely forthright. Instead, A Division opted for the old KGB blackmail technique of secretly filming one of their romantic encounters. Such an undertaking required resources that A Division knew Bennett would oppose.

Bruce James, the Officer in Charge of A Division, visited Bennett at headquarters and, as expected, failed to budge him. Bennett insisted the KGB stood behind the operation and anything the Security Service did would play into KGB hands. He cited Natasha's injudicious use of her home telephone as evidence of deception. The Soviet embassy repeatedly warned its personnel not to talk openly on the telephone, yet Natasha talked love and arranged rendezvous over the phone. She is broadcasting her intentions, which is the last thing she would do if she wanted to keep her affair discreet, said Bennett. "You've got to face the facts of life," he said. "This has to be a provoked operation."

James argued back that Natasha happened to be a type who ignored rules. "Soviets have human frailties too," he said.

When James failed, Vaughn Mackenzie, James's senior NCO, took a run at Bennett. "Okay Jim," said the witty Mackenzie, "you tell me the Soviets are peddling her ass around Ottawa with some god damn cab driver just to deceive the Mounted Police. Can you see that happening? Say the motel burns down and the woman gets caught in there with this cab driver. Who looks bad—us or the Russians? I can't accept anybody doing something like this for so trivial a reason. If her lover sat on the Russian Desk at External Affairs, okay. Maybe. But Joker has no intelligence value at all."

"The Soviets are too well trained to do this sort of thing," replied Bennett. He added that each one is screened and subjected to rigid training before going abroad. Mackenzie responded that the Soviets are not a superrace and face the same pressures as anybody else. The sides hardened.

Bruce James had worked for Bennett as a staff sergeant and like everyone else had lost arguments. Now, a freshly commissioned inspector, he had more clout. James belonged to the oncoming breed of young Mountie who did not automatically defer to Bennett's reputation and toyed with the idea of provoking war with Bennett over Deep Root. James's official line of reporting authority no longer went to Bennett so he could go to Sexsmith without overstepping but no senior officer would side with him without first hearing out Bennett which ultimately meant bareknuckling it out with Bennett, an opponent who outstripped him in rank, experience and prestige. James may not have regarded Bennett with the same reverence his older colleagues did, but nevertheless recognized political realities. To beat Bennett he needed help. Then, suddenly, before James realized it, help arrived and it came, ironically enough, from Bennett himself.

While a demoralized A Division plodded ahead with its film attack on Natasha, Bennett at headquarters concocted a different scheme. Bennett called in two NCOs, Del Klatt and Gerry Armstrong.

"Look," he told them, "Why don't we see if we can squeeze the husband. He's the main target, not the bloody woman. What the hell is she going to tell us? The husband is the one we suspect of being intelligence."

Bennett had a plan.

Natasha's husband, the Russian Desk had learned, had been called back to Moscow and would be leaving in a few days, opening the door to his possible recruitment. After all, Bennett said, he was the KGB Officer, not her. Bennett did not know why Makhotin was returning—

Joker later learned from Natasha it was for "consultations"—but knew it was a special trip, not a vacation or the end of his normal posting, and that he was going without his wife. Conceivably he was in trouble with the KGB, which made him a candidate for defection. If he was not in trouble, Bennett proposed to put him in trouble by anonymously phoning the Soviet embassy with news that he was carrying on a love affair with a woman in Toronto. Bennett had not invented the love affair. It was real. While his wife played around with Joker in Ottawa, Makhotin had a thing going with a member of the Communist Party of Canada in Toronto, something that the embassy might not know. If Makhotin was hiding it, a simple anonymous phone call could land him in trouble that the Security Service could exploit.

In order to work, Bennett's operation had to be mounted within a couple of days otherwise Makhotin would be gone, and to protect against the backlash of failure, Bennett proposed turning off the wiretap on the Russian embassy for about 15 minutes while the anonymous phone call was placed. Should the recruitment attempt fail, the Russians would surely protest about diplomatic interference and External Affairs would complain to the Security Service. With the wiretap turned off, the Security Service could assure External Affairs that it had checked and found no record of such an incident.

Klatt, Bennett's own man, another one of the younger Mounties, argued against his boss and supported A Division's proposal, but Bennett refused to give him the resources to carry it out no matter how loudly Klatt argued. "Shit," muttered Klatt. "I think he's working for somebody. God damn it, I can't understand what's taking place." Klatt declared he would take his case upstairs all the way to Higgitt if necessary.

Bennett never told A Division of his alternate plan but did not have to, for word spread across the Rideau River fast enough. James considered it an intrusion in his affairs and gave him, as officer in charge of A Division, the ammunition needed for battling Bennett although he was so infuriated that at the time he did not view his new strategic leverage in such analytical terms. James stormed over to headquarters for a session with Sexsmith and accused Bennett of undercutting him. "This is an A Division operation," fumed James, "and Bennett had better keep his hands off." Sexsmith summoned

Bennett into his office and, with James glowering in plain sight, laid down the law to Bennett: A Division would carry the ball on Deep Root and Bennett would keep out. Sexsmith's ruling had killed the plan against the husband. "This doesn't change my view," sniffed Bennett. "I still think it's deception and you're not going to be successful."

Now that it had bureaucratic approval, James's filming operation still had logistical problems to overcome. Joker could not be enlisted in the filming, even if he was trusted, otherwise he would not act naturally. The streetsmart Joker constantly suspected the Security Service of tampering with his motel room and each time rejected the first room or two offered. So the Security Service could never be sure which room to set up in advance. For a simple bugging, such uncertainty presented no insurmountable problem because with the help of clamp-on equipment from the CIA, the Security Service could switch rooms in less than a minute. But filming introduced a new dimension. A strategically placed pinhole had to be drilled into the wall and a camera mounted behind it, all of which required lead time. So the Security Service had to pick a room in advance and with the help of the motel manager manipulate Joker into the wired room. As expected, Joker rejected the first key from the manager but took the intended one. The ploy worked.

"It's my wife and not me who should be watching this," quipped one Mountie in the screening room.

Natasha's composure never cracked when Deschenes appeared at the next rendezvous instead of Joker. She did seem slightly uneasy, not out of embarrassment but of not knowing what to expect from the Canadian authorities. For someone with a dirty deed to do, the personable Deschenes acted with mindful politeness while still ensuring she understood that the Security Service had filmed her secretly making love in a motel room. If she chose to remain in Canada, he counselled, the Canadian government would welcome her with citizenship, financial assistance and opportunity. Deschenes avoided the drastic word 'defect' and did not spell out Canada's expectations for her to divulge everything she knew. He did not need to. Natasha understood perfectly the meaning of Deschenes's offer.

Natasha said she would not become a traitor and spy against her own country. Deschenes told her she was in trouble if the embassy discovered her liaison but Natasha, unruffled and calculating her options, replied she would be in bigger trouble if the embassy discovered her cooperating with the other side. Besides, she said, she had an eight-year-old daughter in Moscow and could not bear leaving her. Deschenes realized strong arm tactics would not work and did not descend into naked blackmail. Since the direct approach was not working, he kept the conversation light and friendly while disengaging himself. "Maybe sometime we'll get together with our families," Natasha said before he left. The remark and her attitude surprised Deschenes. Although she had turned him down, she had not locked the door. Her invitation left room to develop a friendship and keep the effort alive. While the attempt had not succeeded, neither had it exploded into an incident. The fact that she had carried on with Joker suggested nonchalance and led A Division to believe she would not tell the embassy what had happened, sparing at least a diplomatic incident. Natasha had a powerful incentive to hush up the encounter with Deschenes. The minute she told the embassy she would be put on the next flight to Moscow for carrying on an illicit affair with a foreigner and lose the man she loved.

A Division's optimism proved ill-founded. A distressed Natasha suddenly phoned Joker with the news that she was returning to Moscow. Her anguish seemed directed more at losing her lover than anything else. Under escort from Yuri Perfiliev, an identified KGB officer, Natasha was put onto a flight to Moscow where she would be joining her husband who would also be staying in Moscow. It seemed the Russians had learned about the Security Service's approach. Conceivably she had reported it, in which case her recall was normal, but nobody in A Division believed she had. If she had not reported it, then the embassy must have learned some other way. The Soviets, strangely, did not launch a protest with External Affairs. Maybe her husband's affair in Toronto had been passed on to the embassy by one of the KGB's informers in the Communist Party of Canada and landed him in sufficient trouble for recall and Natasha now was merely joining him. Although possible, the timing was too coincidental. One or two Mounties even thought that a sullen Bennett had tipped off the embassy in order to show he was right and A Division wrong.

Each new failure hurt and caused more despair inside the Security Service. Was it one big cancer or a collection of small ailments?

Nobody in the divisions across the country could pinpoint their worry yet when somebody murmured that the KGB must have an agent inside the organization someone else usually picked it up. Mounties travelled and met NCOs in other divisions and traded stories and slowly discovered that others had similar setbacks and suspicions. One investigator in Vancouver who had lived through the consecutive failures of Apple Cider, Moby Dick and Top Hat, and an assortment of smaller collapses, retired out of frustration when Vancouver's next big operation—a case in which a double agent from Seattle was making third-country meets in Canada with a KGB officer posing as a sailor from a Soviet freighter docking in Vancouver—fizzled out like the others had. Everybody acknowledged that the Security Service of old lacked expertise, so were not too surprised when their cases fell apart. The Security Service in the meantime had come a long way and by the late 1960s operated with reasonable professionalism. So members asked themselves, if they had improved so much, why did their operations keep failing? People sensed that something was basically wrong but hated to think the system had been contaminated.

Something about the Bennett persona had always bothered some of his colleagues. They did not know why, but when the subject of penetration arose, long before people worried about it happening to their own organization, their focus shifted to Bennett. A mystery surrounded him. He rarely talked about his family or previous professional experience. He had an international flavour, had known Kim Philby (everybody assumed—wrongly—he had worked for Philby and met him in a number of exotic places in the Far East). People wondered about his style, his aloofness, solitariness and even his British accent. He stood so much apart that people could not help but notice him. One staff sergeant in the Security Screening Branch who had never worked with Bennett or spent a day in B Branch and knew little or nothing of its failures, one day on impulse pronounced Bennett a spy. Even one of Bennett's "boys" who followed his dictates and defended him against the rising dissent would years later acknowledge: "I always thought he could be a spy. There was something about him." As a foreign civilian, Bennett had a handicap to overcome. But part of the perception was Bennett's fault: he had nurtured a mystique and encountenanced a series of myths to bolster his superior image. People thought he had gone to university, worked for MI6 and run counterespionage cases in his pre-RCMP days, and Bennett did nothing to dispel these myths or illuminate his real background. Almost everybody else had come from the same boot camp in Regina, so not surprisingly they speculated about Bennett's professional origins.

When Kim Philby, from the safety of Moscow, published his memoirs of how he had fooled MI6, a local Ottawa newspaper ran a picture of a contented Philby standing in Red Square. At a distance he resembled Bennett a little and some unknown person posted the picture on B Branch's fourth-floor bulletin board with a caption: "Is this our Jim?" The anonymous act displayed bad humour and even worse manners, given the environment, and it came down quickly but not before people noticed.

Don Atkinson, the first Mountie to voice serious suspicion over Bennett, had retired and left Ottawa but others had picked up the theme. Little groups speculated about the failures and in not so hushed tones as they once did. Conjecture over the mole theory, with Bennett as the mole, had virtually seeped into the open. Sandy McCallum and his assistant, Howard Gillard, discussed withholding daily Watcher Service strategies from Bennett. In case Bennett was a mole they wanted to deny the KGB the surveillance techniques the watchers would be using on any given day. McCallum spent hours analyzing the legacy of failure with his colleague, Vaughn Mackenzie, and the two kicked around explanations. "The French have been penetrated and so have the British and the Germans," said McCallum. "The States is having trouble. Yet here we are, the youngest and least experienced and superclean." They looked around for various mole candidates and the suspicion always returned to Bennett. The commissioned officers above him had been transferred in and out like a revolving door. Compartmentalization denied broad access to the NCOs below him. Maybe Sexsmith, but he had spent two critical years in Hong Kong and his early years with the satellites denied him knowledge of most Soviet cases. Besides, they decided, he lacked the capacity to lead a double life. He was exactly what he appeared to be. The common denominator through all these years of failure was Bennett. He had always worked at the core and knew every Soviet case that ever came to the Security Service. The more they thought about it the more they considered it possible.

Something radical had caused the Soviets to whisk Natasha home.

The complexion of that case changed too suddenly. Although if Bennett was a mole, why did the Soviets not withdraw Natasha before the filming? It was a sticky question. Bennett knew of the filming well in advance and could have warned the KGB. If the Russians were going to withdraw her quickly, they would have done it before the incident could develop. Maybe Bennett felt he could divert the investigation away from her and onto the husband and by the time he failed he had run out of time to warn the Soviets. Then, when the Soviets realized Natasha had not reported the Deschenes's approach and, worse still, not absolutely ruled out defection, they felt compelled to spirit her away from temptation. It was not a convincing explanation and McCallum and Mackenzie were tempted to get drunk and forget about their suspicions. Not only was their thesis leaky, but by pursuing it they would have to push the matter to the commissioned level and challenge not only Bennett but the soundness of the officers' decisions promoting Bennett. Deep Root was not the biggest failure, only the most recent one. They felt they had seen enough, so Mackenzie visited his superior, Bruce James, and told him he had something to bring to his attention.

The failure rate under Bennett disturbed James too and he could not help but worry that something was amiss and did nothing to discourage Mackenzie, although he did warn him that Bennett made a perfect victim for KGB deception. The two agreed that if a mole was spoiling the operations, the KGB would work to shift the blame away from the real mole and onto somebody else who was vulnerable and that Bennett made a good fall guy. The KGB would specifically aim at the Security Service's most valuable soldier and Bennett had invested many hours and invented innovative tactics against the Soviets. The KGB would insist on covering every operational failure with a plausible explanation. Nevertheless small clues, unnoticed at the time, would inevitably emerge over a stretch of years and form a trend that even KGB deceptions could not mask. It happened that way with Philby, Maclean, Burgess, Felfe and virtually every KGB penetrator. James sighed in a wistful manner that one needed to go back to the files and starting with Operation Keystone, review the history of Security Service cases and see what emerged. A couple of days later Mackenzie told James he proposed doing exactly that—reviewing the files. James did not stop him. As the senior NCO in charge of counterespionage in

A Division, Mackenzie enjoyed virtually the run of the filing system. He would tell no one he was pulling certain files. Aside from James and McCallum, no one would know about Mackenzie's private investigation.

Mackenzie selected half a dozen of the most prominent counterespionage cases and started jotting down notes as he leafed through them. He by-passed cases like Deep Root, Gold Dust and Carrot Top because he already knew them through personal involvement. He passed over Keystone because he had learned about it through the grapevine. More than a decade later Security Service men still talked about Keystone. Before getting too far he first wanted to satisfy himself that other operations had followed the pattern of failure. He studied the files of cases like Top Hat, Blue Skies and Apple Cider and as he examined them he was struck by a phenomenon that he long knew about but had never before questioned. Now it dumbfounded him. Masses of paper inundated the entire Security Service, choking the filing system and clouding the organization's ability to perceive developments. Mackenzie could hardly comprehend the files because each operation contained volume after volume of trivia, negative information and reports on dead-end leads. Every time Bennett dispatched an investigator to follow one of his leads, a detailed investigative report went into the file even though it produced nothing. Mackenzie flipped through report after report of non-productive leads before finding a development and then through another battery of reports before discovering the next development. One Watcher Service report described a KGB officer walking down a street with a copy of Time magazine, stepping off a curb at one corner, blowing his nose at another and so on. One discovered six pages later the fellow had merely gone out for a walk. The system discouraged file reading and review. Mackenzie figured if the KGB wanted to cover a trail, it could gum up the filing system and strangle the lifeline of the Security Service. Bennett himself inadvertently acknowledged the unwieldiness of the filing system by keeping his own private summary of each active case. His insistence on meticulous reports for every lead had good reason, though. The Watcher Service report on the KGB officer walking down the street may be worthless on that particular day but six months later the Security Service might need to know precisely what he did that afternoon. So it did hold potential long-term importance for the

Security Service but at the same time, masses of extraneous material camouflaged failures and hid trends, which could also benefit a mole.

By going back and re-reading reports, Mackenzie pieced together the thrust of each case. After finishing a particular file he realized that not only had the Soviets terminated each operation but they had never seriously tasked any of the agents. If the cases he reviewed formed a representative sample then the degree of failure had exceeded his fears. He now felt, more than ever, something had to be wrong. He also realized he had no evidence, only speculation, but figured in this business that court quality evidence would never arrive, so speculation would have to do.

Mackenzie's findings placed James in a difficult position. "What the hell do I do with it?" whistled James.

Confronting Bennett over the strategy in Deep Root was one thing; questioning his loyalty was another. They were questioning the guru himself, the man who monitored the pulse and held every counterespionage secret in the organization. One had to be awfully sure before climbing out on such a limb. James wanted to press ahead but without evidence realized he could not take on Bennett. Mackenzie tore up his notes.

Everyone assumed Operation Deep Root died with the hasty recall of Natasha. But the unpredictable Joker still had a surprise or two left. He revealed that he was taking his wife to Russia to visit Natasha and her husband. The love-starved Natasha had written letters urging him to come and later telephoned. Joker and his wife worked nights and took extra jobs to raise money for the passage. Natasha seemed to have freedom phoning and writing from Moscow and Joker had no problem getting a Soviet visa, so it all could be a deception setup. But why would the KGB bother? How could the Soviet Union deceive Canada through the visit of an Ottawa cab driver and his wife?

Until now, James, Mackenzie, Deschenes and the others at A Division had to concede that maybe Natasha had confessed to the embassy. The invitation to visit Russia changed their thinking. They now felt more certain she had not talked. Would Vladimir Makhotin invite Joker to visit his wife in Moscow if he knew what had really happened in Ottawa? "What do you think her husband would say to Joker when he got to Moscow?" One Mountie asked sarcastically. "How good the old lady was? Can you imagine Joker telling him:

'Gees, you've got some lady there.' I don't think they'd have an awful lot to talk about." If her husband did not care about Natasha's extra-marital endeavours, his employer, the KGB would. If the wife of a KGB officer admitted carrying on an illicit affair in contravention of the rules and being entrapped and propositioned to defect, the KGB, even if it trusted her loyalty, would quarantine her from further outside contact for punishment alone. The last visitor permitted into her Moscow flat would be the Canadian lover who precipitated the breach.

"What the hell is going on?" asked one Mountie when he heard about Natasha's invitation. "It's totally inconsistent and when things aren't consistent I don't like it."

Joker's upcoming trip to Moscow changed things. It revived the old question: If Natasha had not told the KGB, then who had? James started thinking he had better move his suspicions up the ladder.

19

Operation Gridiron

THE SECURITY SERVICE considered setting up Joker as a double agent for the purpose of sniffing out the reason for Natasha's return. Time and home surroundings might loosen her tongue and maybe even the tongue of her husband. The Makhotins would undoubtedly say something about it and even if they parroted the KGB deception line, the Security Service would at least know something. The stumbling block was Joker. A Division could compensate for KGB deceit but without a trusted double agent the fabric grew too complex and threatened to confuse or even entangle the purpose. Joker might reveal to Makhotin, and thus to the KGB, his cooperation with the Security Service and thus give the other side another advantage in the war of lies. So rather than manipulating Joker, A Division decided instead to abort his plans for Moscow.

The RCMP lacked the power to cut off the trip through legal procedures. Besides, if Joker suddenly could not get a passport the KGB would figure out the Canadian government had intervened and from that conclude that the authorities knew something. A more subtle way had to be found. Without showing its hand, the Security Service needed to scare off Joker. Convincing a stallion like Joker to forego a prize filly like Natasha needed some doing, but A Division came up with a plan.

The Security Service brought in an elderly Russian-language translator from its office in Toronto and instructed him to telephone Joker and pretend to be a friend of the Makhotins visiting Canada with a scientific delegation. The translator would invite Joker to meet him in Confederation Square on some urgent business. "It doesn't matter what Natasha tells you in her letters," the RCMP translator would say in his best Russian accent at the meet, "she doesn't really want you to come." The Security Service figured the translator had enough cover to fool the clever Joker for only about three minutes, so they gave strict instructions—give his warning and disappear thirty seconds later.

The translator should have returned to his debriefing spot at the Beacon Arms Hotel about ten minutes later but did not. When he failed to return an hour later, the Mounties set out on a search. "Aw shit," said one of the investigators, "we were looking all over town for this guy and couldn't find him. He was supposed to be back. We went over it fifty times: 'Here's what you're going to say. Thirty seconds and you get out.'" The search team finally spotted him wandering in a drunken daze south of the Lord Elgin Hotel. He had lost his directions. By this time Joker had contacted Deschenes demanding to know what kind of stunt his outfit was pulling. It seemed Joker saw through him almost immediately, invited him for a drink and, despite his briefings, the translator accepted, had too much and confessed everything. "He was very dumb and didn't handle himself well," Joker would eventually say. Back at the hotel the translator admitted to a drinking problem and was soon fired. The Mountie responsible for handling him had a drinking problem of his own and had missed an appointment and was transferred to police duties on the Prairies. In the aftermath of the shambles, Joker and his wife went to Moscow.

Before leaving, Joker contacted his Member of Parliament, John Turner, the Minister of Justice, and got a letter of introduction to the Canadian embassy in Moscow, and when he arrived an embassy car picked him up at the airport. He met Ambassador Robert Ford and only later, when dined by one of Ford's diplomats, did the embassy discover he was not a VIP but a cab driver. The embassy shot off a telegram to Ottawa demanding to know what was happening. If the embassy was miffed over Joker, the feeling was mutual. Joker described his dinner host as "rather dumb." "He had nothing good to say about Russia, not one thing," recalled Joker. "During dessert I told him that if he wanted Vladimir [Makhotin] to come and join us for a visit he should phone and invite him. He figured that was impossible." Joker arrived back in Canada trying to sell his story, figuring the RCMP could pay his trip expenses and leave him a tidy profit. "Get lost," Deschenes told him. "We're interested but not that interested."

Bennett's fortunes had been dwindling and the defeat over the Natasha filming hastened the decline. Before Joker had left for Moscow, Bennett had reached for the backing of someone who would surely support his view of Operation Deep Root, namely defector Anatoli Golitsin who perceived deception in almost everything the KGB did. Bennett proposed bringing him to Canada to review cases and offer advice on the practice of counterintelligence. His original attempt to tap Golitsin in the mid-1960s had been stymied by Kelly who could not swallow Golitsin's adamant claim that the KGB had faked a phony rift between Russia and China to fool the West. Times had changed. In mid-August 1969, as Joker scraped together funds for his Moscow trip, Kelly, now Deputy Commissioner, was retiring and so Bennett did not have to try hard to get Golitsin this time because the CIA supported him and Golitsin himself wanted to come. Two months later, Bennett, by himself, picked up Golitsin, also alone, at the Ottawa train station and welcomed him to Canada.

Bennett took his bulldoggish-looking guest to his home and, with Shev and his two daughters at the table, served him dinner, entertained him for the evening and later delivered him to a comfortable and electronically swept suite in the Chateau Laurier. From his perch overlooking the locks of the Rideau Canal next to Parliament Hill's East Block, Golitsin held court and for the next four days rarely moved outside. With Golitsin ensconsed, selected visitors dropped by to call on him, including John Starnes, the diplomat whom Prime Minister Trudeau had freshly designated as the next head of the Security Service. Bennett and four of his NCOs at headquarters showed up with a load of selected case files of failed operations, which Golitsin pondered one by one. He pored over the files on the Soviet embassy's infamous "stud squad", the three hard-drinking KGB officers who boorishly lunged after women wherever they went in Ottawa. The Security Service had never encountered anything like it and could only conclude that they were trying to distract the organization. In this instance, almost everybody supported Bennett's claim of deception. After one look through the files Golitsin did too.

Golitsin always moved slowly, as if measuring each action, and the

Mounties discovered that he also read files slowly. A man with such a dominating personality and iron will could not be pushed, so his deferential hosts waited with anxious patience for every verdict. Golitsin meanwhile plodded along oblivious to the anxiety around him. He grasped the thrust of the cases well but sometimes flipped past significant events to zero in on fine detail, almost trivia. When Golitsin wanted a break, everybody broke. As they adjusted to his pace the Mounties understood why the CIA had experienced trouble handling him. He read a few pages and flipped back, forward and back and in his thick Ukrainian accent asked questions as he went. Each case absorbed several hours. "Deception," he barked after laying down the file on Operation Carrot Top. Bennett had called it deception too and A Division had disputed it. Golitsin did not elaborate why he thought Carrot Top was phony. He pronounced his conclusions without much explanation and nobody cared to dispute his authority.

All the cases Golitsin studied were dead except for one—Operation Deep Root. Bennett sought Golitsin's opinion on Natasha's liaison with Joker and Golitsin did not disappoint him. He flatly said she had been dispatched and that the KGB controlled her affair with the cab driver. With the filming of Natasha long over, Golitsin's support came too late to help Bennett win his way but it did bolster his argument.

Bennett carried the scar from another battle wound, even before Deep Root. When Sexsmith took over B Branch he soon thereafter took control of the Featherbed file. Featherbed was top secret but among top-secret files it was more secret than the others. It did not sit in Central Registry with the other files. Featherbed had always rested in the head of B Branch's office safe but since Charles Sweeny's departure in 1964, it had fallen under Bennett's control. He tended to it with another civilian, Janette Keir, until, as one observer put it, "the Mounties took over Featherbed," meaning that Sexsmith had moved to take possession. Bennett as assistant officer in charge of B Branch still had access to Featherbed but Sexsmith ran the show.

Featherbed started in the early 1950s while Terry Guernsey ran B Branch. Guernsey believed that many communist spies had escaped the disclosures from Soviet defector Igor Gouzenko since Gouzenko exposed only the operations of military intelligence and did not touch the KGB (then called the NKVD). If Gouzenko exposed only a corner and not the whole that meant that several or more agents remained in place for every agent he uncovered. Virtually all the agents he revealed were ideological recruits co-opted on the strength of their religious-like belief in communism, so the undetected KGB agents would likely be similarily motivated. By now they would have embedded themselves so deeply in the civil service under a false flag that normal investigation could not uproot them. Most secret ideological agents once had been open communists who attended party meetings and distributed leaflets on street corners before "dropping out" of the open party and apparently abandoning communism to go undercover. They could hide their real beliefs and the passing years would dim peoples' memories but they could never totally erase the past, so they lived with an achilles heel that always threatened their cover. Guernsey worked on the idea that by searching back into the 1930s and 1940s one could uncover the open communists of that generation and compare their names with current civil servants and thereby develop leads toward identifying the undiscovered KGB agents inside the government.

When Guernsey, then a junior officer, tried to get investigators he found his proposal turned down. The RCMP hierarchy refused to support Featherbed. It felt such a search would embarrass the Force in the eyes of the government. Subsequent attempts to rekindle the investigation were also stopped from on high, so Guernsey's idea deteriorated to the status of a passive holding file. If a piece of information flowed across his desk, Guernsey slipped it into the slender Featherbed file, which rarely left his office safe. For the next half dozen years the file never accumulated more than three or four sheets of paper.

The original name to make it into Guernsey's file was E. Herbert Norman, the Canadian ambassador and friend of Lester Pearson who committed suicide in 1957 after the witchhunting United States Senate Subcommittee on Internal Security named him publicly for the second time. Guernsey and George McClellan interviewed Norman after the U.S. committee first publicized his name in 1951, confirmed that he had been a communist at Cambridge University in the 1930s and pinned down a few other suspicious things, but Norman denied being an agent or betraying Canada. He said his university days were behind him. Norman returned as ambassador but Guernsey and McClellan harboured doubts and put his name into the Featherbed file.

The second name in the Featherbed file belonged to the late O.D.

Skelton, the Undersecretary of External Affairs generally known as the father of the civil service. His record showed a trace with the Communist Party of Canada back in the 1920s but his appointments at External Affairs showed no evidence of packing the department with suspected communists. The names of one or two other living senior civil servants filled the Featherbed file. The information did not prove anything and may not have been accurate but contained enough fragments to keep the file around. In 1960, Howard Draper, the junior inspector from the Countersubversion Branch looked at the file and shook his head. Draper said it was a shame the Force refused to devote resources to it and vowed that if ever he rose high enough he would untie Featherbed. Featherbed started taking on life in the 1960s first with Sweeny and later under Bennett who, with Keir, expanded it to a series of files with scores of names. As leads came in, they were investigated and stored away for future reference. After Sexsmith took away Featherbed, Draper finally reached his senior post and the restrictions fell off.

Overnight Featherbed grew from an orphan to a spoiled child, getting not only full-time investigators but the choice of almost anybody in the house. Harry Brandes and Ray Lees, two of the best counter-espionage investigators, joined Featherbed shortly after returning from university and in turn were joined by the hardworking Neil Chadwick and Ian MacEwan, another latter-day university product. Since Featherbed dwelled heavily on the Communist Party of Canada, D. Branch (countersubversion) got a representative and nominated the capable Neil Pollock. Later Archie Barr, the baby-faced but fearsome intellectual, would switch to Featherbed and so would Bill Cliffe.

Featherbed, which never before had had an office, took over the "penthouse," a nest of four offices in headquarters' most secret nook; a square turret hovering over the main entrance one floor above roof level. The locks were changed and since the penthouse had no elevator, nobody visited it by accident, which made it an ideal base for a secret operation. The transformation took place quietly. People wondered why Featherbed's secrets had stopped leaking out.

The new secluded Featherbed went back in time, culling the files for leads of longterm Soviet penetration of the Canadian government and starting with a more thorough investigation of Herbert Norman. The Security Service suspected Norman had committed suicide in 1957 to avoid recall and another investigation for fear he could not withstand it. Now in the late 1960s Featherbed uncovered allegations that Norman had secret communist membership which he had withheld from Guernsey and McClellan in 1951. At the same time the CIA passed along information from an informant quoting Norman shortly before his death in Cairo as saying he could not talk without betraying colleagues. These colleagues of Norman's did not have to be agents but the remark heightened the suspicion Norman had been holding back.

The Featherbed search widened beyond the civil service, expanded into the general public and eventually produced a list of 262 alleged secret communist party members including doctors, lawyers, economists and academics suspected of performing various tasks short of espionage. They belonged to the so-called "secret clubs" with no membership card. Featherbed also delved into the Waffle wing of the New Democratic Party—after seeing the KGB subtly cultivate some members—on the theory that the KGB had recruited British agents from the left wing of the Labour party and would try to do the same in Canada. Featherbed would eventually get its knuckles rapped for interfering in the affairs of an open conventional political party. The incident showed how Featherbed had grown and how strongly the investigators feared Soviet disruption in Canadian society. "If I had my life to live over again," said one Featherbed officer, "I might just shrug my shoulders everytime I saw a Russian somewhere and say: 'If he's not physically stealing something it's all right. He can go and talk to anyone he wants.'"

The more Featherbed looked the more mesmerizing became the thought that the Canadian government had been overrun by KGB agents, and the more tantalizing yet frustrating the search became. Some potential informers, who once told the RCMP to go to hell, now had second thoughts and started talking, which helped push the investigation forward. One who finally cooperated was Grif, the KGB talent spotter in Toronto who helped Bourdine recruit Green as Gideon's only agent. But each step forward was usually matched by a step backward. "One of the things I regret like hell is not getting to Norman Robertson," said one Mountie of the powerful Undersecretary of External Affairs. "He was dying of cancer. So much doesn't get put on paper and External Affairs had so much going on." People had died; others forgot. Evidence disappeared, usually innocently but sometimes not. Investigators scrambled through quarter-century-old telephone books for evidence of who owned certain telephone numbers. Such leads provided suspicion but no proof. Featherbed was paying the price of nearly two squandered decades. The evidence would never satisfy a court but the investigators felt the thrust of the material was unmistakable. Detached outsiders never saw the files so an impartial referee could not determine whether the files would open one's eyes to the breadth of KGB espionage and subversion or merely smear peoples' names with poisonous gossip and innuendo based on hearsay evidence appealing to conspiratorial minds.

As Featherbed spread out, Jim Angleton's counterintelligence group at the CIA was running in high gear, and the CIA's belief that high-level penetration in the Canadian civil service subverted foreign policy on issues like Cuba, as well as time, inevitably drew them together. Angleton and Sexsmith exchanged material through a special communications link so secret that the official liaison officers had no access to it. Angleton had certain operations in the wind that he was withholding from the CIA's Soviet Bloc Division in order to exclude the suspected mole, but he cut in the Security Service on the condition it restrict the knowledge to a handful of insiders. With an assurance that the information would not seep out of the Featherbed unit, Angleton divulged a big secret: he was receiving communication from an entrenched source behind the iron curtain that from time to time coughed up clues toward Soviet disruption and disinformation in the West and gave positive intelligence as well. Angleton believed in the integrity of the source and felt he had pulled off an end-run around the Soviet deception campaign. The source did not produce a full crop or harvest easily. It served up only partial information and tended to refer to ancient history. It could not be interrogated, and so it dispatched its intelligence erratically at intervals of its own choosing. Aside from the logistical problems of getting its message to the outside, the source had not penetrated the Soviet government to the inner soul, but was burrowing and might get there. In the meantime it offered to help the West. Angleton, who propagated hybrid orchids and waited up to seven years for a single result, treated the source with patience and tenderness for the day it burst into bloom.

Angleton felt he had pierced the iron curtain with a hole that might eventually grow big enough to expose the KGB's campaign of deception and disinformation. When that happened the West could retaliate with a deception program of its own and Angleton had the plan ready. "It takes a mole to catch a mole," said one CIA officer and history proved him at least partially correct. Soviet defectors had exposed more and bigger spies in the West than had the unassisted efforts of all the western counterintelligence agencies. Angleton hoped that with time the source behind the iron curtain might expose the KGB's mole in the CIA if the mole lurking inside the CIA did not destroy his source first. Whose mole would expose the other? Angleton felt that the CIA must put its house in order and, in the meantime, protect the source.

Normally the code name for Angleton's source would have come off the approved master list of code names but requesting one would in itself automatically tell a few people outside Featherbed that a source of one kind or another was being run out of the penthouse. Sexsmith treated Angleton's source with such delicacy that he spurned a code name and simply called it the source.

Angleton's warning about the need to protect the source came as the complaints and suspicions from NCOs in B Branch kept growing. The protesters no longer whispered clandestinely and the accusations had reached high into the commissioned ranks. At least one NCO announced he could no longer work under Bennett. "All right," counselled Draper, "we'll make some changes." The Security Service had reacted reluctantly to the mole suspicion because such a penetration, if substantiated, wreaked massive damage to the organization and challenged the judgment of the officers who had invested in Bennett. Even Sexsmith had hesitated when confronted by the suspicion. Sexsmith along with others would look foolish if Bennett had been sabotaging the organization all those years under their noses. Now circumstances had changed. Howard Draper was a new broom in charge of the Security Service's operations. He rose from D Branch and had no investment in protecting Bennett. More significantly, accusations from NCOs coupled with Angleton's security requirements forced Featherbed to look at itself. If the NCO's suspicions were correct, then Angleton was being let down and his source put into jeopardy because as Assistant Officer for B Branch, Bennett periodically presided over Featherbed and knew what was happening. Featherbed felt it had to clean its own house first and that meant resolving the Bennett innuendos. As they reviewed the superficial evidence the

Featherbed investigators arrived at the conclusion Mackenzie had come to: that despite the lack of proof, the Security Service could not afford to let the suspicion linger.

Suspecting a mole is like discovering cancer, once you suspect the problem all restrictions fly away and only one priority remains: to rid yourself of the disease. The organization that had leisurely ignored the signs now checked the vital indicators and started to race to make up for lost time. Featherbed made the perfect base from which to explore the Bennett suspicion. It already had the best investigators and, cordoned off both physically and professionally, could start an internal inquiry without people knowing a thing. Except for one matter—when Sexsmith was absent, Featherbed reported to Bennett. Featherbed had already been hiding from him its impromptu querying but this could not continue long. Bennett had to be moved out of the nerve centre to be investigated properly and Draper had already, for personnel reasons, decided to transfer him. But where? He could not rise higher in B and moving him out of the counterespionage field after sixteen years would certainly alert a mole and make him freeze, which was the last thing Featherbed wanted. Draper found himself tied. He could not leave Bennett in place to do a proper investigation, but moving him might skewer the investigation. Draper resolved the dilemma with a decision that left everyone blinking.

Either Draper had pulled off a brilliant coup or committed a colossal blunder. Few denied that his decision carried the touch of genius. Whether it worked or not was another matter. Some feared Draper had been too clever by a half. Draper started with the premise that Bennett could not be investigated discreetly as long as he remained in B Branch. Aside from giving him access to Featherbed, he knew where everybody was and could watch investigators being diverted from their regular work into something mysterious, which he would soon figure out. Yet B Branch was the elite of the Security Service and shifting him to any other branch diminished his prestige. Draper would be giving him a thousand reasons for the transfer and raising Bennett's suspicion with each one of them. Aside from counterespionage work, Bennett had experience in electronic and technical matters from his communications days at GCHQ and the Security Service's technical facilities had grown into a series of small fiefdoms in various corners each too small for somebody with the authority of Superintendent. The system was not satisfactory. The technicians in the bugging section worked by themselves independently of the logistics people who engineered clandestine entries that allowed the technicians to install their bugs safely while the bugs were monitored by the processing section, which resided elsewhere. Meanwhile D Branch complained that B Branch hogged the Watcher Service. Draper figured this grab bag collection of support services needed to be combined into one super branch and run by an officer who understood the needs of B Branch, the opportunities of radio equipment and the intricacies of physical surveillance. Draper felt Bennett met the requirements so well he would hardly suspect anything, especially since the transfer moved him from an Assistant Officer up to Officer in Charge of the new E Branch, which overlooked all the support services, including the Watcher Service.

"Is this a demotion?" asked Bennett.

"Hell no," boomed Draper. "It gives you the opportunity for advancement."

Bennett seemed satisfied and told colleagues he was pleased. As the man running E Branch he presided over the largest section in the Security Service.

The controversy over the transfer lingers still. Some say a transfer like that would not fool a mole because beneath the veneer he was not being promoted but kicked upstairs. "You might be a corporal in charge of a drug section in Vancouver and get promoted to Sergeant in charge of a headquarters desk where you escort people in to see the Commissioner," says one B Branch veteran. "Yes, you got a promotion and more money, but man, you're on the skids." E Branch might have been big but got its bulk from the mass of low-paid civilians in the Watcher Service and the processing section and was relegated to a function of assisting B and D Branches carry out their cases. The real action happened in those two branches and Bennett, who all his career had been an initiator, now responded to others' initiatives. Rather than control cases he acted as an executive technician.

On the other hand Bennett continued to wield immense power from his new base on the third floor. Because he controlled the support services, everybody came running to him with requests. Bennett never had enough Watcher Service units to go around and his technicians could install only so many listening devices and his transcribers listen to a finite number of bugged conversations. So when B and D quarrelled over the available resources, Bennett heard the arguments and played the role of Solomon. Sometimes he could control a case by the way he doled out his resources.

If E Branch represented banishment, Bennett suffered a lofty—and, to many, an enviable—exile. The size of the Watcher Service alone exceeded B Branch and, overall, Bennett had four times as many people as Sexsmith. Elsewhere, he controlled the black bag people, known as E Special, who entered buildings clandestinely and also had another section for special operations. Bennett brought with him to E Branch his cherished Movements Analysis program, which was about to go onto computer. Between fusing together a new branch, steamlining operations, straightening out personnel problems, mounting his support operations, converting Movements Analysis to computer, introducing computers to the rest of the Security Service and sitting on committees, Bennett had enough work to absorb his time. Draper had deliberately overloaded him so he lacked time to speculate about what might really be happening.

Maybe Draper's tactic not only worked but worked so well that in his desire not to alert Bennett he gave away too much. The transfer moved Bennett from one sensitive post to another and actually increased his circle of knowledge. Every sweaty deal passed through E Branch. In B Branch he knew all the counterespionage cases. In E he learned about both counterespionage and countersubversion cases. "Now he had not only one room but the whole house," says one Mountie. As a mole Bennett could compromise more secrets than before. Even the detachment from Featherbed was not quite absolute. Soon Featherbed would be bombing Bennett with every investigative aid in the book—the Watcher Service, bugs, wiretaps and even closed-circuit television—and Bennett directed most of them. With Bennett removed, Featherbed launched Operation Gridiron and focussed solely on the hunt for the mole.

Gridiron never fooled itself that investigating Bennett would be easy. For starters, if Bennett was loyal, the investigation would flail away uselessly and frustrate the investigators. On the other hand, if Bennett was a mole embedded for decades, smoking him out would be Herculean and probably equally frustrating. Gridiron did not know how long the probe would run so it budgeted a year. The Philby search exhausted more than a decade of stops and starts and the search into former MI5 chief Sir Roger Hollis at that point was still running after six years. Gridiron would start at the beginning by combing the files and hoping that following up the leads did not take too long.

The investigation started on the granddaddy file of them all, Operation Keystone. It was established that Gideon had been sold out by Mountie traitor Long Knife but a patient review of the file uncovered indicators muddying what had seemed to be clear water. Evidently more lay behind Gideon's betrayal than the simple actions of Long Knife. From the day Gideon undertook training in Moscow, he had been earmarked to settle in the United States but never did. Nobody believed the KGB would invest so much in the legend of an illegal and change course after he had been put into the field. Several theories at the time attempted to explain why the KGB had shifted Gideon from the United States to Canada: one, the Soviets encountered trouble in the final stages of documenting Gideon's phony status in the United States so kept him in Canada until it could be worked out; another, the sweep of American McCarthyism intimidated the Soviets into holding Gideon back; and, lastly, Gideon had done so well legitimizing himself in Canada the KGB decided to promote him from a radioman to full intelligence officer and keep him where he was. Now, long after the event, a more plausible theory emerged when the investigators overlaid the experiences of Gideon with the story of the infamous Soviet illegal, Rudolph Abel, who had operated in New York City for nine years.

Abel, a KGB Colonel, landed in North America at Quebec City as Andrew Kayotis and settled in the United States mostly as Emil Goldfus but sometimes as Martin Collins. He worked diligently on behalf of Soviet intelligence and became so busy that he needed assistance in carrying out routine functions. Moscow sent Reino Hayhanen who for five years had been building up cover in Finland as Eugene Maki. The Russians in those days liked to run illegals in groups of three: an intelligence officer (Abel), a courier (Hayhanen) and a radioman (who had not arrived). Six months after Hayhanen came to the United States to help Abel, Moscow sent Gideon to North America with instructions that, after documenting himself in Canada, he would move to the United States as a radioman for an illegal whom it did not identify. When Moscow told Gideon to stay in Canada, Abel instructed

Hayhanen to learn Morse code and set up cover in a one-man photo shop, which resembled uncannily Gideon's cover in Montreal. Evidently Abel wanted Hayhanen to take up radio even though he had not been trained for it.

If Abel needed a radioman it made no sense for the KGB to convert Hayhanen and simultaneously transform an existing radio operator like Gideon into an intelligence officer when neither Hayhanen nor Gideon had been schooled for their new functions. It made no sense except under one scenario: Gideon had been destined to become Abel's radioman except the KGB had learned about his defection and changed his assignment. If the KGB knew about Gideon's change of loyalty it had to change plans and divert him in order to save Abel. Fortunately for the KGB, Gideon volunteered to stay in Canada, which made the change convenient. If Gideon could not be trusted to work with anybody else, what choice did the KGB have but to promote him to intelligence officer where he could work independently. Radiomen had to work for other people, which in Gideon's case the KGB would not permit if it knew he had turned into a double agent. These events pointed toward an early exposure of Gideon, much before Long Knife betrayed him, and raised a disturbing question: how had the KGB learned about Gideon's secret defection. Gridiron had to assume another agent compromised Gideon very early when the circle of knowledge was small. Something else struck the investigators as strange. The Soviets never did provide Gideon with the promised high-speed transmitter. After promising it, they said it would come after he returned to Moscow. It seemed later that Moscow had dangled the transmitter as a lure to get the RCMP to send Gideon to Moscow. The transmitter also had been promised before Long Knife entered the case.

Another disturbing item cropped up—the KGB had never fully exploited Long Knife. The KGB should have wrung every drop of intelligence out of a well-placed mole like Long Knife. Instead it dropped him after a few haphazard sessions. Maybe Don Atkinson had been correct, that the KGB already had a mole elsewhere and merely used Long Knife to take the blame. The Security Service in those days was so small the KGB could do little without jeopardizing a mole, and Long Knife, who was being exiled to police duties, had become expendable. So maybe Long Knife did not so much betray Gideon as give the KGB an opportunity to pull back an already-exposed agent.

While reconstructing Keystone, Gridiron tripped across the fact that Bennett knew about the case earlier than the investigators had thought—while he still worked for GCHQ in England. The Security Service files contained no record of it. Gridiron discovered it only through investigation and started to wonder if Bennett had covered up this fact. As a mole he has reason to do so.

Why had Bennett come to Canada? It seemed strange somebody as ambitious as Bennett would abandon a good career at GCHQ to take a flyer on a country he had never visited. Furthermore, why did he stick it out at the RCMP where he could never become Commissioner and had to answer to officers with less experience and intelligence. Most civilians with his talent quit and took jobs with more equitable conditions and higher rewards. The RCMP once offered to make Bennett a Mountie but he declined. Mounties were routinely transferred from branch to branch and around the country. Bennett evidently preferred sitting on the Russian Desk even if it retarded his advancement and relegated him as a civilian to second class citizenship.

Then there was the question of the empty room in the Soviet Embassy. After Guernsey had bugged the new embassy following the great fire of 1956, why had the Soviets left the wired room empty? Somebody might have told the Russians about the bugs which explained why they did not use the room. Neither could they tear the bugs out. In those days the Russians lacked the sweeping equipment to allow them to find the bugs so they could not dismantle them without jeopardizing a mole. Maybe the Soviets left the room empty until they acquired the technology to properly find them. In the meantime the Security Service monitored an empty room.

Who told the Russians about the bugs? Long Knife had to be the primary suspect except he had been transferred out of Ottawa six months before the fire and nearly a year before the bugs had been planted in the new building. Nevertheless he could have learned about it from old colleagues while visiting Ottawa. Long Knife's signed confession did not touch the subject, so Gridiron reinterviewed him with a lie detector. Long Knife swore he knew nothing about it. If Long Knife did not tell the Russians, who did? Bennett had worked on

Operation Dew Worm and knew the precise locations of each installation. One more piece of circumstance had been added to the suspicion against him but the case still rested on speculation rather than evidence. Gridiron had not yet proved anything.

The first big break arrived by accident almost six months later at CIA headquarters when Neil Pollock, one of the original Featherbed investigators who was transferred to Washington when the focus shifted onto Bennett, was talking with Clare Edward Petty, one of Angleton's counterintelligence officers. Petty was described as a "walking computer" and could claim to have actually identified a mole. Through reviewing files he pinpointed Heinz Felfe as a KGB mole inside the BND, West German intelligence, before defector Golieniewski confirmed it.

Pollock made a crack at Bennett. "You have some doubts?" asked Petty.

"No, not really," replied Pollock. "He's just such a martinet. He keeps everything to himself."

"I'll tell you a story," volunteered Petty, "that will probably get me into trouble." Petty revealed that Bennett, while head of the Russian Desk a while back, had dispatched a message through a special cable channel asking the CIA to put surveillance on a local Soviet agricultural attaché named Bagramov as he toured South America and attached with the message Bagramov's travel itinerary as submitted to External Affairs. Soviets posted to Ottawa usually did not travel to South America but it was unusual also for Bennett to request CIA surveillance of somebody not identified as an intelligence officer. The CIA's Soviet Bloc Division made a big effort to fulfill Bennett's wish and reported an uneventful trip. Then, when the Bagromov surveillance had been finished and forgotten, Bennett delivered another message. This time he said he had been sitting in his office chatting about the movement patterns of Soviet staffers and while describing Bagramov's route through South America, his guest, Heinz Herre, the BND's Liaison Officer in North America, suddenly turned white, lost his composure and nearly dropped his cigarette.

Bennett's report worried the CIA because Herre was the BND's official link in Washington and if he was contaminated, the CIA had a security problem. Checking back, the CIA discovered the reason for Herre's discomfort: he had recently travelled through South America along an amazingly similar route. The coincidence, and the fact that it obviously disturbed him, immediately threw him under suspicion and the suspicion increased when Herre and his wife later travelled on vacation to Denver and Jackson Hole, Wyoming, at about the same time a New York-based Soviet officer known to have been in contact with Bagramov travelled with another Soviet through Denver and Jackson Hole. Two coincidences seemed more than coincidence and the CIA nearly asked the BND to withdraw Herre when cooler, more senior, heads at the CIA concluded the case lacked substance.

Herre had fallen under suspicion before and been cleared. Defector Goleniewski, who exposed more important Soviet operations than any other defector in history, had once said a KGB officer told him ex-patriate Ukrainian nationalist Stefan Bandera had been murdered in a KGB plot by somebody who invited him out to dinner and then administered poison. Mystery had shrouded Bandera's death for a while. An investigation showed that prior to his death Bandera had been taken out to dinner by his BND control officer, Heinz Herre, who had also been a suspect of the Munich police. So evidence pointed at Herre. A few years later KGB assassin Bogdan Stashynsky fell in love with a German woman, defected and confessed to shooting Bandera with a double-barreled gas pistol. Originally disbelieved, Stashynsky produced overwhelming evidence that dispelled any doubt and a West German court sentenced him to eight years in prison.

It seemed the KGB with its phony poisoning story had tried to frame Herre through an unwitting Goleniewski. Herre was ripe for a set up. He was a Russophile who spoke better than passable Russian and who many years earlier, before Germany attacked the Soviet Union in 1941, had received Russian training. "With his background we all had our suspicions about him," explained one CIA officer who was later satisfied that Herre was innocent. Moles over the years had troubled the BND and it now looked as if the KGB wanted to tear up the organization with a hunt for a possibly non-existent mole. The Stashynsky defection had spoiled the first attempt and it looked like the KGB was trying to make another pass at Herre. The way it unfolded implicated Bennett because it was hard to believe he acted unwittingly. On the other hand it was hard to believe a mole would show his hand so boldly as Bennett had.

Until now Gridiron had withheld the Bennett investigation from the

CIA but the Herre incident proved too big a lead not to follow and it required taking the Americans into the investigation. Angleton had always trusted Bennett implicitly and saw him as his man inside the RCMP. But Angleton had also trusted Kim Philby in the early 1950s and after the Burgess and Maclean defections still failed to implicate him. A redneck, gun-toting colleague, Bill Harvey, had suspected him instead. Having missed the twentieth century's most infamous mole under his nose, Angleton's mystique as a mole hunter would suffer if he overlooked Bennett too. Angleton became an instant hawk on Bennett and from then on the Security Service had a partner in the Bennett investigation, and an aggressive one at that.

Angleton launched a number of inquiries. He first consulted his alter ego, Anatoli Golitsin, who during his visit to Ottawa the previous fall had spent hours alone with Bennett in his home and, like Angleton, never suspected anything. Now Golitsin told Angleton that Canada could have a mole. Gridiron investigators interviewed Golitsin but his information was too soft to help. "We couldn't pin it down," says one Mountie. "After naming about 625 agents in NATO countries, how could he miss this one. Most of the other cases he identified in the western world had a fair number of clues. But here he had no other information. All he had was a suspicion and the suggestion that we must have one."

If Bennett was a mole, what kind of recruit to the KGB was he? More than intellectual curiosity asked the question because the correct answer could help the investigators unearth evidence against him. Any number of factors caused people to betray their country. An agent might have succumbed to blackmail—homosexuality, an extramarital affair or any embarrassing secret—and having served the KGB once, become forever entangled in the espionage net. The need for money, as in the case of Long Knife, could drive somebody to the KGB; or narcissism, vindictiveness or just plain rebellion. Gridiron virtually ruled out money. Bennett spent little, had no big secret bank account to be found, and showed no excessive craving for money. Narcissism did not fit either. A man who worked such long hours could not be self indulgent. He lacked the detachment to be an egotistical agent selling out the system as an act of defiance. Maybe he had betrayed out of vindictiveness. As a civilian Bennett had been passed over in favour of Mounties with less experience and fewer attributes and maybe he revenged the injustices in the most devastating way possible. But his behaviour over the years showed no tinges of revenge.

Recalling the Labour party's stronghold over South Wales, and its socialist leanings, Gridiron tabbed Bennett as an ideological agent who many years ago had been recruited to the communist cause. Philby and most of the great twentieth century Soviet spies worked out of philosophical commitment. Ideological spies usually acquired their communist religion late in adolescence or early adulthood and once recruited into espionage buried their ideology on instructions from their Soviet controllers. To cover up his student activism at Cambridge University, Philby in the 1930s became a neo-fascist supporter of Adolf Hitler. Philby could cover up his years as an open communist but could not erase them because too many witnesses had seen him at the time. Philby could only hope that authorities never had reason to check his university days. If Bennett was an ideological agent he too would have left some clues behind. Gridiron decided as a top priority to check into Bennett's early years and see what emerged.

A look at Bennett's personnel file produced little information prior to 1954 other than his place of birth, name of parents and a bare sketch of employment history. Prominently missing were the security screening results usually accompanying personnel files. The RCMP routinely carried out field checks on all applicants to check the accuracy of their claims. After reviewing records and interviewing neighbours, the checkers put a report into the file. Bennett had been an exception. Because he came to the RCMP as a fresh immigrant, the Force had no background in Canada to check, so in 1954 it had turned to the British who answered the Canadian request with a one-line telegram stating that Bennett had been cleared for access to special materials. A special materials clearance was one level higher than top secret. The telegram did not say he had been given a field check and how many years the check went back. Since Bennett had already been indoctrinated into special work, the RCMP had accepted the British clearance without batting an eye, assuming he could not have received Britian's highest security clearance without being screened and field checked. But sixteen years later, the Gridiron investigators searched into the background of the British clearance and got one big shock.

Gridiron discovered that the British had no record of Bennett ever being field checked. The emergency of war pulled him into Signals without scrutiny and, once inside, he graduated up the ranks and at war's end transferred to GCHQ. If GCHQ vetted his background it had no record of it, not even an army file. The British started field checking as a policy only after Bennett had become entrenched. It appeared the RCMP had relied on GCHQ, which relied on the army, which during the crisis of 1940 had not carried out a check. Nobody could explain it.

The British apologized profusely but in 1970 could not undo a mistake of the 1940s. The responsible individuals were long gone and the Security Service itself deserved some blame for not questioning in 1954 the basis of the British clearance. At this point the Security Service could only ask the British to conduct a thorough if belated investigation. An embarrassed MI5 did not need prodding. It volunteered to probe into Bennett's background in Penrhiwceiber and pick up the remnants that thirty years later might shed light on Bennett's tendencies as a youth.

Some formidable barriers impeded the way. MI5 in those days never bothered keeping a list of Communist party members and knew so little about Bennett's personal history it could not launch a thorough investigation and keep it discreet. Field investigators usually followed the information supplied by the subject but in this case the subject had never been required to supply such information and now could not be asked to do so without arousing suspicion. The probe needed to know the names of his uncles, aunts, boyhood friends and check their backgrounds to assess the milieu that shaped his early years. Only Bennett could realistically supply those details but how could Gridiron ask him without explaining why.

Sexsmith had an idea: introduce Positive Vetting to the Security Service and apply it universally. If everybody had to supply information about their backgrounds, Bennett would not necessarily get suspicious. The British invented Positive Vetting after they realized how deeply the Soviets had penetrated their civil service. It required civil servants in sensitive areas to sit down in front of a tape recorder and recount their personal histories and list every conceivable detail remotely affecting their security status. The subject took as much time as he needed and once satisfied he had divulged everything signed the transcript. He would be re-interviewed periodically and any deviation from his original statement would land him in trouble. Withholding pertinent information would put himself into extremely serious trouble if caught. Positive Vetting confronted the old ideological agent hiding a forgotten communist association with a dilemma: he either divulged his hidden skeleton and chanced losing his security clearance and job or risked more serious consequences by lying. Either way, the agent walked a precarious line.

Sexsmith felt confident Bennett would never suspect the introduction of Positive Vetting. The idea had kicked around for years and been proposed by, among others, Bennett himself. He would not grow wary over one of his own recommendations. Many of Bennett's colleagues had noted the irony that the Security Service did security screening on the government but ignored itself. Once an RCMP recruit passed the original security screening examination that got him to boot camp, he was in and never drew a second look, even when transferred into the Security Service. The organization needed Positive Vetting and by introducing it now could squeeze double duty from it.

Mike Spooner, the Office in Charge of Positive Vetting, sent out a general circulation memo with revised A-48 Personal History Forms attached requesting background information from everybody in the Security Service whether civilian or Mountie. The yellow A-48s required more family information than the original form. Spooner started the program by interviewing Draper, the Deputy Director, to demonstrate that nobody was exempt. Half a dozen people would sit down in Spooner's office before Bennett's time "randomly" came up.

"Jim, we'll have to get you on Positive Vetting before too long," warned Spooner. The interviews were supposed to be sprung on short notice to prevent rehearsing but people had meetings and deadlines and Positive Vetting became one more item marked into their appointments calendar.

The tape recorder sat primed and waiting when Bennett arrived for his appointment. Spooner led off with basic questions—where was he born? who were his parents? what were their political leanings?—mere pump primers to get Bennett talking. Bennett described first his father, in his seventies, and how he went off to fight in World War One and in the 1920s supported the Independent Labour party and later the traditional Labour party although never held a membership card in either organization. He then switched to his mother who had died the previous year and described her support for the Liberal party and her gradual conversion to Labour. He touched on Uncle Albert, his father's deceased older brother who had worked as a miner's agent and had been a long time elected Labour party member of the Mountain Ash municipal council and pointed out that Uncle Albert later had the opportunity to become the local Labour member of Parliament but felt a younger man with better health should run. Bennett said Uncle Albert had been a lifelong pacificist who opposed both world wars and during World War Two belonged to the anti-war coalition called the Popular Front. Bennett added that his uncle's views did not stop two of his uncle's brothers from fighting in World War One nor his two sons from enlisting in World War Two. He also mentioned that Uncle Albert had a close friend named Justin Lewis who had left the Labour party to become a communist. Bennett turned to Uncle Ernest, one of his father's two younger brothers and said that after the war he heard his mother call him a communist. He said he knew nothing about it and did not believe it. Bennett quickly mentioned his father's other brother, Uncle Bill, and his three sisters, Aunt Winifred, Aunt Beatrice and Aunt Doris.

Bennett said while working for the Mountain Ash Urban District he encountered a voluble communist named Foster[1] who worked as the District's rent collector and had unsuccessfully tried recruiting him into the communist-run Left Book Club. He declined although at the time he did not know the club's connection with the Communist party. Bennett said another employee took him aside and described Foster as a dangerous person and warned him to stay clear of him. Bennett said he accepted the advice but in any case found Foster personally disagreeable. Spooner interrupted Bennett to ask about the functions of the Left Book Club and Bennett explained that it was a local club used by the Communist party to attract members and generate sales. Bennett said he never again saw Foster after leaving Wales in 1940.

Bennett described volunteering for the army with the hope of getting into the engineering corps and then having to wait for the draft and being stuck into the Signal Corps. He said while posted at the Intelligence School in Heliopolis, Egypt, he met Brant[2], a tall, rugged individual with a dominating voice and an unconcealed belief in

---

[1] Foster is a pseudonym used by the publisher to protect the identity of the real person.

[2] Brant is a pseudonym.

communism. Although not close friends, they argued politics occasionally and sometimes ventured to Cairo together to haunt bookstores
and visit the Services Club. He said Brant never seriously attempted to
convert him. Years later, while working with GCHQ, Bennett said he
discovered that Brant had remained with the peacetime army and risen
to the rank of Major and become involved with secret special wireless
regiments, and years later still, after he had joined the Security Service,
reported both Foster and Brant to Harry Stone of MI5. He said Foster
did not worry him because his employment gave him access to no state
secrets but felt Brant posed a real threat, which is why he alerted Stone.

Bennett talked about his post-war career with GCHQ and before
listing his string of international postings said he had served simultaneously in Istanbul with Kim Philby. He said he met Philby a few
times but worked in a different organization and did not really know
him, but nevertheless reported this coincidental posting to Harry
Stone of MI5 and Maurice Oldfield of MI6 and informally discussed it
with RCMP officers Norman Jones and Bing Miller. After finishing
off his overseas travels and describing the circumstances of arriving in
Canada and joining the Security Service, nearly two hours had passed.
The interview was over.

With material to work from, MI5 searched into his youth in Wales
while the Security Service followed up the Canadian leads to his
Philby story. Norman Jones had died but the Security Service could
ask Bing Miller about Philby. When interviewed, Miller denied ever
being told by Bennett about Philby. Soon MI5 reported back that both
Harry Stone and Maurice Oldfield also denied Bennett's Philby story.
As well Stone said Bennett never reported Foster and Brant. There
was more. Bennett indicated MI5 had interviewed him about Philby
but MI5 records turned up no interview. In fact following Philby's
defection the British circulated a memo asking anybody who had
known Philby to report their experiences. Bennett had not responded.
The investigators concluded that Bennett had covered up the Philby
connection and wondered why he would do it other than to spare
himself investigation.

MI5's field check in Wales took more time and MI5 had to move
slowly and talk to old acquaintances carefully to avoid tipping its hand.
The verdict on Bennett's youth would have to wait a few months.

While MI5 dug into Bennett's past, the Front de Liberation du

Quebec struck with two political kidnappings in Quebec and the federal government invoked the War Measures Act. The October Crisis of 1970 moved virtually the entire Security Service onto an emergency footing except for Gridiron whose internal investigation hardly missed a beat. As Head of E Branch, Bennett controlled the Watcher Service, which played a big role following suspects in the hope of leading them to the hideout of the kidnappers of British Trade Commissioner James Cross but most of Bennett's time concentrated on looking for hidden messages in Cross's dispatches and analyzing the pattern of drop off points used by the abductors. At one point Bennett went into the cabinet room to explain the nature of his operation and the leads being followed. Few knew the irony in the Prime Minister and his cabinet being briefed by a suspected KGB agent. With Bennett commuting between cities, simultaneously working on the hostage crisis in Montreal and running his branch in Ottawa, the long hours gave him no time to snoop or speculate about events happening elsewhere.

Meanwhile Operation Kit Bag in Edmonton drew no closer to resolution. The Security Service still had not caught Mihalcin making a single revealing contact. Since meeting Shalnev in Montreal, he started listening to coded Soviet broadcasts but his listening soon stopped and now, like the other B Branch failures, where cases jerked along in fits and starts, Kit Bag seemed to have finally collapsed. Five years had produced nothing, not a new suspect, not even a successful lead, so Sexsmith decided to roll up the case and finally confront Mihalcin with questions.

As Mihalcin drove home from work, a car cut him off and three Security Service officers jumped out. One Mountie took Mihalcin's keys and drove his car away while the other two drove him to a motel for interrogation. Mihalcin quickly acknowledged he had been dispatched to Canada as a KGB spy. He said he suspected surveillance at the Brockville meet in 1965 and went on ice for two years until the KGB called him to Montreal in 1967 and reactivated him. After Montreal he listened to Moscow's broadcasts but a communications foul up caused a misunderstanding which again caused him to stop listening. By this time, he said, he had become disillusioned about spying and communism and let matters slide. He said he had defected intellectually but was afraid to approach the Canadian authorities so did nothing. Mihalcin surrendered his one-time cipher pads, his microdots and other spy paraphenalia and the Security Service made a belated effort to turn him into a double agent but too much time had passed for it to work. The Security Service could do nothing but accept his story. As matters stood, even with Mihalcin's cooperation, Kit Bag merely added to the Security Service's list one more failure.

If the investigation into Bennett seemed to be catching momentum the long-awaited MI5 field report untracked everything, at least for the moment. After scouring his background, MI5 uncovered no evidence of a politically alienated youth or any sign of radicalism. The British investigators reported he had grown up a typical youngster showing normal interests and had not been disaffected by the surrounding poverty. Furthermore, they could unearth nothing to substantiate the claim of Bennett's mother that Uncle Ernest had been a communist. However, the MI5 report revealed that Bennett had neglected to tell Spooner that Uncle Albert had been expelled from the Labour party for supporting the Popular Front and that the Popular Front had been controlled by the Communist party. Gridiron suspected the late Uncle Albert, now a communist suspect, may have secretly recruited Bennett, which may account for the lack of communist footprints in his background. It was speculation rather than evidence but the investigators would not ignore any possibility.

Bennett's background did not fit the mold of an ideological agent. Philby, Burgess, Maclean and Blunt were born into upper class families around 1910 and attended university during the early depression years when pessimism was spreading and the world seemed to be splitting into two adversarial ideological camps, communism and fascism, as the centre melted away. People were starting to choose sides and many liberally educated young idealists threw their lot in with the bright utopia of communism. The Soviet experience later disillusioned most of them but the ones recruited by the Comintern could not turn back. Bennett was born a decade later and grew up in a different world. He never attended university where the recruiting was heaviest and his interests focussed not so much on political theory but on earning an engineering education to escape the mines. When Hitler invaded Poland, Bennett volunteered for the army; it was a time when communists uniformly denounced World War Two as an "imperialist War."

Almost every point against Bennett could be balanced off by a counterpoint in his favour. For example, the fact that Bennett's early knowledge of Operation Keystone did not appear on file could be explained simply. The Security Service in the 1950s kept sparse records that carried little detail. Many other details also went unmentioned. Bennett's quitting of GCHQ and Britain in 1954 was unusual and could be viewed with suspicion but at the same time also made him look innocent. He had successfully embedded himself in one of the U.K.'s most sensitive organizations and the KGB would never permit an asset like that to quit and immigrate blindly to another country. The Bennett hawks rationalized it away with two explanations. One was that the KGB already had GCHQ so well penetrated that another mole was superfluous and it therefore directed him to Canada on the hope of infiltrating the newly emerging CBNRC. But the KGB is cautious and never thinks it can have too many moles. It would use them to check up on each other as insurance against disinformation from a phony mole. The other explanation had Bennett immigrating to Canada as a British agent. This theory had even greater flaws. Britain and Canada exchanged so much security and intelligence information that the British already got almost anything it wanted. Besides, why did Gridiron enlist the help of the British to investigate Bennett if he was their mole? The empty room in the bugged Soviet embassy was another piece of information that could just as easily make Bennett look good. The Soviets may have left the room empty because they did not know the exact location of the microphones. Bennett knew precisely where each bug had been planted.

If Bennett was a KGB spy why had he not appeared in the big post-war cipher break? Philby appeared under the code name Stanley, Maclean as Homer, and other people such as Klaus Fuchs, the Rosenbergs and Alger Hiss could be recognized and identified from the clues. No code name or agent identity could be conceivably linked to Bennett. Absence of incriminating evidence did not clear Bennett. The American cryptanalysists opened only some windows on Soviet cable traffic and maybe missed the dispatches referring to Bennett. Yet many other things accumulated in his favour, such as not being named by a single defector during three decades of disclosures. In addition to their solid information, defectors usually brought along a storeful of clues that, when analyzed, open up leads. The first defector pointing at Philby arrived in 1938 and another in August 1945. These clues later hurt Philby. No such hints had built up against Bennett. Even Golitsin offered not a scrap when he defected. Neither did Goleniewski who had felled so many others.

Some little things did not fit Bennett as a mole. Although his wife was a practising Catholic and their two daughters were being brought up in the Catholic faith, Bennett never hid his lack of religious conviction. An ideological agent would probably exploit the religion around him to further cover up his own beliefs.

Ideological agents were driven by political belief, which gave them supreme personal confidence. Bennett tried to reflect an aura of aplomb but sometimes the poise waned. While waiting for the start of meetings he showed his nervousness by pacing the room and lecturing always seemed to give him the jitters and for the first few minutes made his voice quiver. He displayed other nervous gestures like wetting his upper lip and giggling artificially when unsure of himself. Overall he lacked the cocksureness that true believers had.

Bennett did some things that made it hard to believe he acted under Soviet instruction. He helped negotiate the RA Club constitutional amendment stripping Soviet embassy personnel of associate membership status, thus eliminating one of their most lucrative agent-recruiting pools. He helped scare off External Affairs from giving the Soviet Union a trade office in Vancouver, thus denying the KGB a diplomatically protected espionage base in western Canada. Bennett personally initiated the licence-plate numbering system for diplomatic vehicles and introduced the random sighting program with his wallet-sized cards that complicated the life of Soviet intelligence officers. Bennett devised the on-line cipher system that turned the observation post on the Soviet embassy into one of the most valuable counterintelligence tools. Whenever the Soviet embassy asked External Affairs for the right to transmit to Moscow by radio, Bennett belonged to the group harshly opposing it. Consequently the Soviets continued communicating by telex, which gave the cryptanalysts a clean text for code-breaking attempts. When experts discovered that the Soviets might be able to intercept telephone calls going through Bell Canada's microwave system because its path crossed over the roof of the Soviet embassy, Bennett belonged to the group that argued in favour of the costly alternative of rerouting the path. Some people argued that the Soviets could not effectively exploit the opportunity. Bennett said the system carried confidential government telephone calls so the risk could not be taken. Finally Bell was persuaded to build another tower that doglegged the route around the embassy. Why would a mole invest effort to restrict the Soviets' ability to operate in Canada? A mole would have to appear to be something he was not and on some of these incidents Bennett could have anticipated a hawkish outcome and jumped onto the bandwagon. But nothing compelled him to introduce the licence-plate system and the on-line relay. Nobody would have suspected a thing had he chosen not to introduce them, and other measures. Introducing restrictive measures damaged the Soviets more than they built up his cover.

Bennett had a broader outlook than his colleagues and did not focus only on catching spies. He preached that containing the Soviets through preventative measures accomplished more than running operations. Many Mounties did not understand the fundamental importance of preventative measures and viewed counterespionage work simply as running cases. Only a foolhardy mole would try rousing an organization out of such a deceptive sleep.

Bennett continually stressed the need for upgrading the security of the Watcher Service radio communications, particularly in the free-wheeling early days. He felt radio threatened the integrity of cases more than anything else. The Soviets only had to find the Watcher Service frequency and tune in. The KGB even had portable monitoring equipment for the times the embassy was out of radio reach. When he could not buy secure enough equipment off the shelf, he ordered custom-made gear with sophisticated anti-monitoring features. Such action would not hurt the Soviets immediately if Bennett was a mole because he already knew everything. But the KGB always looked to the future when its mole would be gone.

If Bennett was working for the KGB why had he allowed Mikhail Klochko to defect in 1961? The Soviets hated losing defectors more than almost anything. Defectors hurt their pride and damaged their world image. Bennett could have scotched Klochko with a simple anonymous telephone call to the head of the Soviet delegation. Given the looseness of the defection and NRC's uncooperative attitude, nobody would have suspected anything sinister.

It seemed improbable that a mole would have boldly fingered BND officer Heinz Herre the way Bennett did. Bennett's behaviour looked suspicious but if conspiratorially motivated it fit neither the Bennett nor the KGB style. Both of them operated with more finesse. A mole of Bennett's age still had more than a decade's service, which the KGB would not want jeopardized.

The Security Service had failures all right but it did not follow that they belonged to Bennett. Betrayal did not have to come from the head man on the Russian Desk. If a mole bedevilled the organization the damage could originate from other quarters such as the Watcher Service, which had extraordinary access yet whose members were overworked, underpaid, suppressed and, as "special constables", held even less equal status than the maligned civilian members. As untouchables, the watchers represented the easiest pickings for the KGB. Since the watchers numbered in the scores and were always quitting for better jobs elsewhere, the KGB had a good selection of recruitment targets. Or the mole could be somebody in the processing section who translated and transcribed the bugged conversations. Since few cases did not use bugs or wiretaps, the people attached to the "Mini-United Nations" on the fourth floor knew a lot and, like the watchers, were civilian specialists with no upward mobility in the RCMP. "That's a minefield you walk through when you get people with linguistic capabilities," said one officer. "They are not all made in Canada." They listened to tape recordings all day and learned the intimate secrets of other people's lives. They were not supposed to talk about it but they worked in a group and had lunch, coffee breaks and free time with the same people and the stories their headsets picked up were just too funny, too sad or otherwise too good not to pass on. A traitor in the processing section could inflict remarkable damage.

Did the failures have to be caused by a mole? Did lack of success equal betrayal? Nobody, not even the most hawkish Gridiron investigator, could argue it necessarily did. Other western agencies also stumbled against the KGB, some as badly as the Security Service. The CIA had enough anomolies and outright failures to precipitate a super mole hunt. FBI cases crumbled with remarkable consistency and, in Britain, MI5's cases miscarried for so long that insiders secretly launched an investigation into the head man, Sir Roger Hollis. If Hollis had been a spy, it went a long way toward explaining the Security Service's failures because MI5 knew most of the Canadian cases. All three organizations to some extent blamed their failures on moles, but it seemed unlikely the KGB had penetrated all of them. The Russians had at one time penetrated virtually every European agency but that did not mean they did the same across the Atlantic. North America is different from Europe, which has large indigenous communist parties. The Russians feel less comfortable in North America.

The KGB could conceivably discover the Security Service's cases in many ways. Hardly a case developed where Security Service investigators did not enlist outside help of some kind, whether through acquiring informers or somebody's home as an observation post. They tried to be discreet but KGB officers looked for the signs. Or could the problem be communications? If Soviet cryptanalysists broke the Security Service code not a single operation would escape exposure.

Sometimes the operations failed in a way that was inconsistent with the kind of access the Soviets would have with Bennett as their mole. Take, for example, Operation Top Hat where the KGB ran Aquavit, the German immigrant, for seven years before dropping him. With Bennett as its mole, the KGB would know from the start about Aquavit's duplicity and could react immediately by either slowly dropping Aquavit or by playing him back as an unwitting deception agent. The KGB did neither. The KGB did not phase out Aquavit and did not use a series of time-consuming non-productive leads as it often did in deception operations. Maybe the case was real. After all, bringing Aquavit to Moscow consumed KGB resources. On the other hand, one could argue that maybe the KGB felt it had to carry on to protect its mole. The problem with that theory was that the operation died such a bizarre death that it actually fuelled speculation about a mole.

The fact that Aquavit's agent running officers grew increasingly-fearful the last three years foretold trouble. The worrying started when the Security Service, under Director William Kelly, started expelling exposed intelligence officers with public fanfare. The Soviets disliked expulsions and disliked even more public expulsions and did what it could to avoid them. Aquavit's last meet with the fretting Soviet officer Mike followed only by a few months the Watcher Service's successful hit on Bower Featherstone. Evidently the KGB knew enough about the Watchers' new surveillance techniques to fear them but not enough about operations to know the Security Service had a blanket policy of not using the Watchers on Top Hat. Apparently the KGB knew some things but not others, which would preclude Bennett as the leak because he knew everything. An individual watcher who knew the surveillance techniques but not about Top Hat fit the clues much better. As a mole, Bennett would have long ago assured the Soviets that Aquavit's meets were not being surveilled. So why did Aquavit's officers spend three years worrying about surveillance and, particularly, why did Mike behave at that last meet as if he was standing in the middle of a fishbowl?

The Gridiron investigators also had to examine one other possibility: maybe Bennett dragged down the organization not through treason but with incompetence. In some ways this scenario hurt the most because if incompetence produced the problem why had his colleagues —including the Gridiron investigators—not challenged him much earlier. People might not spot a mole, but lack of ability had to emerge over the years except if the people around him were also incompetent. For a long time only Sexsmith occasionally questioned him. While Bennett manufactured an image and overplayed his experience, education and almost everything else, he did possess native intelligence and a superior command of counterespionage knowledge. He could both conceptualize broadly and assimilate detail. One could always tell who in the Security Service visitors from foreign agencies respected as they gravitated past more senior officers to get to Bennett. If Bennett was so good how could he be incompetent? How could the operations fail so badly unless he was deliberately spoiling them? Bennett might be incompetent only depending on how one defined competence.

Bennett gambled by chasing long shots. His decision to sit back and wait for Mihalcin in Edmonton turned out to be wrong but would have appeared brilliant and made him a hero if it had uncovered a network of illegals. One could argue that poor decision-making is investing a lot of manpower without getting results. Bennett had done a good share of this kind of thing. He often got carried away pursuing detail to the final end. Such meticulousness can waste resources but occasionally trips across a major discovery. So was Bennett imprudent or a brilliant operator short on luck? Bennett's doubters could claim a track record no better. A Division's filming of Natasha had not worked, as Bennett predicted. Bennett at least proposed a more innovative plan with better potential. Bennett may have fallen too far into the Angleton school and oversold the power of the KGB, but the investigators could not sustain an argument that he had violated fundamental rules or run operations badly.

Bennett's record as an administrator was different. He possessed a good analytical mind but had trouble delegating. He could not keep his hands off operations. If the Watcher Service uncovered something, he grew ecstatic and started fitting together the nuts and bolts. Every small detail crossed his desk and the staff did little without his approval. The system worked well in the early years when the Russian Desk was small and needed little administration. By the late 1960s the Security Service had ballooned into a bureaucracy and even a workaholic like Bennett had to let go or be dragged down.

As the Russian Desk expanded, Bennett should have shifted his priorities from operations to running the desk and keeping his case officers equipped and happy. He already had senior NCOs whose jobs included assisting the case officers. Instead Bennett worked harder, longer and under greater pressure and grew more demanding and less flexible. His staff became increasingly experienced and capable without receiving a commensurate reward of authority and when Bennett forced upon them assignments they considered irrelevant they grew alienated, critical and rebellious and, eventually, suspicious. Administrative incompetence did not explain failures but magnified Bennett as a target when fingers started being pointed.

Bennett may not have utilized his men to full advantage but it was not all his fault. He worked under an inappropriate system, which often tied his hands. The RCMP's command structure required the head of the branch to sign every telegram and piece of instruction going to the field. Sometimes the officer did not read the document or even query its contents, yet subordinates still had to wait outside his door for approval. So if Bennett overcentralized operations he did it in the tradition of the RCMP.

Sometimes the RCMP promotion system arbitrarily coughed up men who should have kept their police uniforms. Since they could not be trusted they had to be watched and told what to do. A corporal on the Russian Desk might spend two years studying Russian intelligence officers and as he started mastering his assignment get promoted to sergeant for which only Central Registry had an opening. The paramilitary system could not accommodate another sergeant on the Russian

Desk. Meanwhile the sergeant who created the vacancy in Central Registry had become a staff sergeant after several years of learning the filing system and been moved elsewhere where he had to start over. The system could not raise the pay of both men and leave them in place to utilize their experience. Promotions tripped off chain reactions and the Russian Desk always had rookies needing training. So if Bennett interfered, the system often encouraged him to do so.

The simple fact was that the KGB conducted espionage more professionally than the Security Service stopped it, and Bennett could not be blamed if the reasons were institutional. Espionage represents a major thrust of Soviet foreign policy. The KGB has almost a blank cheque and picks from among the brightest and most promising people in the land while the RCMP selects non-educated policemen and puts them into the Security Service without a day's training. The Canadian government has historically tolerated security work as a bothersome necessity and the senior policemen managing the Security Service's budget lived by the laws of working on the cheap. In the mid-1960s when a string of minor scandals briefly exposed the inadequacies of the RCMP and when the technicians were crafting bugging equipment out of spare parts, the RCMP refused a gratuitous government offer for more money. A handful of Mounties had kept the peace in the old West while the U.S. Army needed divisions south of the border. The RCMP believed it could handle the KGB on a shoestring budget too. The most competent administrator on the Russian Desk could not overcome such handicaps. As head of E Branch Bennett's record as an administrator improved dramatically. He did not meddle or make unreasonable requests. In fact he streamlined procedures.

Howard Gillard, the new head of the Watcher Service, called in his most seasoned surveillers for a special briefing. Normally Gillard did not tell his people to keep their mouths shut because in their line of work that was assumed. This time Gillard counselled them to tell nobody—not even other watchers—what they were about to hear. Gillard revealed that Bennett was under investigation and being put under surveillance and that they would be doing it. The watchers over the years had encountered some breathtaking assignments but never before had they surveilled the man who was ultimately their own boss. Bennett, as Officer in Charge of E Branch, oversaw the Watcher Service although he looked after budgets and rarely visited the unit's secret headquarters. Gillard did not spell out the nature of the investigation but the watchers knew it had to be serious. They had to be extremely careful because Bennett recognized most of them.

Surveillance churned up all kinds of petty details about Bennett's personal habits but nothing to implicate him as a spy. Bennett kept an amazingly regular pattern. He rose each morning before dawn and took an early walk. He left for work around seven-thirty A.M. and usually left the office at the end of the day. Evenings normally kept him at home except when he drove his daughters somewhere or returned to the office for late work. When first established, the observation post on his home noticed the house lights switching on and off in the middle of the night and the investigators initially thought he was sending signals until they found out a recurring knee injury from a cricket game in 1956 had flared up to keep him awake at night and, for a while, he passed time by reading and wandering through the house flipping the light switches as he went. Weekends, when Bennett broke from his rigid daily pattern, proved no more incriminating. Bennett made no suspicious encounters and, furthermore, never looked for surveillance, which suggested he had no reason to fear it. The bugs and wiretaps also turned up nothing. J Branch mounted a hidden closed circuit television camera above his desk to catch him stuffing material into his pocket. If he did, he did it out of camera range. As 1971 came to an end the investigation had carried on nearly two years and still had uncovered no evidence of contact with any Soviet or even dredged up a clue of how he might have communicated with the KGB. It found no radio, no dead letter drops and no live letter box. Gridiron could only continue surveillance and hope for a break. Then something happened.

Driving home from an RCMP party at a private home in the West End late one weekend night, Bennett pulled onto a side road, parked his car and shut off the lights for about an hour before continuing home. The unusual stop violated his pattern of behaviour and seemed unexplainable. An explanation emerged when Gridiron investigated the incident. Bennett had parked close to the home of defector Mikhail Klochko. Maybe he had stopped for a secret rendezvous. Maybe Angleton was correct in believing Klochko had been a dispatched defector sent to propagate the myth of the Sino-Soviet dispute. Klochko could be not only a false defector but Bennett's KGB control officer. He had perfect cover and it explained why back in 1961

Bennett had by-passed an opportunity to snuff out Klochko's defection.

One day soon after, Bennett was on the phone with Mountie Warren Huget. "What are those strange noises on the phone? It's clicking," exclaimed Huget.

"I can't hear anything," replied Bennett.

"Ah, somebody's tapping your phone."

Later, Draper pulled Huget aside. Bennett's phone was being tapped. Huget sat with Bennett on the Telecommunications Committee and saw him frequently but never again joked about his telephone being tapped.

After coffee break one morning part of the video equipment over Bennett's desk slipped and knocked one of the ceiling tiles a little outside its metal slot. A technician with a step ladder neatly positioned the tile back in place while Bennett ate lunch in the mess.

Eventually, the fact that Bennett was being watched began to show in public. One evening at a party in the home of a CIA man in Ottawa, he accidentally collided with a tray of drinks. He went to the kitchen to get cleaned up, and when he ambled back into circulation a bolt of heckling struck him. "Look at the jowls of the man already," called out Harry Brandes, one of the Gridiron investigators. Bennett ignored the remark and went over to John Starnes who was engrossed in conversation with the chairman of the Joint Intelligence Committee. Starnes brushed him off.

Bennett could be fooled only so long. Sexsmith knew it and as the investigation dragged on he grew increasingly worried that Bennett had found out. Bennett could not miss the growing hostility and could—although no one knew whether he did—notice the flow of material from B Branch dwindle. Of course, maybe the Watcher Service, the bugs, wiretaps and television camera drew blanks because Bennett was loyal and had nothing surreptitious to be discovered. On the other hand, the investigators could not disregard the possibility that a perceptive person like Bennett had caught on to the investigation and put himself on ice. A mole would always sniff the winds for danger and freeze at the first warning. The signs had started before his transfer to E Branch and now accumulated quickly. Bennett had to notice that people did not stop by his office to talk like they once had. The investigation that started with a handful of insiders had expanded into scores. Besides the CIA and British being cut in, Sexsmith used his

Hong Kong connection to backcheck Bennett in the early 1950s. Surveillance had brought in the watchers; bugging the technicians and the processing section. As the investigation widened Bennett's colleagues were indoctrinated one by one. Even old colleagues who had quit years ago were questioned in retirement about things Bennett had done or failed to do. Each time the investigation took a new turn a few more bodies became involved. Over the months all Bennett's senior NCOs and his best friend, Howie Jones, joined the conspiracy. How long could secrecy be maintained? Bennett had to find out eventually.

Ottawa's harsh winters had always plagued Bennett. He suffered a debilitating neo-asthmatic condition that had progressively worsened and in the last few winters effectively emasculated him. Snow shovelling or sometimes simple walks in the cold left him gasping for air. Bennett's skin started turning grey and during the final stages of the investigation his body grew so weak he had to nap during the day. During the last stages not a month passed where cold viruses did not keep him in bed for a day or two, and away from work. Had the stress of work caught up with him at last, or was the stress of living a double life finally taking its toll; or did he see the net closing in and start buckling under the strain?

If Sexsmith could not catch Bennett in the act of meeting the Soviets or even sending messages, he had another plan to pin him down. Sexsmith would set a trap which, depending on Bennett's reaction, could settle the mystery for good.

Nonchalantly holding a single sheet of paper with the top-secret red stripe down the righthand side, Sexsmith dropped by Bennett's office. "Jim," he said handing over the document, "it's possible we may want some Watcher Service assistance. I'll let you know later if we need it." Bennett read the document matter of factly. It carried the breathless news that a Soviet defector would rendezvous that weekend in Montreal. For such a delicate event Sexsmith wanted coverage from the best surveillance people, which meant importing watchers from Ottawa. Bennett showed little reaction and quietly returned the document. "Let us know and I'll set it up," he said.

The document was phony. There was no defector and no rendezvous. The entire operation had been created by Sexsmith to entrap Bennett. Sexsmith never did get back to Bennett and had never intended to. He had forewarned Bennett about possible surveillance as a pretext for feeding him a non-existant case. He had planted a litmus test and now could sit back and watch if the operation changed colour. Only eight people knew about the defector and only Bennett laboured under the impression it was real. If the Soviets did anything to stop it or reacted in any way, then they too would think it was real, which would point the tip-off in Bennett's direction. The document Bennett had seen referred to the defector only by code name, which would give the Soviets an incentive to appear on the scene to see who it was.

Sexsmith cordoned off the area with discreet observation posts. Nobody could arrive at the rendezvous sight without passing through one of the traps. The observation posts merely wanted to keep score of who showed up. When the appointed hour arrived, a snowstorm unloaded over Montreal and a member of the local Soviet consulate who had been identified as a KGB officer passed through the trap.

20

Interrogation

TRUE ENOUGH, A KGB officer had appeared at the scene of the bogus defection but what did it mean? The entrapment operation was supposed to have been foolproof but the more the Bennett investigators analyzed the results, the more holes they poked in their litmus test. It seemed the outcome told more about the quality of the litmus than Bennett's loyalty. The Russians travelled around Montreal a great deal and could easily have passed through the area innocently. It did not mean much for a KGB officer to pass through a central location. The test would have meant more had Sexsmith chosen a city like Toronto, which had no Soviet consulate and which would have forced the Soviets to file a travel plan with External Affairs. If Bennett had made errors of judgement in running operations over the years, so had his investigators.

The investigators agreed the Soviets would not want to expose their hand so blatantly if they had a mole to protect. While George Blake worked as a KGB mole inside MI6 he secretly compromised the infamous tunnel under the Berlin Wall before it had been dug. Yet the Soviets allowed the tunnel to tap into the East Berlin telephone system and expose a mass of Soviet military secrets. The hemorrhaging continued nearly a year before they "accidently" discovered the tunnel. The hardbitten KGB operated with finesse when protecting moles and would shelter a key man like Bennett. The KGB would do nothing without weighing the danger for its mole.

If, as the investigators suspected, Bennett knew he was under suspicion, his sharp questioning mind with its bent for conspiracy had probably smelled something wrong the minute Sexsmith started setting him up. Nobody in the Security Service knew counterintelligence like he did and enjoyed the game as much. Sexsmith's "preliminary" approach—itself suspicious—had purposely given him several days to contact the Soviets. If Bennett had sensed the trap, the last thing the Soviets would do would be to send a man to the scene. On the other hand, if the plan fooled both Bennett and the Soviets, the KGB would act subtly and probably ask Bennett to find out what he could about the identity of the defector and then it would move to stop him or feed him disinformation. Under very rare circumstances would the KGB react so blatantly as to send someone onto the scene.

Eight people, including Bennett, knew about the event. Of course, the mole, if he existed, could be one of the other seven in which case the KGB would mischievously show up to injure Bennett and further protect the real mole. Conceivably one of the other seven could have anonymously attracted the Soviets to the scene on the pretext of settling an old score with Bennett. Bennett over the years had acquired enemies yet it seemed unthinkable that a Mountie would mix with the KGB for personal vindictiveness. Mounties valued loyalty too highly for that. Possibly one of the seven believed so strongly in Bennett's guilt and, convinced the rules of evidence were protecting a traitor, decided the western concept of fair play that had shielded Philby for so long were insane and by himself decided to even the balance in the state's favour by doctoring the evidence through tipping off the Russians. It was unlikely, but Mounties could justify acts for the national good they would never contemplate for selfish reasons.

By itself, the litmus test held little importance. Needed was a series of litmus tests. Only if the Soviets showed up after each one, could they rule out the possibility of coincidence. With time a pattern would emerge to resolve the doubt. But the patience of John Starnes had nearly run out.

The investigation had stretched two years and Starnes told Sexsmith he had to wrap it up. Sexsmith asked for more time, got a short reprieve and hurriedly unleashed a few small litmus tests but nothing happened. Either Bennett was innocent, or aware or the Soviets simply were not tempted by the small bait. With nothing working, the investigation was forced to confront Bennett and see what happened.

Interrogation might break Bennett. Some agents confessed only too willingly, as if thankful for the opportunity to unburden themselves of an oppressive load. Klaus Fuchs, the atomic spy, divulged minute details of his secret life and helped convict his accomplices. Even a hardened mole like George Blake confessed when confronted with circumstantial information. And none other than Kim Philby, the master mole, yielded a limited confession when finally challenged by his old friend Nicholas Elliott when he could have stonewalled longer. So Bennett also might succumb to circumstantial evidence. On the other hand many agents stubbornly proclaimed their innocence in the face of overwhelming evidence. One could not predict Bennett's reaction until the morning of March 13, 1972, when two years of investigation would test him out in the interrogation room.

March 13 started like a normal Monday for Bennett. He arrived in his office at about seven forty-five A.M. He had already taken his in and out baskets from the office safe when Howard Draper arrived.

"Good morning Jim," he called out. "John Starnes wants to see you."

Bennett locked his office door and walked with Draper up one flight of stairs and along the long corridor to the Director-General's office at the other side of the building where Starnes waited grimly. Starnes made no small talk and offered no introduction.

"We're lifting your security clearance," Starnes said rigidly. "There are some doubts about your loyalty. We want you to be interviewed."

Bennett showed almost no reaction, remaining calm, too calm as far as Starnes and Draper were concerned. He looked first at Starnes and then at Draper, and still said nothing. Then he wilted slightly and turned limp.

"I don't understand," he said. "But if there are any doubts I'm prepared to cooperate fully and cast any doubts to the four winds."

"That's good," replied Starnes with unbending stiffness, "but your security clearance is lifted."

Bennett asked what it was all about but Starnes said that would be covered at the "interview." Starnes divulged no more than the minimum.

Starnes advised that his assistant, Al Nowlan, would be taking over his work and instructed him to cover his absence by saying he was leaving on special assignment. The meeting lasted a few minutes. In the meantime Gridiron investigator Neil Chadwick had slipped into Starnes's outer office to escort Bennett back to his office and from there to the interrogation. Dorothy McDonald, a civilian aide and longtime friend, waited outside Bennett's office for some advice. Bennett quickly gave her instructions, returned his in and out baskets to the safe, called his secretary to explain his absence, locked his office door and gave the key to Nowlan. As he started to leave he surrendered his building pass to Chadwick. Chadwick did not ask but Bennett gave his CBNRC pass as well.

"We're going downtown," advised Chadwick.

Chadwick drove Bennett to the Embassy Apartment Hotel and escorted him to a safehouse in Suite 1109 where Sexsmith and Ian MacEwan waited. Sexsmith, a colleague for eighteen years, looked uncomfortable and subdued. He treated Bennett with politeness and a measure of deference as the three sipped coffee in the lounge.

"We have something we want to go over with you," explained Sexsmith. "It could take a number of days. We want to take this in sequence. We'll break for lunch and you'll be free to go out for lunch on your own and then when we finish for the day you can go home. Tomorrow you can drive in and park and we'll continue again until we're through."

With coffee and explanations out of the way, the three moved to a rectangular table. Bennett sat back comfortably with his chair pushed away while Sexsmith and MacEwan leaned forward over their notepads across the width of the table. A one-half inch thick brief and a small stack of files accompanied them. Occasionally they jotted down a note but did not copy Bennett's statements. A hidden microphone picked up every word.

Interrogating an old colleague came with the business but was still tough, although Sexsmith would show fewer emotional scars than most. Nature had never intended the loud, aggressive Sexsmith as an interrogator. Breaking an entrenched mole needed subtlety and finesse. Lacking the firepower to come out shooting, the interrogators had to act politely and persuade Bennett to cooperate. If he talked freely and the interrogators listened attentively and pounced at strategic moments, they might fashion a credible case and break down his story. They could set traps but somebody as knowledgeable and astute as Bennett could probably sidestep them. The interrogators had to build on their strengths and Bennett's weaknesses, the interrogators' strengths being the series of counterespionage failures and Bennett's weaknesses, his leftist background that could have recruited him as a KGB agent. Rather than confronting him or entrapping him, Sexsmith and MacEwan tried to wear him down bit by bit, starting with the political influences of his youth and leading eventually to bad judgement on the Russian Desk. Sexsmith hoped each bit of evidence would erode his denials a little until he could no longer plausibly deny the allegations.

Interrogation at this level is an art. The interrogators must sense every reaction and know when to squeeze and when to ease up in the interest of wringing out every scrap of information. Classic interrogations worked in teams with a polite interrogator carrying the load while a nasty partner waited ominously in the wings. The subject opened up to the nice fellow to avoid the nasty guy. The technique was so effective it worked even when the subject saw through the strategy. Sexsmith had been around a long time and knew all the failures. More importantly, he knew Bennett. He had to be part of the interrogation team and with his personality qualified perfectly as the axeman. But Sexsmith was a Superintendent and the officer running Gridiron and would not be playing number two. This interrogation team had no number two. Sexsmith and MacEwan divided their work not by function but by subject matter. Sexsmith questioned Bennett about the failed cases while MacEwan handled the family background and only occasionally would they try to unbalance him by alternating questions.

MacEwan kicked off the interrogation by asking Bennett about his youth. MacEwan carried a big police build and had a crescent scar under his eye from a car accident. After growing up in Saskatoon, he joined the RCMP almost out of high school and the Force later sent him to university on salary. He was intelligent, thoughtful and clever but two handicaps belittled him in front of Bennett. He lacked long experience in counterespionage work and despite his physique, gave off almost no sense of presence. An effective interrogator, like an actor, needs the force of appearance to impress his subject and MacEwan simply fell short.

MacEwan ponderously guided Bennett through his youth, his employment with the Mountain Ash Urban District, the army and GCHQ. At this stage he did not challenge Bennett on any information, he was only duplicating Mike Spooner's Positive Vetting interview to check for discrepancies in his story. If Bennett had lied to Spooner the ensuing eighteen months might have dimmed his memory enough to trip him up on detail. Or else Bennett, not knowing what incriminating information the interrogators had discovered, might panic and through loss of composure contradict his earlier story. Catching a contradiction would poke a hole in his story. The support team listening to the interrogation would study transcripts for inconsistencies, lies, evasions, weaknesses and any claim that could be challenged.

Bennett revealed that as a youngster he sympathized with the Labour party but had never been a member of any political party and during those years had no communist friends. By the time Bennett finished describing his father and uncles and recounted his personal history up to this arrival in Canada, the morning had nearly ended.

As Sexsmith had told him, Bennett left the safehouse free to eat anywhere he wanted but freedom was a relative concept. He did not go entirely alone. Letting Bennett out by himself gave the Watcher Service a chance to observe his reaction. Nobody expected Bennett to flee or sly a signal but he might commit suicide. The Security Service would intervene before he could do anything dramatic.

Undoubtedly aware that hidden eyes traced each move, Bennett walked in the direction of Elgin Street and ate a snack at a lunch counter. He did not look for surveillance. Slush and water filled the street gutters and a cold March wind froze the city. After lunch Bennett hurried back to the hotel early. The warm interrogation room offered him a better sanctuary than the miserable outdoors.

The examining room itself turned frosty as MacEwan, who in the morning had questioned Bennett passively to compare the answers he had given Spooner, started to probe in adversarial style. MacEwan started working Bennett for an admission his background was not what he claimed, implying for starters that the social concern that inspired his father's volunteer work with the Legion Benevolent Fund was politically motivated. Bennett replied that his father was not a communist and that his contributions to the British Legion were a reflection of the man and not ideology. MacEwan's manner hardened when he raised the subject of the Independent Labour party, which Bennett had said his father once supported. MacEwan alleged the ILP was a communist party. "Is that so?" retaliated Bennett. "I didn't realize that." In fact MacEwan was wrong. The ILP was merely a ginger group within the Labour party but Bennett did not challenge Mac-Ewan's faulty history.

Bennett's attitude puzzled his interrogators. He remained limp and defended himself only passively. He answered the questions but his responses carried no fight. Sexsmith sat back quietly pondering the meaning of Bennett's behaviour. Maybe Bennett did not challenge MacEwan over the ILP because he did not know better or maybe he did not care.

MacEwan felt he had engineered a tactical victory of sorts in forging a link between the ILP and the Communist party and now sought to paint his father a philosophical adherent to the communist ILP. If he could make his father into a communist he would have a base for making the case that Bennett was one too. MacEwan threw out the name Keir Hardie, who had been the local member of Parliament and for some time the ILP's only sitting MP. Bennett admitted Hardie set the valley aflame in rhetoric and that his father had supported him, and because Hardie had sometimes been branded a Red for his progressive views, he became another stitch in the fabric of communist persuasion MacEwan was trying to weave against Bennett. Then MacEwan asked Bennett if his father took him to political meetings and Bennett acknowledged that he had. Although Bennett said they were few in number, MacEwan seemed satisfied he had shown that Bennett's father felt strongly enough to take his son to leftist political rallies. MacEwan then pressed, asking if his father ever took him to political meetings featuring Fenner Brockway, a pacifist whose opposition to war sometimes drew cries of treachery. Bennett said he knew Brockway's name but could not remember attending any meetings of his, although he could remember listening to a speech by George Lansbury, a pacifist in the Brockway mold. Bennett repeated that the meetings he attended were few and that he had never been approached or enticed into joining any communist group. MacEwan stressed Bennett's poor youth and the widespread radicalism of South Wales and how it must have affected him. Bennett said it affected him but did not induce him toward extremism. His family had been better off than most. Since switching his sympathy away from the Labour party in 1952, he said he always supported the Liberal party, both in Britain and Canada.

MacEwan inquired whether his father had friends who were communists. Bennett responded that none were close, at which point MacEwan raised the name Charlie Bull. Bennett said his father knew him and that he himself had visited Bull's home three years earlier when in Wales for his mother's funeral. He said he had accompanied his father who was interested in the condition of Bull's health but did not think his father and Bull were close. He said he personally had never visited Bull's home before or since. As for other communist acquaintances of his father's, he said his father sat for some years on the executive of the Penrikyber (sic) Old Age Pensions Society with the late Richard Morgan who had been a communist, but he did not think they were close.

Continuing with the hypothesis that Bennett had been a long time secret communist, MacEwan turned his attention to Uncle Albert, the oldest brother of Bennett's father, and focussed on his role as a miners' agent and Labour party aldermen on the Mountain Ash District Council from 1926 until his death thirty-six years later. Bennett had already reported Uncle Albert as a lifelong pacifist who in the late 1930s joined the Popular Front's campaign against the coming war. MacEwan alleged and Bennett acknowledged that the Popular Front had support from the communists who, given an opportunity, would exploit this coalition to attain power through democratic means and then consolidate control. Bennett said his uncle, like many non-communists, had been taken in by the Popular Front. Then MacEwan laid before him a 1941 newspaper article from the Aberdare *Leader* revealing that things had gone a step further. Uncle Albert had publicly supported the Communist's Vigilance Committee against World War Two and been repudiated and expelled from the Labour party. MacEwan stressed the fact that the Vigilance Committee had been clearly communist. Bennett had said nothing to Spooner about the expulsion, which portrayed Uncle Albert in a more radical light, and the newspaper article surprised him. Was he surprised that Uncle Albert had been expelled or had he known all along and was now surprised by being caught withholding it? During 1941, Bennett said, he had been cut off in Malta and fighting for his life against enemy bombers and had never known about the Vigilance Committee. He vaguely recalled receiving a letter from his mother saying Uncle Albert had been expelled from the party but had not been told the reason. He said he had not suppressed the information; he had not told Spooner because, not knowing the reason behind it, did not think it worth mentioning. Bennett said his mother used to send him local newspapers but many of the ships were torpedoed and he could not recall getting anything about this matter. He added that Uncle Albert later kept being re-elected to the Mountain Ash Council as a Labour party candidate after the war, so obviously he had recanted.

Around the time of Uncle Albert's wartime expulsion, Justin Lewis, his good friend, fellow councillor and political ally, bolted the Labour party and joined the Communist party. Lewis resigned his council seat and ran again as a communist, comfortably reclaiming the position. For years Uncle Albert, Lewis and Phil Thomas, another Labour councillor, had taken leisurely walks every Sunday morning through a local beauty spot called Twmpy where they discussed the problems of society, and the weekly strolls continued after Lewis' defection. MacEwan dwelled on this relationship and tried to establish that Justin Lewis had at least manipulated Uncle Albert and possibly recruited him outright and, since the Labour party refused to tolerate admitted communists, turned him into a secret agent of influence and talent spotter inside the Labour party. Bennett replied that Uncle Albert was an open and straightforward man incapable of exercising such subterfuge. He said he always went public with his beliefs and never concealed his Sunday morning walks.

"He had no influence on me," replied Bennett. "Therefore in terms of security clearance it had no validity."

"Well, you must have been close to your uncle," pressed MacEwan. "He lived not far from you."

Indeed, Uncle Albert had at one stage lived eight doors away and always within half a mile but Bennett said Uncle Albert's union work and political career and his willingness to help anybody who came to him so monopolized his time that he had little left for his family and none for his relatives. He said he always viewed Uncle Albert as a grey man and had never been close to him.

Bennett was correct. In security investigations a relative whose loyalty was questioned had to have influence on the subject before it became relevant. Bennett, a veteran at examining others' security clearances, had deftly deflected MacEwan's advance by voluntarily declaring Uncle Albert's influence to be nil, which frustrated MacEwan because he could strike back with no contrary evidence. There may not have been any influence but MacEwan did not want to accept Bennett's word. Even if influence existed, proving it more than thirty years later was almost impossible. As one investigator put it: "How do you get inside a person's head?" MacEwan had scored some points but not nearly enough. Not only did he lose out on the question of influence, but he failed to establish that Uncle Albert had been a communist.[1] Even if, as MacEwan implied, Justin Lewis had recruited Uncle Albert during World War Two, Bennett by this time had permanently left home. Lewis could have recruited Uncle Albert before the outbreak of war while Lewis, presumably, worked as a secret communist, but there was no evidence for that. The afternoon ended with Bennett having suffered a few bruises over the expulsion, The Vigilance Committee, and Charlie Bull, but he remained in good condition for the next round.

MacEwan started off the next morning inquiring about Uncle Ernest, one of Bennett's father's two younger brothers whom Bennett had reported his mother had called a communist in 1945. The investigation unearthed no evidence of Communist sympathy from Uncle Ernest. All it found was a quiet apolitical man dominated by his wife and interested primarily in his two daughters, gardening, fishing and tending his chickens. MacEwan wondered whether Bennett had deliberately created a straw man in Uncle Ernest. If the allegations against Uncle Ernest were discredited the case against Uncle Albert, Bennett's father and Bennett himself would suffer. Bennett's mother died three years earlier so it could never be proven that she made such an allegation. MacEwan asked Bennett why, if he had known about the allegation, he had not reported Uncle Ernest when he got his GCHQ security clearance. Bennett said the information was not required and in any event was hearsay that he had dismissed as untrue. He said he had never heard Uncle Ernest discuss politics and added that if he was

[1] On Uncle Albert's political philosophy, Gordon Bennett, his son, says the following: "Dad was not a communist or fellow traveller. He may have had some sympathy and understanding of some facets of communism. He once told me that true theoretical communism could be a perfect way of life but, until a perfect human being was developed, it wouldn't be practical. Then it wouldn't be necessary anyway."

a communist he was the quietest and most harmless one the party ever had.[2] Uncle Ernest, he said, had absolutely no influence over him. MacEwan, with nothing to go on and not certain it was a genuine lead, made no effort to develop Uncle Ernest as he had done the day before with his father and Uncle Albert.

Having finished with Bennett's relatives, MacEwan moved to the subject of Foster, the municipal rent collector whom Bennett had known while working with the Mountain Ash Urban District. Foster's sister, Mabel, was married to Justin Lewis. Bennett explained that his job had nothing to do with Foster but all staff members had to belong to NALGO, the National Association of Local Government Officers, which is how he met him. Bennett said his first exposure to Foster occurred at a NALGO meeting where he found himself supporting Foster on an issue that he could no longer remember. The issue was not political because NALGO dealt only with staff matters and, besides, he later changed his mind and opposed Foster in the end. A few days later, Foster, at a chance meeting in the office, tried to enroll him in the Left Book Club and although not aware of the political nature of the club, he had been warned by Percy Bailey, an accountant, to stay clear of Foster. Bennett said Foster was persistent and may have tried again unsuccessfully to enrol him but never sought to interest him in the Communist party. MacEwan tried doggedly to cement a connection between Bennett and the Left Book Club. If he could get Bennett to admit an attraction to the club he might chisel a further admission of having read the literature and been closer to Foster than he had previously acknowledged. From there he might be able to parlay that concession into evidence of communist leanings, which set the stage for recruitment as an agent. But Bennett conceded nothing, saying he did not like Foster and found him humourless and shrill. He said he had heeded Percy Bailey's warning and stayed away and, besides, he was too busy and already belonged to the Penrhiwceiber library. Bennett allowed that the Left Book Club probably sent its literature to the library but said he did not recall reading it. His

---

[2]"Uncle Ernest was not a communist but he might well have been one," says Gordon Bennett. "Apart from his sense of humour, which all my uncles had, he had a touch of fire. He could and did get very angry and would rant and rave about injustice. Somehow he lacked the drive to put his ideas into action. He was much more content to feed his chickens or tend the vegetables on his plot of ground. Besides, I think he was a bit 'hen-pecked.'"

interests, he said, were historical novels, mystery thrillers and travel books, not political theory.

MacEwan next pinpointed Bennett's friendship with Brant, the open communist who served with him in Egypt. Bennett had mentioned Brant to Spooner and now under hostile questioning said their friendship had not been very close; their interests diverged and Bennett found Brant too argumentative and overbearing. Bennett said they had gone book hunting to Cairo together on occasion and agreed with MacEwan that they probably had discussed the problems of society and the future of Britain but said he could not remember much political discussion. In any case, said Bennett, Brant did not try to convert him and had no influence on him, adding that he spent less leisure time with Brant than with other friends. MacEwan chipped away at trying to uncover a philosophical link and establish that Brant had sought to manipulate the army's compulsory current affairs discussion meetings but Bennett flatly denied it. He said of the hundreds of men he met during four and one-half years overseas, Brant was the only one he knew to be a communist. MacEwan pressed that a friend who was an argumentative, overbearing communist with whom he spent leisure time and discussed politics had to influence him. Bennett steadfastly denied that he had and offered the diaries he kept during part of the war years as proof. MacEwan did not place much stock in Bennett's offer because he figured an agent would omit anything incriminating from a diary, but nevertheless, curiosity and the thirst for new leads compelled him, so he accepted.

Bennett repeated the claim he made to Spooner and again to MacEwan that in the late 1950s he reported both Foster and Brant to Harry Stone of MI5. MacEwan asked why so many years later he had suddenly reported his association with these two communists. Bennett replied that when it became clear the Soviets had penetrated the British government more deeply than anyone had initially suspected he started thinking back about people he had met and wondered about the two of them since they were capable of talent spotting on behalf of the KGB. He said Brant especially worried him when he discovered that he had stayed in the army after the war, risen to the rank of Major and become involved with secret radio work.

Now MacEwan unleashed his heaviest punch. He told Bennett that Harry Stone emphatically denied being warned about Foster and

Brant. Bennett looked uncomfortable and MacEwan sensed that he had scored a tactical victory. Bennett remained silent momentarily, seemed to flag and then mumbled that he thought he had told them. MacEwan pressed for an explanation but Bennett, missing the old confidence of the man who knew everything, had no answer to give. MacEwan felt vindicated. First he had shown that Bennett had withheld the expulsion of Uncle Albert, then established that he had a communist friend, Brant, with whom he discussed politics, and now, according to Stone, had lied about reporting Brant and Foster. MacEwan believed he had torn some of the fabric from Bennett's story.

MacEwan moved quickly to exploit the moment, going straight on to his relationship with Kim Philby, confident he could deal Bennett another setback. Bennett had earlier put himself on the record as having told a variety of people about his simultaneous posting with Philby in Turkey. MacEwan showed him part of the transcript from the interview with Spooner claiming that MI5 had interviewed him about Philby. MacEwan said the record could find no interview. Bennett read the transcript portion and acknowledged that there had been no interview and that his statement appeared to be in error; he had not tried to mislead anybody. He said while talking to Spooner he tried to put into context the cooperation he had given MI5 over the years in general terms while the transcript made it appear he was referring specifically to Philby. MacEwan, not hiding his scepticism, asked why, if he had tried to cooperate over Philby, had he not at the time of Philby's defection answered Britain's general circulation memo asking all members of the security and intelligence community for information. Bennett said he did not remember seeing any memo. MacEwan wanted to know how the head of the Russian Desk could have missed it. "What the hell happened to Higgitt or George B. McClellan?" asked Bennett. "Did they step forward? They knew Philby far better than I did." MacEwan pestered Bennett about hiding his knowledge of Philby to avoid having his own background investigated but Bennett countered that he had never covered it up because there was nothing to cover up; it was a matter of record that GCHQ had sent him to Istanbul in 1947 while Philby was there for MI6. If the British cannot maintain records they were in worse shape than he imagined. Besides, Bennett said, as he already told Spooner, he had talked about Philby to Maurice Oldfield, of MI6, Harry Stone of MI5 and Security Service officers such as Norman Jones and Bing Miller.

MacEwan had been waiting for Bennett to repeat that claim for by doing so he had fallen into his own trap, which MacEwan would now spring. MacEwan announced that Oldfield, Stone and Miller all denied his claim. Everybody had repudiated him except Jones who was dead. The news crippled Bennett. He said he thought he had told them and could not understand why they could not remember. MacEwan said they had looked for evidence of him talking about Philby and could only dredge up one passing reference Shev had made in 1967 to Peter Wright of MI5. Bennett said he was sure he had told others such as Janette Keir and John Dawe, both civilian colleagues in the Security Service, and had definitely not concealed meeting Philby just as he had not boasted about it.

Had Bennett covered up Philby, or had he simply acted with modest prudence? In fact he had done both. "After Philby defected in 1963," recalls one Mountie, "I do recall Jim saying he knew Philby. He said that in an office with about four people around. That was when Philby was an issue and the halls were buzzing about his defection. Jim just casually mentioned something to the effect that he knew the bastard." Says another colleague: "He didn't like it known he knew Kim Philby. Somebody once asked whether he had worked with Philby and Bennett said never to mention that name." MacEwan knew of neither incident. He dropped the subject satisfied that he had punched another hole in Bennett's credibility.

Sexsmith increasingly had been slipping in questions but now took control, moving Bennett ahead to an argument he had had in the Washington home of Maurice Oldfield when he was the MI6 Liaison Officer to North America. After debriefing Golitsin during the day, Bennett and Higgitt were partying in Oldfield's living room with Golitsin, Angleton, Ray Rocca, Angleton's assistant, and Arthur Martin of MI5 when Bennett mentioned how horrified he had been to learn upon arriving in North America the way McCarthyism had wrongly blighted peoples' lives. Angleton and Rocca claimed McCarthy had cleared many radicals out of society and improved the country's capability to combat espionage and subversion. Bennett said it blackened the American image around the world and ultimately hurt the United States. As Angleton and Rocca defended McCarthyism,

Bennett spelled out its evils, citing his ultra-conservative brother-in-law as a typical American who defended McCarthyism. Soon the two sides argued loudly, particularly Bennett and Rocca. Bennett got up from his chair and moved next to Rocca, sitting down on the arm of the sofa overlooking him. Rocca stood up as if ready to throw a punch. Angleton pulled at Rocca's sleeve to cool him down while Oldfield came over to quiet down Bennett.

Sexsmith and MacEwan questioned Bennett about his anti-McCarthyism as if it indicated evidence of underlying sympathy for communism that needed probing. Bennett said it had nothing to do with defending communism but defending innocent people, and pointed out that Golitsin had supported him that evening. The interrogators were making no headway and moved on to the circumstances that brought him to Canada.

The interrogators scrutinized Bennett about leaving GCHQ for Canada. Bennett replied that Shev's health had not adapted to the English climate and he wanted to quit GCHQ for various reasons, including its failure to reimburse him for money he had spent opening a new post in Hong Kong. As well, he said, the pioneering years of the post-war transition had ended and GCHQ had settled into a comfortable bureaucratic organization full of red tape. He preferred Australia but Shev did not and with advice from Joe Gibson they chose Canada. Sexsmith and MacEwan spent the next several hours quizzing every detail including all the people who had even a remote hand in the move including Joe Gibson, the CBNRC Liaison Officer posted to England, Mary Oliver, the CBNRC Personnel Officer in Ottawa who encouraged him about a job, Rod MacAskill, the more senior administrator who overruled her, Roy Batchelor, the former GCHQ man who helped Bennett settle into Ottawa, Mark McClung and Don Wall, the two RCMP civilians who interviewed him, and Terry Guernsey, the head of B Branch who finally hired him as a research assistant. Then they searched the possibility that he had come to Canada on instruction as an agent either of the Russians or the British. Bennett maintained that catching on with the RCMP had been fortuitous because he had applied for an array of jobs with private industry and other government departments. The interrogators stressed that Bennett had good prospects of landing a job with CBNRC.

Day two had run out. It had clearly belonged to the interrogators, thanks mainly to MacEwan's telling attacks on Bennett's credibility. If they could continue discrediting his claims they might break him before the week was out. That night Bennett retrieved from his basement eight army-issue notebooks each having 100 lined pages of daily entries from Malta to Egypt. He handed them to Neil Chadwick and also voluntarily surrendered Canadian and British passports dating back to 1946, when he got his first.

The next morning Sexsmith, for the first time in the interrogation, explored operational cases and examined Bennett over mistakes and "lapses of judgement." Throughout his questioning, Sexsmith controlled his emotions, remaining cool and calculating, and loomed as a more formidable adversary than Bennett had expected. His poker face, which left Bennett unsure whether he believed or doubted his statements, put Bennett at a disadvantage. Sexsmith started with Operation Keystone and promptly asked why Bennett had given the CIA the wrong date for Vladimir Bourdine's involvement in the case.

In 1958 Bennett had compiled a chronological review of Keystone that wove into the file for the first time Long Knife's meetings with Ostrovsky so that the two cases could be studied side by side. The document became the Security Service's standard working brief on Keystone for the next decade. In 1967 the RCMP finally disclosed Keystone to the CIA but still did not want to admit that a Mountie had sold out to the Russians. Consequently, Bennett rewrote his 1958 review for CIA eyes and deleted every reference to Long Knife, leaving the impression that the case died for undetermined reasons. In preparing the sanitized report Bennett listed Bourdine as Gideon's Soviet controlling officer in the wrong year. The CIA later got the full original report with the Long Knife details, noticed the discrepancy over Bourdine and suspected the date had been altered deliberately to foil analysis.

"Why did you put down Bourdine as the officer controlling the case when he wasn't," asked Sexsmith.

"All I can say," replied Bennett, "is that when I prepared that particular review it was during the time of Expo 67 and I was probably doing ten different jobs at the same time and probably worked overtime on that one. It was probably just one of those little errors. It certainly wasn't intended."

Sexsmith backed off almost sheepishly, leaving Bennett wondering what kind of case they had, to be clutching at such straws. Sexsmith rebounded quickly with an allegation that he hid the fact that he had known about Keystone at GCHQ. Bennett denied hiding his prior knowledge, saying that he had explained to Guernsey and Sweeny how he had verified Gideon's signal plan. Sexsmith shot back that both Guernsey and Sweeny denied it. Bennett, contradicted once more, again could only say he thought he had told them. Once more Bennett's credibility had been challenged.

Sexsmith then asked why he had continued his close friendship with Long Knife after his transfer for stealing the Bell Telephone money, and after Guernsey had warned him about the disgraced Mountie. Bennett said he had never been warned; Guernsey merely told him one day that Long Knife had financial problems, not that he had stolen money. Bennett said he had applied for vacation leave a few months after Long Knife's transfer and filled out a form saying he was staying at Long Knife's home and the application was approved. He said when he returned he talked around the office about his duck hunting experiences with Long Knife and described how wet and cold the weather had been. Once Long Knife had been exposed as a traitor Bennett said he submitted a report about his relationship with him. Sexsmith wanted to know why it took so long to mop up Keystone after Long Knife's treachery became known. Long Knife confessed in early 1958 but nearly two years passed before the Security Service interrogated Green and Gideon's live letter box. By the time Gideon's landlord was interviewed, Gideon's possessions had long been packed and moved and for some time the Security Service did not know where or by whom. Sexsmith thought the case had been misdirected. Bennett said he wanted to roll up the case but could not get approval from Higgitt who felt the KGB, not knowing about Long Knife's confession, might send Gideon back as a triple agent. Bennett claimed the delay frustrated him and others and as soon as he got clearance he moved.

Sexsmith never once asked Bennett about setting up Long Knife as the fall guy for Keystone's failure. In the preceding months, Long Knife had voluntarily submitted to a lie detector test and did not change his original admission that he approached Ostrovsky and not the other way around. Long Knife would eventually reverse himself but not for a few more years.

Sexsmith asked Bennett why he continued monitoring Operation

Dew Worm's bugs in the Soviet Embassy long after it was obvious they were not producing intelligence. Bennett said movements in and out of the empty room raised hope it would soon be occupied, possibly even by the military, although Bennett conceded that in retrospect the Soviets had probably dangled a carrot to excite interest. He said the bugs occasionally produced useful data such as the time the Soviets used the room to prepare their annual report. In this instance Dew Worm allowed a good insight into the range of Soviet interests in Canada and their estimates of the size of ethnic groups and the number of Canadians of Soviet background who had returned to the Soviet Union. Bennett said the decision to continue the tap belonged to the officer in charge of B Branch who wanted to squeeze the operation for all it was worth.

At this point Sexsmith confronted him over the unexplained late-night incident at Klochko's home. Sexsmith asked why he had parked his car there at such an odd hour. Initially, Bennett said he did not know what he was talking about and only when Sexsmith cited chapter and verse did Bennett seem to understand. Bennett said a string of his NCOs had been simultaneously promoted and he felt obliged to attend each promotion party so went hopping from one event to another. The last party, in the West End, had been the best and as he drove home he realized he had consumed too much drink and should not be driving. He parked his car on a sidestreet, fell asleep, and later woke up feeling better able to continue. The explanation sounded strange but Bennett said he had never done this kind of thing before and had no idea he had parked in the vicinity of Klochko's home. Sexsmith tried to get him to admit that he went there to contact Klochko, but Bennett refused.

When questioning resumed the next morning Bennett's diaries had been read and digested and, as Bennett had indicated, had nowhere mentioned Brant's name. However the diaries opened a new lead concerning one of Bennett's other friends and Sexsmith and MacEwan now turned their attention to him. Bennett's best friend during his two years at Malta had been a radio operator named Cedric Homer and in his diary he referred to Homer as a "gay bird." The interrogators now probed for evidence of a homosexual relationship.

Bennett said under no circumstances was Homer a homosexual and that he had used the term gay bird to emphasize his interest in the opposite sex. Homer had a fiance, Margaret, back in Britain and worried his absence might cost her affection. When Sexsmith and MacEwan kept pressing, Bennett said gay bird was an acceptable term for the day and then had no connotation of homosexuality. The interrogators showed him a March 25, 1943, excerpt about Homer: "At Music For All, we discussed communism—although he poses as a Red he is an Independent Reformist with socialistic tendencies." The interrogators said his own evidence cited him as a communist, although Bennett denied it, and tried to work an admission out of him that Homer had recruited him either through ideological persuasion or homosexuality. Bennett said that was nonsense and maintained that the passage described Homer as appearing more radical than he was. Bennett said he himself could not have been a communist because communists never used the term Red. If anything, he said, it was evidence he was not a communist.

Other diary entries supported Bennett's claim that he was not a communist. In 1942 he wrote: "...I am what is termed an Independent. I know that the difference between the classes of Britain is too high and wish to alleviate, but Socialism is a mild form of Bolshevism and Dictatorship, and is treated nowadays as National Socialism. Soon the Socialist Party of Britain will split; the views of reformists and extremists are unlinkable." The entry supported Bennett's claim but did not prove it. An agent could leave false evidence in his diary. Or he may have been recruited after he wrote that passage. The interrogators worked at breaking down Bennett's denials but he insisted Homer was neither a communist nor a homosexual, and neither was he.

After ninety minutes on the diaries, Sexsmith returned to case failures and questioned Bennett on why former Ambassador John Watkins had died under interrogation. If Watkins had been a KGB agent, the KGB might want to kill him before he talked. Bennett's report had tended to clear Watkins while a few others reading the same evidence thought Watkins had been guilty. Sexsmith had to tread carefully because Bennett's fellow interrogator was Harry Brandes who now belonged to the inner circle investigating Bennett. Brandes could be a stooge while Bennett—as the CIA believed he might have done—had switched the pills Watkins took for his heart condition.

"Well," replied Bennett, "he just died because of his heart condition.

Nobody was more surprised than Harry and myself. Certainly I had done nothing to provoke his death. I hadn't slipped him a tablet. I hadn't changed his tablets."

No autopsy had been performed because the Security Service at the time had sought to avoid publicity and did what it could to cover up the circumstances behind the death. The lack of an autopsy now deprived the investigation of evidence it wanted. Sexsmith could never prove his suspicion and moved to the next issue.

Sexsmith asked why Bennett had not accepted the CIA's story about Olga Farmakovsky being a planted agent and Bennett replied that both he and Higgitt examined the CIA's claim and could not support it. He said the CIA had been asked to substantiate the allegation and refused. He said he had made the recommendation but the final decision belonged to Higgitt. Sexsmith did not push the issue. Angleton's influence had got him to raise the subject but he personally did not buy the CIA claim.

Sexsmith quickly introduced another Angleton theme: why had Bennett not "taken more positive steps to identify Golitsin's leads." Golitsin had brought with him five Canadian leads and all had been resolved except the one alleging an External Affairs person had been recruited while serving in Moscow. Golitsin offered no other leads except the KGB's Russian language code name. The Security Service had catalogued the names of all External Affairs employees in Moscow during the 1950s, produced about twenty-five possibilities, and prepared poop sheets on all of them. Then through investigation they were reduced to about five prime suspects who were bugged, wire-tapped and, occasionally, surveilled, all with no positive results. Golitsin had been re-interviewed and shown documentation and the names of even distant suspects in the hope of prodding his memory, but he coughed up nothing more. One Mountie spent months trying unsuccessfully to identify the agent and when he gave up, Sexsmith took a shot and advanced the search no further. The case was eventually put on the shelf and allowed to linger. Now Sexsmith, who had been part of the search, bore down on Bennett for not doing more.

"Damn it all," retaliated Bennett, "you know the positive information Golitsin had to offer. We did go back to him time and time again."

Bennett sparked to life for one of the few times during the interrogation. The exchange threatened to become personal so Sexsmith backed off and changed subjects.

During one of the early debriefings, the Security Service showed Golitsin a list of names with matching photographs of Soviet personnel in Ottawa. Golitsin could not personally identify any intelligence officers. Later, on second perusal, Golitsin pointed to Ivan Khoroshilov, the Agricultural Counsellor, mainly because his beautiful daughter, Victoria, had accompanied him to Ottawa as his translator. Golitsin thought there was more to Victoria. "His daughter must be involved in the recruitment of a high-ranking Canadian," he said. Her presence was unusual and Golitsin theorized that back in Moscow she must have seduced a Canadian diplomat and had now come to Ottawa to continue the liaison on behalf of the KGB. Her father showed no sign of being an intelligence officer and, in fact, seemed to do a first class job as Agricultural Counsellor. Bennett, on the strength of Golitsin's analysis, added daughter Victoria to the watch list.

Scrutiny unearthed nothing. The Security Service found no relationship with any Canadian nor caught her fulfilling any intelligence function, leading to the conclusion that Golitsin must have been wrong. Maybe she had been sent genuinely as her father's translator. Her father, the fourth or fifth highest ranking official in the embassy, spoke poor English.

A few years later she returned to Canada to work in the Soviet pavilion at Expo 67 in Montreal, which seemed plausible since she spoke good English and knew Canada. Golitsin, after it was all over, did not think so. He felt Expo 67 gave her a good cover to carry out an assignment and that she had fooled the Security Service, which had not covered her return visit. Since the Security Service had not covered her, Golitsin's suspicion could not be discredited.

"Why did you oppose coverage of Victoria Khoroshilov during her period of attachment during Expo 67?" asked Sexsmith.

Bennett said he had not opposed coverage, merely invested coverage in other areas with better potential. Victoria Khoroshilov had not been identified as an intelligence officer, he said, while maybe as many as fifty others attached to Expo 67 had been, and needed coverage in addition to the thirty or so intelligence officers working out of the embassy.

Sexsmith next alleged Bennett had "taken little positive action to examine and establish the possibility of counterintelligence penetration of the RCMP." In other words Bennett had not looked hard enough for a mole, presumably because he was the mole. This allegation infuriated Bennett because nobody had preached the fear of penetration more than he and mostly to an apathetic audience. Bennett hardly gave a formal lecture without listing hostile penetration as one of the greatest dangers confronting them. He preached so adamantly that Don Atkinson considered it excessive and wondered whether he was the mole. Bennett had done more to combat penetration than had Sexsmith, his accuser. Ironically, Bennett was now suspected as a mole for, among other things, not doing enough. Bennett explained haughtily that he had continually looked and urged his staff to look for signs of infiltration, had tightened file handling and supervised further compartmentalization to contain the damage a mole could do.

Bennett's emotions perplexed Sexsmith. Accusations of treachery did not provoke him but suggestions of incompetence or mere lapses in judgement aroused anger and awakened his spirit.

MacEwan asked Bennett why he dragged out Operation Kit Bag in Edmonton so long and Bennett replied that he had wanted to document Mihalcin's tasks before pulling him in for interrogation. Hindsight had shown that Bennett had misjudged the case and let a good case disintegrate. Kit Bag represented an ideal failure to challenge Bennett with—except for one thing: Sexsmith ran B Branch for the last half of the operation and had supported Bennett's policy of letting it run. Sexsmith sat back while MacEwan asked the Kit Bag questions.

Bennett had fared well in the morning session. Except for the questions about Homer, Sexsmith and MacEwan had not really touched him. The afternoon session promised to be different. Sexsmith was holding back his knockout punches until after lunch.

Sexsmith opened the afternoon by confronting Bennett over his bizarre intervention against German BND officer Heinz Herre. He asked Bennett why he had requested CIA surveillance on Bagramov's trip to South America. Bennett said he had not specifically asked for coverage, instead he passed along information the agency might find relevant and might want to follow up, hoping the CIA would keep the RCMP informed of what it did. Sexsmith said it amounted to a request for coverage, which the CIA treated seriously enough to expend a great deal of effort accommodating him. Furthermore, Sexsmith alleged, the request was unusual given that Bagramov had not been identified as an intelligence officer. Bennett countered that the trip had been unusual; never before had he seen a Soviet Agricultural Attaché in Ottawa travel abroad like that. Bennett said he felt it important to learn what lay behind it and felt the CIA would be interested too. Then Sexsmith asked why he had reported Herre to the CIA. Bennett said Herre turned white in front of him when he mentioned the Bagramov trip, which was an abnormal reaction and possibly significant, so he reported it to Jim Smith, one of the CIA's Liaison Officers in Ottawa. Next Sexsmith wanted to know why he mentioned Bagromov's trip to Herre in the first place. Bennett said he always spoke warily to West German officials because of their history of Soviet penetration, but in this case Herre and he were talking about unusual movements so he used the Bagromov trip as an example since it had been posted with External Affairs. Sexsmith implied that he had picked on a vulnerable target to mislead the CIA but Bennett maintained that he tried to do nothing of the sort. Sexsmith could not substantiate his allegation yet felt he had scored a minor victory of sorts. Bennett had given answers that properly covered himself but otherwise did not ring with conviction. He hoped the momentum was beginning to swing back to his side.

When Sexsmith introduced Operation Deep Root and the contested filming of Natasha his voice grew slightly tense and his speech a little clipped. Bennett's senses pricked up too. The eruption in Sexsmith's office had happened more than three years ago but scars remained and the emotional fallout from both sides had not fully dissipated. The filming, as Bennett predicted, had failed and Sexsmith, who had overruled Bennett, would now try to build a case alleging that it miscarried because Bennett had sabotaged it. Sexsmith seemed to brace himself and then asked why he had tried to undercut the attack against Natasha. Bennett said he had not undercut A Division but proposed an alternative plan because Natasha was obviously a provocation agent while her KGB-officer husband had real intelligence value and was also blackmailable.

"Why did you discuss it?" Sexsmith asked.

"Because it was an alternative plan," replied Bennett. "It could have been a pincer operation."

Sexsmith started quizzing him about why he proposed to cut the wiretap on the Soviet embassy. Bennett said phoning the embassy was the most expedient way to put Natasha's husband into trouble for his secret love affair in Toronto and temporarily dropping the wiretap would leave no record of the call in case the plan backfired and the Soviets complained to External Affairs.

"You phoned the embassy to screw up that case," charged Sexsmith.

"I didn't in any shape or form," responded Bennett. "Under no circumstances have I ever phoned anybody."

Sexsmith refused to back off and accused Bennett of engineering his alternate plan as a cover to lift the wiretap long enough to warn the embassy. His plan was overruled but Sexsmith alleged that he went ahead and lifted the wiretap of his own volition and warned the Soviets, which resulted in Natasha's sudden departure from Canada. Bennett denied it, but Sexsmith asked why else would be concoct a plan to call the Soviet embassy.

"Damn it all," shot back Bennett, "this is no bloody different than when we tried to recruit Tchelernysken. We arranged that there would be no record anywhere of your phone call. It's no different than that."

Bennett had counterattacked and landed a hard blow. Sexsmith froze momentarily. He had not expected such retaliation and thought Bennett had hit a bit low. Back in May 1963, when Sexsmith was still a sergeant, Leonid Tchelernysken, a thirty-one-year-old KGB support officer, had been drinking in his car in an Ottawa park with his friend Vladimir Cheremisinov, when an RCMP squad car not connected with the Security Service passed through the area on routine night patrol. Tchelernysken panicked and took off so fast he hit the nearby Hog's Back Bridge. Tchelernysken was uninjured and the car suffered only about $200 damage but his friend Cheremisinov, an exchange scientist, gashed his head and died instantly. Tchelernysken, too junior to have diplomatic immunity and badly shaken by the death of his friend, was charged with drunken driving and thrown in jail. He was in trouble with the Canadian law but in even deeper trouble with the embassy and no doubt dreaded the consequences of returning to Moscow. All of this made him ripe for defection.

The best chance lay to talk to him while he feared for his future in an Ottawa jail cell but that opportunity vanished when the Ottawa City Police notified the embassy too quickly. Bennett and Sexsmith devised a strategy between them to recoup the lost opportunity. While Tchelernysken packed his belongings in preparation for his return to Moscow, Sexsmith would call him at home and offer asylum while Bennett would turn off the wiretap. The scheme was hatched and proceeded flawlessly except that in the end Tchelernysken told Sexsmith he was not interested.

"I arranged it and you went ahead with the phone call," said Bennett. "It's the same thing."

"It's different," bristled Sexsmith.

"It isn't," argued Bennett. "It is exactly the same. If we had done this with Makhotin there would be no record on the board in case of a protest from External Affairs. Nobody in the organization would have known about it."

Sexsmith tried to press ahead but Bennett's counterattack had at least partly deflated one of his best cases. Still, Sexsmith still had one last good case to raise, the litmus test in Montreal, which he now introduced.

The litmus test did not prove a lot but it did carry good shock value and might stun Bennett into confession. Sexsmith asked Bennett to explain why a Soviet intelligence officer showed up for a phony meeting only *he* had reason to believe was genuine. Bennett said he could not explain it because he had nothing to do with it. Sexsmith demanded to know how many people he had told and Bennett replied none, so that if a leak occurred it originated elsewhere.

"Only eight people knew about it," charged Sexsmith. "So therefore it would have to be you who told the Russians."

"Do you think if I had been a KGB agent the Russians would be so bloody stupid to compromise me in something of that nature," retorted Bennett.

The two sparred aimlessly for half an hour with neither side prevailing. In reality Sexsmith had lost. He had fired his loudest shot and missed and had nothing more to fall back on. Had he pulled out a string of litmus results the onslaught might have overwhelmed a KGB mole until he could no longer deny the emerging truth. Sexsmith had tried other litmus tests and received no reaction. Out of evidence, Sexsmith had to face the consequence that he had suspected all along: Bennett was probably loyal.

The next morning, Friday, Sexsmith asked why Bennett had

opposed the setting up of an Illegals Desk. A mole of Bennett's stature would report to an illegal and Sexsmith wanted to check whether Bennett may have thwarted the search for illegals in order to protect himself. Bennett replied that illegals could be better handled under the existing structure where the Russian Desk looked for Soviet illegals, the Czech Desk for Czech illegals and so on, adding that the CIA evidently agreed with his approach because it had an Illegals Section and had abandoned it. After hearing Bennett recite how he had tried to identify illegals, the interrogation had effectively ended. Sexsmith spent the next few hours tying up loose ends about the McCarthyism argument in Washington, Klochko, Kit Bag and a few other incidents. As lunch time approached the interrogation had run out of gas.

"If you want to talk to me again, you're welcome," offered Bennett. "I'm here to clear up any doubts."

Bennett also volunteered to submit to a polygraph examination and Sexsmith promised to pass on the offer to John Starnes, the Director-General.

"The decision about you returning to work is entirely up to the DG," counselled Sexsmith. "He'll be in touch with you."

Sexsmith advised him not to leave town without checking with the Security Service.

Bennett looked sombre but felt triumphant and vindicated. Inside Sexsmith felt sorrow over interrogating a colleague but maintained a stoical expression until slight watering in the corner of his eyes spoiled the front. He had worked with Bennett almost continuously since 1954 and the two had been pillars of B Branch. Despite their clashes, they had usually formed an effective team and had grown to respect the other's strengths and differences. Sexsmith knew that whatever he said about the DG deciding, the DG's ruling would be a formality because the outcome was not in doubt: Bennett was finished as a counter-espionage officer and would be forever banned from any kind of national security work. The results of the interrogation did not matter; the only result that counted was the fact he had fallen under suspicion in the first place. The suspicion he had been a KGB agent would stain him so indelibly that it was now part of him and nobody would trust him again. Counterespionage work does not forget suspicions. Convicting a mole might be difficult, but proving loyalty was more difficult, if not impossible. Winning back questioned trust lay beyond comprehension.

"I don't believe in any way you have been a KGB agent," said Sexsmith.

He looked sorry that he had ever gotten into the mess. The grim expression on MacEwan's face did not agree. MacEwan had pushed hard during both the investigation and interrogation and grown frustrated by his lack of success. No long history with Bennett softened his emotions. He had known Bennett only a few years and mostly as a suspect.

While Sexsmith and MacEwan remained back in the safehouse, Bennett left the hotel and went home to await the Director-General's inevitable verdict.

21

The Aftermath

BENNETT HAD NOT been home long when another shock arrived. Shev, his wife of twenty years, announced the next day that she was leaving and returning to Australia. She had contemplated leaving for some time and thought that now, with everything coming apart, was the best time. Bennett reacted to the break-up of his marriage the way he had reacted to the interrogation—with limp acceptance. Disheartened, he agreed, with hardly a murmur, to sell the house and split evenly the proceeds. He would also fortify her with a quarterly stipend of $800 while she took Vivienne, nearly fifteen, and Hilary, eleven, to Australia.

Bennett told Shev he did not want to return to work inside the shell at the RCMP, even if Starnes took him back, and also hoped to move to Australia if he could find a job. He had spent eighteen years with the RCMP and pensionable time began after twenty years although a medical pension would let him leave Canada with a reasonable annuity. After a few days, as Shev started planning the logistics of moving three people to Melbourne, Bennett said he would apply for a medical discharge. He wanted to retire and settle in Perth but figured a pension, even a medical one, would not allow him the luxury of full retirement and Perth held limited employment prospects for his skills.

A similar grimness hung over the atmosphere in Starnes' office at headquarters a few miles away. While Bennett tried to figure out his future, Starnes, Draper and Sexsmith huddled together on the fourth floor with the same objective, but from a different perspective.

"Damn it," grumbled Starnes, "I've lost confidence in the guy."

The Security Service had not made its case against Bennett, but Starnes believed Bennett had not made his case either. Draper also held reservations.

"I was so sure he would have no difficulty," remarked Draper, "but he dug holes for himself."

Sexsmith said he too had not been happy with Bennett's answers but added that it did not have to be sinister.

While Bennett had emerged relatively unscathed, the interrogation had produced gaps and inaccuracies that a mole could conceivably hide behind. Bennett had merely shrugged his shoulders in reply to some of the discrepancies. Everybody in Starnes' office felt he could have done better. Bennett was normally meticulous and articulate and could think on his feet, so why had he not performed better? He had handled other people's security clearances a long time and been critical of similar lapses.

The interrogation had occasionally provoked Bennett into fits of rancour but he never lost his temper or showed sustained bitterness. "If somebody accused me of being a Soviet spy I'd probably pop him in the nose," declared Draper. Bennett's defence for the most part lacked spirit and it bothered his jurors who agreed a red-blooded guy would likely get hopping mad or fall on his knees and confess. So why had Bennett remained so passive? Maybe it was part of his personality. Many people over the years had poked personal insults at him in the office or at parties and he always brushed them off. Maybe he was just that kind of guy.

Bennett had not always given satisfactory answers, but in many instances he had given more information than necessary. Nobody would have suspected Uncle Ernest if he had not reported his mother's description of him as a communist. Bennett could have omitted reference to Foster and the Left Book Club, as well as Brant, with almost 100 percent safety from discovery. Yet he failed to disclose Uncle Albert's expulsion from the Labour party in spite of the fact that it was a matter of public record and highly traceable. The Cedric Homer suspicion arose out of Bennett's volunteered war-time diaries.

To some extent Bennett composed his own difficulties at the interrogation, which is not something a calculating mole would do.

Starnes decided he could not keep Bennett around. Bennett, he said, had disqualified himself from national security work. Besides, Starnes added, he could not in good conscience keep Bennett and expect to keep the trust of foreign agencies. Skewering yourself was bad enough, he said, but screwing your friends was unpardonable.

The next Friday, a week after the interrogation ended, Starnes, with Draper at his side, met Bennett in the same safehouse and told him he could have his lie detector test. By this time Bennett had started pressing the issue. Bennett had also been asking for the right to seek guidance from Inspector Vince Cain, a lawyer in the RCMP's legal branch. Starnes okayed that as well.

Starnes informed Bennett that he did not doubt his loyalty but questioned his judgement for failing to disclose earlier his family background and his connection with Philby. Furthermore, he said, he had been indiscreet in talking to Long Knife about the bugging of the Soviet embassy. During the interrogation Bennett admitted having fantasized to Long Knife about television cameras going into the embassy when Long Knife came back in 1956 and offered help on the bugging operation. Bennett had said he merely responded to Long Knife's offer of help. Starnes insisted that such lack of judgement precluded his reinstatement into the organization. It would be best, he said, for the Security Service, its relations with other services, and Bennett's own welfare that he work elsewhere in the civil service. Starnes said he had already talked with John Carson, the chairman of the Public Service Commission, about a transfer to a position with approximately equal salary. Bennett replied he would act in the best interest of his family but first wanted to clear his name. Then, he added, he would prefer a medical pension so he could move to a warmer climate.

The following Wednesday, back at the safehouse again, Sergeant Holmes unpacked his portable polygraph unit and patiently told Bennett how a lie detector test worked. He counselled him to relax and then attached one lead wire to his hand, another to his neck and a third to his chest. With everything in place, Holmes, a polygraphist from the police side of the RCMP, asked first his name, then his place of birth, the names of parents and a few more simple questions to give his machine a normal response.

Holmes moved quickly and quietly. Unlike Sexsmith's and Mac-Ewan's probe two weeks earlier, he sought simply to record Bennett's responses for analytical purposes and did not seek to break the man. Had he been a communist? Had he been a socialist? What were his political philosophies as a youth? How did he find school? Did he have boyfriends? Did he have girlfriends? Did he play sports? Holmes shifted to his father, mother and uncles and when finished with Penrhiwceiber, asked about his experiences in the war, GCHQ and, finally, the RCMP. Who did he not get along with? What unpleasant things happened to him?—anything that might cause him to bolt to the Russians. By mid-afternoon Holmes focussed in on homosexuality and sexually deviant activity, taking Bennett back to his early years, then to his relationship with Cedric Homer in Malta, then to two homosexual colleagues during his posting with GCHQ in Hong Kong. After that Holmes delved into his sexual relations with his wife.

The next morning, before Holmes could re-attach the wires, Bennett announced he would answer no more questions on homosexuality and sexual deviation. Bennett said the preoccupation with the subject disgusted him and that the inquiry had wandered beyond the boundaries of need and had no cause to belabour the issue. He also served notice he would not answer speculative questions about friends and colleagues.

Bennett's terms did not trouble Holmes who routinely carried on with the test. He now confronted Bennett directly with a series of root questions about his allegiance. Have you been loyal to the RCMP? Have you been loyal to Canada? Then for the first time Holmes asked the most fundamental question of all. "Have you ever been a member of the Russain Intelligence Service?" No, said Bennett. Holmes continued: Romanian, Bulgarian, Polish, Chinese, British. Bennett said no to each. When Holmes had finished, Bennett told him he had missed East German Intelligence Service. After Bennett assured him he had never worked for the East German service, Holmes said the examination was finished.

"How did I do?" asked Bennett.

"You didn't do too badly at all," replied Holmes.

Vince Cain, the Mountie lawyer, carried a reputation for being an independent character, and he usually spoke his mind freely. For an in-house lawyer whose first responsibility belonged to the RCMP, Cain represented as good a choice as Bennett could pick. He advised Bennett to prepare a formal written rebuttal answering each allegation for the record so that his disclaimers remained permanently on file. Bennett accepted the advice and hurried out to the Library of Parliament to read up on incidents of treachery to help marshal his defence.

John Carson of the Public Service Commission did not know the candidate visiting his office was a suspected spy. Starnes' letter of introduction merely said Bennett had worked in the "arcane" field of security and was considering a change. Carson had an amended curriculum vitae. The original one prepared by the Force so offended Bennett he prepared his own and submitted it. Bennett's revised curriculum vitae ran ten pages and listed an array of experiences and skills the RCMP had neglected.

"My god," exclaimed Carson, "you have experience at so many things, haven't you?"

Bennett told Carson he had not come to reject or accept any job, but came because Starnes had written the letter. Bennett said he had applied for a medical pension and, if successful, would leave Canada. With the preliminaries cleared up, Carson narrowed down Bennett's interests and told him the public service must have employment to suit his desires and a few weeks later, through an intermediary, offered him a position on the Public Service Appeals Board. The job dropped Bennett's salary about $5,000 a year, so he rejected it.

Bennett finished drafting his defence rebuttal in early May and Cain personally handed it to Commissioner Higgitt.

"Please ensure that Jim knows that this is being handed to Draper and [Ray] Parent," replied Higgitt. "And also ensure Jim that he knows that if he ever wants to see me at anytime the door is open to him."

Bennett's rebuttal started with an affidavit denying he was a communist agent.

AFFIDAVIT

I solemnly swear that I have never been an open or secret member of a communist party or any of its front organizations; a supporter of the international communist movement; a witting tool of the aspirations of the international communist movement including its security and intelligence arms or a witting agent of a foreign power with particular reference to communist countries. In addition, I wish to give similar assurances that since coming to Canada I have not acted as an espionage agent or agent of influence on behalf of either the British or U.S. governments or any other foreign government. As no valid evidence has been produced by the Security Service of the RCMP in support of its allegations this reinforces, in my opinion, my plea of complete innocence. It is respectfully submitted that my record of dedicated anti-communist work, involving family and personal sacrifices, in the employ of the British and Canadian governments over the past twenty-six years should be adequate testimony against these false and untenable accusations.

I also wish to place on record the fact that I have never purposely withheld information relevant to my security status, and, that I have offered every cooperation necessary to assist the Security Service investigation, including the furnishing of my World War II diaries, my British passports, and, the voluntary undertaking at my behest of a polygraph examination, which took place on March 29 and 30, 1972.

I am prepared to afford any further assistance necessary to the Security Service of the RCMP and, any other appropriate organization, in order to remove any lingering doubts concerning my loyalty.

Witness:	Inspector V. Cain,	L.J. Bennett
	Legal Branch, RCMP	2 May, 1972.
	HQ, Ottawa	

Bennett's presentation had five parts, the main one being volume two, a forty-page single-spaced typewritten rebuttal of each point raised against him, starting with the allegations about Uncle Albert and finishing with a blow-by-blow defence of his managing of counter-espionage cases. "It needs to be stated.... that any mistakes and lapses of judgement have not been motivated by witting support of the international communist movement," Bennett's defence said. "In the peaceful atmosphere of retrospection it is so easy to criticize decisions taken in operations, a retrospection so devoid of all the essential elements such as atmosphere, ignorance, personalities, policies, information and reasons for those decisions."

Later Cain delivered to Commissioner Higgitt another sealed envelope adding to Bennett's submission.

AFFIDAVIT BY MRS. HEATHER E. BENNETT

I solemnly swear that my marriage separation from my husband, Mr. Leslie James Bennett, is due to incompatability of long duration and cannot be attributed to any doubts concerning his loyalty to Her Majesty and Canada. The crisis caused by the recent action of the Security Service of the RCMP against my husband certainly brought to a head the decision to separate. I wish to add my full support to his plea of innocence of the wrongful accusations of communist sympathizer, communist intelligence agent and British intelligence agent as submitted by him to Commissioner W.L. Higgitt in Appendix I-Affidavit dated 2 May, 1972. Throughout the twenty years of marriage his demonstration of anti-communist dedication has been self evident through the not inconsiderable sacrifices, both personal and family, he has made in discharging his RCMP responsibilities to the fullest extent. With respect to the suggestion of possible homosexual tendencies in his part, I wish to state categorically that these are totally unfounded as his heterosexual interests have been displayed consistently throughout our married life. In supporting his attestation of innocence I wish to reiterate my preparedness to render any assistance necessary to remove any lingering doubts concerning his loyalty.

It is essential that his reputation and loyalty be cleared for the sake of the family, and also to ensure that there is no vestige of impediment left to disbar me or my children from seeking gainful employment in order to achieve a decent standard of living.

Witness: Vince Cain,   H.E. Bennett
          Inspector, RCMP   24 May, 1972.
          Ottawa

By this time Bennett's medical tests had come back and he had already submitted form A-159 for a medical discharge. Befitting a man of his thoroughness, Bennett typed out sheets of notes on his medical condition, including a 150-word medical history going back to 1925 when he was five. Yet when past illnesses were discounted, Bennett's case looked thin. Bennett cited three medical deficiencies: 1) his difficulty with cold weather; 2) his tendency to catch cold viruses; and 3) his allergies. A complete medical examination a few weeks earlier declared him in good physical condition. He had many ailments but did they render him unfit to continue work? His personal doctor could contribute the best opinion and his report defended Bennett's application with restrained support.

Commissioner W.L. Higgitt,
RCMP Headquarters,
1200 Alta Vista Drive
Ottawa, Ont.

Re: Mr. Leslie James Bennett

Dear Sir,

The above mentioned patient was first seen by me in 1964 because of reactions to local anesthetics. At that time we had positive skin tests to Xylocaine and nupercaine and a passive transfer test confirmed these reactions. During the course of this examination some mild wheezing was heard in his chest but he denied a history of previous allergies although his father had had asthma and one brother had exzema.

He was seen again in 1969 with typical allergic rhinitis both seasonal and perennial and wheezing on exertion and in the cold.

Skin testing at that time revealed multiple reactions to dust, feathers, dog, wool, ragweed, moulds and summer weeds.

It was obvious from the history and particularly his history of propensity to get reactions to chemicals that the etiology of his asthma was both intrinsic and extrinsic. Getting rid of their dog improved the situation. Taking injections therapy for a number of extrinsic allergents also improved the situation but on review in 1971 and 1972 it was found that he was still wheezing, particularly in the cold weather and on exercise.

The patient's history indicates that he has considerable trouble with this in the winter time and I consider that it is unlikely that he will be completely free of it under the present situation. Therefore, I would support his request for retirement on medical reasons and his plan to move to a warmer climate.

Yours truly,
E.C.R. Purchase, M.D.

Draper looked at the papers once and shook his head. "You've got as much chance as a snowball in hell," said Draper. "There's no way."

Bennett suffered during the winter, had weakness in the lungs, a series of allergies, and experienced a lot of sickness, but had nothing fundamentally wrong. The report from Bennett's doctor mentioned nothing about long-range problems. Bennett said he needed the extra $4,000 a year from a medical pension in order to leave Canada for a warmer climate and thought the Force could do something to help arrange a medical pension.

"There's no way in the world I could ever see a board doing this," replied Draper. "I hope your doctors are prepared to stand by these scanty notes because they don't say very much." Don Saul, the RCMP administrative officer, echoed Draper's comments.

Just as the RCMP seemed paralyzed over what to do with Bennett, the medical board unexpectedly resolved the problem by approving the medical pension. "He appears very tense and anxious," noted the medical board report. Bennett weighed 11 pounds less than he had upon joining the RCMP in 1954 and the report noted that he looked older than his fifty-two years. "Freedom from his responsibilities will probably relieve him of his anxiety state," concluded the report.

People in later years assumed the medical discharge had been fixed. But it had not. "There are a lot of people who think that those things can be manipulated," said one RCMP officer. "I wouldn't want to be the one who ever tried it. They've got some pretty crusty old people on that pension thing. The medical types there take their own world very seriously." Bennett's medical pension looked rigged but had stood on its own merits and somehow had been approved.

The medical discharge required Bennett to come to headquarters and sign separation forms. His desk had been cleared out for him, so this would be his first visit since the morning of the interrogation and it presented a delicate problem. Most Security Service personnel still did not know what had really happened to him and both the RCMP and Bennett had an investment in maintaining the official story that medical impairment had forced his early retirement. But now, without his security clearance, Bennett could not walk in the main door and had to be checked in and escorted like any other visitor; his cover would be jeopardized. An indoctrinated NCO waited at the door to whisk him casually into the building. "Where have you been?" asked one of the guards. "We haven't seen you for ages." Bennett politely replied that an assignment had taken him away.

Upstairs, Bennett signed the forms severing him from the RCMP, but the Security Service neglected to present him the de-indoctrination forms that would prohibit him from discussing the secrets he had learned from his job. So a few days later Bennett had to return to the safehouse for a final meeting with Starnes and Draper. Bennett delivered a short message declaring he was not a Soviet agent.

"I've been accused of all sorts of things in the interrogation, none of them are true," proclaimed Bennett. "You of all people should know that. What has happened is a bad reflection on the professional capacity of the RCMP and particularly you."

Starnes' expression hardened. Bennett had more to say.

"If you're looking for an agent inside the organization, you'd better smarten up because I've never been that agent. And if there is one in the organization, then you'd better find him. You've wasted time looking at me."

"We still have reasons to doubt your loyalty," shot back Starnes.

"I could put this case before the appeal board if I wanted to," said Bennett.

Bennett's threat may have been empty but it struck a sensitive chord. Going to the appeal board was tantamount to telling the government what happened. The Security Service had told the government nothing about its mole suspicion or even of the record of failure over the years. The Security Service adopted the attitude of a proud family: the shame is too great, so you tell nobody.

"It wouldn't be in your interest to do so," threatened Starnes. "Lots of things would come out."

"It would be more damaging to you than to me," retorted Bennett.

"Your army friend, the gay bird," barked Starnes, referring crudely to Cedric Homer in Malta.

"You must be pretty stupid to take that as meaning homosexuality."

Starnes said he had used some pretty unusual terminology.

"What about Dew Worm?" asked Starnes.

"You have no evidence Dew Worm died because of me in any shape or form and you know it," maintained Bennett.

"You've been indiscreet in talking with Long Knife," Starnes emphasized.

"Yes," acknowledged Bennett, "and I've already admitted that. But he went voluntarily to the Russians. He was the one who spilled the beans. He knew about Dew Worm."

Starnes said Long Knife did not know about Dew Worm until Bennett told him.

"The compromise on the Dew Worm operation must come back to you," insisted Starnes.

"That's absolute nonsense, Long Knife already knew about the operation."

"Oh no, he didn't," said Starnes. "He denied it entirely."

"Do you believe a traitor?" asked Bennett.

Bennett's question carried an irony. Starnes seemed prepared to believe a proven traitor over somebody who could not be shown disloyal.

"You talk about my being indiscreet," said Bennett, "what about your indiscretion with Maurice Oldfield?"

Starnes bristled. Bennett did not have to spell out the indiscretion. A few years earlier, MI5 had shared with the Security Service news of an extremely sensitive operation on an eyes-only basis and Starnes had told Maurice Oldfield of MI6. When MI5 discovered that its opposite number had been told, it filed a memo of protest to the Security Service for violating the trust. "The British service was madder than hell," said one officer. "They were absolutely uptight."

"If at any stage in the future," threatened Bennett, "I find that what has happened is used against my wife or my children to deny access to classified information then I will raise absolute hell. I don't care about myself because I have no interest in getting back into that form of security."

"Oh," replied Starnes, "there will be no problem there."

"Also," added Bennett, "if I went and found employment with airport security, what would the Force do? Would they write something that had an adverse impact?"

"There would be no problem," Starnes promised.

Bennett signed the de-indoctrination forms, stood up and without saying another word left the safehouse for the last time.

"This is to certify that you served with the Royal Canadian Mounted Police as a Civilian Member from July 1, 1954 to July 28, 1972," said Bennett's official letter of acknowledgement from the RCMP, "the date you were discharged in consequence of having been compulsorily retired under the provisions of Section 10 (2) (b) of the Superannuation Act, by reason of having become medically disabled for further service in the Force."

Epilogue

What Happened to Bennett

The cover-up could not last. Rumours overcome any bureaucracy and, once started, the speculation could not be stopped. Bennett had disappeared too quickly and too completely; the Force had not given him a visible send-off party. All kinds of wild stories about Bennett as a Soviet agent started to spread. Many people knew about the investigation but only a few knew the results. Many questions were asked. Some of the officers who knew refused to answer. Others got mad and told the questioners to mind their own business. Some looked the questioner straight in the eye and said flatly that Bennett had never been a suspect and retired for the reasons stated.

Nobody believed the denials, especially when a general housecleaning removed Bennett's closest friends and colleagues from their operations. Joe Yoblonski, one of Bennett's two senior NCOs, was moved to Vancouver. Vic Wallwork, his other senior NCO, was transferred to Halifax but, suffering from terminal cancer, was allowed to stay for the remaining months of his life. Dick Rowan, a colleague and close friend, was transferred to A Division. Dorothy McDonald was moved. So were friends outside E Branch such as Ken Green and Aussie Gee. Janette Keir, one of his closest friends, was herself interrogated but deflated the allegations against her and was rehabilitated. Of Bennett's close friends, only Howie Jones, who collaborated with Operation Gridiron, kept his position.

Eventually the gossip had to leak outside the Security Service. A year after Bennett's departure from Canada, Tom Hazlitt, a reporter with the Toronto *Star*, picked up the rumours and flew to Johannesburg to ask Bennett if he was the "Canadian Philby." Bennett emphatically denied it and told Hazlitt he had been retired early for medical reasons alone. Bennett typed out and signed a brief statement:

> This is to certify that I have never been at any time during my life either a witting or unwitting supporter of the Communist cause, and, as such, never a member of the Soviet-bloc intelligence services.
>
> This is also to certify that any rumours to the effect that my retirement from the RCMP was related to such activities are completely untrue and thus without any factual foundation.
>
> In support of this statement I would add that my record of anti-communist dedication from 1940 to 1972 in the employ of the British and Canadian governments is sufficient testimony, as can be eloquently supported by those intimate associates in government.
>
> It is my most sincere hope that for the sake of my two young children that the persons who are pursuing this line of investigation will now desist so that they can be spared any further suffering in addition to that caused by marriage separation. The future belongs to them and it is only right that they should be allowed to pursue their careers without any muckraking which would be detrimental to their futures.

Bennett did tell Hazlitt before he left that he was questioned as a possible security risk but wrote it off as a normal updating of his clearance, which the organization did routinely. After Hazlitt reported the denial in the *Star*, Bennett, on the invitation of his journalist friend Peter Worthington, wrote an article in the rival Toronto *Sun*.

"I retired after eighteen years of service for reasons of ill health," Bennett's article said. "My respiratory and allergic problems, freakish in their entirety, respond well in a warm climate along with regular injections. For health reasons I could no longer continue to work in the cold environment of my beloved country.

"The *Star* stated that before resignation I was investigated as a possible security risk and interrogated on the possibility that I had some connection with a foreign intelligence service.

"I made it clear to Mr. Hazlitt that the RCMP would be remiss not to update security clearances in accordance with government policy and that I would not expect to be immune from such an investigation because of my length of service and seniority."

Hazlitt could not challenge Bennett's disclaimer. He knew only the vague outlines of Operation Keystone and Long Knife and had nothing more than a feeling that Bennett's cases might have failed. Hazlitt still believed Bennett was a mole but when he denied being the Canadian Philby his story collapsed.

Back in Canada, Hazlitt, a distinguished journalist of the "old school", wanted to pursue the Bennett story further and develop it into a book but he had terminal cancer, and so joined forces with Ian Adams, a younger breed of journalist who had opted-out of the professional mainstream. Since Hazlitt had sources inside the Security Service and Adams had an interest in the organization and a desire to pursue the Bennett story, the two entered into a pact. Hazlitt would introduce Adams to inside sources while Adams did the legwork and the writing.

Hazlitt's health deteriorated almost as soon as the project started and before long he died. In the meantime Adams concluded that an outsider could not write the Bennett book and in November 1977 produced a novel entitled *S, Portrait of a Spy*, which featured the main character S, a Superintendent in the RCMP Security Service with a striking resemblance to Bennett, as a Soviet mole inside the Security Service turned into a triple agent for the CIA. The book became an overnight bestseller and caused such a public controversy that Ottawa had to respond.

By this time Bennett had moved to Australia and in an interview with Barbara Frum on CBC Radio's "As It Happens" again downplayed the nature of his interrogation. By coincidence, the Solicitor General and top RCMP officers appeared before the House of Commons Committee on Justice and Legal Affairs the next evening.

"There have been, of course, a number of allegations made both inside the House of Commons and outside the House of Commons concerning Mr. Bennett," testified Solicitor General Francis Fox. "Mr. Bennett did leave the Force in 1972. The allegations and innuendoes that have been flying are completely unfair to Mr. Bennett. Mr. Bennett left the Force on a medical discharge, and in spite of rumours to the contrary, he was not paid off and not ordered to get out of the country. Contrary, once again, to allegations and innuendoes, there is no evidence whatsoever that Mr. Bennett was anything but a loyal Canadian citizen. I would suggest that the treatment given to Mr. Bennett to date has been most unfair."

A few seconds later Robert Simmonds, the new-broom RCMP Commissioner, jumped in with his own endorsement.

"In a general way," said Simmonds, "I am rather appalled at seeing the way a man's reputation can be pilloried in public, based on a lot of rumour and speculation. All the events surrounding Mr. Bennett's career in the Force occurred long before I was in headquarters and long before, of course, I was Commissioner of the Force. But a review of the file and conversation with people in the Security Service who were present at the time have given me every assurance that there was absolutely no evidence on which to base any charge of any sort — criminal, internal or anything else — in connection with his departure."

But fifteen minutes later, Mike Dare, the inept successor to Starnes as head of the Security Service, undercut his superiors and spoiled the cover up by divulging that Bennett had been interrogated for four days (actually it was five days) and that the procedure was not customary.

"There was a possibility in certain minds that because of certain events, he might have been a security risk, and because he held such highly sensitive positions, as a very senior civilian member in the Force, he was very closely examined before the release," said Dare. "There was no evidence found, as I think has been repeatedly said by both the minister and me."

When the committee met again the following week, Dare agitated the speculation further by incorrectly implying Bennett had been fingered by a defector.

"Did the defection of [Yuri] Nosenko form any part in the events leading up to the interrogation of Superintendent Bennett?" asked MP Erik Nielsen.

"No, Mr. Chairman," replied Dare. "The matters that lead to Mr. Bennett's interrogation had to do with, which I think the minister has made abundantly clear in the House, the over-all concern of the western intelligence community as to possibility of penetrations at a high level, which were the results of matters which were disclosed by a high-level KGB defector to one of our major allies. So though the information did not come from Nosenko, it came from some other defector. Thank you."

"If a defector has come out with any sort of information whatsoever," Bennett told "As It Happens" the next day, "all I can say is that the information is totally false. Because I have never been a traitor in any shape or form to Canada and never would."

His cover decimated, Bennett admitted publicly for the first time, "the RCMP thought they had a case which obviously they had to proceed with and interrogate me until such time as they're satisfied."

Early in 1978 Bennett launched a libel suit against Adams and his publisher for $2.2 million in damages that the fictional KGB agent "S" was actually meant to be him. A settlement nearly two years later gave Bennett $30,000 plus a disclaimer in future copies of *S, Portrait of a Spy* that S was not intended to be him.

After having lived in Sydney for a while, where he was vice-president of a local constituency of the Liberal Party of Australia, Bennett now lives in Perth, Australia, where he lives off his medical pension and income from part-time self employment as a credit counsellor to small companies.

What Happened to the Others

James Angleton, the Chief of Counterintelligence who stood behind the great mole hunt, was fired on December 20, 1974, by CIA Director Bill Colby who thought Angleton's theories had damaged the organization.

Aquavit, the Double Agent who visited Moscow in Operation Top Hat, is a successful small businessman in greater Vancouver.

Don Atkinson, the senior NCO who first put together the case against Bennett, retired in 1967. He now is an administrator in the Customs and Excise Branch of Revenue Canada.

Archie Barr, one of the investigators in the Bennett probe, is working on the transition team that is converting the Security Service into a separate, civilian agency and is expected to have a senior position in the new organization.

Heather Bennett, Bennett's former wife, lives in Melbourne, Australia.

Ted Bennett, Bennett's father, retired from mine work in 1962 and now lives with his son in Perth.

Harry Brandes, who helped Bennett interrogate John Watkins and later investigated Bennett, has risen to Chief Superintendent and is the head of B Branch.

Carton, the Double Agent who entrapped Vasily Tarasov, the KGB Intelligence Officer who operated in Ottawa under the cover of a correspondent for *Izvestia*, still works in the federal civil service.

Neil Chadwick, the Featherbed investigator who escorted Bennett to the safehouse for interrogation, lives in Greater Vancouver and works for the B.C. Institute of Technology.

Howard Draper, the Deputy Director of the Security Service during the Bennett investigation, retired in 1975 and now lives in Vancouver.

Olga Farmakovsky, Peter Worthington's translator who defected from Moscow, lives in Toronto under another name.

Bower Featherstone, the civil servant convicted and sentenced to prison for two and a half years for his activities in Operation Gold Dust, was released early and now works for a private printing company in Ottawa.

Joe Gibson, the CBNRC Liaison Officer to GCHQ who gave Bennett advice about moving to Canada, returned to Canada in 1956 and still works for the organization, which is now called the Communications Security Establishment.

Anatoli Golitsin, the KGB defector who helped fuel the CIA mole hunt, lives in the United States under a false identity and has reportedly written a book, which he is seeking to publish.

Ken Green, one of Bennett's close civilian colleagues in the Security Service, is retired and living in Ottawa.

Cliff Harvison, the Director of the Security Service whose ultimatum drove Long Knife to the KGB, became Commissioner in 1960, retired in 1963 and died in 1968.

Heinz Herre, the German BND Liaison Officer to Washington who was briefly suspected as a Soviet agent, is retired and living in West Germany.

W. L. "Len" Higgitt, the former head of B Branch and director of the Security Service, became RCMP Commissioner in 1969 and retired at the end of 1973. He is now president of the Canada Safety Council.

Bruce James, the Security Service officer in charge of A Division who battled Bennett over the filming of Natasha in Operation Deep Root, has risen to Chief Superintendent and is the officer in charge of Southern Ontario.

Joker, the Ottawa cab driver whose secret love affair with Natasha sparked Operation Deep Root, is a middle-ranking officer with a federal crown corporation.

Howie Jones, Bennett's former close friend, is now the civilian equivalent of a Chief Superintendent in the Security Service.

Janette Keir, another one of Bennett's close civilian friends, retired from the Security Service in 1976. She lives in Ottawa.

William Kelly, the aggressive director of the Security Service during the mid-1960s, rose to the rank of Deputy Commissioner and retired in 1969. He lives in Ottawa.

Jimmy Lemieux, the director of the Security Service responsible for bringing Long Knife into Operation Keystone, is retired and living in Ottawa and Florida.

Long Knife, the betrayor of Gideon in Operation Keystone, lives with his wife in relative comfort in Canada and does term work for a multinational corporation.

Rod MacAskill, the administrator who in 1954 informed Bennett that CBNRC would not hire him, retired in 1968 as Co-ordinator of Administration and lives in Ottawa.

Sandy McCallum, the head of the Watcher Service through most of the 1960s, retired in 1970 and runs a private security company in Sarnia.

Mark McClung, the director of research who first interviewed Bennett on behalf of the RCMP, left the organization in 1960 and is now retired in Ottawa.

Ian MacEwan, the Gridiron investigator who helped interrogate Bennett, was commissioned in 1976 and is now an Inspector in the Organizational Development section.

Vaughn MacKenzie, the A Division NCO who privately investigated Bennett, retired in 1970 and currently lives in Vancouver.

Mike Mihalcin, the Canadian-born Czech citizen who the KGB sent to Edmonton, drives a truck in Thunder Bay.

Len Nicholson, who brought Long Knife to Ottawa, resigned as RCMP Commissioner in 1959 in a public dispute with Justice Minister Davie Fulton over policing in Newfoundland. He lives near Ottawa.

Mary Oliver, the CBNRC personnel officer who wanted to hire Bennett, is retired and living in Toronto.

Dick Rowan, Bennett's friend and colleague, transferred out of the Security Service and now works for the RCMP in Ottawa as a staff sergeant.

Murray Sexsmith, Bennett's long time colleague and interrogator, succeeded Draper as Deputy Director of the Security Service in 1975 but in 1977 was transferred to the police side of the RCMP and made the Commanding Officer in charge of Southern Ontario. He retired in 1982 and at the time of this writing is moving from Toronto to British Columbia.

John Starnes, the director of the Security Service while Bennett was investigated and interrogated, retired unexpectedly in 1973. He lives in Ottawa.

Charles Sweeny, Gideon's controlling officer and later the head of B Branch, transferred out of the Security Service in 1964 and retired in 1973 as an Assistant Commissioner. He lives in Ottawa.

Henry Tadeson, the head of B Branch during the mid-1960s, retired as an Assistant Commissioner in 1977 and works in Toronto as Director of Security for TransCanada Pipelines.

Joe Yoblonski, one of Bennett's senior NCOs in E Branch, retired shortly after his transfer to Vancouver. He lives in Greater Vancouver and owns a private security company.

Index